PARLEY P. PRATT
and the
MAKING OF MORMONISM

PARLEY P. PRATT
and the
MAKING OF MORMONISM

Edited and with contributions by
Gregory K. Armstrong, Matthew J. Grow,
and Dennis J. Siler

THE ARTHUR H. CLARK COMPANY
An imprint of the University of Oklahoma Press
Norman, Oklahoma
2011

Library of Congress Cataloging-in-Publication Data
Parley P. Pratt and the making of Mormonism / edited and with contributions by Gregory K. Armstrong, Matthew J. Grow, and Dennis J. Siler.
p. cm.
Based in part on a conference held in 2007 in Fort Smith, Ark.
Includes index.
ISBN 978-0-87062-401-8 (hardcover : alk. paper) 1. Pratt, Parley P. (Parley Parker), 1807–1857—Congresses. I. Armstrong, Gregory K. (Gregory Kent), 1943– II. Grow, Matthew J. III. Siler, Dennis J. (Dennis James)
BX8695.P7P37 2011
289.3092—dc22

2011010911

The paper in this book meets the guidelines for permanence and durability of the Committee on Production Guidelines for Book Longevity of the Council on Library Resources, Inc. ∞

1 2 3 4 5 6 7 8 9 10

Contents

Illustrations

Figures

Map

Table

PARLEY P. PRATT
and the
MAKING OF MORMONISM

Parley P. Pratt, about 1853.
Courtesy of the Church History Library, the Church of Jesus Christ of Latter-day Saints.

Introduction

Gregory K. Armstrong,
Matthew J. Grow, and Dennis J. Siler

Reflecting on his life in a letter to a boyhood friend in 1853, Parley P. Pratt called his history "stranger than fiction," as he had been a "farmer, a servant, a fisher, a digger, a beggar, a preacher, an author, an editor, a senator, a travellor, a merchant, an elder and an Apostle of Jesus Christ."[1] The drama of Pratt's life continued until his murder four years later in Arkansas by the estranged husband of his twelfth plural wife. Through his varied roles—particularly as writer, theologian, missionary, and apostle—Pratt profoundly shaped nineteenth-century Mormon thought and history. Nevertheless, he has received relatively little scholarly attention, perhaps owing to his popular *Autobiography*. The essays presented here in *Parley P. Pratt and the Making of Mormonism* use Pratt's intriguing life as a window onto early Mormonism and, more broadly, American religious and cultural history.

Born in 1807, the third of five sons of Jared and Charity Pratt, young Pratt moved frequently with his family around eastern New York in a largely failed search for economic success. His family's poverty forced his parents to board their teenage sons, including Pratt, with local farmers. As a result, Pratt received little formal

[1] Parley P. Pratt to William Patterson, 9 May 1853, Church History Library, the Church of Jesus Christ of Latter-day Saints, Salt Lake City, Utah.

education, though he became self-educated through voracious reading. Coming to manhood in the tumultuous era of the Second Great Awakening, Pratt inherited from his parents a devotion to Christianity but a suspicion of clericalism and religious denominations. Like many of his contemporaries, he became a religious seeker, on a quest for the primitive and pure Christianity he found in the New Testament.

In the late 1820s, after moving to Ohio, Pratt started to associate with a restorationist religious movement known as the Campbellites, or Disciples of Christ. Resolving to begin a career as an itinerant preacher, Pratt in 1830 began a journey back to eastern New York, now with his wife Thankful Halsey. Along the way, following what he described as divine inspiration, he read a copy of the recently published Book of Mormon and became one of Mormonism's earliest converts. Soon after, he baptized his younger brother Orson. In October 1830, Joseph Smith received a revelation that directed Pratt and three other missionaries to preach to American Indians in Missouri. En route there, Pratt convinced his companions to stop in Kirtland, Ohio, where they taught Sidney Rigdon, a Campbellite preacher who had been Pratt's religious mentor, and many members of his congregation. The Kirtland conversions transformed early Mormonism; Smith and the other New York Mormons soon moved to Kirtland, which served as one of the centers of Mormonism until the late 1830s. In 1835, Smith called Pratt and his brother Orson as members of the newly formed Quorum of the Twelve Apostles, a position they served in for the remainder of their lives. Pratt experienced both Latter-day Saint expulsions from Missouri, first in 1833 and '34 and then in 1838 and '39. During the second conflict between Mormons and Missourians, Pratt was arrested for involvement in an armed clash and subsequently spent eight months imprisoned in Richmond and Columbia, Missouri.

Pratt's calling as an apostle solidified his lifelong devotion to missionary work, and his preaching and leadership played a key role in the expansion and internationalization of early Mormonism. He crisscrossed the eastern and midwestern United States on missions several times, and in 1836 he ventured into Canada, where his teaching led to the conversion of John Taylor, a Methodist lay preacher who became the third president of the Church. From 1840 to 1842, he accompanied several other apostles on a mission to England, where he edited the influential *Latter-day Saints' Millennial Star* and helped supervise the rapid growth of Mormonism. Following the deaths of Joseph and his older brother Hyrum Smith in 1844, Pratt again served missions in the eastern United States and England, primarily to convince Latter-day Saints in those areas to accept the Twelve Apostles as the legitimate successors to Smith. Following this last mission to England, Pratt helped lead the large Mormon trek to Utah in 1847. In territorial Utah, Pratt turned his attention to entrepreneurial and exploring activities by constructing a toll road into the Salt Lake Valley through what came to be known as Parley's Canyon and by leading a fifty-man company that successfully located sites for future Mormon settlements in central and southern Utah. In the 1850s, Church president Brigham Young appointed Pratt to supervise missionary work throughout the Pacific Ocean, including the Pacific coasts of North and South America, helping orient the Church toward Latin America and the Pacific Rim. Pratt thus served two missions to California during the gold rush and a mission to Chile as the first Mormon missionary in Latin America. His constant missions left him and his family in a state of almost perpetual poverty.

Pratt exerted his influence most widely through his writings, which introduced the Mormon message to tens of thousands of people. Besides writing doctrinal and theological texts, Pratt penned poetry, hymns, fiction, and a posthumously published autobiography (1874). His *A Voice of Warning*, a missionary book, was the most widely read Latter-day Saint book outside of the scriptures during the first few generations of Mormonism. During his missions, he frequently turned to print to amplify his message, including writing many short pamphlets and proclamations and editing newspapers. In *Key to the Science of Theology*, Pratt produced nineteenth-century Mormonism's most comprehensive theological treatise. His autobiography recounts Mormonism's early days and his own life in lively prose. His influence is regularly felt today in his popular restoration hymns that are still sung in congregations of the Community of Christ and Latter-day Saints.

Though Pratt remains among the least understood of early Latter-day Saint leaders, he arguably influenced the direction of early Mormonism more than anyone besides Joseph Smith and Brigham Young. The essays in this volume use Pratt's voluminous public and private writings to explore issues ranging from print culture to the internationalization of early Mormonism to the Mountain Meadows Massacre.

Many of these essays began as part of a 2007 conference in Fort Smith, Arkansas, titled "Religion and Reaction: The Life, Times, and Legacy of Parley Parker Pratt," commemorating the bicentennial of Pratt's birth and the sesquicentennial of his death. Organized by Greg Armstrong and Dennis Siler, professors at the University of Arkansas–Fort Smith, and supported by grants from the Arkansas Humanities Council and the National Endowment for the Humanities, the conference included a banquet (complete with a special taped appearance of the Mormon Tabernacle Choir); a country musical tribute to Joseph Smith; a reader's theater; and academic presentations, including a keynote address (adapted here as chapter 1) by Jan Shipps.

Shipps's essay examines the religious environment in nineteenth-century America by tracing Pratt's ancestry and narrating how he, an itinerant preacher, became a firm convert to the new faith of Mormonism. Locating Pratt's conversion within the origins of early Mormonism, Shipps argues that his life illuminates the experiences of early Latter-day Saints and how Smith and his followers created a new religious movement by envisioning both the restoration of New Testament Christianity and Old Testament Israel. Shipps also uses Pratt's story to explain how Mormons came to be perceived by outsiders as a cult or an aberration of traditional Christianity.

In chapter 2, R. Steven Pratt examines Parley Pratt's personal life, with an emphasis on Parley's family and experience with plural marriage. Pratt married twelve women, fathered thirty children, and was one of Mormonism's most vocal public defenders of polygamy. Steven Pratt uses the rich correspondence between Parley Pratt and his wives to examine the domestic dynamics of Mormon plural marriages, including how Parley and his wives viewed their marriages, as well as the relationships and tensions between the "sister-wives."

In chapter 3, David J. Whittaker surveys Pratt's foundational role in the emergence of Mormon print culture. Between 1835 and his death in 1857, Pratt authored many works that described, defended, and explained Mormonism to both Church members and the larger world. By writing the first responses to anti-Mormon literature in both the United States and in England, Pratt established the basic contours of Mormon apologetics. In addition, he was the founding editor of the major British periodical of the Church, published the first important Mormon theological works, and left a manuscript that was perhaps the most significant early Mormon autobiography.

Following the Mormon expulsion from Missouri in 1838–39, Pratt spent eight months in jail before his brother Orson helped him escape. In chapter 4, Alexander L. Baugh examines Pratt's extensive manuscript letters from prison—both to his family and other Church leaders—and places them in the context of the intense controversy over Mormonism in Missouri during the late 1830s. In chapter 5, David W. Grua uses Pratt's writings on the Latter-day Saints' treatment in Missouri to examine the creation of Mormon identity and memory through the rhetoric of persecution. In his influential *History of the Late Persecution* (1839), Pratt argued that Missourians drove out the Latter-day Saints not because of their religion but because they were good republicans. Nevertheless, Pratt also sometimes portrayed the struggle religiously, arguing that Missourians targeted Mormons because they were God's saints. Grua's analysis demonstrates how nineteenth-century Mormons constructed an identity both connected with and opposed to the American republic.

In chapter 6, Jordan Watkins examines Pratt's contribution to the development of Mormon theology by closely examining Latter-day Saint conceptions of theosis (human divinization). He demonstrates how dynamics both within Mormonism and between Latter-day Saint apologists and their antagonists spurred the evolution of Mormon theology. In *Key to the Science of Theology*, Pratt proclaimed his view of theosis by asserting that "Gods, angels and men are all of one species."[2]

In the early 1850s, Pratt became the first Mormon missionary to visit Latin America during an unsuccessful mission to Chile. His writings demonstrated considerable interest in Latin America; he later published the first Mormon pamphlet in Spanish, urged other Mormons to learn Spanish, and encouraged Latter-day Saints to focus their attention on Latin America and the Pacific Rim. Several of Pratt's descendants have also played formative roles in the growth of Mormonism in Latin America. In chapter 7, David Clark Knowlton examines these interactions between Pratt, his descendants, and Latin America.

Pratt's involvement in plural marriage ultimately led to his murder in 1857 by Hector McLean, whose estranged wife, Eleanor McComb, had joined Mormonism and married Pratt. In chapter 8, Patrick Q. Mason situates Pratt's murder within its wider social and cultural milieu, particularly antebellum notions of honor and extralegal violence, to illuminate McLean's motives. Whereas both nineteenth-century Latter-day Saints and their opponents saw Pratt's death as an extraordinary occurrence, Mason argues that placing his murder within the context of the clash between Victorian domestic ideals and national anti-Mormon sentiment reveals cultural norms pervasive in 1850s America.

Pratt's murder shocked the Latter-day Saints and became front-page news across the nation. After Pratt's death, his widow Eleanor and other Mormon authors presented Pratt as a martyr to the cause of truth who had valiantly rescued her from an alcoholic, abusive, and religiously intolerant husband. National newspapers,

[2] Parley P. Pratt, *Key to the Science of Theology: Designed as an Introduction to the First Principles of Spiritual Philosophy; Religion; Law and Government; as Delivered by the Ancients, and as Restored in This Age, for the Final Development of Universal Peace, Truth and Knowledge* (Liverpool, England: F. D. Richards, 1855), 33.

by contrast, saw Pratt's death as a tantalizing story featuring religious fanaticism, sexual deviance, polygamy, and justly delivered violence. These competing narratives, analyzed by Matthew J. Grow in chapter 9, are microcosms of the national furor over Mormonism and the debates about the boundaries of religious tolerance in nineteenth-century America.

Six months after Pratt's murder in Arkansas, Mormon settlers massacred a wagon train of mostly Arkansan emigrants at Mountain Meadows in southern Utah. Newspapers immediately linked the events, claiming that Mormons had exacted vengeance for Pratt's murder. Ever since, historians and journalists have listed Pratt's murder as a cause, and sometimes even the principal cause, for the Mountain Meadows Massacre. In chapter 10, Richard E. Turley disputes such claims and argues that a careful analysis of the sources reveals that Pratt's death played little role in the massacre.

In the 150 years since Pratt's death, his family and descendants have made several attempts to locate his remains and move them to Utah. Early efforts to do so were hampered by hostility toward Mormonism in Arkansas, exacerbated by the Mountain Meadows Massacre, combined with conflicting historical records and local memories about Pratt's exact burial site. Between 2005 and 2008, a group of his descendants used modern scientific technology, including ground-penetrating radar, to pinpoint his probable grave. An archaeological dig in April 2008 determined that Pratt's remains had disintegrated in the Arkansas soil. In this volume's final chapter, Robert J. Grow, who led this recent effort, narrates the historical and recent attempts by Pratt's descendants to find his burial site, an intriguing case study on the convergence of historical memory and modern technology.

These eleven essays—seven focusing on Pratt's life and four on his controversial death—demonstrate how one individual both navigated and shaped the religious and cultural currents of the nineteenth century. Placing Parley P. Pratt within these wider contexts not only illuminates his own life and early Mormonism but also nineteenth-century America more broadly.

CHAPTER 1

Parley P. Pratt and the Coming of a New Religious Tradition to America

JAN SHIPPS

As a Methodist who has been studying the Mormons for almost a half century, I may be one of the few remaining historians thoroughly familiar with the early and mid-twentieth-century distinctive form of the Latter-day Saint biography. I started reading stories of those who were still calling themselves "peculiar" people in the 1960s. Consequently, I came to know this particular form of biography well when I set out to read biographies of as many Latter-day Saints who were involved in politics as I could find. It turned out—as all those familiar with Mormon history know—that this included nearly all the leading Latter-day Saints in the state of Deseret in the years before the Mormon kingdom became the state of Utah.

I found plenty of nineteenth- and early twentieth-century Mormon biographies to read, but my project was not especially enlightening because these biographies had a more or less standard form: the biographer, familiar with the informally canonized history of the Church of Jesus Christ of Latter-day Saints (LDS

Church), nearly always started with the early 1830s and moved forward with the Church's history, emphasizing the story of the biography's subject only at the points where he (and it was virtually always a he) converted, joined the Church, and participated in the historical events that ensued. After reading six or eight such biographies, I realized that they were nothing more nor less than conventional histories of the Church. Usually beginning with a short chapter about the genealogy of the individual subject, each work proceeded with an account of the history of the Latter-day Saint movement. The only thing that turned such works into life stories was that, for all practical purposes, information about the subjects of the biographies was underlined at points where they had taken part in what was going on.[1]

In what follows here, this traditional biographical form will be turned on its head. A sketch of the life of Parley Parker Pratt will be used as a screen on which to view the story of the Latter-day Saints. This approach will allow several questions to be answered. They are: What does Pratt's genealogy, conversion, life experience, and untimely death reveal not just about Pratt himself but also about how the faith he shared with other Mormon converts came into existence, and, to the extent Pratt's experience will reveal, how it became a new religious tradition? Because a religious as well as a cultural context is needed to establish the true significance of the life of Pratt in Mormon and American history, the answers to these questions are indispensable in a book about one of Mormonism's most influential Latter-day Saints.

Who Was Parley Pratt?

Parley Pratt, born in 1807, was a descendent of William and Elizabeth Pratt, members of the congregation of Thomas Hooker, a nonconformist Puritan pastor-preacher. In 1635, Hooker moved

[1] It is possible, even likely, that one reason Fawn McKay Brodie's *No Man Knows My History* (New York: Knopf, 1945) was quickly acknowledged by non-Mormon readers as the most reliable and complete scholarly biography of the Mormon prophet is that it departed so radically from the conventional Mormon biography.

with his congregation from Cambridge, Massachusetts, to Connecticut, where the ecclesiastical shepherd and his flock founded the town of Hartford. Two years later, the pastor told the state court that his people had the right to choose their own magistrates, an idea that was much advanced for an age in which magistrates were selected by local church authorities and approved by representatives of the English crown. Given this rebellious bent, perhaps it is not surprising that along with the Pratt family, another seventeen of the fifty-five heads of households who settled in Hartford in 1635 were ancestors of Latter-day Saint converts.

Taken alone, this genealogical information does not place the Pratt family decisively among the radical ancestors of the early Mormon converts traced by author Val D. Rust. The Pratts, however, were also descendents of John Lathrop, an English minister who, believing that the Church of England had lost its way, renounced his religious orders to become, first, an Independent, and later, a Separatist pastor. After a stay in prison, Lathrop left for New England and eventually settled in Barnstable, Connecticut, where ancestors of the Pratts lived, along with the ancestors of Oliver Cowdery, Wilford Woodruff, and the Mormon prophet Joseph Smith, Jr., himself. The Pratt family likewise descended from Anne Marbury Hutchison of religious dissenter fame.[2]

The radicalism of many ancestors of the early converts to Mormonism was not civic but religious, for these were persons disappointed in all the existing Christianities—Presbyterianism, Congregationalism, Methodism, Anglicanism (later Episcopalianism), Baptist churches, and a variety of short-lived Christian groups. They were "seekers," not only attempting to find New Testament Christianity but also anxious to discover that the heavens were again open so that direct communication could be reestablished between humanity and divinity. Using Pratt as an exemplar supports the premise that the religious movement headed by Joseph Smith was not a mere alternative to other groups of Christian

[2] Val D. Rust, *Radical Origins: Early Mormon Converts and Their Colonial Ancestors* (Urbana-Champaign: University of Illinois Press, 2004), esp. chapter 5.

Primitivists nor an alternative to a different restorationist group like the Disciples of Christ, which held out the hope it would become the denomination to end all denominationalism.[3] In due course, the movement led by the Mormon prophet would separate itself from every other existing form of Christianity, taking Pratt and his brother Orson with it. But unlike the Disciples who, ironically, became just another Protestant denomination, Mormonism never became a Christian denomination or even a Christian church analogous to Roman Catholicism.[4]

With its novel truth claims of having additional scriptures and of being led by a prophet, Mormonism would become something new under the sun, a new religious tradition. Moreover, the genealogical origins of the Pratt brothers placed them directly in the nucleus of the set of seekers whose so-called radical origins allowed Rust to argue that—as far as the independence of thought was concerned—the ancestors of converts to Mormonism inhabited the margins of colonial culture. In one case after another, they were not among English colonists satisfied to re-create Old England in the New World. With regard to the rights of settlers and the relationships between the civil and religious dimensions of society, they held that *New England* and, indeed, the United States of America should be truly new.

Pratt's radical genealogical location generated in him a true hunger for knowledge about nearly everything, but most especially spiritual things. In his *Autobiography*, Pratt told readers that as a boy he learned to love books and would consume their contents morning, noon, and night. His concern for the state of his soul was more important than anything else. Reflecting on his youth, Pratt expressed it this way: "I felt a weight of worlds, of *eternal* worlds resting upon me; for fear I might still remain in uncertainty, and at

[3] Led by Thomas and Alexander Campbell, the Disciples of Christ claimed to be the only true church. This pattern of contention that a new religious group, or "sect," is the "sect to end all sects" is discussed at length by William A. Clebsch, "Each Sect the Sect to End All Sects," *Dialogue: A Journal of Mormon Thought* 1 (Summer 1966): 84–89.

[4] See Jan Shipps, *Mormonism: The Story of a New Religious Tradition* (Urbana: University of Illinois Press, 1985), chapter 3.

last fall short and still sleep on in the cold embrace of death; while the great, the good, the blessed and the holy of this world would awake from the gloom of the grave and be renovated, filled with life and joy."[5]

After he married Thankful Halsey, the couple moved to Ohio where Pratt became associated with Sidney Rigdon, who, in turn, followed Thomas and Alexander Campbell. Rigdon's teachings were restorationist in a legalistic sense, seeking to re-create early Christianity as described in the New Testament. This, however, did not satisfy Pratt's genuine desire to discover the correct canons of faith. In his understanding, that had to await his leaving Ohio and traveling to New York with his wife in the late summer of 1830.

During this trip, Pratt met a Baptist deacon who told him about "a very strange book" that he had in his possession. The deacon allowed Pratt to borrow it, and thus it was that the future Mormon missionary propagandist extraordinaire came about his knowledge of Joseph Smith and the movement he founded. Reading the volume night and day, Pratt became convinced that it was precisely what it claimed to be: an ancient document translated by Smith by the "gift and power of God."[6]

This conviction led Pratt to travel to Palmyra, New York, where the book had been published, to discover what he could about Smith, the "author and proprietor" of this peculiar and perplexing tome that seemed to reveal truths about the restoration that Pratt had theretofore no knowledge. To his disappointment, neither the prophet nor his father were in Palmyra or in the surrounding geographical area when he arrived, though he did meet Smith's brother Hyrum. From him, Pratt obtained his own copy of the Book of Mormon and heard the particulars of its coming forth. Within a week or so, he was baptized into the Mormon movement's new Church of Christ.[7]

---

[5] Parley P. Pratt, *Autobiography of Parley Parker Pratt, One of the Twelve Apostles of the Church of Jesus Christ of Latter-day Saints, Embracing His Life, Ministry, and Travels, with Extracts in Prose and Verse from His Miscellaneous Writings*, ed. Parley P. Pratt, Jr. (New York: Russell Brothers, 1874), 19.

[6] Ibid., 37–38.

[7] Ibid., 38–41.

Pratt rapidly became a key figure in the religious movement led by the Mormon prophet. Here again, Pratt's experience prefigured and/or mirrored the experiences of a host of early Latter-day Saints who were, in modern parlance, Book of Mormon converts. These were folks who somehow came by a copy of the Book of Mormon, read it, and coming upon what is now the fourth verse of the final chapter of the volume's final book followed instructions to "ask God, the Eternal Father, in the name of Christ, if these things are not true" and had manifested to them "the truth of it . . . by the power of the Holy Ghost."[8]

What happened after Pratt's baptism also reflects the experience of many other new converts. Because the movement was so young, many positions of leadership were open. In the same month that he was baptized, Pratt and three others were sent to the West (which at that point would have been the Midwest) on a mission to carry the gospel to the American Indians in accord with the purpose spelled out on the title page of the Book of Mormon.[9] Although the missionaries did not appear to have succeeded with the Native peoples, Pratt's missionary eloquence and his steadfast position regarding the truth of the claim that the Book of Mormon was holy writ helped lead to the conversion of his former Campbellite pastor, Sidney Rigdon, and many of the members of his congregation. During the same missionary expedition, partly as a result of Pratt's robust testimony, many other Ohioans joined the new church. They, too, would become influential in the Mormon movement, whose members increasingly used the descriptive name "Latter-day Saints."[10] During the early 1830s, Pratt virtually

[8] The first edition of the Book of Mormon was not divided into chapters and verses. The cited passage is familiar today as Moroni 10:4. Pratt does not specifically mention this passage in his *Autobiography*, but his description of coming to believe the book parallels many accounts of reading the book, praying about it, and concluding that it is precisely what it claims to be. Modern missionaries point to this verse as a means of discovering the truth of the work.

[9] The three other missionaries were Oliver Cowdery, Peter Whitmer, Jr., and Ziba Peterson.

[10] Pratt's eminence in the new movement is made clear throughout Jan Shipps and John W. Welch, *The Journals of William E. McLellin, 1831–1836* (Provo, Utah: BYU *Studies*; Urbana-Champaign: University of Illinois Press, 1994).

became itinerant as he moved back and forth between the Church's centers in Missouri and Ohio.

Most of the twenty (or more) biographical accounts of Pratt's life focus on his success as a missionary and his elevation to the new church's Traveling High Council, which became the Council of the Twelve Apostles. Nearly all of these accounts tell of his composing *A Voice of Warning and Instruction to All People, Containing a Declaration of the Faith and Doctrine of the Church of the Latter Day Saints, Commonly Called Mormons*, a missionary pamphlet that went through some thirty printings.[11] But they all give short shrift to the impact on Pratt of the years he traveled back and forth from Ohio to Missouri and how they shaped his perception of Zion in the New World. This is a remarkable oversight because these years were a great deal more significant than a simple period of transition between Pratt's converting Rigdon and his followers in late 1830 to his becoming a member of Zion's Camp—an attempt to regain land in Jackson County, Missouri, from which the Saints had been expelled—in the late spring of 1834. Indeed, if Pratt is considered as an archetypal Latter-day Saint whose life is a guide to the development of Mormonism as a new religious tradition, these transitional years are critically important because they clarify the unconventional thought processes that turned the members of the Church of Christ into a chosen people.

As an organized entity, the Mormon movement had become the restored Church of Christ in April 1830. Less than a year later, revelations to the prophet Joseph Smith started to add a second sort of restoration to this new movement, the restoration of Israel.[12] During Pratt's first month as a member of the Mormon movement, Smith received a revelation calling for the "gathering of the elect . . . in one place upon the face of the land."[13] The revelation stated

[11] Biographical treatments of Pratt are listed in *Studies in Mormon History, 1830–1997*, ed. James B. Allen, Ronald W. Walker, and David J. Whitaker (Urbana and Chicago: University of Illinois Press, 2000), 870–71.

[12] See Jan Shipps, *Sojourner in the Promised Land: Forty Years among the Mormons* (Urbana and Chicago: University of Illinois Press, 2000), chapter 14.

[13] Doctrine and Covenants of the Church of Jesus Christ of Latter-day Saints: Carefully Selected from the Revelations of God (Salt Lake City: The Church of Jesus Christ of Latter-day Saints, 1981) (hereafter Doctrine and Covenants), 29:8.

that the gathering would permit the Saints to escape tribulation as they awaited the opening of the millennium. At the same time, as Richard Bushman, Smith's pre-eminent biographer said, "[This revelation] brought all the routine activities of everyday life into question," and nearly all historians of early Mormonism agree.[14]

Historians describe the two-pronged move of Smith's followers that led them to settle in Kirtland, Ohio, and Independence, Missouri. That move was one of the revelation's consequences. But another result not often mentioned because only time connects the two more or less directly, is that the gatherings in Ohio and Missouri set the stage for a series of revelations that placed an Old Testament restoration layer over the Saints' newly restored New Testament church. Issuing through Joseph Smith, one of these revelations included God's designations for the sites of temples rather than meeting houses or structures in the style of New England churches and pledged that when His covenant people are gathered (in Kirtland and in the New Jerusalem, i.e., Missouri), He would come to His temple(s).[15] A further revelation assured the Saints that God would give them "a land of promise, a land flowing with milk and honey upon which there will be no curse when the Lord cometh," a land that will be the land of their inheritance and that of their children.[16] A revelation likewise called Joseph Smith, Sr., to be the Church patriarch, and in his patriarchal blessings, Saints would be informed of their Hebrew genealogy. This is to say, they were told from which tribe of Israel they were descended.[17]

If Pratt was not present when these revelations were first made known, he was close enough to the center to have learned of them right away. The revelations about the New Jerusalem were especially critical, for they became the basis of defining Missouri as Zion. What this meant for those who traveled from Missouri to

[14] Richard L. Bushman, *Joseph Smith: Rough Stone Rolling* (New York: Alfred A. Knopf, 2005), 122–23.

[15] Doctrine and Covenants 42:35–36; and 84:2–3.

[16] Doctrine and Covenants 38:18–19.

[17] Irene M. Bates and E. Gary Smith, *Lost Legacy: The Mormon Office of Presiding Patriarch* (Urbana and Chicago: University of Illinois Press), chapter 2.

Ohio and back again is that Zion became a real place rather than a metaphorical one. Despite the reality of assaults on the Saints by the old settlers of Independence and subsequent attacks in Clay County and the Far West, Missouri, region, Pratt and his fellow missionaries called the land "Zion" and spoke not of going to and from Missouri, but of going to and from Zion.[18]

David Brion Davis and other historians familiar with the history of religion in New England have pointed to the similarity of the experiences of early Latter-day Saints and the Puritans.[19] In fact, there is considerable similarity in the manner in which the Puritans perceived the undertaking in which they were engaged as an "errand" into the wilderness while Smith's followers found themselves busy building up Zion. Some of the colonial settlers experienced the New World as the Promised Land, but the parallels drawn by the Puritans and their contemporaries on the one hand, and the followers of the Mormon prophet on the other, are more superficial than they might first appear because both groups used the same words. For the Puritans and other colonial settlers, the notions of the Atlantic Ocean as the Red Sea, and the Massachusetts Bay Colony as the wilderness and/or Promised Land, were metaphors, often spelled out in sermonic arguments that used logic as well as scripture. For the Saints, the Promised Land was absolutely authentic for they were convinced that "the heavens were no longer brass," that through their prophet, God was speaking directly to them.[20] They were convinced they were a covenant people, as chosen as the Hebrews in the Old Testament. In addition, the mythological dimension of the Mormon faith did not entirely depend on revelations defining Zion, namely, calling for the construction of temples, promising inheritances of land, and describing members of the restored Church of Jesus Christ as members of the

[18] In addition to Pratt's *Autobiography*, evidence of the way Smith's followers referred to going to or living in Zion is found in Shipps and Welch, *Journals of William E. McLellin*.

[19] In particular, see David Brion Davis, "The New England Origins of Mormonism," *New England Quarterly* 26 (June 1953): 147–68.

[20] Shipps, *Mormonism*, 37, 177.

household of Abraham, Isaac, and Jacob. Of at least equal consequence were revelations that situated the Garden of Eden in the New World and located the site where Adam and Eve went when they were dismissed from Paradise in Daviess County, Missouri, in a place called Adam-ondi-Ahman. As Klaus Hansen said in summing up what happened, "Smith assigned the entire antediluvian history of the Old Testament to the New World."[21]

Pratt and his compatriots accepted the designation of biblical places and the biblical story to the New World, but they did not see it as the act of the Mormon prophet. Joseph Smith was merely a conduit; God sent direct messages that turned the topography of Missouri into Zion. Thus, they did not believe that Missouri was reminiscent of or like Zion but that Missouri *was* Zion.[22] This knowledge, plus the physical reality of the Kirtland temple, sustained the veracity of the claim that the Saints were God's people, directly chosen through revelation.

Pratt's *Autobiography* describes multiple journeys from Kirtland to Missouri, including his traveling with the Camp of Israel, that unsuccessful "Zion's Camp" expedition led by Joseph Smith in 1834 to find some means of assisting the Saints who were driven from the town of Independence into nearby Clay County.[23] Sandwiched between missions to the East, to Canada, and to Great Britain, these journeys were unquestionably decisive in magnifying in Pratt's mind the veracity and authenticity of the Mormon gospel with its dual claims that the movement was both the restoration of Christianity and the restoration of Israel.

---

[21] Klaus J. Hansen, *Mormonism and the American Experience* (Chicago: University of Chicago Press, 1981), 66.

[22] Among many Latter-day Saints today, especially those born "under the covenant," the notion that Missouri is Zion remains a part of the their belief system insofar as there is an understanding that when Christ returns, he will appear first "in Jackson County."

[23] While this endeavor was ultimately unsuccessful, it still managed to convince those who were closest to the prophet that Missouri was Zion. For a description of the impact of Zion's Camp on the prophet's closest associates, see Thomas G. Alexander, *Things in Heaven and Earth: The Life and Times of Wilford Woodruff* (Salt Lake City: Signature Books, 1991), 28–32.

One fruit of this total confidence in the prophet's mandate—the absolute authority of the priesthood and the legitimacy of the Book of Mormon—was *Voice of Warning*, the missionary tract that Pratt composed in 1837, which became the most effective and widely distributed Mormon tract in the nineteenth century. Although no other missionary was so prolific a writer as Pratt, his experiences as a missionary were by no means isolated instances. In these early years, the pattern could almost be described in a saying familiar to twentieth-century Saints: "every member a missionary"; only in Pratt's day, it would have been "every male member a missionary." The missionary encounters that led to conversions, healings, and the creation of Church organizations strengthened the understandings of many Saints that they had done the right thing to form a union with others who believed implicitly in Joseph Smith as prophet, the Book of Mormon as scripture, and their own bond with God's chosen people in the overture to the end times.

In 1838, Pratt removed his family to Missouri, where a hot war that resulted in the massacre at Haun's Mill and Pratt's imprisonment (along with the prophet and other Saints) allowed him to see that just as the ancient Hebrews had discovered they would have to liberate their Promised Land from the "Philistines," so the Saints would need to liberate the Promised Land that God had given them from the Gentiles. While they continued to believe that they were living in the "winding-up scene," Pratt and others came to realize that the Saints might not gain possession of Missouri, their Promised Land, in their lifetimes.

Mormonism Becomes a New Religious Tradition

In examining Pratt's entire life, the Missouri troubles can be seen as a prelude to other events and encounters that he would have to go through with the Saintly community, which would push him (and them) ever further away from other American Christians. The death of Joseph Smith in 1844 preceded more occurrences, drawing Pratt and the Saints deeper into a spiritual and physical vortex that ensured that being Mormon was their birthright and their legacy. In the aftermath of Smith's murder, the Saints left Nauvoo, Illinois, under duress, traveled across the Plains to the Great Basin, and built a wall of separation between themselves and the rest of the nation, composed not only of distance and a geographic barrier, the Rocky Mountains, but also a time differential—a discrepancy in perception—the result of living through the pioneer trek experience that carried the prophet's followers backward in time.

Many of them walked across the Mississippi dry-shod as the mighty river froze out of season, providing the Saints with an experience that was remembered as comparable to the time dry-shod Hebrews crossed the Red Sea. Then, as the Saints struggled across Iowa, their hunger was assuaged by the arrival of multiple coveys of quail and by harvesting honey dew, a manna-like substance, giving them reassurance that as the Hebrews had escaped from Egypt, they were escaping from Babylon. This experience itself, or stories about it, deepened the Saints' understanding that they were truly God's chosen people. Such understanding was the fruit of patriarchal blessings and the ordinances in which they participated during temple ceremonies held in the days just prior to the Saints leaving Nauvoo.

One additional consequence of these shared happenings was that those who went through them were able to accept the Mormon prophet's final set of revelations restoring the "ancient order of things" that, among much else, included plural marriage.[24] In the end, this led to Pratt's death in Arkansas at the hands of the

[24] This third and final restoration "layer," sometimes called the "fullness of the gospel," included such rituals as baptism for the dead; ancient ordinances performed in temples under the authority of the Latter-day Saint priesthood; and the doctrines that together make up the Mormon "Plan of Salvation." Some of the Saints in Nauvoo and many of the Saints who did not go west never accepted this part of Mormonism, believing that Joseph Smith had become a "fallen prophet" before these things were revealed. See my chapters on Joseph Smith and the creation of Mormon theology in *Makers of Christian Theology in America*, ed. Mark Toulouse and James Duke (Nashville: Abingdon Press, 1997), 210–17, 373–78.

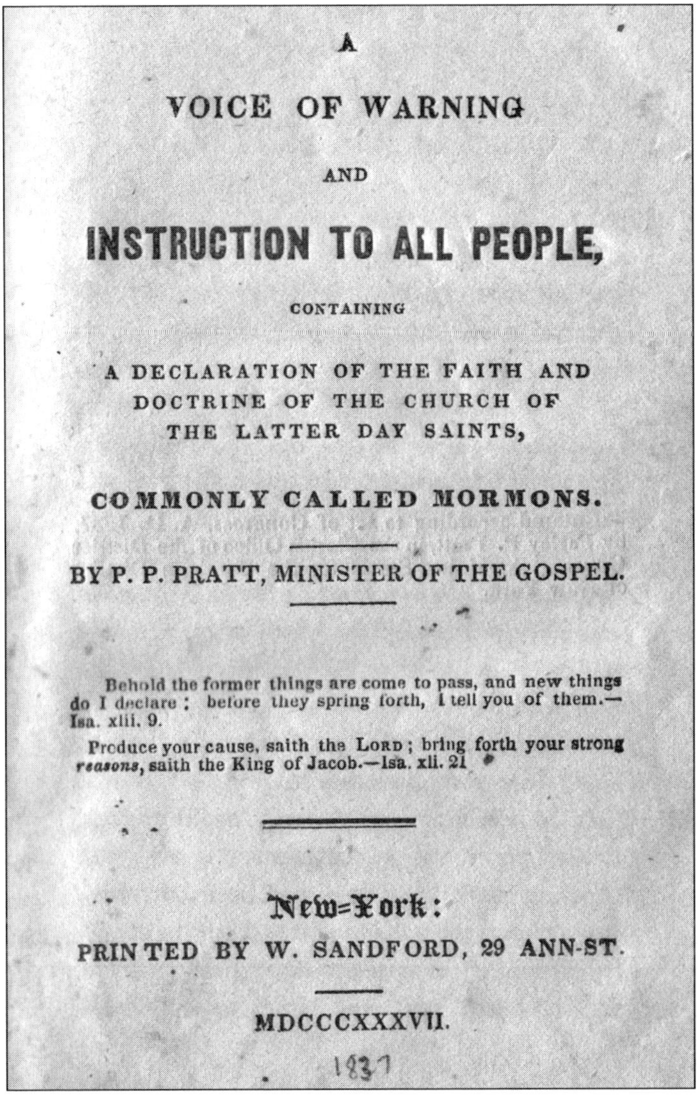
A

VOICE OF WARNING

AND

INSTRUCTION TO ALL PEOPLE,

CONTAINING

A DECLARATION OF THE FAITH AND DOCTRINE OF THE CHURCH OF THE LATTER DAY SAINTS,

COMMONLY CALLED MORMONS.

BY P. P. PRATT, MINISTER OF THE GOSPEL.

Behold the former things are come to pass, and new things do I declare: before they spring forth, I tell you of them.—Isa. xlii. 9.

Produce your cause, saith the LORD; bring forth your strong *reasons*, saith the King of Jacob.—Isa. xli. 21

New-York:

PRINTED BY W. SANDFORD, 29 ANN-ST.

MDCCCXXXVII.

1837

Title page, Pratt's *Voice of Warning*, 1837.
Courtesy of the L. Tom Perry Special Collections, Harold B. Lee Library, Brigham Young University, Provo, Utah.

estranged husband of Eleanor McComb McLean, the twelfth and last of Pratt's wives. Another consequence is that he became an archetypal Latter-day Saint, as will be discussed further on with reference to the religious situation in colonial and nineteenth-century America. Pratt's direct experiences reveal how the religious situation changed after 1787, when the United States started to take shape after the passage and ratification of the U.S. Constitution and, most especially, after the passage of the Bill of Rights whose First Amendment commenced the process of separating church and state.[25]

Pratt's experiences make it possible to distinguish between new forms of existing religious organizations and an authentically new religious movement, clarifying the difference and describing the process by which a new religious movement comes into being. In addition, his experience reveals very clearly what it meant to be an insider, a follower of the Mormon prophet Joseph Smith and, in time, Brigham Young. Moreover, his encounters with folks who were not Mormons expose—in a particularly poignant manner—the way the world of Mormondom was perceived from the outside at different points in time.

The settlers who came from the Old to the New World in the early seventeenth century were adventurous in the political and economic sense. At the same time, they stood in the vanguard of the Protestant Reformation, a sixteenth-century movement that had generated many new forms of Christianity without separating politics and economics from religion. As a result, an "establishment" that amalgamated politics, economics, and religion generated a social order that combined religious and secular authority. So thoroughly integrated were the two that while citizenship and church membership were separate, for all practical purposes, they were two sides of the same coin. Alternative forms of Christianity were tolerated, but taxes supported the Anglican establishment

[25] Although before the American Revolution Virginia and Rhode Island had separated the church from the state, the First Amendment separated church and state only at the federal level. These two fundamental institutions were not finally separated in every state in the Union until 1836.

(i.e., the English church), and its establishment was in charge. Yet, as would become clear at the time of the American Revolution, dissenters challenged the establishment and not just in the political arena.

Because American Indians were regarded as relatively unimportant in the grand scheme of things, the experience of living on land that appeared to be unoccupied gave the colonists the sense that they were living at the beginning of time. This perception had an enormous impact on colonial religion. So many new forms of Christianity existed in North America by the time the colonists gained their independence that religious diversity was a hallmark of the new United States. This diversity led to the separation of church and state, foundational legislation that laid the groundwork for an incredibly complicated religious landscape, with institutions ranging from extremely conservative to very radical. Still, until the emergence of Mormonism, virtually if not entirely all of these institutions were simply various forms of Protestant Christianity. Stephen Marini, a brilliant scholar of American religion, wrote a fine history, *Radical Sects in Revolutionary New England*, in which he described numerous forms of American Protestantism. Although some of these groups came close enough to make an argument that they were new religions, Marini concludes that they were all "idiosyncratic forms of Protestant Christianity."[26]

Mormonism, of course, is not merely a different type of Protestant Christianity. In the first place, while Mormonism is Christian, it is not Protestant. Neither is it Catholic nor Orthodox. It does not fit into any of the Christian categories that existed in 1830. The reasons are probably varied, but it is likely that the ancestors of the people who became Mormons came from the radical segment of the Protestant Reformation. They had been Antinomians, Anabaptists, Quakers, and members of the Family of Love and other ephemeral groups, many of whom had been ostracized from their communities. Some, including Pratt's ancestors, left Massachusetts

[26] Stephen A. Marini, *Radical Sects of Revolutionary New England* (Cambridge, Mass.: Harvard University Press, 1982).

Bay Colony because they did not fit in religiously; others who did not leave were whipped, mutilated, or even hanged for their beliefs. This could help account for the willingness of Pratt and his followers to accept a totally new form of Christianity whose roots are as Hebraic as they are Christian. But it is necessary here to make clear distinctions between a radically new religious movement that differs from every other form of Christianity existing on the earth and simply new forms of older Christian institutions.

Because freedom makes a place for religious questioning, by the early years of the nineteenth century, religious "seekers" were everywhere challenging the status quo. There were two levels of questions: second order and first order (fundamental) questions. Second order questions lead to disagreements in existing religious groupings. These are questions that deal with doctrine and ritual: Has the religious institution of which I am a part got it right? Do we understand the scriptures correctly? Is our church organized in the New Testament way? How does a person become equipped to be ordained as a member of the clergy? How about the church's ritual life? Is "sprinkling" a satisfactory way to baptize folks—adults and children? Or is immersion necessary? Should the Eucharist be passed to persons sitting in the pews, or do they need to kneel at a communion rail to receive the bread and wine? Should it really be wine? And what kind of bread is acceptable? When a sufficient number of individual members of an existing Christian institution ask such second order questions and agree that the institution to which they belong is wrong, the result is often schism, which leads to the creation of sectarian movements. This process explains the great bulk of religious diversity in nineteenth-century America as well as the incredible level of religious diversity in the nation today.

Mormonism, however, did not emerge as a result of the posing of second order questions. Joseph Smith was not asking whether or how questions. The things that concerned him had to do with truth. Moreover, the answers he received did not simply rearrange the furniture on the decks of an existing institutional boat, to use a clichéd metaphor. The answers that came to him had to do with the nature of God. The young farm boy was provided with access to a new source of religious information: the Book of Mormon. In addition, and this is critically important, the movement that Smith's followers put in place was not a break off from an existing institution. The members of the restored Church of Christ started things all over again. Just as early Christianity was not the result of a schism, neither was this new Christian movement. As early Christianity had been, the movement that coalesced around the prophet was a cultic movement. It came together around a new set of truth claims, and it would eventually become a new religious tradition. To summarize, sects grow up to be churches while cults grow up to become new religious traditions.

Getting from a new religious movement to being a new religious tradition is much more complicated than establishing a new church organization. This requires a four-part process, one that I refer to as the "four R's."[27] In sequential order these are the *reiteration* of the Christian story from the perspective of how Christianity emerged from its Hebraic heritage to become a new tradition; *reinterpretation* of the meaning of the scriptures; *recapitulation* of the key events of the biblical story in a new geographical and linear context; and *ritual re-creation*. This is very different from the sectarian model in which "a saving remnant" withdraws (often ostentatiously) from an existing church body and forms another institution. The four "R" process makes reappropriation of the basic story possible so that it is at once the same sectarian model of a new, different institution and a different institution that is not at all the same.

According to Andrew Jenson in his *Latter-day Saint Biographical Encyclopedia*, Pratt was intimately involved in three of the four parts of the generative process that led to Mormonism's becoming a new religious tradition. To be precise:

- With regard to reiteration, from his youth forward, Pratt was a reader of the scriptures. His youthful days were characterized by soberness and thoughtfulness.

[27] See Shipps, *Mormonism*, chapter 3.

- As for reinterpretation, discovering the Book of Mormon, Pratt was convinced of its truth. He also believed that many plain and precious things were missing from the Old and New Testaments. When he found the Church leaders, he asked for baptism by immersion. He accepted not only the prophet's reinterpretation of the scriptures (such as Joseph Smith's revisions of the biblical text), but also his additions to holy writ, which would eventually become a part of the Pearl of Great Price.
- Of greatest importance, Pratt was involved in the recapitulation of the biblical story as it occurred in the lives of the early Mormons. Along with many other Latter-day Saints, he not only knew the biblical story; he literally lived through the biblical story again. He became a missionary preacher in the pattern laid out by the disciples of Jesus; he went to Missouri and, among much else, "stood on the choice land where the city of Zion would be built"; he gathered with the Saints and traveled through the wilderness to reach the promised land. There, like Abraham, Isaac, and Jacob, he became a polygamist and, between missions, lived with his multiple wives in the kingdom in the tops of the mountains. He was elected to the legislature of the State of Deseret and afterward to the territorial legislature. Finally, Pratt was murdered for his beliefs/actions in entering into a plural marriage with a woman who was still legally married to someone else.[28]

Because his murder came too soon, Pratt was never really involved in the *ritual re-creation* of the biblical story in a new context, with new rituals to mark the recapitulation of the Saints living through both the Old and New Testament stories once again. (For example, the Saints' July 24 celebrations not only mark their arrival in the Salt Lake Valley but their traversing of the wilderness and their arrival in the land of promise.)

Finally, there is the question of how people from the outside saw what was going on. In the beginning, despite the Book of Mormon and the claims of prophetic agency that supports the restoration of the priesthood and the Church, this new movement was seen as just one more sectarian rendering of Protestantism. In the burned-over district of western New York, LDS Church members were more competitors than anything else. Joseph Smith and his

[28] Andrew Jenson, *Latter-day Saint Biographical Encyclopedia: A Compilation of Biographical Sketches of Prominent Men and Women in the Church of Jesus Christ of Latter-day Saints* (Salt Lake City: Andrew Jenson History Company, 1901), 1:83–85.

compatriots were subjected to "persecution," but most of it was the sort of persecution that fits into the category of words.

Pratt was never truly part of the western New York scene. He experienced real persecution in Missouri; he went back and forth across the Midwest from Missouri to Kirtland or vice versa. Although he was often on missions, he was clearly a part of the "gathering" that caused outsiders in the Kirtland and Independence areas to recognize that the followers of Smith had many new beliefs that did not fit into the standard Protestant model.

Although virtually all of the Saints in the 1830s were American citizens, Smith's followers were increasingly seen as not quite American. Like the Jews, the Saints were increasingly seen as "other" in the anthropological sense of the word. And as the comparison of Joseph Smith and Mohammad was progressively more a part of the newspaper coverage of the Saints, the members of this particular Church of Christ were increasingly seen as foreign. The way that William E. McLellin put it in the first of his six journals is extremely revealing. McLellin was an Illinois schoolteacher who was entranced by the idea of Mormon preacher missionaries. Yet even as a Gentile about to choose to be chosen, he referred to them as those "*quear* beings."[29]

This perception intensified as a third Mormon restoration took shape, that is, the inauguration of what the Saints call the "fullness of the gospel," or "the restoration of all things." In the eyes of outsiders, the followers of the Mormon prophet had been competitors first, then "other" or "foreign," as much outside as the Jews. But with the restoration of all things, including plural marriage, they were ever more intensely other, or as some wags put it "not us (U.S.)." Practicing that "relic of barbarism," polygamy, and subscribing to a doctrine they called "blood atonement," the Saints seemed so dangerous to so many that huge numbers of otherwise good American citizens decided the Saints would have to be destroyed "root and branch."

In ordinary space and time, Parley Pratt's murder was simply the taking of the life of a bigamist. But in the context of the Saints'

[29] Shipps and Welch, *Journals of William E. McLellin*, 29.

belief system, he suffered and bled to death. In the eyes of the Saints, this made him a "noble martyr," a great man who died for the cause of the truth he had so untiringly advocated for twenty-seven years.[30] So it is that even the death of this Latter-day Saint proved to be a window onto the story of the Mormons. The half century after his death would see the Saints still vilified for their beliefs, even as they built up the kingdom. Pratt's murder prefigured the reality that to be fully functioning members of the larger American community, the Saints themselves would have to give up polygamy and their organized kingdom.

[30] Jenson, *Biographical Encyclopedia*, 1:85.

CHAPTER 2

The Family Life of Parley P. Pratt

A Case Study of Mormon Plural Marriage

R. Steven Pratt

Parley P. Pratt wrote a short sketch of his life in 1853, telling a boyhood friend, "Its plain simple truths would be far more strange to you, than the thousand volumes of Modern Fiction." One of the "simple truths" Pratt knew would surprise his friend involved his unconventional family. Pratt wrote:

> I have been Married a dozen times and have now seven living wives and am the Father of near thirty Children. It would do you good to see my family circle assembled for family worship in our great parlor. One of my wives is a native of New Hampshire, another of New York, one of Pennsylvania, one of Ohio, two of England, one of Scotland; my little boys and girls are fine good children as can be found. We generally live in love and harmony, and I have very seldom a wife who would be willing to live aside from the society of the others. They love and mutually assist each other and so do the children.[1]

[1] Parley P. Pratt to William Patterson, 9 May 1853, Parley P. Pratt Papers (hereafter PPP Papers), Church History Library, the Church of Jesus Christ of Latter-day Saints, Salt Lake City, Utah (hereafter LDS Church History Library).

Though Pratt portrayed his life as a polygamous husband as idyllic, the unusually rich sources on his family life also demonstrate the complications and difficulties of early Mormon plural marriage. His experience, both as a monogamist husband before the introduction of polygamy and as the head of a large plural family, provides important examples of the complexities and intricacies of early Mormon family practices.

Parley Pratt and Thankful Halsey, 1827–1837

At the age of twenty in 1827, Pratt married a thirty-year-old widow, Thankful Halsey. The previous year, Pratt, recently baptized into the Baptist Church, had left his boyhood home in New York for the West, where he hoped to preach and convert American Indians to Christianity. He settled in Russia Township, Loraine County, Ohio, where he spent a winter in a small hut in the woods near the township reading the Bible and other literature.[2] When spring came, he bargained for a piece of forest land, promising to pay over a period of years, and built a small house. He then returned to Columbia County, New York, to ask Thankful, who resided in Ghent, New York, a short distance from his old home in New Lebanon, to marry him. Pratt described her as a tall, slender woman with an oval-shaped face, clear complexion, large eyes, and dark hair. Additionally, she had a "mild and affectionate disposition" and was full of "energy, perseverance, industry and cheerfulness." In July 1827, he arrived at her door and asked her to walk with him a short distance. After describing his house in the wilderness and his plans for preaching to American Indians, he stated, "In view of all these things. If you still love me and desire to share my future you are worthy to be my wife. If not, we will agree to be friends forever; but part to meet no more in time."

---

[2] Parley P. Pratt, *Autobiography of Parley Parker Pratt, One of the Twelve Apostles of the Church of Jesus Christ of Latter-day Saints, Embracing His Life, Ministry, and Travels, with Extracts in Prose and Verse from His Miscellaneous Writings*, ed. Parley Pratt, Jr. (New York: Russell Brothers, 1874), 26–28; and "Beware of Imposters," *Painesville Telegraph*, 14 December 1830.

Thankful replied, "I have loved you during three years absence, and I never can be happy without you." On September 9, 1827, they were married by Elder Electa Palmer, a lay minister of the Flat Brook Baptist Church of Canaan, New York.[3]

Joined by Pratt's younger brothers Orson and Nelson, the couple returned to Ohio a month after their wedding. They used Thankful's savings to pay an installment on the land; Orson and Nelson boarded with farmers and found other work in the area.[4] By 1829, Parley and Thankful had built a small frame house on their property, and Thankful taught school in the original home her husband had constructed. That same year, Pratt was swept up into a religious movement led by Sidney Rigdon, who proclaimed a restorationist New Testament Christianity of faith, repentance, baptism, and the promise of the Gift of the Holy Ghost. Rigdon exhorted his followers to reject all creeds and take the Bible as the sole norm of faith. He was associated with the Disciples of Christ movement, which was led by Thomas and Alexander Campbell and Walter Scott. His doctrines, including the coming millennial reign of Christ, "delighted his audience with things new and old" and won many converts. On hearing the message, Pratt felt that he had found "the Ancient Gospel in due form" and soon joined the group, though he was convinced that the authority to minister was not on the earth and must be restored.[5]

Notwithstanding his doubts, Pratt embraced his newfound religion and felt a duty to preach. In August 1830, he closed out his business, leaving him and Thankful with only ten dollars. Some of his financial obligations must have remained unresolved, as later that year he was arrested for unpaid debts. He and Thankful decided to return to Canaan before he began his formal ministry.

[3] Pratt, *Autobiography*, 29–30; and Minutes of the Flat Brook Baptist Church, Canaan, New York, 1820–1822.

[4] Elden J. Watson, ed., *The Orson Pratt Journals* (Salt Lake City: Elden Jay Watson, 1975), 7–8; Pratt, *Autobiography*, 30; and Rev. Frederick W. Chapman, *The Pratt Family: or Descendants of William Pratt, One of the First Settlers of Hartford and Say-Brook* (1864), 160.

[5] Milton Backman, "A Non-Mormon View of the Birth of Mormonism in Ohio," *BYU Studies* 12 (Summer 1972): 346–64; and Pratt, *Autobiography*, 31–33.

While on the Erie Canal, Pratt told his wife that the "Spirit" had whispered for him to leave the boat and labor in the region around Rochester. Thankful agreed to go to their "native Place" while Pratt preached. Soon after, Pratt encountered the Book of Mormon and joined the new Mormon movement on September 1, 1830. He then journeyed on to meet Thankful and other members of his family in Columbia County, where he baptized his brother Orson, who had also returned to New York from Ohio. Parley and Thankful then traveled to Fayette, New York, the headquarters of the Church, where Pratt was called to a mission to the American Indians.

Beginning a pattern that characterized their marriage, Parley left Thankful in the care of the Whitmers, a family central to early Mormonism, as he performed a mission in Ohio and Missouri. In Kirtland, Ohio, Pratt was instrumental in converting to Mormonism many seekers in the area, including his former religious mentor Rigdon. He then traveled to Missouri to preach to the American Indians before returning to Kirtland in May 1831, where he met up with Thankful again; she had been baptized into the Mormon Church during his absence. Thankful was ill, as she often was during their marriage, but happy to see him. With the help of neighbors and sixty dollars of her savings, the Pratts moved to Kaw Township, Missouri, where the Church was establishing its Zion community.[6]

Arriving in Missouri on August 1, 1832, Pratt purchased lands and then turned them over to the Church and was deeded back a portion under the lease-loan system in operation in the Mormon community at the time.[7] He worked that winter in harvesting, planting winter wheat, building a cabin, and teaching school to the Mormons in the new Jackson County settlements.[8] However, Lewis Abbott, who had apparently helped the Pratts move to Jackson County, demanded full payment immediately, taking

[6] Pratt, *Autobiography*, 49, 85.

[7] Leonard Arrington, "Early Mormon Communitarianism," in Marvin Hill and James B. Allen, eds., *Mormonism and American Culture* (New York: Harper & Row, 1972), 37–45.

[8] Pratt, *Autobiography*, 88; and Eleanor M. Johnson, "Gathering of the Mormons in Jackson, County" (master's thesis, University of Nebraska, 1927), 31.

everything the couple had, including eighty acres, except for one cow.[9] Pratt and his wife tried to eke out an existence with the small wages he received from the students; soon, however, Pratt was called to preach in Greene County, Illinois, leaving Thankful to run the school.[10]

After his return from that mission, Parley and Thankful became embroiled in the problems between the old settlers of Jackson County and the Mormons. When a group of Missouri vigilantes attacked a Mormon settlement on the Big Blue River, Pratt gathered sixty men to defend the community. While posting guards, he was struck over the head by Robert Johnson, a local Missourian, with the barrel of his rifle. As blood streamed down his face, Pratt commanded the Mormon guard to seize Johnson and a friend, though they were released the following morning. On November 6, 1833, after unsuccessfully seeking redress from Missouri judge John F. Ryland, Pratt was forced to flee his cabin by a mob in the middle of the night. John Lowry, a Latter-day Saint who had a permit from Missouri officials to move his family in a covered wagon, concealed Pratt in the wagon and carried him to the Missouri River, where he hid in a cave.[11] Worried about Thankful, Parley sent a young man back to find her.[12] She had joined with a group of women and children and escaped under the leadership of Solomon Hancock, riding the final fifteen miles to safety with the help of the young man, and was reunited with Pratt in the cave. At the "risk of his life," Pratt returned for his household goods but lost

---

[9] Pratt, *Autobiography*, 88; and Lewis Abbott, "Petition to Congress," L. Tom Perry Special Collections, Brigham Young University (hereafter BYU), Provo Utah.

[10] Far West Record, 32–33, LDS Church History Library; and Pratt, *Autobiography*, 88.

[11] *Evening and Morning Star Extra*, February 1834, 1; Pratt, *Autobiography*, 88–103; Parley P. Pratt, *History of the Late Persecution Inflicted by the State of Missouri upon the Mormons in Which Ten Thousand American Citizens Were Robbed, Plundered, and Driven from the State, and Many Others Imprisoned, Martyred, &c. for Their Religion, and All This by Military Force, by Order of the Executive* (Detroit: Dawson and Bates, 1839), 7–25; William E. McLellin to Samuel McLellin, August 4, 1832, LDS Church History Library; and H. S. Salisbury, "History of Education in the Church of Jesus Christ of Latter Day Saints," *Journal of History* 15, no. 3 (July 1922): 269.

[12] Pratt, *History of the Late Persecution*, 23; and Pratt, *Autobiography*, 101.

his house and field of wheat. He and Thankful pitched a tent and began living in a new community the Mormons called Liberty. The ordeal left Thankful sick and helpless much of the time.[13]

Pratt quickly constructed a house and supported himself and Thankful through "day labor, jobbing, building and wood cutting."[14] At a Church conference at Pratt's house on January 1, 1834, Pratt and Lyman Wight volunteered to travel to Kirtland to report the Jackson County situation to Joseph Smith and other Mormon leaders. As a result, Smith organized Zion's Camp, a paramilitary company that hoped to restore the Saints to their lands in Jackson County, and designated Pratt to recruit participants. During the recruitment, Pratt visited his in-laws in Ghent to calm them down over the situation in Missouri. Thankful's mother, also named Thankful, had written to Joseph Smith about her daughter and was answered by Oliver Cowdery that Thankful Pratt "was in a low state of Health" (which probably did little to comfort the anxious mother) but otherwise in comfortable circumstances.[15]

Following his participation in Zion's Camp, Pratt returned to Liberty, where he served as a high councillor in Clay County.[16] Because of Thankful's illness during his absence, she had amassed a large debt that Parley worked to repay.[17] After petitioning Joseph Smith for advice, Pratt received instructions from Smith to move his family to Kirtland, Ohio, which he did in October 1834 with literally no money and an ill wife. They settled in New Portage, a small town fifty miles from Kirtland, where Pratt built a temporary cabin. Their debts from Missouri, however, stalked them, as Church leader William W. Phelps wrote Joseph Smith and suspended Pratt's license to preach for lack of payment for debts.

---

[13] John Corrill to Oliver Cowdery, December 1833, *Evening and Morning Star*, January 1834; Edward Tullidge, *Women of Mormondom* (New York: Tullidge and Crandall, 1877), 164–65; Pratt, *History of the Late Persecution*, 23; and Pratt, *Autobiography*, 103.

[14] Pratt, *Autobiography*, 103, 107; and Pratt, *History of the Late Persecution*, 22–23.

[15] Pratt, *Autobiography*, 107–13; and Oliver Cowdery to Thankful Halsey, 4 March 1834, Oliver Cowdery Letter Book, No. 27, Huntington Library, San Marino, California.

[16] Pratt, *Autobiography*, 117.

[17] W. W. Phelps to Brethren, 24 August 1834, *The Evening and the Morning Sta*r, September 1834; and Far West Record, 49–50, LDS Church History Library.

After presenting his case to Smith in February 1835 at Kirtland, Pratt not only received forgiveness and a return of his license but was also ordained by Smith, Oliver Cowdery, and David Whitmer as one of the original Twelve Apostles of the Church.[18]

At this time, Pratt was building a larger house in New Portage, which would be the first permanent house he had built since they left Russia Township. Thus, Pratt initially hesitated when he received a call to accompany the newly called apostles on a mission to the eastern states in March 1835, as he felt his family (which now included his mother, Charity Dickinson Pratt, who had recently arrived to live with him) needed his help. As he pondered whether to accept the mission call, his unfinished house, a two-story frame building full of lumber and shavings, caught fire one night and burned to the ground. Pratt viewed it as a providential sign for him to go on the mission, so he again left his wife and mother with a friendly family and departed.[19]

After returning to Ohio, Pratt moved with his wife to Kirtland in October 1835 and purchased some lots with the help of Joseph Smith and again began building a home. In January 1836, Jonathan and Caroline Crosby moved into Kirtland from Wendell, Massachusetts, and boarded at Pratt's house until March 1836. While Jonathan and Parley attended meetings almost every night, Caroline and Thankful spent much time together. Caroline stated that she enjoyed herself with Thankful, whom she described as a "very sociable interesting woman, but had very delicate health," as she "was afflicted with severe spells of sick headache, which came upon her monthly."[20]

In April 1836, Parley was home with Thankful, wondering what he should do about another mission call, this time to Canada.

---

[18] Pratt, *Autobiography*, 117–27; and Minutes of Quorum of Twelve, Patriarchal Blessing Book, 14–27 February 1835, LDS Church History Library.

[19] Parley P. Pratt to Asael Smith, 21 July 1835, George A. Smith Papers, University of Utah Special Collections; and Minutes of Quorum of Twelve, 26 April 1835 to 28 August 1835, LDS Church History Library.

[20] Jonathan Crosby, Journal, 9 January to March 1836, LDS Church History Library; and Caroline B. Crosby, Journal, 9 January to March 1836, LDS Church History Library.

Thankful was still ill and they were in debt to Smith and others. Heber C. Kimball knocked on the door and once inside prophesied that Thankful would be healed and would give Parley a son and that Parley's mission to Canada would open the door to missionary work in England. This greatly affected the thirty-nine-year-old Thankful and her twenty-nine-year-old husband, as they had no children during their nine-year marriage. Parley went on the mission, even taking Thankful with him on one of the trips. His Canadian venture resulted in the baptism of future Church president John Taylor and many others. Seven days after her fortieth birthday on March 25, 1837, Thankful gave birth to Parley P. Pratt, Jr. The day before, Thankful related to her husband a dream that she was going to paradise and said she longed for death to relieve her suffering. Three hours after the birth, Thankful was dead, leaving Parley overwhelmed with grief and loneliness. Thankful was buried in the churchyard near the temple.[21]

Parley Pratt and Mary Ann Frost, 1837–1843

Pratt now faced the prospect of living alone plus caring for his new son, Parley. He initially left his son in the care of a Sister Allen and went back to Canada to check on the mission and overcome his grief.[22] On his return to Kirtland in April 1837, he courted Mary Ann Frost Stearns, who had moved to Kirtland in July 1836 along with her daughter, Mary Ann Stearns.[23] Parley and Mary Ann had become acquainted in August 1835 when they both attended a Church conference in Saco, Maine (a short distance from her hometown of Bethel, Maine). Mary Ann's first husband, Nathan Stearns, had died two years earlier, leaving her a widow with a

[21] Pratt, *Autobiography*, 130–68; *Latter-day Saints' Messenger and Advocate* (May 1836), 377–97; Parley P. Pratt to John Taylor, 27 November 1836, John Taylor Papers, LDS Church History Library; *Messenger and Advocate* (April 1837), 496; and Wilford Woodruff, Journal, 26 March 1837, LDS Church History Library.

[22] Pratt, *Autobiography*, 183.

[23] *Messenger and Advocate* (May 1837): 512; and Parley P. Pratt, "Family Record of Parley Parker Pratt," PPP Papers.

four-month-old baby. Parley and Mary Ann were married on May 14, 1837, by Frederick G. Williams.[24]

The newlyweds' happiness was short-lived, as financial problems again plagued Pratt. He had joined the Kirtland Safety Society, a banking institution, and had purchased some lots from Joseph Smith and Brigham Young, who had arranged a deal with Claudius Stannard for the title.[25] When Pratt was unable to complete payment for the lots, Smith was forced to foreclose because Stannard was pressuring him for payment. Sidney Rigdon, acting as an agent of the bank, served Pratt notice. Infuriated, Pratt sent a scathing letter to Smith, accusing him of land speculation and trying to destroy him.[26] By June 15, 1837, Pratt and his brother Orson had joined with leaders opposed to Smith in giving speeches in the temple against the prophet and his land dealings.[27] Finally after persuasion from John Taylor and Smith, Pratt confessed to Smith his error and took his wife Mary Ann and her daughter to New York on a mission.[28]

Arriving in New York on August 5, 1837, the couple rented an apartment and Pratt began writing and preaching. From August to October, Pratt wrote his influential pamphlet, *A Voice of Warning*.[29] While Parley carried on his mission duties, Mary Ann traveled to Bethel, Maine, to visit her parents and family, where she spent most of the winter. Parley had intended to go to Maine to

[24] Mary Ann Stearns Winters, "An Autobiographical Sketch of the Life of the Late Mary Ann Stearns Winters," LDS Church History Library.

[25] Geauga County Land Record, Record of Court of Common Pleas, Geauga County, Ohio, Book U, 585–86; and Kirtland Safety Society Stock Ledger, original in Chicago Historical Society, microfilm copy, L. Tom Perry Special Collections, BYU.

[26] Parley P. Pratt to Joseph Smith, 23 Mary 1837, *Zion's Watchman*, 28 March 1838.

[27] Mary Fielding to Mercy Fielding, 15 June 1837, Mary Fielding Papers, LDS Church History Library; and Lyman E. Johnson and Orson Pratt to Newel K. Whitney, 29 May 1837, Newel K. Whitney Collection, BYU.

[28] B.H. Roberts, *Life of John Taylor* (Salt Lake City: Bookcraft, 1975), 39–41; Pratt, *Autobiography*, 184; Mary Fielding to Mercy Fielding, 5 July 1837, LDS Church History Library; and Mary Russell to Isaac Russell, 17 July 1837, Isaac Russell Papers, LDS Church History Library.

[29] Parley P. Pratt to Don Carlos Smith, 3 October 1837, *Elders Journal* 1 (October 1837): 8–9; Pratt, *Autobiography*, 168; and Winters, "Autobiographical Sketch," 5.

meet his in-laws and then travel back with Mary Ann to Kirtland. By November, though, the winter prevented him from doing so, so he wrote to Mary Ann that he would not able to come but would try to come that spring. In addition, he stated that he missed her and her young daughter terribly and wished they could be with him always.[30] In the spring, Mary Ann rejoined her husband, and they moved to Far West, Missouri, where the Saints were gathering.[31] At Far West, they built a home and Mary gave birth to a son, Nathan, on August 31, 1838.[32]

Happiness was again fleeting, as Pratt soon became embroiled in the renewed clashes between Mormons and Missourians. As a member of a Mormon militia company, he participated in the Battle of Crooked River on October 25, leading to his arrest, along with a group of other Mormon leaders, on various charges.[33] Before leaving Far West for Independence, Pratt was allowed to see his wife. He later recalled:

> This was the most trying scene of all. I went to my house, being guarded by two or three soldiers; the cold rain was pouring down without, and on entering my little cottage, there lay my wife sick of a fever, with which she had been for some time confined. At her breast was our son Nathan, an infant of three months, and by her side a little girl of five years. On the foot of the same bed lay a woman in travail, who had been driven from her house in the night, and had taken momentary shelter in my hut of ten feet square—my larger house having been torn down. I stepped to the bed; my wife burst into tears; I spoke a few words of comfort, telling her to try to live for my sake and the children's; and expressing a hope that we should meet again though years might separate us. She promised to try to live. I then embraced and kissed the little babes and departed.[34]

[30] Parley P. Pratt to Mary Ann Frost Pratt, 25 November 1837, PPP Papers.

[31] Pratt, *Autobiography*, 169–73.

[32] Pratt, Family Record.

[33] Pratt, *History of the Late Persecution*, 33–40; Joseph Smith, Jr., *History of the Church of Jesus Christ of Latter-day Saints*, ed. B.H. Roberts, 2nd ed., rev., 7 vols. (Salt Lake City: Deseret Book, 1971), 3:169–99; Pratt, *Autobiography*, 173–98; and *Document Showing the Testimony Given Before the Judge of the Fifth Judicial District of the State of Missouri, on the Trial of Joseph Smith Jr. and Others, for High Treason and Other Crimes Against the State* (Washington, D.C.: U.S. Printing Office, 1841), 281.

[34] Pratt, *Autobiography*, 207.

Pratt and the other prisoners were taken to Independence where they were treated better than expected. To Mary Ann, Parley poignantly wrote: "Our greatest Pain Is for our families and the Church, knowing that you are Exposed to danger to famine and perhaps to Death; But we Can Only Pray for you, and Leave you in the hands of God, and May the Lord god Bless and preserve you and us and Spedily Restore us to the Bosom of our families."[35] In Independence, Pratt, Joseph Smith, and other prisoners were tried before a court of inquiry that bound Smith and others to Liberty Jail on the charge of treason, and Pratt and four others to Richmond on the charge of murder for his participation in the Battle of Crooked River.[36] While in Richmond Jail, Parley asked Mary Ann, then in Far West, to live with him in prison because he thought it would be much cheaper and more comfortable for her than remaining alone in the leaking hut in Far West with no help.[37] She complied with Parley's request and on December 9, 1838, arrived with their new baby, Nathan, and daughter, Mary Ann (Parley, Jr., was still with Sister Allen). She and Parley then wrote a lengthy letter to her parents, projecting themselves as safe, though in prison. They claimed to feel privileged to suffer afflictions for the "gospels Sake." Mary Ann reassured her parents: "I never lost one minuts sleep through all the trouble. I believed that the Lord would protect us."[38]

From December 1838 through March 1839, the Pratts stayed at the Richmond Jail along with the other prisoners and some of their wives. The prisoners were sometimes abused and threatened, and their mail was carefully examined by the guards. Because of the security, Pratt was writing an account of the Mormon experience in Missouri in secret. Aware that he had been writing extensively, the guards set up a time to search his belongings. Parley hid the manuscript in a pillowcase that was attached to Mary Ann's undergarments "in the form of an apron." When they saw the

[35] Parley P. Pratt to Mary Ann Frost Pratt, 4 November 1838, PPP Papers.

[36] Smith, *History of the Church*, 3:200–205; Pratt, *Autobiography*, 209–15; *Document Showing the Testimony*, 1–47; and Pratt, *History of the Late Persecution*, 43–47.

[37] Parley P. Pratt to Mary Ann Pratt, 1 December 1838, PPP Papers.

[38] Mary Ann Frost Pratt to Aaron and Susan Frost, 9 December 1838, PPP Papers.

guards coming to conduct the search, they decided to remove it from Mary Ann's person and hide it in a straw bed in the dungeon. As Pratt ascended the ladder, his six-year-old stepdaughter was close behind him. When Pratt lifted the huge trap door, it slipped from his grasp and fell on her, leaving her head and arm bruised. Pratt realized instantly that this accident could be used to save the manuscript and instructed his wife to run below with the manuscript hidden on her. At the same time, he yelled to the guards who were outside of the jail that their daughter was hurt and that her mother "wished to go out instantly for some spirits to put in her camphor bottle to bathe the bruised child." The guards allowed Mary Ann, with the manuscript and her daughter, to leave. Parley feared that she would be searched upon her return so he asked the wife of fellow prisoner Luman Gibbs to take her a note that read: "Mrs. Pratt let the truth remain with the people of Main." Parley also removed his shoes and asked the guard to give them to Mary Ann to have them mended. When his wife received the message, she knew what to do. She took her husband's shoes and the manuscript to a shoemaker named Sylvester B. Stoddard, a secret disciple of the Church from Maine, thus saving the manuscript.[39] Mary Ann and her children finally left the prison on March 17, 1839, arriving in Quincy, Illinois, the latter part of April.[40] Pratt and his fellow prisoners were transferred to a jail in Columbia, Missouri, in late May 1838, and on July 4, 1839, Pratt ended his imprisonment by escaping and traveling to Quincy, where he was reunited with his family.[41] Parley and Mary Ann then moved to Commerce, Illinois (soon renamed Nauvoo).[42]

Within a month, Pratt and his family left on a mission for England with the other apostles. While waiting in the East for the ship to sail, Pratt published his book on the Missouri "persecutions"

---

[39] Morris Phelps, "Account from October 1838 to April 1839," LDS Church History Library, 17–19; and Pratt, *History of the Late Persecution*, 66–68.

[40] Pratt, *Autobiography*, 225–42; and Smith, *History of the Church*, 3:319–23.

[41] On Pratt's letters to his family during his time in prison, see chapter 4 in this volume.

[42] Pratt, *Autobiography*, 294–302; and Parley P. Pratt, "Sketch of Travels in America and Voyage to England," *Latter-day Saints' Millennial Star* (July 1840): 49–52.

and visited Joseph Smith in Washington, D.C., and Philadelphia, where Smith taught Pratt the doctrine of eternal marriage.[43] Smith told Pratt, who had been troubled over the relationship between himself and Thankful in the world to come, that Thankful could be "secured to him for time and all eternity."[44] This greatly excited Pratt, but it was three more years before Smith fully explained the doctrine of eternal marriage.

Pratt went to England while Mary Ann stayed in the East. Upon arriving in England in April 1840, he was appointed the first editor of a new British periodical, the *Latter-day Saints' Millennial Star,* and also designated to run a bookstore and press.[45] Parley hoped Mary Ann would soon follow him to England but in July learned that she was ill with scarlet fever and wanted him to come and be with her. On July 10, the apostles voted to allow Pratt to return to New York to bring his family to England. Mary Ann and the children, who had recovered from the illness, were overjoyed and surprised to see him. After visiting her family in Maine, the Pratts returned to New York, accompanied by Olive, Mary Ann's sister, who agreed to help tend the children. They arrived back in England in October and moved into the *Millennial Star* office.[46]

During the two years in England, the Pratts increased their family with the addition of a daughter, Olivia, on June 2, 1841.[47] Each family member assisted in the publication of the *Millennial Star,*

---

[43] Pratt, *Autobiography*, 297–99; and Parley P. Pratt to Joseph Smith, 22 November 1839, Joseph Smith Papers, LDS Church History Library.

[44] Parley P. Pratt to Mary Ann Frost Pratt, 6 April 1840, PPP Papers.

[45] *Times and Seasons* 1 (June 1840): 119–22; Smith, *History of the Church*, 4:114–20; Woodruff, Journal, 14–17 April 1840; Parley P. Pratt to Brigham Young, 4 May 1840, PPP Papers; Parley P. Pratt to Mary Ann Pratt, 6 July 1840, PPP Papers; and Pratt, *Autobiography*, 303–29.

[46] Pratt, *Autobiography*, 308–309; Woodruff, Journal, 5–11 July 1840; William Clayton, Journal, 10 July 1840, LDS Church History Library; Elden J. Watson, ed., *Manuscript History of Brigham Young, 1801–1844* (Salt Lake City: Smith Secretarial Service, 1969), 78–79; and Brigham Young, discourse, 31 August 1856, *Journal of Discourses of Brigham Young, President of the Church of Jesus Christ of Latter-day Saints, His Two Counselors, the Twelve Apostles, and Others*, 26 vols. (Liverpool, England: F.D. Richards and S.W. Richards, 1854–1886), 4:35–36.

[47] Pratt, Family Record.

as even the older children, daughter Mary Ann and son Parley, helped fold the papers. By the time the family left on October 29, 1842, Mary Ann was three months pregnant. The journey home was precarious, and several Mormon immigrants perished aboard ship. After arriving in New Orleans, the group chartered a steamer bound for St. Louis. The various deaths loomed large, as the Pratts' young Olivia had developed whopping cough.[48] The family disembarked at Chester, Illinois, and Pratt hurried 240 miles to Nauvoo to get help for his pregnant wife and sick family.[49] Soon before their arrival in Nauvoo, Mary Ann delivered a baby girl named Susan.[50]

Plural Marriage in Nauvoo

When Pratt and his wife disembarked with their family, including their week-old baby, Susan, in Nauvoo on April 12, 1843, Joseph Smith openly wept as he greeted them. Smith took them to his own home and instructed his bodyguards to place Mary Ann in a chair and carry her.[51] One to two months later, Smith introduced Pratt to his most startling doctrinal innovation—plural marriage. According to biographer Reva Stanley, Pratt first opposed the doctrine and told Smith so; however, after an all-night prayer and a vision of Thankful visiting him and instructing him to accept it, Pratt did so.[52] Pratt also became somewhat aware of the doctrine through accounts of a rumored relationship between his sister-in-law Sarah Marinda Bates Pratt, wife of Orson Pratt, and either Joseph Smith or John C. Bennett, as well as a controversy surrounding Brigham Young and Martha Brotherton the previous

[48] Winters, "Autobiographical Sketch"; Parley P. Pratt to Thomas Ward, 21 January 1843, *Millennial Star*, 3 (12 April 1843): 206–207; and Mary Ann Pratt, "Olive Grey Frost," *Historical Record*, 6:235.

[49] Pratt, *Autobiography*, 328–29; Smith, *History of the Church*, 5:265–70; Parley P. Pratt to *Times and Seasons*, 19 March 1843, *Times and Seasons* 4 (15 April 1843): 162–65; and Levi Richards, Journal, 8–29 March 1843, LDS Church History Library.

[50] Pratt, Family Record.

[51] Smith, *History of the Church*, 5:354–57; and Winters, "Autobiographical Sketch," 11.

[52] Vilate Kimball to Heber C. Kimball, 29 June 1843, Heber C. Kimball Papers, LDS Church History Library; and Reva Stanley, *The Archer of Paradise: A Biography of Parley P. Pratt* (Caldwell, Idaho: Caxton Printers, 1937), 163–64.

year.[53] In the summer of 1842, Orson had been almost driven to suicide over competing allegations regarding his wife Sarah—one being that Smith had proposed a polyandrous marriage with her, and the other that she had been involved in an affair with John C. Bennett, formerly associate president of the Church; both allegations were horrifying to Orson. While the truth of the situation is clouded by contradictory accounts, the events demonstrate the confusion and secrecy of early Nauvoo plural marriage.[54]

Pratt was well acquainted with Thomas and Sarah Brotherton, who had worked with him in England before they and their daughters, Martha and Elizabeth, left for Nauvoo in September 1841.[55] Eighteen-year-old Martha, who had known Brigham Young in England, claimed she was approached by Young, Heber Kimball, and Joseph Smith and asked if she would be Young's plural wife. The feisty Martha told them she wanted to consider the proposal. This disturbed the leaders and they swore her to secrecy, but Martha soon told her parents and several others.[56] Church leaders warned the Saints in an April 1842 conference not to believe everything she said. With Bennett's encouragement, Martha decided to publish her story, which started appearing in newspapers in July 1842.[57] All of the Brothertons except for Elizabeth abandoned Mormonism;

---

[53] Brigham Young to Parley P. Pratt, 17 July 1842, Brigham Young Papers; and Elizabeth Brotherton to unnamed recipient, 20 April 1842, *Millennial Star*, 3:74.

[54] Breck England, *The Life and Thought of Orson Pratt* (Salt Lake City: University of Utah Press, 1985), 77–82.

[55] Joseph Fielding to Parley P. Pratt, January 1842, *Millennial Star*, 3 (August 1842): 76–80; Thomas Brotherton to Edward, 7 December 1841, *Millennial Star*, 2 (February 1842): 156; William Clayton to William Hardman, 30 March 1841, *Millennial Star*, 3 (August 1842): 74–76; and "Apostasy," *Millennial Star*, 3 (August 1842): 73–74.

[56] Martha Brotherton to John C. Bennett, 13 July 1842, *St. Louis Bulletin*, 15 July 1842; *Sangamo Journal*, 22 July 1842; *Warsaw Signal*, 23 July 1842; John C. Bennett, *The History of the Saints; or, an Expose of Joe Smith and Mormonism* (Boston: Leland & Whiting, 1842), 236–40; and John McLlwrick to Brigham Young, 27 August 1842, Brigham Young Papers.

[57] *Times and Seasons*, 3 (15 April 1842): 763; "Affidavits and Certificate Disproving the Statements and Affidavits Contained in John C. Bennett's Letters, Nauvoo August 31, 1842"; 27 August Affidavit of Heber C. Kimball, 27 August Affidavit of Brigham Young, 30 August Affidavit of Vilate Kimball, LDS Church History Library; and John E. Page to Joseph Smith, 8 August 1842, Joseph Smith Papers.

Martha left Nauvoo and settled in St. Louis, where she married and raised five children. While there is no doubt that Martha exaggerated somewhat, the basic facts seem to confirm her statement about a Young proposal. Martha's sister, Elizabeth, took the story as truth. (In 1886, after Martha's death, Elizabeth had Martha's dead children sealed, or ritually connected in a temple ceremony, to Young.)[58] While Martha was incensed by Young's proposal, Elizabeth viewed plural marriage quite differently. On April 20, 1842, she wrote Pratt, still in England, accusing her sister of spreading "falsehoods of the basest kind" and reaffirming her faith. She also suggested that Pratt would have the opportunity to know for himself. "I believe it is your privilege," she wrote, perhaps a guarded reference to plural marriage. She continued, "O! how I long to see you and enjoy your society, and unbosom all my care to you."[59]

Soon after Smith told him of plural marriage, Parley began to consult with Mary Ann about prospective wives, including Mary Wood, Mary Aspin, and Elizabeth Brotherton. On June 27, 1843, he wrote to Mary Wood, a twenty-five-year-old Scottish convert whom he and Mary Ann had known in Manchester: "Mrs. Pratt wishes me to say particularly that she wants you to live with us and have one of our upper rooms to follow your trade, which she thinks will be good here; and I think myself that it would give me great pleasure to see two spirits so congenial, so like, each other, live so near as to enjoy other's daily society."[60] Wood accepted the Pratts' offer and arrived in Nauvoo on March 1, 1844; on September 9, 1844, Brigham Young married her to Parley as his fourth

[58] Martha Brotherton was sealed to Brigham Young by proxy on 1 August 1870. Salt Lake Endowment House Record; W. Bigler to Elizabeth B. Pratt, 22 April 1886, PPP Papers; James G. Bleak to Elizabeth Pratt, 10 April 1889, PPP Papers; James G. Bleak to Elizabeth B. Pratt, 3 October 1889, PPP Papers; and Elizabeth Brotherton Pratt: "Autobiography of Elizabeth B. Pratt," *Woman's Exponent* 19, no. 12 (1 December 1890): 94–95; *Woman's Exponent* 19, no. 13 (15 December 1890): 102; and *Woman's Exponent* 19, no. 14 (1 January 1891): 110–11.

[59] Elizabeth Brotherton letter, 20 April 1842, *Millennial Star*, 3 (August 1842): 74.

[60] Parley P. Pratt to Mary Wood, 27 June 1843, cited in "The Fourth Wife: Mary Wood Pratt" by Leah P. Call and Amy P. Romney of Mary Wood Pratt, http://pratt-family.org; and Kate B. Carter, ed., *Parley P. Pratt and His Twelve Wives* (Salt Lake City: Daughters of Utah Pioneers, January 1974), 213–15.

wife and second plural wife. To better understand plural marriage, the Pratts visited Vilate Kimball, who reported to her husband Heber on June 29:

> I have had a visit from brother Parley and his wife. They are truly converted it appears that J——h has taught him some principles and told him his privilege, and even appointed one for him, I dare not tell you who it is, you would be astonished and I guess some tried. She has been to me for council I told her I did not wish to advise in such matters. Sister Pratt has ben rageing against these things, she told me her self that the devil had ben in her untill within a few days past, she said the Lord had shown her it was all right. She wants Parley to go ahead, says she will do all in her power to help him; they are so engaged I fear they will run to fast. They asked me many questions on principle. I told them I did not know much and I rather they would go to those that had authority to teach. Parley said he and J . . . were interupted before he got what instruction he wanted, and now he did not know when he should have an oppertunity. He seemed unwilling to wait, I told him these were sacred things and he better not make a move until he got more instruction.[61]

Mary Ann also accepted plural marriage. William Clayton wrote on August 20 that Pratt "has through his wife made proposals" to Mary Aspen, "but she is dissatisfied." Mary Ann told Aspen that the "Twelve would have more glory than" Clayton.[62]

Along with plural marriage, the Pratts learned of the full doctrine of eternal marriage after arriving in Nauvoo. On June 23, 1843, Hyrum Smith sealed Mary Ann and Parley for eternity, but he did so without the approval of his brother Joseph, who possibly had other plans for Mary Ann.[63] Smith—motivated by the controversies involving John C. Bennett, Sarah Pratt, and the Brothertons—had put several apostles, including Heber Kimball, John Taylor, and perhaps Orson Pratt, through a type of loyalty test by asking for their wives to become his own plural wives. In addition, he wanted to select plural wives for himself who he knew would

---

[61] Vilate Kimball to Heber C. Kimball, 27–29 June 1843, Heber C. Kimball Papers.

[62] George Smith, ed., *An Intimate Chronicle: The Journals of William Clayton* (Salt Lake City: Signature Books, 1995), journal entries of 9 June 1843 and 20 August 1843, 107, 118.

[63] Pratt, Family Record; and Vilate Kimball to Heber C. Kimball, 27–29 June 1843, Heber C. Kimball Papers.

Pratt and his third wife, Elizabeth Brotherton, in 1854. *Courtesy of the International Society, Daughters of Utah Pioneers.*

not betray the secrecy as Brotherton had done.[64] Mary Ann, Pratt's stepdaughter, remembered that Smith told Parley while he, Mary Ann, and her sister Olive were aboard a steamboat excursion in May 1843: "It is the will of the Lord that these two sisters should never be parted (meaning that they should both belong to one man)."[65] Olive Frost later married Joseph Smith.[66]

On July 24, 1843, Pratt had married twenty-seven-year-old Elizabeth Brotherton as his first plural wife in Brigham Young's house

[64] Orson F. Whitney, *Life of Heber C. Kimball* (Salt Lake City: Kimball Family, 1888), 333–35; Daniel W. Backman, "A Study of Mormon Practice of Plural Marriage Before the Death of Joseph Smith" (master's thesis, Purdue University, 1975); Lawrence Foster, *Religion and Sexuality* (New York: Oxford University Press, 1981); Kathryn M. Daynes, *More Wives Than One* (Urbana: University of Illinois Press, 2001); and Richard S. Van Wagoner, *Mormon Polygamy: A History* (Salt Lake City: Signature Books, 1989).

[65] Mary Ann Stearns Winters, "Autobiography," *Relief Society Magazine* (1916): 580–81.

[66] *Historical Record*, 6:235.

in an ordinance performed by Hyrum Smith in the presence of Mary Ann and Mary Ann Young. At this time, Mary Ann was also sealed to Pratt and stood as proxy for Thankful Halsey to be sealed to Pratt.[67] Mary Ann was later sealed to Joseph Smith after his death in February 1846. Elizabeth did not move into the Pratt home but continued to live with her sister and brother-in-law. In October 1844 or 1845, Elizabeth decided not to move to nearby Warsaw. Pratt wrote approvingly, "Stay here and enjoy the Society of the Saints, and be useful to them, instead of serving the Gentiles." He encouraged her to be "employed in doing good to the poor, and nursing the Sick," and added, "When you can Get wages do So, and when you Cannot get wages, be buisy in doing good, and God will bless you, and I will bless you, and you Shall want for no Good thing." Pratt further promised her that she would soon "have a house and home and enjoy more and more of the Society of those you love."[68]

In December 1843, Pratt became a member of the Holy Quorum, a group that met almost every week in Joseph Smith's brick store and received instructions on various principles including the higher ordinances of the temple.[69] Brigham Young received these ordinances with his wife on January 14, 1844, and was instructed to administer them to all of the apostles.[70] On January 21, Smith said that Pratt "had no wife sealed to him for Eternity and asked if there was any harm for him to have another wife for time & Eternity as he would want a wife in the Resurrection or else his glory would be clipped." After the group debated Pratt's situation, Smith again reiterated that Pratt "has no wife sealed to him for Eternity. He has one living wife but she has a former Husband and did not wish to be sealed to

[67] Pratt, Family Record; Mary Ann Pratt Smith Affidavit, Joseph F. Smith Affidavits, LDS Church History Library; and Elizabeth B. Pratt, "Autobiography of Elizabeth B. Pratt."

[68] Parley P. Pratt to Elizabeth Pratt, 7 October 1844, PPP Papers.

[69] Watson, *Manuscript History of Brigham Young*, 2 December 1843, 155–56; and Woodruff, Journal, 2 December 1843.

[70] Watson, *Manuscript History of Brigham Young*, 158; and George A. Smith, Speech, 25 December 1874, St. George Temple, LDS Church History Library.

Parley for Eternity."[71] This statement may suggest that Mary Ann had been promised to Smith for eternity. In addition, neither she nor Elizabeth Brotherton had received their temple endowment, so they could not receive the further temple rituals with Pratt.

The refusal of Mary Ann to be sealed to him weighed heavily on Parley's mind. When he went East to campaign for Joseph Smith's presidential campaign in 1844, Parley wrote to Mary Ann:

> My heart is on my kindred and my friends, the aged parents and the helpless Infants, on the tender wife of my Bosom. in short the helpless family which God has commited to my care. And for whose welfare in time, and in Eternity I feel a Great Responsibility. Aside from them and the Saints the world to me is all a dreary waste, a confused wilderness of bewildered human beings very few of whom are in a situation to be benifited by the Light of Truth. . . . My Dear Wife, I realy desire from the Bottom of my heart to retire for ever, from this wilderness—this sea of confused, and Deranged Inteligences who neither know nor can be taught, and to Devote my principle attention to my family, my kindred, my Ancestors and my offspring, and to those who love the truth.[72]

Mary Ann and Parley remained close after Parley's return from the East following Smith's death. Amidst their initial involvement in plural marriage, Parley and Mary Ann faced a series of personal crises. Tragedy struck the Pratt family when little Nathan was in the construction site of their new home and fell into the cellar, breaking his leg; he soon contracted a fever and died on December 12, 1843.[73] This devastated Parley and Mary Ann. Parley wrote a short article for the *Times and Seasons* about his son. Eliza R. Snow composed a poem to console Mary Ann, and Joseph Smith visited the family to mourn with them.[74] In August 1844, Mary Ann and one-year-old Susan were afflicted by cholera and Susan also died.[75]

[71] Woodruff, Journal, 21 January 1844; and Devery S. Anderson and Gary James Bergera, eds., *Joseph Smith's Quorum of the Anointed*, 1842–1845 (Salt Lake City: Signature Books, 2005), entry for 21 January 1844, 55–56.

[72] Parley P. Pratt to Mary Ann Pratt, 26 April 1844, PPP Papers.

[73] Winters, "Autobiography," 579; and Pratt, Family Record.

[74] Eliza R. Snow, "To Mrs. Mary Pratt on the Death of Her Little Son," *Times and Seasons*, 5 (March 1844): 463; Parley P. Pratt, "Biography of Nathan Pratt," *Times and Seasons*, 5 (15 January 1844): 414–15; and Smith, *History of the Church*, 6:153.

[75] Pratt, Family Record.

Sisters Susan and Hannahette Snively came to assist the struggling family. The Snively house, a few doors from the Pratt home, had become a type of Nauvoo hospital with the Snivelys caring for many sick children.[76] Hannahette was particularly concerned with the Pratts and came to their house several times to care for Mary Ann and the children. Pratt later wrote: "Coming to the house and kindly taking care of the sick never shall I forget that time. It opened an acquaintance and laid the foundation of a friendship which will be as durable as the throne of Jehovah."[77] Parley soon entered into two more plural marriages, first to twenty-five-year-old Mary Wood on September 9, 1844, and then to thirty-two-year-old Hannahette Snively on November 2, 1844; both sealings were performed by Brigham Young at the Pratt home.[78]

In late September 1844, Belinda Marden arrived in Nauvoo from Boston. She had recently left her husband Benjamin A. Hilton—who had renounced Mormonism and tried to force her not to attend her meetings—and traveled to Nauvoo with the aid of Church leaders. Though she did not obtain a divorce, she considered her marriage to Hilton over. Belinda had known Pratt in Boston and soon renewed her acquaintance with him. Three weeks after his marriage to Hannahette, Parley married Belinda on November 20, 1844, in a secret ceremony (because of the lack of a formal divorce) in Erastus Snow's house with only Snow and Young as witnesses.[79] Ten days after the sealing, Pratt left on a mission for the eastern states to help consolidate the authority of the Twelve Apostles in the era following the death of Joseph Smith and to bring into control problems caused by William Smith and George J. Adams related to plural marriage.[80] The situation partly

[76] Henrietta Hope Russell Platt, "Hannahette Snively Pratt," in Carter, *Twelve Wives*, 215–16.

[77] Parley P. Pratt to Hannahette Snively Pratt, 5 June 1845, PPP Papers.

[78] Pratt, Family Record.

[79] Belinda Marden Pratt, Autobiographical Sketch, 17 February 1884, 1–3, Belinda Marden Papers, LDS Church History Library; and Gary James Bergera, "Identifying the Earliest Mormon Polygamists, 1841–44," *Dialogue* 38 (Fall 2005): 19–24.

[80] Wilford Woodruff to Brigham Young, 9–14 October 1844, Brigham Young Papers; and Pratt, *Autobiography*, 337.

revolved around the question of who had authority to authorize plural marriages.

This was a critical moment in the relationship of Parley and Mary Ann. Mary Ann was ready to deliver Parley's fifth child after they had lost two children within the previous year. Likely adding to Mary Ann's strain was that Hannahette had become pregnant, and Parley was taking Belinda with him on his mission to the East (though Mary Ann may not have known this).[81] From Wheeling, Virginia, Parley wrote Mary Ann a bittersweet letter on December 18, 1844: "I never left home with more intense feelings, Nor under more trying Circumstances than the present, except the time I went to prison and to death Leaving you Sick of a fever with a babe 3 months old and to the mercy of Savages." He promised Mary Ann: "Now My Dear, what Shall I say to you, you Shall ever be with me and all I have is thine and I am thine for ever and you Shall forever Reign in Glory and in a fulness of Joy with those you love. So be of good Cheer and you Shall not often have trials hereafter but Shall be blessed; for you have sacrifised enough and a day of blessing awaits you." Parley also sent a brief message through Mary Ann to "Sister Wood and Others": "My Love to them and God bless them and he knows what is in my big heart though only expressed in those few words."[82]

When Pratt finally arrived in the eastern states, he succeeded in correcting some of the problems with William Smith and George J. Adams. Brigham Young believed that only he possessed the authority to authorize plural marriages, while Pratt felt that the Quorum of Twelve members could perform sealings in the absence of Young.[83] This had to be clarified later in a series of

---

[81] Pratt, Family Record; Belinda Marden Pratt, Autobiographical Sketch, 1–7.

[82] Parley P. Pratt to Mary Ann Pratt, 18 December 1844, PPP Papers.

[83] Minutes of the Trial of George J. Adams before the High Counsel, Brigham Young Papers; Trial of Samuel Brannan, 24 May 1845, Miscellaneous Minutes, Brigham Young Papers; Brigham Young to William Smith, 10 August 1845, Brigham Young Papers; Parley P. Pratt, "Proclamation," *The Prophet*, 4 January 1845, 2; Parley P. Pratt to Brigham Young, 10 April 1845, Brigham Young Papers; and Brigham Young to Parley P. Pratt, 26 May 1845, PPP Papers.

Pratt and his sixth wife, Belinda Marden.
Courtesy of the Church History Library, the Church of Jesus Christ of Latter-day Saints.

meetings, with Young's view prevailing.[84] Nevertheless, Pratt performed no sealings in the East.[85] When Belinda became pregnant, the two hurried back to Nauvoo in August 1845.[86] During this mission, Parley also met twenty-two-year-old Phoebe Soper in Long Island, who would later become his plural wife.[87] Upon

[84] Meetings, November–December 1847, Miscellaneous Minutes, Brigham Young Papers.

[85] Parley P. Pratt, "This Number Closes the First Volume of the Prophet," *The Prophet*, 24 May 1845.

[86] Pratt, Family Record; and Belinda Marden Pratt, Autobiographical Sketch, 1–7.

[87] Phoebe Soper Letter, Undated, BYU Special Collections; and Parley P. Pratt to Family, 22 September 1846, PPP Papers.

his return, Parley learned that Hannahette had delivered a baby named Alma. To maintain the secrecy of polygamy, Parley must have kept Hannahette in seclusion, perhaps in the home of Erastus Snow, though she later moved back to her former home not far from the Pratt's house.[88] Belinda and Mary Wood, both pregnant, moved into the upstairs of the Pratt home. On October 15, he married an additional plural wife, twenty-three-year-old Sarah Houston, a native of Ohio. The James and Sarah Houston family lived a few blocks from the Pratt home. Three of their five daughters, including Sarah, entered plural marriages with Church leaders.[89]

Tensions between Parley and Mary Ann, especially over Parley's attention to his plural wives, increased during this time. As the various ordinances of the temple became available to a broader spectrum of Latter-day Saints from December 1845 to February 1846, all of the wives who had already been sealed to Pratt were resealed to him in the temple except for Mary Ann. Meanwhile, Sarah Marinda Bates Pratt, Orson Pratt's wife, who viewed plural marriage as adultery, was chiding Mary Ann because Sarah knew that Belinda had delivered a son named Nephi on January 1, 1846.[90] Orson, unaware of Parley's secret marriage to Belinda, agreed with Sarah's interpretation of their relationship as adulterous. The tensions exploded during a temple session on January 11, 1846. Orson felt that Parley was the cause of many of the rumors circulating about Sarah's alleged affair with Bennett. Parley accused Sarah of being an apostate, speaking against the heads of the Church, spreading rumors about his relationship with Belinda, and ruining and breaking up his family by influencing Mary Ann against him. Orson denounced Parley for lying and misrepresentation. Angry, Parley defended his conduct and proclaimed his innocence. As a

88 Pratt, Family Record.

89 Belinda Marden Pratt, Autobiographical Sketch; Pratt, Family Record; and James and Mary Houston Family Record, http://earlylds.com.

90 Pratt, Family Record; Sarah Pratt to Bathsheba Smith, 4 April 1850, Bathsheba Smith Papers, LDS Church History Library; and Orson Pratt to Brigham Young, 12 January 1846, Brigham Young Papers.

result, the apostles temporarily banished Orson from the temple. The next day, Orson wrote a letter to Brigham Young accusing Parley of various misdeeds and vowing they were enemies.[91] This rift did not end until 1853 when the two brothers made amends.[92]

The confrontation in the temple was only the capstone of the problems between Parley and Mary Ann. Heber Kimball and Brigham Young tried to reconcile them but it was useless.[93] Finally, Young called them to a meeting on February 6, 1846. According to Parley, Mary Ann confessed she had been spreading falsehoods about him and promised to quit, for which she was "frankly forgiven by her husband and then by the mutual consent of both parties and by Brigham Young's advice she was sealed to Joseph Smith (the deceased president of the Church) for Eternity and to her former husband for time, as Proxy." Mary Ann and Parley never reconciled completely after this meeting even though they put on appearances of such.[94]

Two days later, Pratt was sealed to Phoebe Soper, who had arrived in Nauvoo from Long Island two days earlier, at night in a secret ceremony by John Taylor.[95] Taylor and Pratt likely kept the sealing secret because Brigham Young had already closed the temple ordinance work that morning and may not have authorized the sealing. In 1851, Young resealed Phoebe and Parley in the endowment house in Salt Lake.[96]

Pratt's early experiences with plural marriage in Nauvoo demonstrate the problems that arose with the new marriage system because no precedent had been established as to procedure. One of the pressing problems was who could seal or perform plural marriages. Most Mormons aware of polygamy likely felt that Young was

---

[91] Orson Pratt to Brigham Young, 12 January 1846, Brigham Young Papers.

[92] Parley P. Pratt to Orson Pratt, 25 May 1853, Orson Pratt Papers, LDS Church History Library; Orson Pratt to Parley P. Pratt, 10 March 1853, PPP Papers; and Meetings November–December 1847, Miscellaneous Minutes, Brigham Young Papers.

[93] Heber C. Kimball, Journal, 27 November 1845, LDS Church History Library.

[94] Pratt, Family Record.

[95] Ibid.

[96] Endowment House Record, 26 February 1851, LDS Church History Library.

the only person who could authorize sealings; even Pratt defended this notion on numerous occasions. However, he and John Taylor also felt that in the absence of Young, other apostles held equal authority and could perform sealings.[97] This posed problems for Taylor and Pratt as the exodus across Iowa commenced.

Plural Marriage at Winter Quarters

The Pratt family left Nauvoo and crossed the Mississippi on February 13, 1846, as part of the large Mormon exodus.[98] Mary Ann and her children set out with the family but then returned to Nauvoo. Parley tried several times to persuade her to rejoin the family but she refused.[99] Parley, meanwhile, had settled the rest of his family at Winter Quarters under the care of George Whitaker and John VanCott (his first cousin) as he, Orson Hyde, and John Taylor served a mission to England in the winter of 1846–47.[100] Before they left, Young told the apostles, "No man has the right to attend to the ordinance of sealing except the President of the Church or those who are directed by him so to do and that ordinance should be confined to Zion or her stakes."[101] Pratt and Taylor believed that part of the instruction—"or those who are directed by him so to do"—gave them authority to perform new plural marriages,

---

[97] Brigham Young to William Smith, 10 August 1845, Brigham Young Papers; Brigham Young to Parley P. Pratt, 26 May 1845, Brigham Young Papers; Minutes of Meetings, 6 June 1847, 6 May 1848, LDS Church History Library; and Parley P. Pratt, "Proclamation," *The Prophet*, 3 January 1845.

[98] Phoebe Soper Pratt Letter, BYU Special Collections; Winters, "Autobiographical Sketch," 14–15; Pratt, Family Record; and Juanita Brooks, ed., *On the Mormon Frontier: The Diary of Hosea Stout 1844–1861*, 2 vols. (Salt Lake City: University of Utah Press, 1964), 1:122.

[99] Winters, "Autobiography," 641–45; Parley P. Pratt to John Van Cott, 29 March 1846, PPP Papers; and Pratt, Family Record.

[100] Woodruff, Journal, 11–30 July 1846; George Whitaker, "Life of George Whitaker, a Utah Pioneer, as Written by Himself," LDS Church History Library; and Mary Haskin Parker Richards, Journal, 1846–47, LDS Church History Library.

[101] Willard Richards, Journal, 24 July 1846, LDS Church History Library; Woodruff, Journal, 24 July 1846; and Watson, *Manuscript History of Brigham Young*, 24 July 1846, 272–74.

though Hyde felt that sealings could be performed only when Young was present.[102]

On the way to England, Pratt wrote to his family regularly. At first he kept quiet about plural marriage in the eastern states because of legal entanglements caused by Benjamin Hilton (Belinda's former husband) and financial problems Pratt had incurred.[103] From Boston, Parley revealed his feelings to Belinda following his separation from Mary Ann and his newly acquired family via plural marriage:

> I certainly would Sooner die than Live in this world one day with no one to Love or Care for me, or to be beloved by me. I have been led for a moment to doubt whether any person on earth Could be relied on with much certainty or assurance: but I Came to the Conclusion on reflection that there are two Spirits in Oposition and the fact that some are Overcome by the one is a proof that Others will be Led by the Other. therefore the very oposition prooves that Some will attain to the good and some to the evil. but O the fearful Struggle; and O the joy and blessedness of those who finally overcome, and How much Greater will be our Confidence and Love for such.[104]

Once Parley had gone to New York, he was also met with the anti-polygamy preaching of George J. Adams and James J. Strang.[105] Adams, a polygamist with at least three wives before his excommunication in 1845, claimed he had been deceived by the Twelve.[106] Another dissenter from the leadership of the Twelve was Lucian R. Foster, the former Nauvoo temple recorder. He had visited Phoebe Soper Pratt's father, Samuel Soper, on Long Island,

---

[102] Meetings, November–December 1847, Miscellaneous Minutes, Brigham Young Papers; and Pratt, Family Record.

[103] "Archer of Paradise" and "Parley P. Pratt," *Voree Herald*, October 1846; Samuel Richards, Journal, 6 September 1846–47, LDS Church History Library; Franklin D. Richards, Journal, 6 September 1846, LDS Church History Library; and Erastus Snow to Brigham Young, 1862, Erastus Snow Papers, LDS Church History Library.

[104] Parley P. Pratt to Belinda Marden Pratt, 4 September 1846, PPP Papers.

[105] Franklin D. Richards, Journal, 8–22 September 1846; and Samuel Richards, Journal, 8–22 September 1846, LDS Church History Library.

[106] George J. Adams Case Before the Nauvoo High Council, 1845, Brigham Young Papers.

told him about Parley's sealing to Phoebe, and warned him that Parley was in the East to "get the rest of the Soper daughters." Parley went to the Soper home on September 21 and described his encounter with Samuel Soper: "Tell Phebe I saw her Sisters last evening. they were well, and in good Spirits—they think of Coming to her next spring, when we return. The old gentleman also thinks of coming. . . . I Beged his pardon for not asking his Consent Owned up to every thing, and finally the Old gentleman Laughed, and said I might have them all, if I would take him also, So it all passed off verry well."[107]

After this encounter with the Sopers, Pratt sailed to England. He wrote frequent letters to his wives and children, whom he referred to as his "Dear Lambs." He wrote Belinda:

> O the dreary ages included in the term; "*Six Months*." what would I not give for one glance at my family Circle, one Sweet words—one kiss—or even a Single line to Say that you live, and that I am remembered—but no—even this Cannot be I must Leave it all to the Mercy of the Lord and remain in Suspence.—O Cruel fate. But Hush this Repining—you *live*, and you will live eternally—you *love*—and you will always *Love*. You are true to me and will always be—well I am happy. . . . O the Camp of the Saints! O My family Circle! O Belinda! Mary! Elizebeth! Phebe! Ette! Sarah!—O Parley! Alma! Nephi! Helaman! . . . How dear to me is you're the fond remembrance of each of you, and the Scenes of Happiness now gone forever, which I enjoyed in your Society. I look back with pleasure on the six Months Spent in Camp as the happiest by far that I ever spent in this Life.[108]

Nevertheless, Pratt found fulfillment in the duties of the ministry. He wrote: "The power and life and joy of the Spirit is poured out upon us while we Speak to that degree that we are all swallowed up in the Ingeligence, Life and joy of the truth. And it thrills through every extremity of our Spirit and Body as it were with a throb of Immortality. In those Moments we hardly know whether we are in the Body or out of it and our sacrifices seem nothing."[109]

---

[107] Parley P. Pratt to Family, 22 September 1846, PPP Papers.

[108] Parley P. Pratt to Belinda Marden Pratt, 1 October 1846, 14 October 1846, 21 November 1846, 29 November 1846, 26 December 1846, PPP Papers.

[109] Ibid.

While in England, Pratt taught two young converts about plural marriage, seventeen-year-old Ann Agatha Walker from Pendleton, Lancaster, and twenty-two-year-old Martha Monks from Rayner, Chester. Little is known of Monks. Walker was trained as a milliner by her mother, Mary. She was five feet six inches tall with dark brown hair, large gray eyes, high forehead, and was very intelligent. When Agatha finally arrived in Salt Lake City, she became one of the first milliners in Utah.[110] Sailing from England on January 19, 1847, Pratt and Taylor arranged passage for several others to accompany them back to Winter Quarters, including Walker, Monks, and sisters Mary Elizabeth and Sophia Whitaker, the latter of whom would marry Taylor.[111] On arriving in Winter Quarters, Pratt found his family struggling to survive in a log cabin. His wives and children had been plagued by sickness (especially scurvy), hunger, and cold and for several days subsisted only on cornmeal. In addition, the Pratts' horses and most of their cows and oxen were dead. Yet the Pratts had been luckier than most, as no family member had died.[112]

After reporting to Brigham Young, Pratt and Taylor were asked to come with him on the first company of pioneers to Utah.[113] They declined, wanting to be sealed to the new wives they had brought from England and to help their struggling families. On April 28, 1847, Taylor sealed Ann Agatha Walker and Martha Monks to Parley.[114] Earlier, Parley had sealed Sophia Whitaker to Taylor.[115] Pratt and his eight wives and five children prepared to depart from

[110] Ann Agatha Walker Pratt, Reminiscence, Ann Agatha Walker Papers, LDS Church History Library; Pratt, Family Record; and Whitaker, "Life."

[111] Franklin D. Richards, Journal, 19 January 1847, LDS Church History Library.

[112] Watson, *Manuscript History of Brigham Young*, 547; Brooks, *Mormon Frontier*, 46; Robert Campbell, Journal, 8 April 1847, LDS Church History Library; Historians Office Journals, LDS Church History Library; Pratt, *Autobiography*, 357; Whitaker, "Life," 1–29; Mary Haskin Parker Richards, Journal, 30–31 July 1846, 6–18 December 1846; Pratt, Family Record; and Patty Sessions, Journal, 1 April 1847, LDS Church History Library.

[113] Pratt, *Autobiography*, 358; November–December 1847 Meetings, Brigham Young Papers; and Brigham Young to Orson Spencer, 12 April 1847, Brigham Young Papers.

[114] Pratt, Family Record; and Ann Agatha Walker Pratt, Reminiscence.

[115] Whitaker, "Life."

Winter Quarters with the large emigration company led by Pratt and Taylor in 1847.[116] Mary Haskin Parker Richards described the Pratt home, with "all of his ladys," as hospitable and friendly.[117] Just before Parley left, he met with Mary Ann, his estranged wife, and arranged for her and his older brother Anson to have equal claim of the sale of his Nauvoo home to the Catholic Church.[118] Parley would not see her for another five years, as she returned to Maine.

During the journey across the plains, Pratt managed the company, and his wives drove the wagons and even put lock chains on the wheels while the wagons went up and down hills.[119] The Pratt wives also attended the prayer meetings organized by Eliza R. Snow, which often included dramatic spiritual manifestations.[120] Just before entering the valley, the Pratt and Taylor group met Young and others who were returning to Winter Quarters. Young severely rebuked Pratt and Taylor for reorganizing their pioneer emigration party, which Young had originally organized on adoptive family principles.[121] Young also chastised them for the sealings they had performed, though he did not mention this to Pratt and Taylor at the time. Later, in meetings between November and December of 1847, from which Pratt and Taylor were absent, Young adamantly stated that they had abused the priesthood and must be reprimanded.[122]

---

[116] Ann Agatha Walker Pratt, Reminiscence.

[117] Mary Haskin Parker Richards, Journal, 21 May 1847.

[118] Daniel Spencer Journal, 13 June 1847; Patty Sessions Journal, 13 June 1847; Parley P. Pratt to Mary Ann Frost Pratt, 22 October 1853, PPP Papers; Pratt, Family Record; Nauvoo Land Transactions, Nauvoo Restoration file, LDS Church History Library; Brigham Young to Mary Ann Pratt, 1 October 1846, Brigham Young Papers; Municipal High Council Minutes, 19, 27 September 1847, Brigham Young Papers; Orson Pratt to Parley P. Pratt, 24 April 1848, PPP Papers; and Parley P. Pratt, "to property delivered to Anson Pratt," PPP Papers.

[119] Ann Agatha Walker Pratt, Reminiscence.

[120] Eliza R. Snow Journal, 1846–49, LDS Church History Library; and Patty Sessions Journal, 1847–48.

[121] Thomas Bullock, Journal, 4 September 1847, LDS Church History Library; Woodruff, Journal, 4 September 1847; Daniel Spencer, Journal, 4 September 1847, LDS Church History Library; Pratt, *Autobiography*, 359–60; and Horace K. Whitney, Journal, 4 September 1847, LDS Church History Library.

[122] Meetings, 16 November to 3 December 1847, Miscellaneous Minutes, Brigham Young Papers, LDS Church History Library; and Parley P. Pratt to Orson Hyde, 9 November 1846, PPP Papers.

Salt Lake City, 1847–1857

After arriving in Salt Lake City in September 1847, the Pratts faced a difficult life. At first they slept in their wagons with the young children. Pratt soon built a cabin to house the various wives during the winter. He was kept busy gathering fuel and exploring the surrounding canyons. The women were occupied just keeping the large family alive. During most of that first year, Belinda was pregnant with twins and caring for one-year-old Nephi; Hannahette was pregnant and caring for the two-year-old Alma; Sarah was caring for six-month-old Julia; Mary was pregnant and caring for one-year-old Helaman (who she prized because he was saved on the road after he was run over by a wagon); Martha was childless and homesick for England; Agatha was expecting her first child; and Phoebe and Elizabeth assisted the others in tending the children. The eight Pratt wives delivered five more children during that first year, bringing the total to ten in a little over two years.[123]

The Pratts fared better than most during the first year in Utah, though they also faced rationing and the destruction of crops by frost and crickets. Agatha described the conditions during the first year in the valley:

> About the eighteenth of March the equinoctial storm set in and it began to rain and it kept on raining for over a week. We were told that there was no rain to speak of in the country, so in building our roofs they were made nearly flat. They were constructed of—first poles put as closely together as possible, then dried grass and weeds, then a good layer of earth which made a warm roof, but alas! Not impervious to rain.
>
> So we had rain out of doors and mud-fall in the house, for the continued fall of rain so thoroughly soaked the earth overhead that the downpour was mud—good-honest—mud. You can imagine the condition our beds and bedding were in. As long as there was a dry spot we would move it there, but after a while there was no dry spot.
>
> One of the family had a babe nine days old; she stayed in bed till it was soaked through; then she placed in a chair before the fire with an umbrella over her head. Sometimes the rain would cease and the sun showed his face and we would put out the bedding to dry. But alas! It would cloud up again and the weather would resume its normal condition. All were not quite as bad off as we were for some had better roofs

[123] Pratt, Family Record.

and one man had built a gabled roof and I can assure you he had plenty of company while the storm lasted.[124]

Pratt built his large home in downtown Salt Lake City on a site originally designed for Orson Pratt's family lot.[125] He completed it by 1853 and also built a smaller house on a back lot for Agatha (to use in her milliner trade) and a house for Sarah Houston near the big field where the Pratt farm was located. Belinda, Mary Wood, Hannahette, Elizabeth, and Phoebe lived in the main house. Parley left the organization of the households to his wives.[126] Mary Ann Frost's departure led to the question of which wife should be principally responsible for Parley P. Pratt, Jr., the son of Thankful and Parley. On March 25, 1848, Parley, Jr., was asked to choose who he wanted to be his mother until he would meet his real mother in the next world. He chose Belinda, the sixth wife, who became from that time on the head of the main household.[127]

Until the 1852 public announcement of polygamy, Pratt kept his plural marriages a "secret" from the outside world, including the families of several of the wives. For example, Ann Agatha's parents, William and Mary Walker in England, had no idea that their daughter was married to Pratt or that she was a mother. Pratt and Taylor had told them before Agatha left England that she would accompany the Pratt family to the West, be cared for by his wife and family, and be a helper to them. On February 28, 1848, having not seen their daughter for over a year, they wrote to her hoping she would be able to "repay Brother Pratt's kindness" for taking her to Utah by "being a comfort to his wife and family." They further asked if she was married, and advised accordingly if not: "Consult your best friends before you take so important step, in every sense of the word."[128] To preserve the secret of plural marriage, a careful response was needed from Parley and Agatha. Writing to her

124 Ann Agatha Walker Pratt, Reminiscence.

125 Parley P. Pratt to Orson Pratt, 25 May 1853, 23 August 1853, Orson Pratt Papers.

126 Pratt, Family Record; and Parley P. Pratt, Journals, 1851–56, PPP Papers.

127 Pratt, Family Record.

128 Mary Walker to Ann Agatha Walker Pratt, 28 February 1848, Ann Agatha Walker Pratt Papers.

parents on April 30, 1849, Agatha expressed her hope they would emigrate soon and told them, "Bro Pratt and his family are well. . . . I am still living with them, and they the same kind friends they always were." Parley added: "Your daughter has been with us every day since our return from England; She is respected and beloved by all our family and numerous circle of friends, because of her noble, generous and amiable disposition and goodness of spirit. She will never be separated from us, and therefore I know no other means for child and parents brothers and sisters to enjoy each others society in the case of her fathers house than for them all to unite in the same naborhood, and in the same ties of eternal friendship in the New and Everlasting Covenant."[129]

Agatha's family came to America in 1850 but stayed in the St. Louis area where her mother died on August 15, 1851. The following year, her father came to Utah and learned that Agatha was married to Parley, a mother of two children, and expecting a third. He lived with Agatha in the little house on the Pratt homestead for a while.[130]

Though Agatha and six of the other plural wives adjusted fairly well to polygamy, Martha Monks did not. During the first year in the valley, five of Pratt's wives were pregnant, including Martha. Four of the wives delivered healthy children so that by the end of 1848 nine children, eight wives, and Pratt lived in an adobe house.[131] Pratt named and blessed each one, taking names for his sons from the Book of Mormon.[132] Agatha said Parley "hailed each newcomer with much pleasure and delight as if it were the only one." She further stated that he gathered his children around him and heard them sing "childish songs," putting as many of the children on his lap as possible.[133] Martha gave birth to a son, Ether, on January 30, 1849, the last of the five children born in the

[129] Ann Agatha Walker Pratt and Parley P. Pratt to Mary Walker, 30 April 1849, PPP Papers.

[130] Ann Agatha Walker Pratt, Reminiscence.

[131] Pratt, Family Record; and Pratt, *Autobiography*, 364

[132] Pratt, Family Record; and Parley P. Pratt to Family, 21 November 1851, PPP Papers.

[133] Ann Agatha Walker Pratt, Reminiscence.

years 1848 and 1849. He died one month later. This was more than Martha could take. According to Pratt's family record, she became "influenced by a wicked spirit through the agency of Jesse Turpin," a church member, and joined a group of men going to California in July 1849. She never returned.[134]

The rest of Pratt's plural wives took on various tasks to support the family. Agatha began a millinery shop; Belinda supervised the main household; Hannahette was the nurse and helped with the farm; Sarah ran the farm; and Mary, Phoebe, and Elizabeth kept busy with child raising. When not on missions, Pratt participated in various civic affairs, constructed the homes, assisted with the farm, and engaged in other pursuits to support his growing family. After Parley and Orson reconciled in 1853, Orson tried to persuade his brother to use writing as a profession. Although Pratt wrote voluminously, his family never received much financial benefit from his writing, and the family remained poor most of Pratt's life.[135]

When Pratt went on a mission, he generally took one or two of his wives with him, leaving the remainder to support themselves. During his mission to California and South America in 1851–52, he took Phoebe and Elizabeth.[136] At this time, the Pratt home was not completed, five of the wives (including Phoebe) were pregnant, and bills were mounting up. Pratt worried constantly on his mission about the wives, even reporting dreams that he returned to his partially finished homes to visit them.[137] His mission to Chile was not as successful as hoped, not only because of language problems and political instability, but also because of Phoebe's illness and the death of her infant son, Omner, who was born in Chile on November 30, 1851, and died there less than two months later on January 7, 1852.[138] His letters and journal from this mission

[134] Pratt, Family Record.

[135] Parley P. Pratt to Orson Pratt, 25 May 1853, 12 September 1853, Orson Pratt Papers; and Orson Pratt to Parley P. Pratt , 12 September 1853, 2 November 1853, PPP Papers.

[136] Pratt, Journal, 16–21 March 1851.

[137] Parley P. Pratt to Family, 13 June 1851, 15 September 1851, PPP Papers; Parley P. Pratt to Agatha Pratt, 27 August 1851, PPP Papers.

[138] Pratt, Journals, 30 November 1851, January 1852.

demonstrate Pratt's highly spiritual and romantic inclinations and his deep affection for each wife. He firmly believed that the love between husband and wife originated with God and would continue throughout eternity among eternal beings endowed with priesthood power. On several occasions he said he felt unworthy of the love and sacrifice of his wives.[139]

A letter Pratt wrote to his family on November 21, 1851, from Valparaiso, Chile, gives a sense of the family relationships. Parley stated that he and Phoebe had rejoiced when they had recently received seven letters from home. He wrote:

> I opened one, it was from Elizebeth. I opened a second it was verry short, dated June 9th and signed Belinda. It gave an account of the arrival of one "Lehi." I could read no more for Joy. . . .
>
> Mary's Letter was excellent, but the poor girl was all most tired to death, and could not write much. I Look for more nextime from her. Bless her, O Could I get my mouth as near her lips as I did in a dream, I would immediately snatch one good Long hearty Kiss, Lest in stoping to smile into her eye I should awake with my mouth within about an inch of hers and go without a Kiss as I did in my dream. . . .
>
> Belinda's letter was a most excelent one, and gave me much satisfaction in regard to the buisiness, and in all else. I was verry sorry concerning the complaint in her head Still troubleing her. Bless her, I dreamed of seeing her several times but she would not speak freely, for her soul was vexed, and I knew not the cause. But the Last time I saw her she was seting in my lap with her arms around my neck in a meak and humble spirit and she said: "*comfort me*." And I did comfort her, with kind words while I enfolded her in my arms and pressed her to my heart. Agatha, How can I speak of your Letter. It was Like yourself, all Love and affection for me. You ask if you will ever be happy in this world again in the society of him you Love. I answer yes, you shall have Joy in this world, and a fullness in the next, and even now we are happier in each other than the Ignorant are when togather.
>
> I sometimes think, and I am now inclined to believe that Our father in heaven never associated in this Lower world of fallen nature, spirits more conjenial, Lovely and happy in each other, than we are as a family. Nor do I believe that a greater Lot of hapiness ever fell to the Lot of mortals

[139] Parley P. Pratt to Family, 31 January 1852, 28 March 1852; Parley P. Pratt to Agatha Pratt, 9 February 1852, 24 June 1852; and Parley P. Pratt to Belinda Pratt, 25 February 1852, PPP Papers.

> than we have, and do enjoy. Others have had riches, Luxuries, and the pleasures of the world, with the honors thereof. But we have learned to endure poverty with cheerfulness, and affliction and crosses with joy. And in these circumstances we have learned to love, and bear with each other, till we feel a union, which links us to each other and with all good beings. Such Lessens were never learned in a School different from our own. O House of Parley, Continue in this school, and persue the Lessons with all meekness and diligence, and no Joy shall be withheld from us. We are heirs to that which neither death nor any thing else can take from us.[140]

Pratt also sent special love letters to his wives in Spanish, using his favorite Spanish word, *besito* (kiss).[141]

During this mission, Parley had reason to be concerned for the welfare of his wives as Hannahette, Belinda, Sarah, Phoebe, and Agatha all bore children between June 6, 1851, and November 30, 1851.[142] When Parley finally received letters that his wives and their new babies were healthy, he wrote a long letter to Belinda pouring forth his love:

> Need I tell any of my family that have not forgotten them! No, they know that I love them ~~and~~ as only one *can* love, who is taught of God. No man ever had a family more worthy of being loved. for them and for the Gospel I live. . . .
>
> [E]very day, and year increases my affection for my children and their mothers. every new developement of eternal principle shows new reasons for loving them, and convinces me, that even the best informed among us know but little how to prise our precious gifts. What! the Gift of *Eternal life* not enough to display the benevalence of our God! But he gives us also eternal beings to mingle with us in eternal Joys!
>
> Not merely the beauties of youth, which dazzle for a moment and fade forever, but the ever blooming, ever increasing beauty of an eternal being springing upwards in all the fragrance of still increasing life inteligence, light and love.
>
> O Daughters of sorrow and of Loneliness! Could you but see yourselves in the Light that I see you, you would Know how I love you. . . .
>
> Yes! it is eternal beings to whom I am writing! Eternal Beings!—and yet they are given into my bosom to Love and cherish forever! O What responsibility![143]

---

140 Parley P. Pratt to Family, 21 November 1851, PPP Papers.

141 Ibid.; and Parley P. Pratt to Belinda Pratt, 23 August 1854, PPP Papers.

142 Pratt, "Family Record.

143 Parley P. Pratt to Belinda Pratt, 25 February 1852, PPP Papers.

Returning to Utah on October 18, 1852, Parley found his family well except Agatha's infant daughter, Marion, whom he never saw, as she had died on October 6.[144] Pratt was also greeted by his two living children by Mary Ann Frost (Olivia and Moroni) whom he had not seen for over five years. Mary Ann had returned to Utah from Maine, and he wanted her to live near him so he could see the children more and help with their education. He asked her again to take up residence with him; he promised her a home but said if she refused again he would not feel any obligation to her.[145] She declined but settled in Pleasant Grove and allowed the children to visit Pratt quite often.[146] She obtained a divorce from Pratt on March 5, 1853.[147]

The Pratt household was full of life from October 18, 1852, until May 5, 1854, when Pratt was called on a mission to California. He participated in temple work, reconciled with Orson, taught Spanish, attended legislative assemblies, and wrote a new volume called *Key to the Science of Theology*.[148] Before he left for California on his mission in 1854–55, Pratt took another plural wife, forty-one-year-old Keziah Downes, who had known Pratt since 1842 when she had joined the Church in England. In England, she was apparently married to a Mr. Hill but either she was separated from her husband or a widow when she emigrated to Utah in 1852.[149] The following letters that Parley wrote to Brigham Young and Keziah illustrate their courtship:

> Prest Young,
> Dear Brother,
> I have in my own mind selected another assistant missionary to assist me in my mission for time and all eternity.—It only requires *your sanction*, the *Lady's Consent*,—and the *Seal of God* to complete the appointment.

---

[144] Pratt, Journal, 18 October 1852.

[145] Parley P. Pratt to Mary Ann Pratt, 22 October 1852, PPP Papers; and Parley P. Pratt Journal, 22 October 1852, PPP Papers.

[146] Winters, "Autobiographical Sketch."

[147] Divorce Certificate, 5 March 1853, Mary Ann Pratt Smith from Parley Parker Pratt, Brigham Young Papers.

[148] Parley P. Pratt, Journal, 18 October 1852 to 5 May 1854; and Parley P. Pratt to Orson Pratt, 25 May 1853, 23 August 1853, 30 October 1853, 30 January 1854, PPP Papers.

[149] Keziah Downes Pratt Papers, LDS Church History Library.

The candidate is a sister from Manchester Eng. heretofore known as Sister Hill.—What say ye?

Your Bro.,
P. P. Pratt

Dear Sister Hill,

I hope you will excuse the Liberty I have taken in presenting the above to Prest. Young. He gave his ready sanction, to the selection, and it now remains for you to say whether you will undertake such a mission, of your *own free will and choice.*

Count well the cost I can promise you nothing but Poverty, hard work, and many burthens in this work which but few can bear.

And be assured your decision either way will never lessen our friendship.

Your Bro.
P. P. Pratt.

P.S. excuse the name Hill. your name I do not know.[150]

Six days later, Parley married Keziah.[151] A good businesswoman, Keziah lived in the main house and served as a scribe for Parley for many of his journals he compiled for his autobiography.[152] A year after their marriage, Keziah wrote him that she felt "happy all the time" and expressed her "best love to Parley."[153] Parley responded on January 19, 1855:

> Continue to be diligent in your mission, & remember you are doing all you do—to assist one of the twelve in a mission. how Many women would have Desired such a Mission as yours, but they died without even seeing such blessed days. Remember too you have the honor of training & assisting to educate young princes & princesses heirs to the Eternal Priesthood. As to Love I have an eternal fountain Laid up for you I love you a little now, & I expect to grow in it forever. As to the eternal

---

[150] Parley P. Pratt to Brigham Young and Keziah D. Hill, 21 December 1853, Huntington Library, San Marino, California.

[151] Pratt, Family Record.

[152] Parley P. Pratt to Keziah Downes Pratt, 19 January 1855, PPP Papers; Parley P. Pratt Journals, 1854–56, PPP Papers; Parley P. Pratt, "After Manuscript," PPP Papers; and Keziah Downes Pratt Papers, LDS Church History Library.

[153] Keziah Downes Pratt to Parley P. Pratt, 18 October 1854, LDS Church History Library.

affections giving does not impoverish, the more I increase in intelligence the stronger & more Lasting is my love.[154]

Visitors to the Pratt household often noted, sometimes shocked, Pratt's pride in his family. Pratt had a painting made in 1851 of all the family that he hung in his parlor.[155] In 1853, Elizabeth Woodcock Ferris, along with her husband, Utah territorial secretary Benjamin Ferris, visited the Pratts. A cultured woman from New York, Ferris later wrote an account of her time in Utah, much of it focused on the "Mormon harem[s]" created by polygamy. Ferris recounted that after she and a companion were "ushered into a large room" in the Pratt home, they were received by Pratt with much sincerity of manner and then were introduced to five of his wives: Belinda, Mary Wood, Elizabeth, Agatha, and Phoebe. Belinda, being "the mistress of the house" took their shawls and asked that they be seated. The other four wives sat in the large parlor knitting while Pratt entertained the group with conversation about his mission to Chile and the peculiarities of the Spanish language. Ferris described Pratt as an engaging conversationalist with a very even flow of language. Pratt read from his manuscript *Key to the Science of Theology* for nearly half an hour, until Ferris grew tired of it. Finally, Pratt showed them his prized painting, pointing out each wife and child in the picture with pride. The experience thoroughly disgusted the puritanical Mrs. Ferris, though she politely bid the family adieu and left.[156]

All of Pratt's wives except Mary Ann Frost and Martha Monks were full of praise for their husband. Agatha was proud to be a plural wife and described their private life: "He was a gentleman, born so. He had an innate reverence and respect for women as the mothers of the souls of men. He loved his wives, not only as the beloved of his bosom but as mothers of his children, whom he loved very dearly. . . . Amid all our poverty, toil and care, and the

---

[154] Parley P. Pratt to Keziah Downes Pratt, 19 January 1855, PPP Papers.

[155] Brooks, *Mormon Frontier*, 2:393.

[156] Martha Spence Heywood, Journal, 21 January 1851, 48; and Mrs. B. G. Ferris, *The Mormons at Home, with Some Incidents of Travel from Missouri to California, 1852–1856* (New York, Dix and Edwards, 1856), 69–171.

difficulties and perplexities and experiences, he would sometime have occasion to reprove or admonish. He would do so in a manner to touch the heart, make a lasting impression, but never leave a humiliating sting. His wives always knew that he respected them and cared for their feelings."[157]

Phoebe added to Agatha's description in a letter to her sister in 1854: "I am blest with a husband of a noble and generous turn of a kind and affectionate heart, one that delights in good acts and kindness and discharging every know duty Esther you told me that you thought that when I got maried if I ever did it would be to some old doting childish person or some tyrant but I must tell you that must it for once I have one of the best men that ever graced this earth or ever will in my humble opinion. . . . I know that my husband is capable and will exalt me and what more do I want."[158]

In 1854, Belinda wrote a pamphlet defending plural marriage, in the form of a letter to her sister. She stated:

> I have a good and virtuous husband whom I love. We have four little children which are mutually and inexpressibly dear to us. And besides this, my husband has seven other living wives and one who has departed to a better world. He has in all upwards of twenty-five children. All these mothers and children are endeared to me by kindred ties; by mutual affection—by acquaintance and association; and the mothers in particular by mutual and long continued exercise of toil, patience, long-suffering, and sisterly kindness. We all have our imperfections in this life; but I know that these are good and worthy women, and that my husband is a good and worthy man: one who keeps the commandments of Jesus Christ, and presides in his family like an Abraham. He seeks to provide for them with all diligence; he loves them all, and seeks to comfort them and make them happy. He teaches them the commandments of Jesus Christ, and gathers them about him in the family circle to call upon his God, both morning and evening.[159]

Though these glowing tributes speak of unity among the plural wives, jealousies inevitably arose. On July 18, 1854, for example, Agatha wrote to Parley to defend herself against an accusation

[157] Ann Agatha Walker Pratt, Reminiscence.
[158] Phoebe Soper Pratt, Letter to Sister Esther, 1854, BYU Special Collections.
[159] Belinda Pratt, *Defence of Polygamy by a Lady of Utah*, 12 January 1854, 9.

Belinda had written to him that Agatha was "makeing money like smoke" in her milliner business. In reality, Agatha wrote, "I have been very busy all summer at my trade have not had a moment to spare." Her efforts had allowed the family to purchase "butter ever since you went away some cheese and etc." In addition, she had to pay "6 dollars for a load of wood, and got three of the children some shoes made."[160]

In 1854–55, Pratt once again served a mission in California, along with his wife Elizabeth, where he met Eleanor Jane McComb McLean, a talented schoolteacher living in San Francisco. Her husband, Hector McLean, was an alcoholic who had forbidden her from attending church meetings, a situation that likely reminded Parley of Belinda's experiences in 1844. McLean consented for Eleanor to be baptized in 1854, before Pratt's arrival in San Francisco. After his arrival, she had Parley baptize her children, which so infuriated Hector that he sent them to her parents in New Orleans in February 1855.[161] Parley helped Eleanor raise money for a ship passage to follow her children. Writing to his wives in Salt Lake, he told them he felt he had found a soul that needed love by a good "Son of God" and asked Belinda to name a daughter after Eleanor, whom he called a "choice friend—a noble spirit of that name who I trust you will all know & esteem."[162] After Eleanor failed to obtain her children in New Orleans in 1855, she came to the Pratt home to stay. On November 14, 1855, Brigham Young sealed the thirty-eight-year-old Eleanor to Parley; she moved into the main house and was well accepted by the other wives.[163] A year later, Parley was called on a mission to the eastern states and Eleanor accompanied him in an effort to regain custody of her children.[164] When Pratt bid farewell to his family on September 11, 1856, he had nine wives living with him, two separated or divorced

[160] Ann Agatha Walker Pratt to Parley P. Pratt, 18 July 1854, PPP Papers.

[161] Steven Pratt, "Eleanor McLean and the Murder of Parley P. Pratt," *BYU Studies* (Winter 1975): 225–56.

[162] Parley P. Pratt to Keziah Pratt, 19 January 1855, PPP Papers; and Parley P. Pratt to Belinda Pratt, 16 May 1855, PPP Papers.

[163] Parley P. Pratt, Journal, 14 November 1855; and Pratt, Family Record.

[164] Steven Pratt, "Eleanor McLean," 225–56.

wives, twenty-three living children, seven deceased children, and one adopted American Indian child. The vast majority of his children were under ten years of age.[165] Eleanor's estranged husband, Hector McLean, murdered Pratt on May 13, 1857, near Van Buren, Arkansas. In his last minutes, Pratt expressed concern for his family and his hope they would be taken care of.[166]

After Parley Pratt's Death

According to Teancum Pratt, the son of Parley and Sarah, Parley Pratt's death brought "much grief to a large family of widows and Orphans as well as to all the Latter-day Saints who knew him," adding that few men had as many warm friends in the Church as his father. A year later, during the move south at the time of the Utah War crisis, in which Church leaders directed the temporary abandonment of Salt Lake City, Sarah moved with her children, including Teancum, to Payson in Utah County. She "married a German Tanner," William Taussig, as a plural wife. Though Taussig "was a very industrious man," according to Teancum, he "could not control his own affairs being under the influence of a woman (his first wife) who sought to overthrow his family & the consequences were soon felt in my mother & her children being deserted by him & shortly after he left Utah & went to California." Sarah was thus forced to raise five children—three by Parley and two by Taussig—while supporting "herself & children by laboring with her own hands, at whatever she could find to do; such as gleaning, washing." Sarah later moved to Goshen and Antimony, Utah, where she died on May 22, 1886.[167]

Sarah's experience illustrates the precarious situation in which Pratt's death left his family. Of Parley's widows, only Belinda, Sarah, and Ann Agatha remarried; Elizabeth, Keziah, Eleanor,

---

165 Pratt, Family Record.

166 Eleanor McLean to Pratt Family, 14 May 1857, PPP Papers.

167 Teancum Pratt, Journal, LDS Church History Library; and Annie Gardner, "Lines to a Spirit Departed: In Loving Remembrance of the Late Sister Sarah H. Pratt, Who Died May 22nd 1886, Widow of Apostle P. P. Pratt," *Woman's Exponent* 15, no. 12 (15 November 1886), 91.

Mary Ann Frost, Mary Wood, Phoebe, and Hannahette did not. Pratt's estate was settled in 1867 through the leadership of Parley, Jr. The estate, worth approximately $26,000, was divided in 260 shares, with each wife and children (including Mary Ann Frost and her children) receiving at least one share and the wives with large families receiving between twenty and twenty-four shares. Additional settlements of Pratt's finances—including proceeds from his *Autobiography*, published in 1874 by Parley, Jr., and from his *Voice of Warning* and *Key to the Science of Theology*—occurred in 1884 and 1889, with the remaining Pratt widows and children receiving cash payments totaling $13,500.[168]

All of Pratt's widows remained in Utah. Mary Ann Frost Pratt spent the remainder of her life in Pleasant Grove, living alternately with her son, Moroni, and her daughter, Mary Ann, before her death in 1891. Elizabeth Brotherton Pratt remained in the Pratt home along with Hannahette and her family in Salt Lake City, where she raised Abish, an American Indian girl she had been given to care for by Parley in 1856. Elizabeth later moved to other areas of Salt Lake City, where she remained until her death in 1897.[169] Mary Wood Pratt also stayed in the Pratt home with her four children (Helaman, Cornelia, Mary, and Mathoni) before moving to the Forest Dale area of Salt Lake City. Like Agatha, she worked as a milliner. Though she received several proposals of marriage from prominent men, she said that the face of Parley always came to her and she could see no other. She died in 1898. Hannahette Snively Pratt (who also died in 1898) and her children, Alma, Lucy, and Henrietta, lived in what was known as the Big Field area of Salt Lake City, where they built a two-story brick home on 1410 South West Temple. They successfully engaged in farming ventures.[170]

---

168 Settlement of the Estate of Parley Pratt, 11 February 1867, E. Smith Probate, LDS Church History Library; Pratt Family to John Taylor, 24 July 1884; and Pratt Family to George Q. Cannon, 4 October 1889, PPP Papers.

169 Elizabeth Brotherton Pratt, Papers and Letters, LDS Church History Library; Carter, *Twelve Wives*; and Elizabeth B. Pratt, "Autobiography of Elizabeth B. Pratt." On Mary Ann Frost Pratt, see "Death of Mary Ann Pratt," *Woman's Exponent* 20 (1 September 1891): 36–37; and Benjamin W. Driggs, "Death of Mary Ann Pratt, August 24th 1891," *Deseret News*, 5 September 1891.

170 Carter, *Twelve Wives*; Pratt, Family Record; and Settlement of the Estate of Pratt.

Belinda Marden Pratt married Thomas Box on July 10, 1858, and went to live with him along with her five children, Nephi, Lehi, Abinadi, Isabella Eleanor, and Belinda. She taught school and became a leader in the local Relief Society before moving to Fillmore in 1870, where she was the first stake Relief Society president in the Millard Stake, an ecclesiastical unit of several local congregations. To be near her children, she later moved back to Salt Lake City, where she died in 1894.[171] Phoebe Soper Pratt moved to the Utah county area, settling in Spanish Fork in the 1870s with her daughter, Phoebe. A midwife, she later moved to Provo, where she died in 1887.[172] Ann Agatha Walker Pratt was only twenty-eight years old at the time of Parley's death and with four small children (Agatha, Malona, Moroni Walker, and Evelyn). She remained in the Pratt home and continued her work as a milliner. Three years later, after receiving counsel from Brigham Young, she married Joseph Ridges, the builder of the Salt Lake Tabernacle organ, and moved to the Sugarhouse area of Salt Lake City. She had two children with Ridges but discontinued living with him after he married her daughter Agatha in 1866. Agatha became heavily involved in church work in the Relief Society, as a member of the Tabernacle Choir, and in the Retrenchment Society. She also kept extensive records of the Pratt family and a journal even when she became blind in old age. She died in 1908.[173]

Keziah Downes Pratt remained in Salt Lake City in one of the three main Pratt homes. By the 1870s, through proceeds from Pratt's estate, she built a store and a house where she kept boarders and taught school. In a letter to her brother in England, she stated, "My school sustains me comfortable, but it is very harassing (to one of my age) consisting of chiefly of boys from 9 to 16 years of

[171] Belinda Marden Pratt, Journals, 1870–87; "Brief History of a Famous Woman," *Woman's Exponent*, 38, no. 9 (April 1910): 70–71; *Woman's Exponent* 1, no. 16 (15 January 1873): 122; *Woman's Exponent* 2, no. 7 (1 September 1873): 53; and *Woman's Exponent* 8 (1 October 1879): 66.

[172] Phoebe Soper Pratt Papers, L. Tom Perry Special Collections, BYU.

[173] Ann Agatha Pratt Papers, Journals and Accounts, LDS Church History Library; and Ann Agatha Pratt, "Reminiscences of Mrs. A. Agatha Pratt," *Woman's Exponent*, 40 (April 1912): 62–63.

age; and this together with my cooking, and housework, keeps me very busy all the time." She died in her residence of consumption in 1877.[174] Eleanor McComb Pratt stayed in Salt Lake City and taught school for the Pratt family and also for the Brigham Young family, assisted at times by Belinda's son Abinadi and her own son, Albert McLean. She spent much time writing on Pratt's death and giving classes in Relief Society before her death in 1874.[175]

Many of Pratt's children also had large families, for a total of 266 grandchildren. All but two of the sons who survived to adulthood practiced plural marriage and six of Pratt's daughters were plural wives. Pratt's descendants now number more than twenty thousand and include prominent Americans such as presidential candidate and former Massachusetts governor Mitt Romney, billionaire philanthropist Jon Huntsman, Sr., and former ambassador to China and Utah governor Jon Huntsman, Jr.

Conclusion

In an autograph book of Martha Spence Heywood, Pratt wrote:

> The greatest Gift to man—Eternal Life
> But Who could *Ever* live without a *Wife*?
> Eternal Life, without Eternal Sealing Is Hell.
> Or man Eternal has no feeling.[176]

Pratt's monogamous marriages to Thankful Halsey and Mary Ann Frost suggest some of the personal family experiences of an early Mormon leader: excitement of the belief in a restoration of God's church and the coming millennium; persistent financial

[174] Keziah Pratt Papers and Financial Record, LDS Church History Library.

[175] Eleanor McLean Pratt Papers, LDS Church History Library; Letters from Eleanor Pratt to Brigham Young, 1858–66, Brigham Young Papers; "Fourteenth Ward Assembly Room," *Woman's Exponent* 1, no. 14 (15 December 1872): 106; "Physiology," *Woman's Exponent* 15 (1 January 1873): 114–15; Meeting Minutes, *Woman's Exponent* 24 (15 May 1873): 186; Meeting Minutes, *Woman's Exponent* 2, no. 4 (15 July 1873): 26–27; "Obituary," *Woman's Exponent* 3, no. 11 (1 November 1874): 84; and Eleanor J. Pratt, "Good Manners," *Woman's Exponent* 13, no. 15 (1 January 1875): 115.

[176] Parley P. Pratt Autograph, Martha Spence Heywood Autograph, LDS Church History Library.

problems; constant missions and other travel, which took him from his family; moves from New York to Ohio to Missouri to Illinois; and clashes with opponents of Mormonism. By the early 1840s, the doctrines of eternal marriage and plural marriage were fundamental to the Mormon message for Pratt. His experience with plural marriage between the early 1840s and his death in 1857 give a glimpse into the dynamics of plural marriage in early Mormonism and the workings of a large plural family. The lack of clear procedures for plural marriage in the Nauvoo era provoked controversy between Pratt and Brigham Young about who held proper authority to authorize such marriages, though Pratt eventually accepted Young's argument that only the Church president held such power. As with many early Mormons, plural marriage brought both happiness and sadness to Pratt and his wives, as it brought them not only the joy of numerous children and the promise of a large family kingdom in the hereafter but also a divorce between Pratt and Mary Ann Frost and eventually the death of Pratt himself.

On January 27, 1857, four months before his death, Pratt contemplated the possibility of death and penned a letter to his wife Belinda and his family, which demonstrates his feelings for his family:

> I feel well, & in a great measure resigned to suffering pilgrimage, poverty, & every thing Providence may see fit to try me with. I am weaned from the world, & the things thereof. I long to do my duty while here & then go to rest in the paradise of God. The world to me is a dreary, & [torn] empty waste. My heart & affections are beyond the grave. I love my family & am willing to stay & do for them. I love the work of God and am willing to stay & do it. But I neather dread nor fear death, But I antisipate changing worlds with joy inexhausible. My very best love to yourself & Mary, & Phebe, & Kesiah. They must excuse me from writing separate answers to their letters now, & consider this, as if written to them as well as to you. My very best love also to Hannah, & Sarah, & Agatha, & Parley & Peter, & Alma & Nephi & Helaman & Julia, & Lucy, & Abinadi & Belinda, & Agatha Jun'r & Cornelia, & Lehi, & Malona.[177]

[177] Parley P. Pratt to Belinda Pratt, 27 January 1857, PPP Papers.

CHAPTER 3

Parley P. Pratt and Early Mormon Print Culture

DAVID J. WHITTAKER

It is possible to detect two important threads in the fabric of Mormon intellectual history. Both began in the earliest years of the Church's history, both reflect the main currents of thought of the time, and both could find reinforcement in the revelations and teachings of Joseph Smith. The first thread was the rationalism of the Age of Reason; the second was the Romantic reaction to the logic, reason, and order of the Enlightenment. The first found truth by turning to natural science and experimental investigation; the second felt more comfortable with nature, poetry, intuition, and revelation. Whereas the first sought answers in study through inductive reasoning and research, the second found insights in feeling and piety. Where the rationalism of the Enlightenment looked for laws and proofs, the Romantic movement revolted against such finality, seeing truth as less confined to theorems and more open to intuitive insights.[1]

[1] Romanticism is a label given by students of history and literature to a broad cultural movement that had its roots in Europe in the eighteenth century. It focused its expressions as reactions to the Industrial Revolution and as a revolt against the more rational forms of a scientific understanding of the world of nature. See further, M. H. Abrams, *Natural Supernaturalism: Tradition and Revolution in Romantic Literature* (New York: Norton, 1971); and Marilyn Gaull, *English Romanticism: The Human Context* (New York: Norton, 1988).

For the first generation of Latter-day Saint writers, these two approaches can be seen in the work of Parley P. Pratt and his brother Orson. Orson wrote mathematical treatises and searched for laws that governed the motion of the planets,[2] while his brother wrote poetry and theological essays that exhibit a serious "playfulness," inviting his readers into an unfolding and open-ended view of the cosmos and man's place in it.[3] Of course we can be guilty of generalization here, but such a comparison can help us in better understanding the religious heritage of the Church of Jesus Christ of Latter-day Saints.[4] Joseph Smith managed to balance the two approaches. Like Jonathan Edwards who saw the Christian life as a dance of the head and the heart, of the intellect and the emotions, Smith encouraged his followers to study from the best books and to use their minds, while also seeking heavenly assistance, which the seeker would "feel" when it came.[5] Studying with the right spirit could be an act of worship.

This essay presents an overview of Pratt's contributions to Mormon thought by focusing on his foundational role in the emergence of a Mormon print culture.[6] Until 1847 Pratt would dominate

[2] For example, see Orson Pratt, *The Key to the Universe; or a New Theory of Its Mechanism* (Salt Lake City: Published by the author, 1879). For the fuller story of Orson Pratt's natural theology and its sources, see David J. Whittaker, "Orson Pratt, Prolific Pamphleteer" *Dialogue: A Journal of Mormon Thought* 15 (Autumn 1982): 27–41. The best biography of Orson Pratt is Breck England, *The Life and Thought of Orson Pratt* (Salt Lake City: University of Utah Press, 1985).

[3] Most fully, see Parley P. Pratt, *Key to the Science of Theology: Designed as an Introduction to the First Principles of Spiritual Philosophy; Religion; Law and Government; as Delivered by the Ancients, and as Restored in This Age, for the Final Development of Universal Peace, Truth and Knowledge* (Liverpool, England: F. D. Richards, 1855).

[4] A recent study of Mormon thought and culture—Terryl Givens, *People of Paradox: A History of Mormon Culture* (New York: Oxford University Press, 2006)—also recognizes these creative tensions.

[5] Doctrine and Covenants of the Church of Jesus Christ of Latter-day Saints: Carefully Selected from the Revelations of God (Kirtland, Ohio: F. G. Williams & Co., 1835) (hereafter Doctrine and Covenants), 9.

[6] The term "print culture" is used to identify the emergence of printed items in early Mormonism that defended, explained, and analyzed the history and doctrines of the Church of Jesus Christ of Latter-day Saints. It considers printed works (broadsides, pamphlets, newspapers, periodicals, and books) published for both internal use and external consumption. The bibliographical guide is Chad J. Flake and Larry Draper,

Mormon print culture and thereafter would share it with his brother Orson. Between 1835 and his death in 1857, Pratt published over forty separate items, founded or edited several Mormon newspapers, edited Mormon scriptures for publication, and composed poems for and helped edit Church hymnals. At the time of his death, he left manuscripts for a play, a number of unpublished essays, and an autobiography. His sermons and correspondence were extensive, and they remain untapped sources for probing his life and thought. Because his papers have been scattered and because some of his published work first appeared anonymously, he has not received the attention he deserves in early Mormon history and thought. In some cases, Pratt's works were pirated by others who then placed their own names on them. Then, too, his brother Orson outlived him by several decades while managing to issue his own works in large editions. This essay surveys the main published works to reveal Pratt's great creative efforts in the shaping of early Mormon print culture.[7]

Because he caught the spark of Mormonism's fire in 1830, Pratt was a student of Joseph Smith. His reading the text of the Book of Mormon as he was investigating Smith's claims surely helped to develop his own literary approach to Mormonism. His appointment in February 1835 to serve in the Quorum of the Twelve Apostles was a major event, calling him as it did to a lifetime of missionary service. But his written works are only part of his story; to better appreciate his calling as a defender of the prophet Joseph Smith as

A Mormon Bibliography, 1830–1930, Books, Pamphlets, Periodicals, and Broadsides Relating to the First Century of Mormonism, 2nd ed., 2 vols. (Provo, Utah: Religious Studies Center, Brigham Young University, 2004). For an introduction to Mormon book history, see David J. Whittaker, "The Web of Print: Toward a History of the Book in Early Mormon Culture," *Journal of Mormon History* 23 (Spring 1996): 1–41.

[7] The seminal work on Pratt's writing is Peter Crawley, "Parley P. Pratt: The Father of Mormon Pamphleteering," *Dialogue* 15 (Autumn 1982): 13–26. As Crawley's friend and colleague, I have drawn on numerous conversations with him over many years as well as on his extensive published bibliographical work: *A Descriptive Bibliography of the Mormon Church*, 2 vols. (Provo, Utah: Religious Studies Center, Brigham Young University, 1997, 2005). References to these volumes will hereafter be cited as Crawley, followed by the volume, page, and item number. I am also grateful for his willingness to carefully read and comment on this essay.

well as his work as a missionary, we would do well to consider this excerpt from a letter he sent to his Canadian converts in 1836:

> One week before [the meeting] word was Publicly given that Br. J. Smith Jr. would give a relating of the coming forth of the Records, and also of the rise of the church and of his Experience[.] accordingly a vast concourse assembled at an Early hour[.] Every seat was crowded and 4 or 5 hundred People stood up in the Aisles[.] Br. S[mith] gave the history of these things[,] relating many particularly of the manner of his first visions, &c[.] The Spirit and Power of God was upon him in Bearing testimony Insomuch that many if not most of the Congregation was in tears—as for my Self I can say that all the reasonings in uncertainty and all the conclusions drawn from the writings of others . . . however great in themselves[,] Dwindle into insignificance when compared with Living testimony[,] when your Eyes and your Ears hear from the Living oracles of God.[8]

Just before leaving for his British mission, Pratt heard Smith address a large congregation in Philadelphia in December 1839. He wrote that Smith "spoke in great power, bearing testimony of the visions he had seen, the ministering of angels which he had enjoyed; and how he had found the plates of the Book of Mormon, and translated them by the gift and power of God. . . . The entire congregation was astounded; electrified, as it were, and overwhelmed with the sense of truth and power by which he spoke, and the wonders which he related."[9] Thus, any discussion of Pratt's life and thought

[8] Parley P. Pratt to the Elders and Brethren of the Church of Latter Day Saints in Canada, 27 November 1836, John Taylor Collection, Church History Library, the Church of Jesus Christ of Latter-day Saints, Salt Lake City, Utah (hereafter LDS Church History Library).

[9] Parley P. Pratt, *The Autobiography of Parley Parker Pratt, One of the Twelve Apostles of the Church of Jesus Christ of Latter-day Saints, Embracing His Life, Ministry, and Travels, with Extracts in Prose and Verse from His Miscellaneous Writings*, ed. Parley P. Pratt, Jr. (New York: Russell Brothers, 1874), 298–99. Unless otherwise noted, all citations to the *Autobiography* are to the first edition. A number of subsequent prints have appeared, perhaps the most useful being *Autobiography of Parley P. Pratt*, rev. ed., eds. Scot Facer Proctor and Maurine Jensen Proctor (Salt Lake City: Deseret Book, 2000). The first biography was Reva Holdaway Stanley, *A Biography of Parley P. Pratt: The Archer of Paradise* (Caldwell, Idaho: Caxton Printers, 1937). Collections of his writings include *Writings of Parley Parker Pratt*, edited and published by his grandson, Parker Pratt Robison (Salt Lake City: Deseret News Press, 1952); and *The Essential Parley P. Pratt*, foreword by Peter Crawley (Salt Lake City: Signature Books, 1990).

must never lose track of the great influence that Smith had on him.[10] In fact, Smith himself voiced concern in 1842 that the Pratt brothers and others were publishing his ideas as their own.[11]

Early Mormon Print Culture

Few Mormon works had appeared in print before 1836.[12] The Book of Mormon, available from its Palmyra, New York, printer in March 1830 was the first Mormon book. It functioned as the first missionary work, as it continues to do today.[13] Prior to 1836, most Mormon missionaries had worked in the settings of the smaller villages and hamlets of New England and the Old Northwest Territory and Upper Canada, the areas of the origins of the earliest converts. In 1831 the first newspaper and printing shop was established; in 1833 an attempt to publish the first collection of Joseph Smith's revelations was made but abruptly ended by mob action in July 1833. In September 1835 the first successful publication of the revelations appeared as the Doctrine and Covenants of the Church of Jesus Christ of Latter-day Saints: Carefully Selected from the Revelations of God, followed quickly by the first Mormon hymnal in February/March of 1836. These pioneering efforts emphasized basic scriptural and worship texts of the Restoration.

The first Mormon newspaper was established in Independence, Missouri. *The Evening and the Morning Star* announced the

[10] Pratt freely gave credit to Joseph Smith, noting that he had "lifted a corner of the veil" and given him "a single glance into eternity" (Pratt, *Autobiography*, 229–30). Pratt traveled with Smith on a mission to preach and recruit men for Zion's Camp in February and March 1834. Pratt later recalled: "As we journeyed day after day, and generally lodged together, we had much sweet communion concerning the things of God and the mysteries of His Kingdom, and I received many admonitions and instructions which I shall never forget" (ibid., 117).

[11] See comments of Joseph Smith, Minutes of the Female Relief Society, Nauvoo, Illinois, 28 April 1842, LDS Church History Library.

[12] For a survey of Mormon printing, see "Mormon Imprints as Sources for Research: A History and Evaluation," appendix A, in Ronald W. Walker, David J. Whittaker, and James B. Allen, *Mormon History* (Urbana: University of Illinois Press, 2001), 199–238.

[13] See David J. Whittaker, "'That Most Important of All Books': A Printing History of the Book of Mormon," *Mormon Historical Studies* 6 (2005): 101–34.

message of the Restoration, printed revelations received or counsel given by the prophet, and provided a forum whereby members could communicate with each other. Its primary purpose was for internal communication. William W. Phelps, as "Printer to the Church," operated the *Star*, controlled editorial policy, and infused this newspaper with millennial fervor.[14] The distance from Kirtland, Ohio (the headquarters of the Church from 1831 to 1838), to Independence meant that the day-to-day decisions regarding the printing business had to be in the hands of those on the scene.

Several general precedents were established in Missouri for early Mormon publishing. The first was the practice of publishing two newspapers, one religious and one secular. Thus, in Missouri, the Mormons issued the *Star* and the *Upper Missouri Advertiser*; in Ohio they published both the *Latter-day Saints' Messenger and Advocate* and the *Northern Times*; and later, in Nauvoo, Illinois, they issued the *Times and Seasons* and the *Nauvoo Neighbor*. Usual access to all of these newspapers was by local purchase or by subscription, and missionaries could obtain their own copies by acting as agents of the publisher.[15]

The second precedent was the group approach to the publishing business that combined a business venture with an economic philosophy of consecration. In its fullest expression, such an effort was called the Literary Firm. Established by revelation in November 1831, this endeavor was to supply the Church with a variety of published items, including a collection of Joseph Smith's revelations, a hymnal, newspapers, an almanac, Smith's revisions to the Bible, and some items specifically intended for children, all from a printing house in Missouri. The Literary Firm did issue the *Star* and was near to finishing the typesetting of the Book of Commandments when angry Missourians destroyed the Mormon press in July 1833. Thereafter, the publishing business moved to Kirtland where the Firm issued the *Messenger and Advocate* and republished (with textual changes) and continued the retitled *Evening and Morning Star*.

[14] Doctrine and Covenants 55:4; and 57:11–13 (current editions).

[15] Parley P. Pratt would break from this tradition in England, serving in 1840 as the founding editor of the singular *Millennial Star*.

It also issued in 1836 the hymnal compiled by Emma Smith. A variety of factors led to the dissolving of the Firm in 1836, the same year that the first clearly identifiable Mormon tract appeared.[16]

Church leaders recognized the potential power of the press when they encountered attacks against their faith in various books and local newspaper articles. But their earliest reaction to these attacks was either to ignore them or to send select individuals on special preaching missions to personally challenge critics to debate and public discussion.[17] Such an approach was appropriate as long as Mormon missionaries remained in smaller villages or among family and neighbors, but by 1836 they were beginning to enter the larger cities of the United States and Canada. In these more urban and cosmopolitan settings, the elders turned increasingly to the press, as their potentially larger audiences seemed to demand a more systematic and sophisticated presentation of their message.

In Toronto, Canada, in August 1836, Orson Hyde published his *A Prophetic Warning to All the Churches, of Every Sect and Denomination, and to Every Individual into Whose Hand It May Fall.*[18] Hyde's work was followed the next year by Pratt's *Voice of Warning* in New York City.[19] Where Hyde's work was a short broadside that, in the first edition, failed to even mention the name of the church he represented, Pratt's work was a small book that examined in detail the basic beliefs of the Church whose message is clear on almost every

[16] See Lyndon W. Cook, *Joseph Smith and the Law of Consecration* (Provo, Utah: Grandin Book Co., 1985), 45–55; and Max Parkin, "Joseph Smith and the United Firm: The Growth and Decline of the Church's First Master Plan of Business and Finance, Ohio and Missouri, 1832–1834," *BYU Studies* 46, no. 3 (2007): 5–66.

[17] See Doctrine and Covenants (1835), 90:225 (Doctrine and Covenants 71:7–10 in current editions), in response to the published letters of Ezra Booth.

[18] This broadside was dated Toronto, August 1836, and its text was published in the *Latter-day Saints' Messenger and Advocate* 2 (July 1836): 342–46, where it is dated 16 June 1836. The only known copy is in the Community of Christ Library/Archives, Independence, Missouri.

[19] Parley P. Pratt, *A Voice of and Instruction to All People, Containing a Declaration of the Faith and Doctrine of the Church of the Latter Day Saints, Commonly Called Mormons* (New York: W. Sandford, 1837). This work was written in July and August, copyrighted on August 26, and appeared in an edition of three thousand copies in October 1837. Pratt stated, "Thousands date their conversion to the fulness of the gospel to reading of that book" (Pratt, *Autobiography*, 184–85).

page. Pratt's *Voice of Warning* signaled a new era in Mormon publishing, in which his own missionary tracts played a central role.

Parley P. Pratt and Early Mormon Publishing

Pratt's earliest published work seems to be a handbill issued in late 1833. While no copy is known, it was reprinted in an extra of the *Star* in Kirtland in February 1834. The reprint refers to the events leading up to the destruction of the Mormon Missouri press in July 1833. The handbill, entitled "'The Mormons' So Called," was signed by Parley P. Pratt, Newell Knight, and John Carrill [Corrill] and dated December 12, 1833. As Crawley suggests, the wording of this handbill reappears in Pratt's later *History of the Late Persecution Inflicted by the State of Missouri upon the Mormons.*[20]

Pratt's first extant published work as a Latter-day Saint was a short pamphlet that described the rough treatment he received by a rowdy crowd when he was preaching in Mentor, Ohio, in April 1835. It seems to be the first Mormon missionary narrative published.[21] The same year, Pratt published the first volume of Mormon poetry in which he presented in a narrative poem the major gospel events plus additional poems, eight of which were later incorporated into the first British Mormon hymnal in 1840.[22] Pratt included excerpts from this work in his 1837 *Voice of Warning*, and in 1840 expanded the work into *The Millennium, and Other*

---

[20] Crawley, 1:42–43 (Items 9 and 10). On the Mormon Missouri press, see Ronald E. Romig and John H. Siebert, "First Impressions: Independence, Missouri, Printing Operation, 1832–33," *John Whitmer Historical Association Journal* 10 (1990): 51–66. On its destruction, see Warren A. Jennings, "Factors in the Destruction of the Mormon Press in Missouri, 1833," *Utah Historical Quarterly* 35 (Winter 1967): 57–76. Pratt's handbill was the first published account of the Mormon expulsion from Jackson County, Missouri.

[21] Parley P. Pratt, *A Short Account of a Shameful Outrage, Committed by a Part of the Inhabitants of the Town of Mentor, upon the Person of Elder Parley P. Pratt, While Delivering a Public Discourse upon the Subject of the Gospel* (Kirtland? 1835?); and Crawley, 1:53 (Item 19). The only extant copy of the pamphlet is in the LDS Church History Library. See also Pratt, *Autobiography*, 138–39.

[22] Parley P. Pratt, *The Millennium, a Poem. To Which Is Added Hymns and Songs of Various Subjects, New and Interesting, Adapted to the Dispensation of the Fulness of Times* (Boston: Printed for Elder Parley P. Pratt, author and proprietor, 1835); Crawley, 1:54 (Item 21).

Poems: To Which Is Annexed, a Treatise on the Regeneration and Eternal Nature of Matter.[23]

His next printed work was a handbill responding to attacks made by an Irvingite preacher, a Mr. Caird, in Kingston, Canada, in October 1836. No copy has been found, but Pratt referred to the encounter in his *Autobiography*, explaining that he only printed the reply, *Doth our Law Judge a Man Before it Hear Him?* when Caird refused to meet him in debate. This short printed reply was probably the first Mormon tract responding to an attack on the missionary's message.[24] It was a transition work, moving as it did from the oral to the written defense of the Church, which had been the norm until then. At about the same time, Pratt had handbills printed advertising the Mormon meetings in Toronto, which also countered Caird's continuing attacks on them.[25]

By the time Pratt began to compose his first major work, *Voice of Warning*, he had experienced the real challenges of missionary work. Written in about two months in New York City, this 216-page text proved to be one of the most popular Latter-day Saint works in the nineteenth century. It provided the ideal pocket reference work for Mormon missionaries and a most useful introduction to the basic doctrines of the Restoration for new members as well as investigators. It was the first work to emphasize the differences between Mormonism and orthodox Christianity, and as Peter Crawley notes, it established the basic formulas for describing the essential doctrines of the Church. In eight chapters, using biblical proof-texts, Pratt began the literary defense of Mormonism, ranging broadly in his discussion of the Church. His chapter on the Book of Mormon was the first to offer both a summary of its contents and to provide some of the first arguments in print for its authenticity.[26] Joseph Smith appears most prominently in the chapter on the Book

[23] Pratt, *The Millennium, and Other Poems: To Which Is Annexed a Treatise on the Regeneration and Eternal Duration of Matter* (New York: W. Molineux, 1840); and Crawley, 1:98–100 (Item 63).

[24] See Pratt, *Autobiography*, 177–80; and Crawley, 1:64–65 (Item 31). On the Irvingites, see n88, this chapter.

[25] See Crawley, 1:64–65 (Item 32).

[26] Parley P. Pratt and John Goodson printed the second edition of the Book of Mormon in 1837. See Crawley, 1:66–68 (Item 35).

of Mormon, but he is presented primarily as part of a larger story foretold in prophecy and now restored to the earth as the Kingdom of God prophesied by Daniel. Pratt presented the story of the earth in a sweeping panorama moving to the grand events of the last days. Here was the core of his message: the heavens were again open and everyone was invited to be a part of the great events of the last days. There have been at least eighty known printings of this work since 1837, and it continues in print today.[27]

When the first anti-Mormon works were published, Mormon missionaries mostly ignored them or responded with oral defenses. Thus, when Ezra Booth's anti-Mormon letters were printed in the *Ohio Star* in 1831 or when E. D. Howe's *Mormonism Unvailed* appeared in 1834, containing serious charges against Joseph Smith's character, no Mormon produced a written response.[28] But by 1838, when Mormons were catching the attention of a wider audience in the larger cities, written responses were called forth. For instance, when LaRoy Sunderland, the editor of the Methodist *Zion's Watchman*, published a series of eight articles in 1838 attacking the Mormons, using material that had appeared in Howe's 1834 volume, and when the articles were gathered into a pamphlet for wider distribution, Pratt answered with the first Mormon work responding to an anti-Mormon publication: *Mormonism Unveiled: Zion's Watchman Unmasked, and Its Editor, Mr. L. R. Sunderland, Exposed: Truth Vindicated: The Devil Mad, and Priestcraft in Danger!*[29] In this retort, Pratt combined specific replies with an

[27] Crawley, 1:69–71 (Item 38). The second edition was issued in 1839 (New York: J. W. Harrison), with several revisions and additions. See Crawley, 1:97–98 (Item 62).

[28] On Ezra Booth's letters, see Dennis Rowley, "The Ezra Booth Letters," *Dialogue* 16 (Autumn 1983): 133–36; Eber D. Howe, *Mormonism Unvailed; or, a Faithful Account of That Singular Imposition and Delusion, from Its Rise to the Present Time* (Painesville, Ohio: Printed and published by the author, 1834); and Dale W. Adams, "Doctor Philastus Hurlbut: Originator of Derogatory Statements About Joseph Smith, Jr.," *John Whitmer Historical Association Journal* 20 (2000): 76–93.

[29] Parley P. Pratt, *Mormonism Unveiled: Zion's Watchman Unmasked, and Its Editor, Mr. L. R. Sunderland, Exposed: Truth Vindicated: The Devil Mad, and Priescraft in Danger!* (New York: Printed for the publisher, 1838). There were at least three additional printings of this work in 1838, suggesting its value for missionary work moving into larger cities. See Crawley, 1:76–79 (Items 45–48).

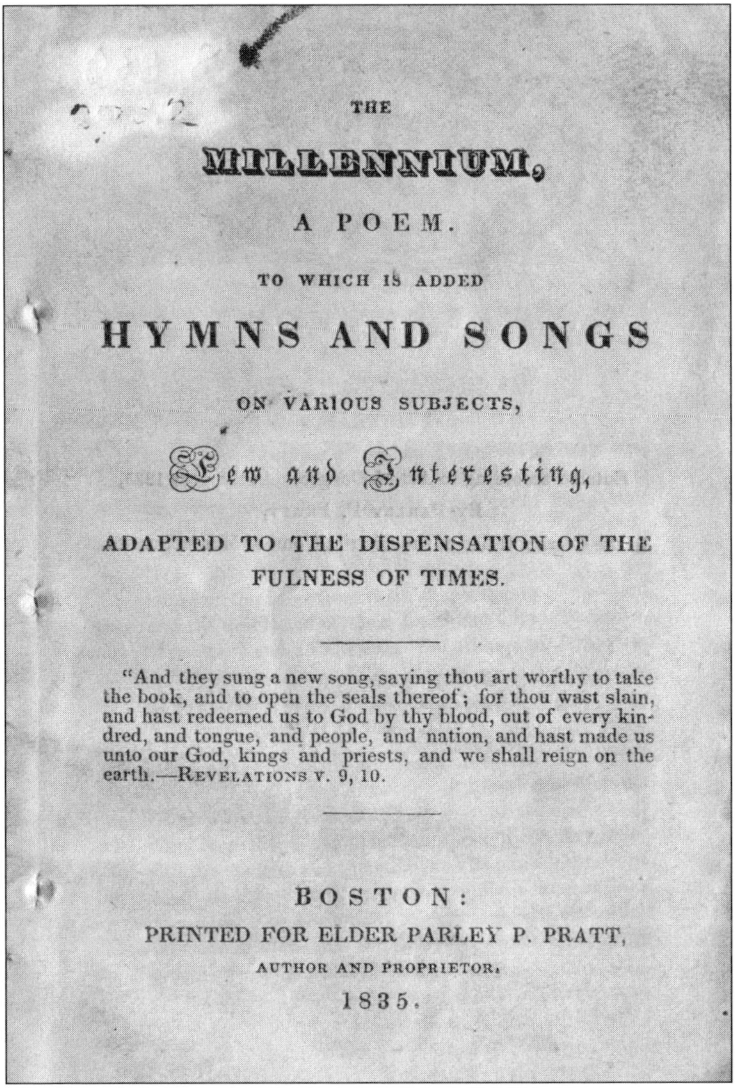

THE

MILLENNIUM,

A POEM.

TO WHICH IS ADDED

HYMNS AND SONGS

ON VARIOUS SUBJECTS,

New and Interesting,

ADAPTED TO THE DISPENSATION OF THE FULNESS OF TIMES.

"And they sung a new song, saying thou art worthy to take the book, and to open the seals thereof; for thou wast slain, and hast redeemed us to God by thy blood, out of every kindred, and tongue, and people, and nation, and hast made us unto our God, kings and priests, and we shall reign on the earth.—REVELATIONS V. 9, 10.

BOSTON:
PRINTED FOR ELDER PARLEY P. PRATT,
AUTHOR AND PROPRIETOR.
1835.

Title page of *The Millennium*, 1835.
Courtesy of the L. Tom Perry Special Collections, Harold B. Lee Library, Brigham Young University, Provo, Utah.

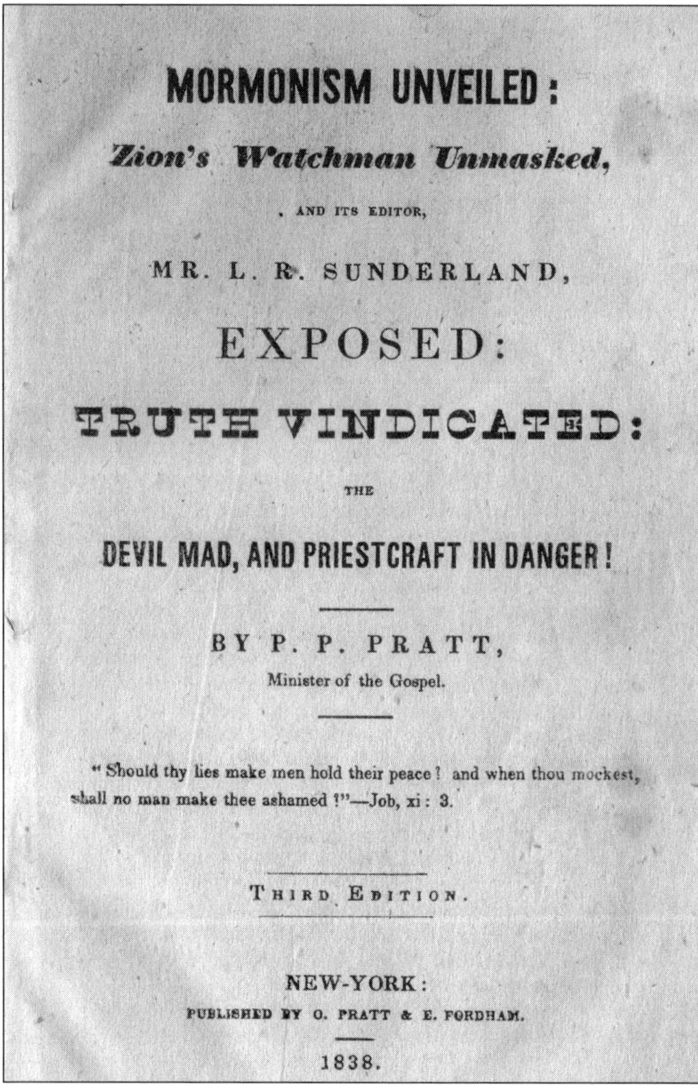

MORMONISM UNVEILED:

Zion's Watchman Unmasked,

AND ITS EDITOR,

MR. L. R. SUNDERLAND,

EXPOSED:

TRUTH VINDICATED:

THE

DEVIL MAD, AND PRIESTCRAFT IN DANGER!

BY P. P. PRATT,

Minister of the Gospel.

"Should thy lies make men hold their peace? and when thou mockest, shall no man make thee ashamed?"—Job, xi: 3.

THIRD EDITION.

NEW-YORK:

PUBLISHED BY O. PRATT & E. FORDHAM.

1838.

Title page of *Mormonism Unveiled*, 1838.
Courtesy of the L. Tom Perry Special Collections, Harold B. Lee Library, Brigham Young University, Provo, Utah.

attack on the religion of the author. He responded to the Solomon Spaulding and Sidney Rigdon theory of the origin of the Book of Mormon by providing details of his early relationship with Rigdon, explaining that Pratt had introduced Rigdon to Mormonism *after* the Book of Mormon was published. Pratt also attacked the Methodist beliefs in the practice of infant baptism and in a God "without body or parts."[30] In his introductory comments, Pratt expressed a frustration that most Mormon writers surely shared:

> When the public are overwhelmed with lying slander of every description concerning the Church of the Latter Day Saints[,] [t]he inquiry often arise, why do the Elders of the Church hold their peace, instead of contradicting them and their principles? The answer is, it would require a standing army of writers, and printers in constant employ; for no sooner are our enemies detected in one falsehood, than a thousand more are put in circulation by them; and there are many who love a lie much more than the truth, that we are quite willing they should enjoy their strong delusion; because, they believe not the truth, but have pleasure in unrighteous; and we know, that those who are seeking for truth, will judge for themselves, by examination of our books, and not allow our opposers to judge for them.[31]

Pratt shared with other Mormons the persecution and forced exile from northern Missouri in 1838–39, and like Smith, he was detained in jail for months. Escaping after eight months in

---

[30] The Spaulding theory was an early attempt by Joseph Smith's critics to claim that Solomon Spaulding had produced a manuscript before 1830 that had been the real source of the Book of Mormon. Sidney Rigdon, an early convert to the Church, was suggested as the person who had secretly obtained this manuscript for Smith. Such an explanation was part of the material gathered into E. D. Howe's 1834 volume, *Mormonism Unvailed*, but until 1884 the actual existence of the Spaulding document was debated. It surfaced then and was placed at Oberlin College in Ohio, where it remains today. See Lester E. Bush, Jr., "The Spaulding Theory Then and Now," *Dialogue* 10 (Autumn 1977): 40–69; and Kent P. Jackson, ed., *Manuscript Found: The Complete Original "Spaulding Manuscript" by Solomon Spaulding* (Provo, Utah: Religious Studies Center, Brigham Young University, 1996). On LaRoy Sunderland, see Edward D. Jervey, "LaRoy Sunderland: Zion's Watchman," *Methodist History* 6 (1968): 16–32. This seemingly larger audience for printed material also called forth a new issuing of E. D. Howe's anti-Mormon volume made up of the sheets of the 1834 edition with only a new title page: *History of Mormonism* ... (Painesville, Ohio: Printed and published by the author, 1840). Apparently Howe's 1834 printing did not sell very well.

[31] Pratt, *Mormonism Unveiled*, 3.

Missouri jails in July 1839, he traveled to Nauvoo, Illinois, and then north to Detroit, Michigan, where he published his account of Missouri Mormon experience.[32] He had written most of this history while in jail, and he was surely moved in this direction by Smith's counsel in the Liberty Jail epistle (Doctrine and Covenants 123). He recalled that writing for him was "a priviledge" [*sic*] that relieved his "full heart like the steam blowing from an over charged boiler."[33] His *History of the Late Persecution* appeared in Detroit in October 1839, and it provided a mostly autobiographical account of some eighty-four pages of the Mormon experience in Missouri, surveying the earliest years but providing a more detailed account of the last months, including the court of inquiry before Judge Austin King in November 1838 and the treatment of the Mormon leaders during this time.[34]

Parley P. Pratt in New York City, 1839–1840

Pratt had been called on a mission to the British Isles with his fellow apostles, and after publishing the account of his Missouri experiences, he traveled to New York City in October and remained there until March 1839 when he sailed for Liverpool, England. His time in New York City and the areas south was short

[32] Pratt devoted a significant amount of his *Autobiography* to these experiences (189–322).

[33] Parley P. Pratt to Mary Ann Frost Pratt, 8 June 1839, LDS Church History Library.

[34] Parley P. Pratt, *History of the Late Persecution Inflicted by the State of Missouri upon the Mormons, in Which Ten Thousand American Citizens Were Robbed, Plundered, and Driven from the State, and Many Others Imprisoned, Martyred, &c. for their Religion, and All This by Military Force, by Order of the Executive* (Detroit: Dawson and Bates, Printers, 1839); and Crawley, 1:89–90 (Item 59). The first serialized history of the Mormon experience in Missouri, initially begun by Edward Partridge and printed in the *Times and Seasons* 1 (December 1839 to October 1840), was interrupted by Partridge's illness and death in May 1840. This forced the editors to gather extracts from other sources, including Pratt's *History of the Late Persecution*. Thus, extracts appeared in the April 1840 issue (1, 6:81–82) taken from *History of the Late Persecution*, 26–29, and in the June 1840 installment (1, 8:113–16) taken from *History of the Late Persecution*, 33–40. The April issue specifically mentioned the Detroit edition of Pratt's work as the source. See also Dean C. Jessee, "'Walls, Grates, and Screeking Iron Doors': The Prison Experience of Mormon Leaders in Missouri, 1838–1839," in Davis Bitton and Maureen Ursenbach Beecher, eds., *New Views of Mormon History: A Collection of Essays in Honor of Leonard J. Arrington* (Salt Lake City: University of Utah Press, 1987), 19–42.

but very important for his own writing and growing understanding of Mormonism. Increasingly concentrating on more doctrinal matters, he issued a second edition of his *Voice of Warning*, a new edition of his Missouri Mormon history, and a much expanded edition of the 1835 collection of poems. It was during this time that several developments in Mormon print culture emerged. The first was the use of printed items to finance proselytizing missions; the second was the notion that authorship could provide a means to support the missionary-writer's family. The third development, a direct outcome of the teachings of Joseph Smith during his trip to the East Coast during the winter of 1839–40, was the appearance in Mormon writing of new and expansive doctrines. All of these are reflected in Pratt's writings prior to his departure for England.

First Pratt prepared a second edition of *Voice of Warning*. Joseph Smith had spoken in September 1839 "concerning some errors in Br. P. P. Pratt's works,"[35] and the textual alterations in Pratt's new edition no doubt reflected Smith's concerns.[36] He next produced an expanded (215-page) edition of his Mormon Missouri history, retitled *Late Persecution of the Church of Jesus Christ, of Latter Day Saints*. Issued by the same printer who published the second edition of *Voice of Warning*, this edition reprinted the Detroit imprint and added several items, including an introduction, some newspaper excerpts, and an appendix taken from John P. Greene's recently published *Facts Relative to the Expulsion of the Mormons*, which included the eyewitness account of the Haun's Mill Massacre by Joseph Young.[37] Perhaps the most important addition to this small book was the fourteen pages in the introduction, which provided his readers with a short history of the Church and a brief

[35] B. H. Roberts et al., eds., *History of the Church of Jesus Christ of Latter-day Saints: Period I, History of Joseph Smith, the Prophet, by Himself*, 6 vols. (Salt Lake City: Deseret News, 1902–12), 4:7 (hereafter HC), citing Joseph Smith, 1839 Illinois Journal, 1 September 1839, LDS Church History Library.

[36] For a short discussion of the textual changes to the second edition of Pratt's *Voice of Warning* (New York: J. W. Harrison, 1839), see Crawley, 1:97–98 (Item 62).

[37] Greene's work was published in June/July 1839 as *Facts Relative to the Expulsion of the Mormons or Latter Day Saints, from the State of Missouri, Under the "Exterminating Order"* (Cincinnati: R. P. Brooks). Greene had been appointed by a May 1839 Church conference to provide leadership in New York City. While on his way, he published this work, which he obviously shared with Pratt when he arrived.

summary of basic Mormon beliefs, the first short framing in print of the fundamentals of Mormonism.[38] A copy of the first edition of Pratt's Missouri history was submitted to Congress with the other Mormon petitions for redress that Joseph Smith and his colleagues took to Washington, D.C., in November 1839.

Pratt's interaction with the Mormon leader during his visit to the East Coast during the winter of 1839–40 exerted a powerful influence on his thoughts and writings. Joseph Smith's own more public outreach during this period likely spurred Pratt's efforts to use the printed word to address a public that was increasingly interested in the Mormon prophet and his message. This renewed effort at missionary work no doubt led Pratt to add the doctrinal introduction to this *Late Persecution*. Orson, who was then traveling with Smith, invited Pratt to come to Philadelphia.[39] Pratt did so for several days and while there gained greater insights into the doctrines of the Restoration. And Pratt was not the only one, as several Mormon writers published pamphlets during this time that contained hints at what Smith was then teaching, doctrines that would be more publicly taught to members during the last years of the prophet's life.[40]

For Pratt, these short months prior to his departure for England saw the emergence from his pen of some of the most important essays on Mormon thought. In February 1840, Pratt used the

[38] Parley P. Pratt, *Late Persecution of the Church of Jesus Christ, of Latter Day Saints. Ten Thousand American Citizens Robbed, Plundered, and Banished; Others Imprisoned, and Others Martyred for Their Religion. With a Sketch of Their Rise, Progress and Doctrine* (New York: J. W. Harrison, 1840), [iii]–xvi; and Crawley, 1:100–102 (Item 64).

[39] See Orson Pratt, letter to his wife, 6 January 1840, published in excerpt in the *Times and Seasons* 1, no. 4 (February 1840): 61; and Pratt, *Autobiography*, 328–31.

[40] See Samuel Bennett, *A Few Remarks by Way of Reply to an Anonymous Scribbler, Calling Himself a Philanthropist, Disabusing the Church of Jesus Christ of Latter-day Saints of the Slanders and Falsehoods Which He Has Attempted to Fasten upon It* (Philadelphia: Brown, Bicking & Gilbert, Printers, 1840); and Benjamin Winchester, *An Examination of a Lecture Delivered by the Rev. H[enry] Perkins on the Religious Opinions and Faith of the Latter-day Saints and Some of the Most Prominent Errors and Mistakes Corrected* (Philadelphia?: n.p., 1840). Bennett asserted the Saints' belief in a corporeal, anthropomorphic God, whereas Winchester referred to the idea of the pre-mortal existence of spirits. Along with Pratt's work, Bennett's and Winchester's pamphlets reinforce the idea that Joseph Smith was beginning to preach more openly about these key doctrines, which would be taught more fully in Nauvoo before Smith's death in 1844.

doctrinal introduction to his *Late Persecution* in *An Address by Judge [Elias] Higbee and Parley P. Pratt. Ministers of the Gospel, . . . to the Citizens of Washington*. Dated February 9, 1840, this work seems to have appeared shortly after Joseph Smith preached a public sermon on February 5, 1840, in Washington, D.C. It was reprinted in the *Times and Seasons* and, with slight modifications, at least six more times in the following three years. The *Address* proved very popular among Mormon missionaries, some of whom incorporated it in their own works.[41] It would be the first tract Pratt printed in the British Isles, and its summary of Mormon beliefs clearly influenced Orson Pratt's listing in his important September 1840 Edinburgh, Scotland, pamphlet, *A[n] Interesting Account of Several Remarkable Visions*, which in turn influenced Smith's listing of Mormon doctrines in his Wentworth Letter of 1842, now known as the Articles of Faith.[42]

Prior to his departure for England, Pratt also printed a new edition of his 1835 collection of poems, though in a much expanded version.[43] Increased from about fifty to slightly over 150 pages, this new printing added more poems (many written while in jail in Missouri), a journal account of Pratt's trip to the White Mountains of New Hampshire, and a fifty-page essay on "The Regeneration and Eternal Duration of Matter." This essay, written, he said, "to comfort and console myself when death stared me in the face," was more personal and in the Romantic tradition of reflection than as a theological discourse, although it was both. A masterpiece, it drew on several of Joseph Smith's earlier revelations, which taught that the elements were eternal, but then provided an extended personal essay on the meaning of the doctrine. Pratt discussed ideas that had never

---

[41] Parley P. Pratt, *An Address by Judge Higbee and Parley P. Pratt, Ministers of the Gospel, of the Church of Jesus Christ of "Latter-day Saints," to the Citizens of Washington and to the Public in General* (Washington? 1840); and Crawley, 1:104–106 (Item 67). In spite of having Elias Smith listed as a co-author, the work is clearly the creation of Parley Pratt, as he noted in his *Autobiography*: "I published an address in a printed circular to each member of Congress, and the President of the United States and his cabinet, setting forth our principles in plainness and bearing testimony of the truth" (328). See also *Times and Seasons* 1, no. 5 (March 1840): 68–70.

[42] David J. Whittaker, "The 'Articles of Faith' in Early Mormon Literature and Thought," in Bitton and Beecher, *New Views of Mormon History*, 63–92.

[43] Pratt, *The Millennium, and Other Poems*. This work appeared in early January 1840. Crawley, 1:98–100 (Item 63).

before appeared in a Mormon publication, including that matter and spirit can neither be created nor annihilated; that the world was not created ex nihilo but organized out of existing matter; and that even God is bound by eternal principles. His essay presented a much more developed concept of the nature of God than had yet appeared in Mormon publications. Such ideas were expanded upon in several of Orson's tracts but defended through scientific logic.[44] Pratt also printed a broadside poem of millennial hope, *Farewell Song*, published just before he departed with other missionaries for Liverpool and reprinted a number of times thereafter.[45]

Parley P. Pratt and Mormon Imprints in England, 1839–1842

The first Mormon missionaries in the British Isles arrived in the Lancashire area north of Manchester in August 1837. They were very successful in baptizing new converts in the valley of the River Ripple, east of Preston, and when they returned to the United States in April 1838, Church membership had grown to about fifteen hundred. This first mission had resulted from earlier efforts of missionaries like Pratt in Upper Canada, where converts had recently emigrated from England and had maintained contact with friends and family back home. Pratt had helped to convert John Taylor, Isaac Russell, and Joseph Fielding in the Toronto area in 1836. Thus, when Orson Hyde and Heber C. Kimball were sent to England by Joseph Smith in 1837, key individuals like Russell and Fielding accompanied them and sought out their personal and family connections. These efforts laid the foundation for the great missionary harvest that would come in the following decades.[46] The second apostolic mission, 1839–41, brought

[44] For example, Orson Pratt, *Absurdities of Immaterialism* (Liverpool, England: R. James, 1849).

[45] *Times and Seasons* 1, no. 7 (May 1840): 111; and *Millennial Star* 1 (June 1840): 48. It was included in both the Manchester, England, and Nauvoo hymnals. See Crawley, 1:106–107 (Item 68).

[46] See James B. Allen, Ronald K. Esplin, and David J. Whittaker, *Men with a Mission: The Quorum of the Twelve Apostles in the British Isles, 1837–1841* (Salt Lake City: Deseret Book, 1992). Chapter 10 is the basis for much of the discussion here.

nine apostles (including the Pratt brothers) to the British Isles and added another four thousand members to the Church.

The first British missionaries primarily used oral preaching, not the press, to spread their message, reflecting the approaches to missionary work used in the earliest years of the movement. They did distribute Orson Hyde's Toronto, Canada, broadside, *A Prophetic Warning*, possibly printed in New York City before they left for England, and reissued under the title *A Timely Warning* in Preston in August 1837. But they published no other pamphlets during this first mission, even though two pamphlet attacks had been made against them. Joseph Fielding noted, "It appears they want to provoke us to controversy, but we have washed our feet against them all, so they may talk and write until they are tired, or till the Lord puts a stop to them."[47] The second mission, largely as a result of Pratt's involvement, would take a much different approach.

By the time the second group of missionaries arrived in England, both the content and direction of Mormon imprints had changed. Pratt, who had been particularly active in these changes, continued in England as a key figure, both as author and editor, as he published a dozen additional pamphlets, served as the founding editor of the Church newspaper there, and functioned as a key member of the publishing committee set up by the Quorum of the Twelve Apostles.

The arrival of the second wave of missionaries in 1840 changed dramatically the Mormon mission in England, giving it new energy and organization.[48] The apostles added their own considerable talents to the effort and brought fresh ideas and experiences to the tasks that confronted them. They gave the mission better organization at the April 1840 conference in Preston, including establishing a publishing committee that planned to issue a hymnal, a periodical, and the Book of Mormon. By the time the majority of the Twelve departed in April 1841, Wilford Woodruff noted that

[47]Joseph Fielding, Diary, 1 June 1838, LDS Church History Library; and Crawley, 1:68 (Item 36).

[48]The apostle missionaries were Brigham Young, Heber C. Kimball, Orson Hyde, Parley P. Pratt, Orson Pratt, John Taylor, Wilford Woodruff, George A. Smith, and Willard Richards.

they had issued 5,000 (actually 4,050) copies of the Book of Mormon, 3,000 copies of a hymnal, 2,500 volumes (probably closer to 1,500) of a Church periodical, and about 50,000 copies of various pamphlets.[49] Obviously, this printed approach to missionary work contrasts significantly with that of the 1837 mission to England.

The apostles moved quickly to initiate a publishing program. While they worried lest they do something that Joseph Smith would not approve of, they moved ahead when long delays were caused by slow mails crossing the Atlantic Ocean. Even before they had left New York City, Pratt had written to Smith seeking permission to publish another U.S. edition of the Book of Mormon as well as trying to obtain general authorization for the Twelve to publish abroad.[50] Pratt had probably discussed these matters with Smith during their interaction on the East Coast the previous winter. Hyrum Smith initially responded, suggesting that they could publish whatever they wanted, but that the Book of Mormon ought to be published in Nauvoo. On May 14, 1840, Joseph Smith gave the apostles full permission to publish.[51] The decision to print a hymnal was approved at the April 1840 general conference in Preston. Brigham Young, Parley Pratt, and John Taylor were assigned the task of choosing the hymns to be included. Even before arriving in England, Pratt had thought of publishing a new hymnal, writing Joseph Smith from New York City that there was "a great call for Hymn Books, but none to be had. I wish that Sister [Emma] Smith would add to the old collections such new ones as is best and republish them immediately." Pratt had offered to oversee the publishing project on the East Coast.[52]

By May the committee in England had moved ahead on the European hymn book, deciding to publish three thousand copies.

---

[49] Wilford Woodruff, Journal, 16 April 1841, LDS Church History Library.

[50] Parley P. Pratt to Joseph Smith, 22 November 1839, Joseph Smith Collection, LDS Church History Library. This correspondence reveals Pratt's thinking about publishing and foreshadows most of the developments in England relating to Mormon printing there. Hyrum Smith responded to Pratt on December 22, 1839. See HC 4:47–48.

[51] Joseph Smith to "Dear Brethren," 14 May 1840, Joseph Smith Collection, LDS Church History Library.

[52] Pratt to Smith, 22 November 1839.

Writing to Brigham Young on May 4, Pratt told of his authoring new hymns every day, hoping to contribute one hundred to the new edition, and adding that "there is indeed a great call for Him [*sic*] Books suited to our worship."[53] Young took the lead in raising money to help with their publishing projects, traveling south with Wilford Woodruff where they borrowed money from new converts John and Jane Benbow and Thomas and Hannah Kington. On July 6, Pratt presented the new hymn book to the general conference in Manchester.[54] This first British edition was exhausted within a year, and the April 1841 conference authorized Pratt to reprint it without alterations (other than typos), which he did in November 1841.[55] This first British hymnal used seventy-eight hymns from Emma Smith's 1835 hymnal, and added 193 others, including forty-four by Pratt, seventeen of which came from the 1840 New York edition of his *The Millennium, and Other Poems.* This Manchester hymnal became the basis for all other Latter-day Saints (LDS) hymnals published in the nineteenth century and was issued in thirteen editions before 1871.[56]

The publishing of the Book of Mormon was undertaken in tandem with the hymnal but took much longer. The 1837 Kirtland edition was published by Pratt, with the financial support of John Goodson, who had brought copies to England with the first mission. But problems with Goodson and his eventual apostasy seem to have prevented many of these copies from being distributed in

---

[53] Parley P. Pratt to Brigham Young, 4 May 1840, Brigham Young Collection, LDS Church History Library. John Taylor seems not to have played much of a role in the work on the hymn book. See Taylor to Willard Richards, 4 May 1840, John Taylor Papers, LDS Church History Library. In his *Autobiography*, Pratt wrote, "I also assisted my brethren in selecting, compiling and publishing a hymn book. In this work was contained near fifty of my original hymns and songs, composed expressly for the book, and most of them written during the press of duties which crowded upon me" (336).

[54] *Millennial Star* 1 (July 1840): 69; and Crawley, 1:121–24 (Item 78).

[55] The conference authorizing the reprint is reported in the *Millennial Star* 25 (25 December 1863): 819. A letter of Parley P. Pratt, dated 19 March 1843, in the *Times and Seasons* 4 (15 April 1843): 163 reported that the second printing consisted of fifteen hundred copies. Crawley, 1:176 (Item 130).

[56] See Peter Crawley and David J. Whittaker, *Mormon Imprints in Great Britain and the Empire* (Provo, Utah: Harold B. Lee Library, 1987), 18–19.

England. When Pratt had written Joseph Smith in November 1839, he requested permission to publish an East Coast edition (as it could not be had "for love or money" there) and, anticipating the mission to England, he further suggested "that the publication of the Book of Mormon in Europe in English, French, German, and other languages be committed to the Twelve, as a committee who shall take charge of the same and whose duty it shall be to secure to you the copy rights in the several governments, and render strict account from time-to-time to the First Presidency."[57] The need for an English edition was only accentuated when the apostles arrived in England. Pratt told Brigham Young in May 1840 that the Book of Mormon was "very much wanted and it is all important to print immediately for why withhold the fullness of the Gospel, in the face of all the prophecies that it shall go to all nations?" Members, he said, "beg and pled for the Book of Mormon."[58]

Young and his colleagues were determined to make the volume available to the British Saints. The project was approved by the same April 1840 conference that had approved the hymnal. The money borrowed from the Benbows and Kingtons was primarily for printing the Book of Mormon, and the apostles moved ahead with the project even though they had not yet heard from Joseph Smith. Young, Heber Kimball, and Pratt were appointed as the publishing committee, and they decided to print 3,000 copies with an index, signing a contract in June 1840 with publisher John Tompkins and Company for 5,000 copies. While Young expected the printing of the Book of Mormon to progress quickly, it proceeded slowly. Part of the problem was Tompkin's changing the width and length of the page, although he was simply reprinting the 1837 Kirtland edition, but Tompkin's growing financial problems were also to blame. It was not until January 1841 that a complete set of galleys was available to Brigham Young and Willard Richards, from which they could compile an index. The index

[57] Pratt to Smith, 22 November 1839. Joseph Smith had requested that the apostles copyright what they published in his name in his May 14, 1840, letter.

[58] Pratt to Young, 4 May 1840; and Brigham Young to Joseph Smith, 7 May 1840, Joseph Smith Collection, LDS Church History Library.

(really a table of contents) was the first to be published as part of a published edition.[59]

The *Latter-day Saints' Millennial Star* finally announced to its February 1841 readers that the volume was ready for sale. While the contract with Tompkins had called for 5,000 copies, he delivered only 4,050. To make up the difference, he promised to print another edition of 950 at his own expense should they agree to order a new edition, but his company failed before he could do so. The volume itself was a faithful reprint of the 1837 Kirtland edition, and though two more editions were to appear in Nauvoo, it was from this Liverpool edition that subsequent LDS editions of the Book of Mormon descend.[60]

Their third project was the publishing of a periodical with Pratt as the natural choice for the founding editor. He had asked Joseph Smith's permission to publish a periodical when he had written to him in November 1839. The April 1840 conference in Preston voted to publish "a monthly periodical in pamphlet form," and Pratt "craved the privilege of editing" it.[61] Assigned as the editor, Pratt lost no time in preparing a prospectus. Received from the printer in Manchester on 27 April, the beautifully printed broadside announced that God had sent forth a holy angel to restore the fullness of the gospel, to bring his wandering sheep into one fold,

---

[59] In 1835 someone prepared a four-page *References to the Book of Mormon* (Kirtland? 1835?), a guide to the 1830 first edition. Some of the first editions have this extended table of contents tipped or glued into them. Following the 1841 British edition of the Book of Mormon, and based upon it, Robert P. Crawford published a twenty-one page *An Index, or Reference, to the Second and Third Editions of the Book of Mormon, Alphabetically Arranged* (Philadelphia: Brown, Bicking & Gilbert, Printers, 1842). See Crawley, 1:60 (Item 24) and 1:204–205 (Item 158). See also Grant Underwood, "The Earliest Reference Guides to the Book of Mormon: Windows into the Past," *Journal of Mormon History* 12 (1985): 69–89.

[60] For the details on the 1841 British edition of the Book of Mormon, see Allen, Esplin, and Whittaker, *Men with a Mission*, 249–52; Whittaker, "'Printing History of the Book of Mormon," 101–34; and Crawley, 1:148–51 (Item 98).

[61] See "History of Brigham Young," 15–16 April 1840, LDS Church History Library; and Young, Discourse, 31 August 1856, *Journal of Discourses of Brigham Young, President of the Church of Jesus Christ of Latter-day Saints, His Two Counselors, the Twelve Apostles, and Others*, 26 vols. (Liverpool, England: F.D. Richards and S.W. Richards, 1854–1886), 4:35.

and to prepare all who would harken for the Second Advent of the Messiah, "which is now at hand."[62]

Pratt wrote in the *Prospectus of the Latter-day Saints Millennial Star* that the periodical was to be devoted "entirely to the great work of the spread of truth." It was to stand aloof from the common political and commercial news of the day; rather its columns were to be devoted to the spread of the fullness of the gospel, which would include information on the Restoration, the gathering, and the signs of the times. Additionally, its pages were to contain extracts from the Book of Mormon as well as from "some of the remarkable visions and revelations which have been given to the saints in this age." Pratt also promised that the periodical would provide a kind of journal for the unfolding of the Kingdom of God by containing letters and news of "our numerous elders."[63]

The *Millennial Star* announced to its readers that the slumber of the ages was broken, that the long night of darkness was ending.[64] Pratt clearly carried his earlier millennial attitudes into his editorial duties. None of the other apostles were as well prepared as he to conduct such an enterprise. His enthusiasm and proven literary skills were surely essential to the project, but the success also depended on more practical matters such as raising the necessary funds. Pratt concluded his *Prospectus* by addressing these more mundane but essential matters: The *Millennial Star* was to be published monthly. Each issue was to be twenty-four pages, with double columns, and printed on good paper suitable for binding at the end of the year. Finally, each issue was to cost six pence, with subscriptions payable quarterly or yearly in advance. Missionaries

[62] Parley P. Pratt, *Prospectus of the Latter-day Saints Millennial Star* (Manchester, England: W.R. Thomas, 1840), broadside, LDS Church History Library. Most of the prospectus was reprinted in the first issue: 1 (May 1840): 1–2. Crawley, 1:108 (Item 70).

[63] Joseph Smith had counseled William W. Phelps, the editor of the first LDS Church periodical, *The Evening and the Morning Star*, to include information on "The Rise, Progress and Faith" of the Church. Phelps did and this set an important precedent for Mormon periodicals. See Smith to Phelps, 11 January 1833, Joseph Smith Letterbook, 18–20, LDS Church History Library.

[64] Pratt composed the popular hymn "The Morning Breaks, The Shadows Flee" for the introduction of this periodical. Pratt, *Autobiography*, 335–36. See further Samuel Russell, comp., *The Millennial Hymns of Parley P. Pratt* (Cambridge, England: University Press, 1913); and Dean L. May, "The Millennial Hymns of Parley P. Pratt," *Dialogue* 16 (Spring 1983): 145–50.

and Church leaders throughout the British Isles were invited to act as agents for the publication, and the first number was to be issued as soon as a sufficient number of subscribers could be obtained. Pratt sent copies of the *Prospectus* to elders, hoping they would begin to act as agents for the publication.[65] But when it came to these practical matters, Pratt was conservative as to how many copies of the first issue ought to be printed. Young did not want to depend on subscribers and told Pratt he was thinking too small when Pratt suggested printing only a thousand.[66] With Young's encouragement, the agreement with the printer, W. R. Thomas, was signed on April 23, 1840, and by May 20 the first numbers of twenty-five hundred copies were available.[67]

To more fully devote his energies to thc publishing business, Pratt established himself in Manchester where he obtained a combined office and living quarters. Pratt had anticipated before coming to England the establishment of a printing enterprise, "in some stake of Zion according to the word of the Lord and the pattern given."[68] His home in Manchester thus became the

[65] Joseph Fielding reported: "On Tuesday I received a Packet of the Prospectus for the Millennial Star from Bro. P. P. Pratt, Manchester, which I have distributed, and have now about 45 subscribers." Fielding, Diary, 2 May 1840.

[66] Pratt had written Young on 4 May 1840, suggesting that twenty-five hundred copies of the first issue would be "rather to[o] large to begin with. It takes a great many names to make 2500 and should we be disappointed for the better, we can reprint some of the first Numbers." In a postscript, Pratt communicated the bids he had obtained for printing, paper, folding, stitching, and binding. In a letter the same day to George A. Smith, Young commented: "I have written to Brother Parley P. Pratt, and I think we shall be able to help him to means, so we won't be under the necessity of getting subscribers but sell the numbers when they come" (LDS Church History Library). Young proved to be right. In his letter to Willard Richards, 24 May 1840, he noted: "The Star is out and about 1300 copies are already gon[e]. If we had on[e] thousand only we should come short of our object" (LDS Church History Library).

[67] The bids and agreements are in the Brigham Young Papers, LDS Church History Library. Thomas printed the first eight issues (May–December 1840), then W. Shakleton and Son became the printers. Crawley 1:107–13 (Item 71).

[68] Pratt to Smith, 22 November 1839. Pratt was probably thinking of Doctrine and Covenants (1835), 89:224 (Doctrine and Covenants 72:20–23 in current edition). In his May 4, 1840, letter to Young, Pratt wrote of his finding "a good House and Shop, on the great Oldham Road" in Manchester for twenty pounds per year. "I think I shall take it for our office and Book Establishment." The agreement, signed May 6, 1840, for the location at 149 Oldham Road, is in the Brigham Young Collection, LDS Church History Library.

quasi-headquarters and book depot for the apostolic mission, and while this printing concern was originally planned to be short-lived, its success laid a broad foundation for most of the LDS publishing in the nineteenth century.[69] Pratt edited the periodical, except for a short period when he returned to the United States to get his family, and his spirit pervades the publication.[70] Even a cursory examination of the longest published periodical in LDS history (1840–1970) reveals how well he established its foundation.[71] In a preface to the first bound volume of the *Millennial Star*, dated April 17, 1841, Pratt noted that his aim had not just been to benefit those who first read it, "but to hand down to posterity a journal" of the events of the developing movement. Today, its pages are

[69] In August 1840, the apostles considered liquidating the "book establishment" (see Willard Richards to Brigham Young, 22 August 1840, LDS Church History Library) and in October 1840 thought it would be best to move the office to London (see Woodruff, Journal, 7–8 October 1840), but neither decision was acted upon. Pratt himself contemplated "retiring from the business" because of the lack of funding (see Pratt to Young, 4 February 1841, LDS Church History Library). Alfred Cordon wrote to George A. Smith that Pratt would leave England in April 1842 "and that no more printing would be done in England" (Cordon to Smith, 26 December 1841, LDS Church History Library). In April 1842, Pratt moved his office to Liverpool where immigration and publication could be centrally located and directed. For its impact, see David J. Whittaker, "Early Mormon Pamphleteering," *Journal of Mormon History* 4 (1979): 35–49.

[70] Pratt's leave was approved by the Twelve on July 7, 1840, and Brigham Young and Heber C. Kimball were appointed as editors in his absence. Willard Richards worked more closely with Young until Pratt's return in October. During this time, Young likely came to see not only how much work editing and publishing entailed but just how valuable the periodical was for Mormon missionary work in England. In June 1840, Young wrote to his wife that he wanted Pratt "to keep it going" (Brigham Young to Mary Ann Angell Young, 20 June 1840, Blair Papers, Marriott Library, University of Utah). In April 1841, it was decided that Pratt ought to remain in England to publish the *Millennial Star* into a second year. In a letter to the Twelve, Joseph Smith approved Pratt remaining in England to continue the *Millennial Star* (Smith to Twelve Apostles, 15 December 1841, LDS Church History Library [incorrectly dated October in HC 4:229]).

[71] The *Millennial Star* was issued monthly from May 1840 until June 1845 when it became a semi-monthly publication. In 1852 it began to appear weekly. For most of the nineteenth century it served as the major Mormon voice for much of the world, but it gradually became the internal publication of the British mission. In 1943 it became monthly again, and in 1970 it was discontinued when the Church consolidated all magazines.

still searched by historians for contemporary letters, conference reports, editorials, reports, and all the material that made up the fabric of the texture of the British Mormon experience. And during the nineteenth century, it also reported regularly the progress of Mormon missionary efforts far beyond England, and not just in continental Europe, but in South Africa, India, Australia, and the islands of the Pacific.

In the first issues, readers were given access to a variety of material that had appeared in earlier LDS publications. For example, material in the *Elder's Journal*, the *Messenger and Advocate*, and the *Times and Seasons* as well as excerpts from Mormon scriptures were republished for a British audience. No doubt, such access helped British converts feel connected to their American co-religionists. In July 1840 Pratt wrote to his wife Mary Ann, telling her of his total immersion in the publishing business: "I am confined entirely at home as Editor of the 'Star' and publisher of the Hymn Book, B. Of Mormon, and all our other Books. . . . [I] employ 3 women in my Back Room as folders." Pratt told his wife that he had not left his house for more than twenty-four hours in three months![72] In an editorial at the conclusion of the first volume, Pratt noted that it had not been possible to cover every item of news relating to the Church; nevertheless, he reflected with appropriate satisfaction: "We have improved our time and space to the best advantage in our power; by endeavoring to select from the inexhaustible variety of chaotic matter laying before us, that portion which seemed best calculated for general edification and information, on the subjects embraced in our prospectus."[73]

A perusal of the first volume also reveals another major role of the *Millennial Star* in early Mormonism: responding to critics of the Church of Jesus Christ of Latter-day Saints. Pratt would often print a reply first in the pages of the *Millennial Star* and then afterward as a separate pamphlet. Toward the end of the first volume of the *Millennial Star*, Pratt noted this reality of their work in Britain:

[72] Parley P. Pratt to Mary Ann Pratt, 6 July 1840, Parley P. Pratt Collection, LDS Church History Library.

[73] *Millennial Star* 1 (April 1841): 312.

"Lies, Slanders, Misrepresentations, etc., in all their varied forms, have been heralded for from the press and pulpit, and have come in upon the world like a flood of water out of the mouth of the dragon, to stop the progress of truth, but all in vain."[74] For an author like Pratt, responding to critics and issuing a Mormon periodical went hand-in-hand. Anti-Mormon publishing had troubled the first group of missionaries that came to England. Richard Livesey, who had spent seven years in the United States, had published an attack in the summer of 1838, summarizing in about eleven pages the arguments of E. D. Howe's 1834 *Mormonism Unvailed* as mediated through the writings of LaRoy Sunderland.[75] Thus, Livesey's tract was actually pasted together from Sunderland's 1838 *Mormonism Exposed and Refuted* and the March 24 issue of his *Zion's Watchman*. The first Mormon missionaries in England saw this work as "nefarious merchandize," and for a time Livesey's work had a damaging effect on missionary work in the Preston area, and it continued to plague the elders in 1840.[76]

The second group of missionaries noted this opposition and responded in print to their critics, with Pratt particularly active in these apologetics.[77] One apostle wrote, "This country is as much flooded with false reports concerning us, as ever America was."[78] Another reported, "Some of the pamphlets . . . which are published against us filled with lies" had stopped some from being baptised.[79] In the larger cities such as Birmingham and Manchester, large quantities of anti-Mormon handbills and pamphlets

[74] Ibid.

[75] Richard Livesey, *An Exposure of Mormonism Being a Statement of Facts Relating to the Self-Styled 'Latter-day Saints.' And the Origin of the Book of Mormon* (Preston, England: J. Livesey, 1838). A testimonial at the end was dated 24 July 1838. A second edition was published in Manchester in 1840.

[76] Heber C. Kimball, Orson Hyde, and Willard Richards, 24 March 1841, in *Millennial Star* 1 (April 1841): 295. See also Fielding, Diary, July–August 1838 and 11 February 1840.

[77] See Craig L. Foster, *Penny Tracts and Polemics: A Critical Analysis of Anti-Mormon Pamphleteering in Great Britain, 1837–1860* (Salt Lake City: Greg Kofford Books, 2002).

[78] George A. Smith to Don Carlos Smith, 18 November 1840, in *Times and Seasons* 2 (1 February 1841): 308.

[79] Woodruff, Journal, 26 November 1840.

were circulated against the Church.[80] Reuben Hedlock wrote from Glasgow, Scotland, in February 1841, "There is plenty of opposition in these parts—the priests cry 'false prophets' from their pulpits,—they generally take their text from the newspapers and pamphlets that are published against us."[81] Pratt noted the opposition press in his letter to Joseph Smith: "Discussions, contentions, lectures, play cards, tracts, books, papers, pamphlets, etc., etc., are flooding the country in great numbers, all containing little else than lies and foolishness of the grossest kind against the cause of truth. . . . In short it is wearisome to notice the multitude of evil and lying publications much more to answer or reply to them. We therefore pass them in silence with few exceptions, and the Lord answer them in his own time, and in his own way [page torn] Bring them to Naught and by doing his own work."[82] As the editor of the *Millennial Star*, Pratt offered missionaries practical advice on dealing with anti-Mormon works. In one editorial he counseled, "Look at Both Sides of the Question"; and, in another, he suggested ways of "answering objections" and "correcting misrepresentations."[83]

But most fully, Pratt published replies to select attacks that appeared in various geographical areas of the country. The first Mormon reply to a British anti-Mormon tract was Pratt's *Plain Facts, Showing the Falsehood and Folly of the Rev. C. S. Bush*.[84] C. S. Bush, a minister of the parish of Peover, had published *Plain Facts,*

[80] See Parley P. Pratt to Sidney Rigdon, 8 January 1841, *Times and Seasons* 2 (1 April 1841): 364–65.

[81] Letter of 1 February 1841, *Millennial Star* 1 (March 1841): 285.

[82] Parley P. Pratt to Joseph Smith, 4 December 1841, Joseph Smith Collection, LDS Church History Library.

[83] In "Look at Both Sides of the Question," *Millennial Star* 1 (October 1840): 156–58, Pratt suggested ways of reading tracts against the Church and specifically requested that these works be sent to his office. In his "Editors Address to his Patrons" (ibid., 1 [May 1840]: 2–3), he gave advice to those who would be "entering into the field of controversy."

[84] The Bush pamphlet is dated 5 February 1840, copy in the Mitchell Library, Glasgow, Scotland. While no author is identified in the pamphlet response, it was clearly Pratt. He so identified himself in his later *A Reply to Mr. Thomas Taylor's "Complete Failure," &c., and Mr. Richard Livesey's "Mormonism Exposed"* (Manchester, England: W. R. Thomas, 1840), 6. Pratt is also listed as the author in the catalogue of publications in the *Millennial Star* 9 (1 July 1847): 208. Crawley, 1:124, 126 (Item 80).

Showing the Falsehood and Folly of the Mormonites in February or March 1840. Responding to written and oral presentations of the Mormon message in his parish, Bush attacked by presenting the Spaulding explanation for the origins of the Book of Mormon. Pratt's response probably appeared in July 1840, and it provided a strong rebuttal to the charges that critics such as Bush were making against Mormonism's claim to new revelation, claims that did not repudiate a belief in the Bible as scripture. Pratt had provided a similar response in his 1838 *Mormonism Unveiled*, but the publishing in 1839 of a letter supposedly written by Spaulding's widow (Matilda Davidson) and published in the *Boston Recorder* had added new life to the critics' arguments against the Book of Mormon. Pratt had responded to this new but small wrinkle in his letter published in the *New Era* in New York City.[85]

Pratt's second British response also addressed attacks being circulated in the Preston and Manchester areas. It was actually a reply to two separate tracts, one by Thomas Taylor and one by Richard Livesey, with a section attacking Methodism. Pratt could not ignore a pamphlet published in his own backyard, as it were.[86] Pratt had briefly responded in the *Millennial Star* to the reissuing of Livesey's tract, but a separate pamphlet, *A Reply to Mr. Thomas Taylor's "Complete Failure", &c., and Mr. Richard Livesey's "Mormonism Exposed,"* allowed him to more extensively focus on this tract as well as on one of the religions that opposed the Latter-day Saints.[87]

[85] Pratt's letter of 27 November 1839 was also printed in the *Times and Seasons* 1 (January 1840): 45–46.

[86] See Thomas Taylor, *An Account of the Complete Failure of an Ordained Priest of the 'Latter-day Saints' to Establish His Pretensions to the Gift of Tongues, Which Took Place October 12, 1840; with an Address to Men of Reason and Religion, Warning Them Not to Be Deceived by the Craftiness of Such Low Impostures* (Manchester, England: Pigot and Slatee, 1840). The only known copy of this work is in the New York Public Library. The second item was the second edition (issued by Thomas Newton) of Richard Livesey, *An Exposure of Mormonism . . .* (Manchester, England: William Shackleton and Son, 1840).

[87] See "Falsehood Refuted," *Millennial Star* 1 (November 1840): 187; and Pratt, *A Reply to Mr. Thomas Taylor's "Complete Failure."* The reply to Taylor appears on pp. 2–4; the reply to Livesey (and Thomas Newton) is on pp. 4–8, with pp. 8–12 (the last five pages) constituting an exposé of Methodism. It would seem that the pamphlet appeared in November 1840. Crawley, 1:135–38 (Item 89).

Pratt's third reply to an anti-Mormon work was published in December 1840. Here he was responding to requests from George A. Smith in the Potteries, a district of Staffordshire about thirty miles south of Manchester, to the effects of a tract written by William Hewitt against the Church. Hewitt had challenged George A. Smith to debate and then had published his attack when Smith declined.[88] In his response, Pratt answered Hewett's criticisms of Mormon belief in the coming millennium, baptism by immersion, and the Mormon's concept of God. Alfred Cordon had reported a "great spirit of inquiry in the region," and no doubt the modest success of Wilford Woodruff and George A. Smith in this area had prompted Hewitt's attack. Pratt apparently expected some payment for his printed work, as he so hinted in his February 1841 letter to Apostle Smith.[89]

Pratt's fourth reply was nearly his last to specific anti-Mormon works during this early British mission. He had written two articles in the *Millennial Star* responding to two attacks, and in July 1841 he issued these in pamphlet form.[90] By this time, Pratt had

[88] William Hewitt, *An Exposition of the Errors and Fallacies of the Self-named "Latter-day Saints"* (Lane-End, England: C. Watts, 1840). The preface is dated October 1840. The tone of Pratt's 18 February 1840 letter to George A. Smith suggests Smith had earlier requested help in responding to this tract. A copy of Hewitt's tract, with Smith's marginal notes, is in the LDS Church History Library. Hewitt's letters to Smith (2, 13 June 1840) suggest an ongoing discussion between them (George A. Smith Collection, LDS Church History Library). It is possible that the "Rev. Hewitt" of England mentioned in the 21 April 1835 letter of Thomas Shaw (*Messenger and Advocate* 1 [May 1836]: 316–17) is the same person. This letter identified Hewitt as an Irvingite (Crawley, 1:139–40 [Item 91]). Edward Irving had founded in 1832 the Irvingites, or more correctly, the Holy Catholic Apostolic Church. The group emphasized a restoration of the spiritual gifs of healing and prophecy, the coming of the millennium, and other doctrines that had some parallel to the Mormon Church. See Robert L. Lively, Jr., "The Catholic Apostolic Church and the Church of Jesus Christ of Latter-day Saints: A Comparative Study of Two Minority Millenarian Groups in Nineteenth-Century England" (D.Phil. diss., Mansfield College, Oxford University, 1977).

[89] Pratt wrote: "I have never Rec'd one *penney* for the 1,000 replies to Hewitt which I printed allmost entirely for the poteries" (Pratt to George A. Smith, 18 February 1841, Pratt Collection).

[90] See Parley P. Pratt, *Truth Defended, or a Reply to the "Preston Chronicle," and to Mr. J. B. Rollo's "Mormonism Exposed"* (Manchester, England: P.P. Pratt, 1841). These responses had appeared in the *Millennial Star* 2 (July 1841): 43–48; and Crawley, 1:166–67 (Item 118).

surely grown tired of responding to the same arguments he had already addressed in his other works. Some of this frustration no doubt was behind the broadside he published in Manchester in December 1840. In the first work of Mormon satire, Pratt crafted his *An Epistle of Demetrius, Junior, the Silversmith, to the Workman of Like Occupation, and All Others Whom It May Concern,—Greeting: Showing the Best Way to Preserve Our Craft, & Put Down the Latter Day Saints*, a work modeled after the opposition of Demetrius, an Ephesian metal worker who opposed Paul in Acts 19 because conversions would decrease the income he received making idols. Pratt made the English sectarian clergy in their opposition to the Latter-day Saints appear as the modern equivalent of the ancient Demetrius.[91] This work was reprinted three times in England and twice in the United States and was reprinted in *The Prophet* in New York City in September 1844. In January 1840 in the *Millennial Star* and later as a pamphlet, Pratt issued the first Mormon work in dialogue format, which attacked other religions, especially Methodists, but did not reply to a specific anti-Mormon work.[92]

In addition to these works of apologetics, Pratt published several missionary pamphlets dealing with the main messages of Mormonism. He also reprinted several of his works that had appeared earlier in the United States. His most effective popular pamphlets were *An Address . . . to the People of England*, issued in ten thousand copies before August 1840,[93] and *A Letter to the*

[91] This was issued as a broadside in Manchester by Wm. Shackleton and Sons, Printers. On its authorship, see Crawley, 1:140–41 (Item 92).

[92] See Pratt's *Dialogue Between a Latter-day Saint and an Enquirer After Truth* . . . (Manchester, England: 1842). This work had originally appeared in the *Millennial Star* 2 (1 January 1842): 129–32. Pratt added to the pamphlet a letter of Thomas Smith dated 30 December 1841. These pieces attacked Methodism, Roman Catholicism, and the Church of England and specifically the evils of infant baptism. Smith's letter described his conversion from Methodism to Mormonism. Pratt had earlier responded to a circular of the Church of England: see *Millennial Star* 1 (May 1840): 17–18; and Crawley, 1:181–82 (Item 138).

[93] The work was dated 18 May 1840 and the publishing information is given on p. 7 of the second printing. This work clearly had its immediate origins in Pratt's *An Address . . . to the Citizens of Washington*.

Queen, ten thousand copies of which were printed in June and July 1841.[94] Both pamphlets addressed the heart of the early Mormon message: *An Address* summarized the basic beliefs of the Church, and *A Letter to the Queen* used Daniel 2 to predict the triumph of the Kingdom of God as the millennial government the Latter-day Saints were expected to establish. In *A Letter to the Queen*, Pratt developed the idea that the Kingdom of God was a real kingdom, destined to replace all other earthly governments. Where Pratt's *Voice of Warning* equated the Church with the Kingdom of God, here Pratt began the written defense of the literal kingdom that was to play such a key role in Mormon political thought in the nineteenth century.[95]

In July 1841, Pratt wrote responses to attacks in the north: the first replied to an article in the *Preston Chronicle* that had reprinted an anti-Mormon article from a U.S. newspaper; the second rebutted an attack of a recently disaffected Latter-day Saint, J. B. Rollo. Rollo had been baptized in Edinburgh in March but had left the Church by June when he published his pamphlet *Mormonism Exposed, from the Word of God* (Edinburgh: Glass, Printer). Pratt had replied to both attacks in the pages of the *Millennial Star* in July 1841 but then issued the replies in a separate pamphlet,

[94] Parley P. Pratt, *A Letter to the Queen Touching the Signs of the Times and the Political Destiny of the World* (Manchester, England: P. P. Pratt, 1841). There were two editions issued, in June and July 1841, totaling ten thousand copies. See *Times and Seasons* 4 (15 April 1843): 163. The tract was dated 28 May 1841 and first advertised in the *Millennial Star* 2 (July 1841): 48. The text was reprinted in the *Times and Seasons* 3 (15 November 1841): 593–96 under the slightly modified title *A Letter to the Queen of England*. Its New York reprinting provided the text for George J. Adams, *A Letter to His Excellency John Tyler, President of the United States, Touching the Signs of the Times, and the Political Destiny of This World* (New York: C. A. Calhoun, 1844). See Crawley, 1:158–60, 167, 212–13, 236–37 (Items 108, 119–20, 166, 195).

[95] Here Pratt's writings helped move the early Mormon interpretation of Daniel 2:44 from a metaphorical to a literal Kingdom of God. Pratt was again influenced by Joseph Smith and his experiences in Missouri. See David J. Whittaker, "The Book of Daniel in Early Mormon Thought," in *By Study and Also by Faith: Essays in Honor of Hugh Nibley on His 80th Birthday*, John M. Lundquist and Stephen D. Ricks, eds., 2 vols. (Salt Lake City: Deseret Book; Provo, Utah: Foundation for Ancient Research and Mormon Studies, 1990), 1:155–99.

presumably because Rollo's tract was creating problems for the missionaries in southern Scotland.[96] At about the same time, additional British printings of Pratt's *An Address . . . to the Citizens of Washington* were issued in England, suggesting the popularity and usefulness of his writings.[97]

In September 1841, Pratt issued the first European edition of his most famous work, *Voice of Warning*. While copies of the early U.S. edition had circulated in England, constant requests for additional copies undoubtedly led him to reprint the work.[98] At least two other items were possibly issued by Pratt in 1842. While it is not entirely clear that he was the author, *The True God and His Worship Contrasted with Idolatry* surely reads like Pratt. The material had appeared in the *Millennial Star* in April 1842 when Pratt was the

---

[96] Parley P. Pratt, *Truth Defended, or a Reply to the "Preston Chronicle." And to Mr. J. B. Rollo's "Mormonism Exposed." Extracted from the Millennial Star for July, 1841* (Manchester, England: Printed and Published by P. P. Pratt, 1841). Rollo argued that the Mormons were adding doctrines to the gospel and that their interpretations of the scriptures were not correct. The *Chronicle's* reprinted article from the *Baptist Register* in New York claimed that the Mormons used force to spread their message. This would be Pratt's last response to an anti-Mormon work until 1852; he had by this time addressed all the major criticisms of his Church then in print. See Crawley, 1:166–67 (Item 118).

[97] This includes *An Address by a Minister of the Church of Jesus Christ of Latter Day Saints, to the People of England* (Bristol, England: Reprinted by James Jones, 1841). Crawley suggests an August 1841 printing for the Bristol edition (Crawley, 1:113–14 [Item 73], 1:152 [Item 101], and 1:170–71 [Items 123, 124]). Pratt's work influenced the very popular (at least twenty printings in the nineteenth century) tract of Lorenzo Snow, *The Only Way to Be Saved* (London: Printed by D. Chalmers, 1841), which, while better written, followed Pratt's in basic structure. Snow had personally used and distributed Pratt's work in London prior to writing his own tract.

[98] Pratt, *Voice of Warning* (Manchester, England: W. Shackleton & Son, 1841). George A. Smith, for example, had said that there was a great call for copies of *Voice of Warning* in the potteries in 1840: see *Millennial Star* 1 (June 1840): 44. This first European edition was taken from the second U.S. edition, published in New York in 1839, with additional material on the history of the Book of Mormon to chapter 4, some of which was taken from Orson Pratt's Edinburgh pamphlet of September 1840: *A[n] Interesting Account of Several Remarkable Visions*. The work consisted of an edition of twenty-five hundred copies per *Times and Seasons* 4 (15 April 1843): 163. It was announced as just published in *Millennial Star* 2 (September 1841): 80. At least five more editions were printed before his death in 1857, with at least thirty-six thereafter. Crawley, 1:172–73 (Item 127).

editor, and like his earlier *Dialogue*, it attacked various religions in England and Scotland, with particular emphasis on the Protestant view of a God "without body, parts or passions." The tract argued that this position was essentially atheism, that is, a belief in a God who does not exist. The work concluded with some practical rules on prayer. The essay may not have appeared in pamphlet form until the 1860s, as there are no known copies of a separate printing until this time. The second item, appearing about the same time, also reprinted parts from an early work. Hence, *The World Turned Upside Down, or Heaven on Earth* was a reprint of the essay "The Regeneration and Eternal Duration of Matter" from the 1840 edition of *Millennium, and Other Poems*.[99]

Publishing and Editing, 1842–1846

Pratt left the British Saints in October, publishing his farewell address in the October issue of the *Millennial Star*. He reached New Orleans in January 1842 and in early February arrived in Nauvoo. During 1842 and 1843, he worked with his fellow apostles as they were brought closer to the First Presidency in matters of Church administration. Pratt took his first plural wives and spent time getting his growing family settled in Nauvoo.[100] He also managed to publish the only really speculative theological work issued during the Nauvoo period.[101] While mostly forgotten today, five essays he wrote under one cover were issued between November 1843 and March 1844 plus a reprinting of his "Address to Queen

[99] *The World Turned Upside Down, or Heaven on Earth. The Material Universe Is Eternal.—Immortal Man Has Flesh and Bones.—Earth Is His Everlasting Inheritance.—To This Bear All the Prophets and Apostles Witness. The Physical Worlds Were Not Formed for Annihilation, but for the Pleasure of God They Are and Were Created* (Liverpool, England: James and Woodburn, [1842]). This work was printed in an edition of three thousand copies and was first advertised in the *Millennial Star* in May 1842.

[100] For information on Pratt's family, see R. Steven Pratt's essay in this volume (chapter 2).

[101] Joseph Smith's April 7, 1844, general conference discourse, the King Follett sermon, was published as an appendix to William W. Phelps, *Voice of Truth* (Nauvoo, Ill.: Printed by John Taylor, 1844). This work was actually issued in 1845. Crawley, 1:309–12 (Item 271).

Victoria" under the title *An Appeal to the Inhabitants of the State of New York, Letter to Queen Victoria.* The first essay grew out of Joseph Smith's invitation on November 29, 1843, to his followers to write to their home states urging support for the Mormon appeals for redress against the state of Missouri. The other three new essays were written in early 1844 and were expansions of earlier essays on the nature and purposes of man and his eternal relationship to God.[102] In "the Fountain of Knowledge," Pratt argued against the notion that all knowledge is to be found in books, however true or sacred or useful they may be, but rather that the fountain of light and truth is in the heavens, and true knowledge is revelation from that heavenly source. In his essay on "Immortality of the Body," Pratt expanded on the ideas in his earlier 1840 essay on the regeneration and eternal duration of matter, arguing that matter is eternal and thus the resurrection is physical in that it deals with material bodies and spirits, possible only through the atonement of Jesus Christ. "Intelligence and Affection" can be read as an essay on the nature of divine and human love, perhaps even a first attempt in Mormon literature to provide a doctrinal foundation for the nature of love between men and women in marriage. Taken together, these essays reveal a positive view of the nature of humanity, an optimistic and Romantic understanding of the divine nature of humankind.

On August 25, 1844, the first work of Mormon fiction appeared in the pages of the *New York Herald.* Less than a week later it was published in *The Prophet*, and on September 25 it appeared in the *Nauvoo Neighbor.* While it appeared without an author, Pratt's *Autobiography* states that while visiting Massachusetts during the spring of 1844, "having a day's leisure . . . wrote a dialogue entitled 'Joe Smith and the Devil,' which was afterwards published in the *New York Herald*, and in various papers in America and Europe. It was finally published and republished in pamphlet form, and had a

[102] Parley P. Pratt, *An Appeal to the Inhabitants of the State of New York, Letter to Queen Victoria, . . . The Fountain of Knowledge; Immortality of the Body, and Intelligence and Affection* (Nauvoo, Ill.: John Taylor, Printer, 1844). See Crawley, 1:247–49 (Item 202).

wide circulation; few persons knowing or mistrusting who was the author."[103] "Joe Smith" reeks of satire against the Christian clergy, who are presented as in league with the devil, who, when the dialogue opens, is posting handbills, advertising for individuals with serious character flaws to work for him against "Joe Smith and the Mormons." Joe Smith then discusses religion with the devil who is a likeable person, and at the end they drink a toast against each other. The lesson seems clear: only Mormonism is the true Christianity, while the rest play the devil's game![104]

In 1844 Pratt composed another work that was unpublished at his death, "The Angel of the Prairies." In his *Autobiography* he referred to this work as "a curious and extraordinary composition, in the similitude of a dream. It was designed as a reproof of the corruptions and degeneracy of our Government, in suffering mobs to murder, plunder and drive their fellow citizens with impunity, etc. It also suggested some reforms. It was read in the presence of President Joseph Smith and a General Council, and was highly applauded."[105]

Owing to the growing maturity of the Quorum of the Twelve Apostles during their British mission, Joseph Smith continued to increase the Quorum's role in every facet of Church and civic affairs following their return to Nauvoo. In January 1842, a revelation through Joseph Smith directed the Twelve to take control of the editorial department of the *Times and Seasons*, an important

[103] Pratt, *Autobiography*, 367.

[104] Parley P. Pratt, *A Dialogue Between Josh. Smith & the Devil!* (New York? 1845?). There were at least two other printings of this work during Pratt's lifetime and a number after 1857, all of which include "Dialogue Between Tradition, Reason, and Scriptus," which had appeared in Orson Pratt's *Prophetic Almanac for 1845*. See Crawley, 1:332–34 (Items 291–293). Crawley suggests that the other two printings were probably done in Liverpool while Pratt was in England between October 1846 and January 1847.

[105] Pratt, *Autobiography*, 367. The work first appeared in print in 1880: *The Angel of the Prairies; A Dream of the Future by Elder Parley Parker Pratt. One of the Twelve Apostles of the Church of Jesus Christ of Latter-day Saints* (Salt Lake City: A[binadi] Pratt Publisher, Deseret News Printing and Publishing Establishment, 1880). In a similar predictive vein was his "One Hundred Years Hence. 1945," *The Nauvoo Neighbor*, 10 September 1845; and *Millennial Star* 6 (15 October 1845): 140–42.

beginning of their full control of Church publishing.[106] Such centralization would be formalized in a statement issued by Pratt in *The Prophet* in January 1845: "Regulations for the Publishing Department of the Latter-day Saints in the East." In the midst of the succession crisis following the death of Joseph Smith, Pratt had been assigned a mission to the eastern states where he found that a number of individuals had written works justifying their rejection of the apostles as the rightful leaders of the Church. Pratt noted that too many people were turning into authors and that many of their works were badly written and often filled with errors. He noted that they were reprinting items already available and were wasting money that was badly needed for the temple being built in Nauvoo. More personally, he noted that much of this independent publishing was out of order because it was having an effect on the sales of those "whose business it is to write and publish the truth." Pratt's statement announced that henceforth there would be only three "great emporiums of light, truth, and news" approved by the Twelve. Only Nauvoo's *Times and Seasons*, Liverpool's *Millennial Star*, and Pratt's own New York *Prophet* were authorized to issue works to be considered "as a standard by the Saints concerning their principles."[107] While such a position would take a few years to fully take effect given the chaos of the westward movement

[106] For the revelation, see Joseph Smith, Illinois Journal, No. 1, 28 January 1842, LDS Church History Library. In his journal entry of 3 February 1842, Wilford Woodruff noted: "After consulting upon the subject the quorum appointed Elders J. Taylor & W. Woodruff of the Twelve to Edit the Times and Seasons & take charge of the whole establishment under the direction of Joseph the Seer." Ebenezer Robinson and Don Carlos Smith had owned and operated the *Times and Seasons* from July 1839 to December 1840. Thereafter, Robinson did the book printing and Don Carlos Smith continued to edit and publish the newspaper. Others assisted for short periods in 1841, but when the Twelve returned from their British mission they voiced their concerns to Joseph Smith regarding its content and Robinson's continuing attempts to publish Mormonism's sacred texts. These concerns and a third meeting with Smith on January 17, 1842, provided the background to the revelatory direction given on January 28. Robinson was paid $6,600 for his share in the printing operation. See Ebenezer Robinson, "Items of Personal History of the Editor," *The Return* (Davis City, Iowa) 2 (May 1880): 252–62.

[107] *The Prophet* 1 (4 January 1845): 2 This was reprinted in the *Times and Seasons* 6 (15 January 1845): 778, with a note, probably by John Taylor, attached: "We shall second the 'regulations' of Elder Pratt: there is nothing like order in the Kingdom of God."

and the early years of pioneering in the Great Basin, it did further centralize Church publication in the hands of the Quorum of the Twelve Apostles.

Connected with the succession crisis, Pratt drafted the 1845 "Proclamation of the Twelve Apostles." In January 1841, a revelation to Joseph Smith had directed that a proclamation to the kings and rulers of the world (Doctrine and Covenants 124:1–12) be issued, but in spite of several attempts to fulfill this request, it was unaccomplished during Joseph Smith's lifetime. Pratt finally drafted and published it in New York in March 1845.[108] He also reprinted or wrote a number of articles for *The Prophet*, including "Four Kinds of Salvation,"[109] "Materiality,"[110] and a number of other essays that would appear in Orson Pratt's *Prophet Almanac, for 1846*.[111]

[108] *Proclamation of the Twelve Apostles of the Church of Jesus Christ, of Latter-day Saints. To All the Kings of the World; to the President of the United States of America; to the Governors of the Several States; and to the Rulers and People of All Nations: Greeting* was dated New York, 6 April 1845, and was printed at the New York office of *The Prophet*. On Pratt's authorship, see Pratt to Brigham Young, 26 May 1846, L. Tom Perry Special Collections, BYU. This sixteen-page pamphlet was issued in both the United States and in larger editions in England and Wales. Wilford Woodruff had it printed in England, and he is often incorrectly credited with its authorship. The pamphlet declared that the Kingdom of God has been restored to the earth and that its authority rests with the Latter-day Saints. The proclamation commanded that the rulers put their treasures at the disposal of this kingdom and that the American Indians were to be civilized and educated so they could assist in building the New Jerusalem in the United States while the Jews rebuilt the old Jerusalem. As Crawley points out, the language of the proclamation hardly reflects the "spirit of meekness" suggested in Document and Covenants 124:4 (current editions). It was first published in *Times and Seasons* 2 (1 June 1844): 424–29. See Crawley, 1:294–96 (Item 256).

[109] This appeared in the 8 March 1845 issue and was reprinted from the earlier *Millennial Star* 2 (June 1841): 21–22.

[110] Issue of 24 March 1845. On 25 July 1845, he published an "Address to the Saints on the East Coast."

[111] Orson Pratt, *Prophet Almanac, for 1846* (New York: New York Messenger Office, 1845). The *New-York Messenger* (5 July 1845 to 15 December 1845) was issued after *The Prophet* ended publication. Crawley suggests that the presence of so many of Parley Pratt's essays in his brother's publication probably means he helped assemble the volume and that it might also provide clues to the authorship of other essays he wrote (see Crawley, 1:306–07 [Item 267] and 1:308 [Item 269]). In his *Autobiography*, Parley Pratt made special note of his essay "Heaven" in the *New-York Messenger* of his "numerous editorials and communications" and in *The Prophet* he noted "Materiality" and "New Proverbs" (376).

Exodus, Colonization, and Exploration

Pratt returned to Nauvoo by August 1845, where he engaged in the cares of his family, finishing his house, carrying out his official duties, and working on and in the temple.[112] On February 14, 1846, he crossed the Mississippi River with his family heading west across Iowa, arriving at Council Bluffs on the Missouri River in July. In the same month Orson Hyde, John Taylor, and Pratt were chosen to deal with various problems that had arisen in England. They arrived in Liverpool on October 14, 1846, and at a general conference three days later Hyde was appointed to edit the *Millennial Star*, and Taylor and Pratt to visit the churches.[113] During these travels Pratt wrote words of comfort to this family at Council Bluffs and published them as a broadside.[114] After the men fulfilled their assignments, they returned to Liverpool in January 1847 and on January 19 began their voyage home. Contrary winds and a sick captain forced their ship to return to Liverpool, thus their second farewell to British Saints.[115]

Pratt arrived in New Orleans on March 6, 1847, and, along with John Taylor, led a large group of pioneers to the Salt Lake Valley that summer, arriving on September 28, 1847. Pratt wrote relatively

---

[112] Pratt, *Autobiography*, 376. Details on the trip west are in Stephen F. Pratt, "Parley P. Pratt in Winter Quarters and the Trail West," *BYU Studies* 24 (Summer 1984): 373–88.

[113] *Millennial Star* 8 (1 November 1846): 102–103. See Crawley, 1:313–15 (Item 273) for a good summary of the British and American Commercial Joint Stock Company and its financial problems.

[114] Pratt described the "letter in blank verse to my family" as "published in England at the time, on a beautiful sheet with a handsome border and designed to be put in a frame as a household ornament; and is frequently seen to this day (1856) as a memorial in the parlours of Saints on both sides of the Atlantic" (*Autobiography*, 386). See the broadside, *An Apostle of the Church of Jesus Christ of Latter-day Saints, Was in the Island of Great Britain, for the Gospel's Sake; and Being in the Spirit on the 21st of November, A.D. 1846, Addressed the Following Words of Comfort to His Dearly-Beloved Wife and Family, Dwelling in Tents, in the Camp of Israel, at Council Bluffs, Missouri Territory, North America; Where They and Twenty Thousand Others Were Banished by the Civilized Christians of the United States, for the Word of God, and the Testimony of Jesus* (London: 1851?); also see in Pratt, *Autobiography*, 387–93, where it is dated 24 November 1846; and Crawley, 2:270–71 (Items 636–37).

[115] *Millennial Star* 9 (15 February 1847): 61; and Pratt, *Autobiography*, 395–96.

little during his time in Utah between 1847 and 1850, as he spent his time exploring Utah, administering Church affairs, exploring, farming, and constructing a toll road up Parley's Canyon. On August 10, 1848, a public feast was held under the Bowery in the center of the settlement for which Pratt composed a "Harvest Song."[116] On March 15, 1849, Pratt was appointed by a general convention as one of a committee of ten to draft a constitution for the Provisional State of Deseret. The document was accepted three days later.[117] In 1849, Brigham Young assigned Pratt to take fifty men and explore "southward." From November 23, 1849, to February 1850, Pratt led the Southern Exploring Company into the southern parts of present-day Utah.

President of the Pacific Mission, 1850–1852, 1854

Pratt had begun to study the Spanish language in 1849, no doubt because Brigham Young had indicated that Pratt was to be assigned another mission. In a letter to his brother Orson, in July 1849, Pratt noted: "I don't know when I shall be sent away. I am studying the Spanish language, and preparing for Spanish America."[118] When the call came, Pratt was appointed to "hold the presidency of all the islands and coast of the Pacific."[119] Between 1851 and 1855, Pratt served twice as the president of the Church's Pacific mission. Although headquartered in San Francisco, the mission embraced

---

[116] Pratt, *Autobiography* (Proctors, eds.), 469–70. The manuscript, dated 10 August 1848, is in the Parley P. Pratt Collection.

[117] See Peter Crawley, "The Constitution of the State of Deseret," *BYU Studies* 29 (Fall 1989): 7–22.

[118] *Millennial Star* 11 (15 November 1849): 343.

[119] See Pratt, *Autobiography*, 414, for the mission call; and Parley P. Pratt to Addison Pratt, 26 July 1851, and Parley P. Pratt to King Kamehameha, 26 July 1851, both in Pratt, *Autobiography*, 429–52. The *Millennial Star* 11 (1 August 1849): 232, cited the First General Epistle of the First Presidency (dated 14 April 1849), which noted that Pratt had been assigned "a mission to the Western Islands." The First Presidency delayed this mission until the next year. For the larger history, see R. Lanier Britsch, *Unto the Islands of the Sea: A History of the Latter-day Saints in the Pacific* (Salt Lake City: Deseret Book, 1986).

the Pacific Basin, including South America and the islands of the Pacific from Hawaii to Australia. Following his earlier approach, publishing would be a central part of his missionary work.[120]

Pratt left Salt Lake City on March 16, 1851, traveled through Los Angeles, and then sailed from San Pedro, arriving in San Francisco on July 11. He was officially sustained as the president of the San Francisco branch on July 20. In a letter to his leader a few days later, he described his surroundings: "We find a great city here and perhaps one thousand vessels in port. A more central point for spreading the Gospel, and communicating with all nations I have not found. . . . We have now an organized Branch here and meetings every Sabbath. Many inquire after the truth, Books, etc. I think of Publishing a General Proclamation."[121] In August he called recently repentant and rebaptized Charles Wandell to accompany John Murdock, whom Brigham Young had earlier called to be president of the Australian mission, to Australia. Because of problems in the Society Islands, Pratt decided not to send additional missionaries there, but he did send more missionaries to Hawaii. With these areas taken care of for the time being, and because he probably expected South America to be as fruitful as early Victorian England had been for Mormon missionaries, Pratt told Young: "I expect to leave this country for South America soon; unless I should be able to go to New York, via the Isthmus, to get some books printed. . . . I am studying Spanish with all diligence, and will, I trust, master it in the course of a few months."[122]

Before sailing for Chile, Pratt wrote the first Latter-day Saint work to be printed in the Pacific region: *Proclamation! To the People of the Coasts and Islands of the Pacific; of Every Nation, Kindred and*

[120] See David J. Whittaker, "Parley P. Pratt and the Pacific Mission: Mormon Publishing in 'That Very Questionable Part of the Civilized World,'" in *Mormons, Scripture, and the Ancient World, Studies in Honor of John L. Sorenson*, Davis Bitton, ed. (Provo, Utah: Foundation for Ancient Research and Mormon Studies, BYU, 1998), 51–84.

[121] Parley P. Pratt to Brigham Young, 25 July 1851, Brigham Young Collection, LDS Church History Library.

[122] Parley P. Pratt to Brigham Young, 28 August 1851, Brigham Young Collection.

Tongue. He gave the manuscript to Murdock and Wandell, who had it published in November 1851 in Sydney, Australia, within a few days of their arrival there.[123] In this tract Pratt called upon his readers to repent and be baptized in the name of Jesus Christ, while declaring the apostasy from the primitive Church of Christ and of the restoration of apostolic authority now held by the Latter-day Saints. Then, in separate sections or chapters, he addressed the Pagans (non-Christians), the Jews, and the "Red Man." In the section to American Indians, he discussed the Book of Mormon and specifically argued that father Lehi and his family landed on the "western Coast of America, within the bounds of what is now called Chil[e]." It was this view that motivated Pratt's own mission there, especially because he strongly believed that eighty or ninety percent of the population of most of the countries of Spanish America were the blood descendants of Lehi.[124]

Pratt's mission to Chile was short and unsuccessful. Accompanied by his wife Phoebe, and Rufus C. Allen, he left San Francisco for Chile on September 5, 1851, arriving on November 8,

---

[123] Parley P. Pratt, *Proclamation! To the People of the Coasts and Islands of the Pacific; of Every Nation, Kindred and Tongue. By an Apostle of Jesus Christ. Published for the Author, by C. W. Wandell, Minister of the Gospel* (Sydney, Australia: William Baker, Printer; Hibernian Press, [1851]). This was the first Mormon publication in Australia and the first Mormon imprint printed outside Europe or North America. See Crawley, 2:262–65 (Item 630), and Crawley, "The First Australian Mormon Imprints," *Gradilis Review* (publication of the Graduate School for Library Science, BYU) 2 (Fall 1973): 38–51. Richard Ballantyne reprinted part of it during his early Mormon mission in India: *Proclamation of the Gospel. Extracted from a Work by Parley P. Pratt*. . . (Madras, India: S. Bowie, 1853). A further curiosity in Mormon publishing reveals that the first Mormon imprint in New Zealand, *Good Tidings, or the "New and Everlasting Gospel"* (1875), though listed as a work by Joseph F. Smith, was a reprint of a four-page tract issued by the *Millennial Star* office in Liverpool—"The Gospel, Illustrated in Questions and Answers"—by Pratt that had first appeared in the *Millennial Star* 1 (June 1840): 25–28.

[124] See Parley P. Pratt to Brigham Young, 13 March 1852, Young Collection; and Pratt, *Autobiography*, 447. Pratt had early felt the need to preach to American Indians, and he had been among the first missionaries officially called in 1830 to do so. He was still thinking in these terms in 1852. This theme was another important dimension to his Romantic outlook that found reinforcement in Mormon doctrine.

sixty-four days later at Valparaiso.[125] Initially optimistic, Pratt wrote to Franklin D. Richards in Liverpool and ordered a variety of LDS literature that he planned to distribute in Chile.[126] The group stayed in Valparaiso long enough for Phoebe to give birth to a son, Omner, on November 30, but the boy died five weeks later. Following a short respite in the small town of Quillota, they returned to Valparaiso where they planned more missionary work. Because Valparaiso was an important way station for ships traveling around Cape Horn and on to California, Pratt surely thought it would provide a public responsive to his message. But the language barrier and the dominance of the Roman Catholic Church forced him to abandon the first Mormon mission to Chile. Pratt later reported to Brigham Young that a Protestant minister had told him that "there was no difficulty in landing religious books or papers and circulating the same, although the press is not free to print or publish any religion but the Catholic."[127] Thus, Pratt's *Proclamation Extraordinary! To the Spanish Americans*, written in January 1852 but not published until his return to San Francisco, contains a strong critique of Catholicism and an even stronger denunciation of the lack of the religious and press freedom that Pratt had generally enjoyed in the United States.[128]

Leaving Chile on March 2, 1852, Pratt had ample time to reflect during the return voyage. Following his arrival in California on May 21, he finished a letter he had been preparing for Brigham Young. The letter summarized his work in Chile, his struggles with the language, and his plans for publishing: "It is in my heart

[125] Pratt's original journal for this mission is in the L. Tom Perry Special Collections, BYU. See also Pratt, *Autobiography*, 429–52; F. LaMond Tullis, "California and Chile in 1851 as Experienced by the Mormon Apostle Parley P. Pratt," *Southern California Quarterly* 67 (Fall 1985): 291–307; and A. Delbert Palmer and Mark L. Grover, "Hoping to Establish a Presence: Parley P. Pratt's 1851 Mission to Chile," *BYU Studies* 38, no. 4 (1999): 115–38.

[126] See his 24 November 1851 letter in *Millennial Star* 14 (15 February 1852): 54–55.

[127] Pratt, *Autobiography*, 445.

[128] Parley P. Pratt, *Proclamacion! Extraodinaria, para los Americanos Espanoles. Por Parley P. Pratt, apostol de la Iglesia de Jesu Christo, de los Postiros Dias Santos . . . Proclamation Extraordinary to the Spanish . . .* (San Francisco: Monson, Haswell & Co., 1852). The work was printed in double columns, one in Spanish and the other in English. This was the first Mormon work in Spanish. Crawley, 2:332–34 (Item 709).

to translate the Book of Mormon, and some other works and to print the same in Spanish as soon as I have the language sufficiently perfect. As [the cost of] printing is very high in all parts of the Pacific, it may be wisdom to go to England and get some printing and perhaps stereotyping done. . . . I study the language all day, and think it, and even talk it loud in my sleep, in which I sometimes learn more that in the day. But it is no small work, to become familiar with the entire grammar, words and style of a foreign tongue, so as to write for publication."[129]

He had wanted to visit Peru, but "an empty purse and imperfect tongue" and a "want of books or the means to print them" forced him to reconsider.[130] Recuperating in the Bay area from May to July, Pratt issued his *Proclamation Extraordinary!* When a review of the work in a San Francisco newspaper questioned the morality of Brigham Young, Pratt responded with a broadside dated July 13, 1852: *"Mormonism!" "Plurality of Wives!" An Especial Chapter, for the Especial Edification of Certain Inquisitive News Editors, Etc.* Because the Church's official public announcement of plural marriage was not made in Salt Lake City until August 29, 1852, Pratt found himself defending the doctrine and Brigham Young's morality without admitting to its actual practice among Latter-day Saints.[131]

In July, Pratt left California for Utah, arriving in Salt Lake Valley in October. He farmed and cared for his growing family and in August 1853 was elected to the territorial legislature. His April 1853 general conference address, "Spiritual Communication," was issued as an eight-page pamphlet apparently long after his death.[132] During the winter of 1853–54, he served as a regent of the University of Deseret, worked on a committee developing

[129] Parley P. Pratt to Brigham Young, 13 March to 29 April 1852, Brigham Young Collection.

[130] Parley P. Pratt to Brigham Young, 13–27 March 1852, in Pratt, *Autobiography*, 442–51.

[131] The broadside was dated San Francisco, 13 July 1852. Crawley, 2:335 (Item 710).

[132] *Spiritual Communication; a Sermon Delivered by Elder P. P. Pratt, Senr. Before the Conference at Salt Lake City, April, 7 1853* (n.d., n.p.). The address was also printed in *Deseret News*, 30 April 1853; *Journal of Discourses* 1:6–15; and *Millennial Star* 27 (11, 18 February 1865): 89–94, 105–109. Crawley, in the forthcoming third volume of his *A Descriptive Bibliography*, suggests that the use of the "Senr" in the printed title (never used when Pratt was alive) means that Pratt's namesake son printed the talk after 1857, possibility as late as 1882.

the Deseret Alphabet,[133] and continued his personal writing and study of Spanish. On April 6, 1854, Pratt was appointed to serve a second mission to California and the Pacific region. He left Salt Lake City on May 5 and arrived in San Francisco on July 2. He spent about one year on this mission, concentrating on more local missionary work and on writing and publishing. In his *Autobiography*, written largely during this time, he summarized his activities: "We now commenced holding meetings, circulating books, tracts, and in every way we could, to notify and warn the people. . . . I devoted the time I could spare from the ministry to writing my history and for the press."[134]

During his year in California, Pratt duplicated the writing and publishing activities of his first British mission. Thus, he moved to establish a Latter-day Saint printing operation in San Francisco, worked to begin an LDS book supply depot for California and the Pacific, and continued his own writing. Brigham Young had encouraged the establishing of a Mormon press in California. This proved difficult for a number of reasons, but a press was finally sent to Pratt. Though arriving too late for him to make use of it, it was important for George Q. Cannon, his successor in the area.[135] For Pratt, a press and a book depot went hand-in-hand, as they had earlier in England. He wrote Brigham Young in February 1855 that

[133] See Douglas D. Alder, Paula J. Goodfellow, and Ronald G. Watt, "Creating a New Alphabet for Zion: The Origins of the Deseret Alphabet," *Utah Historical Quarterly* 52 (Summer 1984): 275–86.

[134] Pratt, *Autobiography*, 458–59.

[135] On Cannon's work, see David J. Whittaker, "Placing the Keystone: George Q. Cannon's Mission of Translating and Printing the Book of Mormon in the Hawaiian Language," in Donald W. Parry, Daniel C. Peterson, and Stephen D. Ricks, eds., *Revelation, Reason, and Faith, Essays in Honor of Truman G. Madsen* (Provo, Utah: Foundation for Ancient Research and Mormon Studies, BYU, 2002), 499–541. Cannon was Pratt's successor, especially in the founding of the Mormon newspaper in San Francisco and in responding to newspaper criticisms of the Church. For a sample of Pratt's articles in the California newspapers, see *Millennial Star* 17 (31 March 1855): 198–200, and Pratt, *Autobiography*, 459–65. Pratt's frustration with other newspaper editors is expressed in his 16 June 1855 letter to Young, but he also showed his awareness that any publicity is better than none. See further Matthew J. Grow, "'A Providencial Means of Agitating Mormonism': Parley P. Pratt and the San Francisco Press in the 1850s," *Journal of Mormon History* 29 (Fall 2003): 158–85.

he was anticipating establishing "A book Depot—Press—& and well conducted Periodical in this central position [which] will, by the aid & blessing of God, be a blessing, & a help to the cause of Zion."[136]

While Pratt was working to establish a printing press in California, he was also anticipating the establishment of an LDS bookstore or distribution center. In April, before he left the Salt Lake Valley for the West Coast, Pratt ordered large quantities of LDS publications from Franklin D. Richards in England. The order was sent to him in July, and Richards enclosed the invoice in a letter he wrote on August 31, 1854. The order included five hundred copies each of the Book of Mormon, the Doctrine and Covenants, the hymn book, and Lucy Mack Smith's *Biographical Sketches of Joseph Smith, the Prophet, and His Progenitors for Many Generations*; three hundred copies each of the Pearl of Great Price, Lorenzo Snow's *Only Way to Be Saved*, Pratt's *Voice of Warning*, and Orson Spencer's *Letters*; one hundred copies of Spencer's *Patriarchal Order*, plus a variety of other tracts and periodicals.[137] The total cost came to just over £340, much of which would be left to George Q. Cannon to discharge. Pratt had informed Richards that he intended to publish a Mormon newspaper in California, and his fellow apostles had encouraged his efforts: "I hail with great pleasure the opening of your book store, and the establishment of the 'Mormon Herald.'"[138]

Pratt's preparation of his *Autobiography* occupied much of his time in California. In August 1854 a number of returning Hawaiian missionaries, including Cannon, arrived in the Bay area. Pratt invited Cannon into his home and hired him to copy his personal history. By September 21, four hundred manuscript pages covering

[136] Pratt to Young, 15 February 1855. See also Young to Pratt, 19 August 1854, and Young to Pratt, 19 September 1854, both in Pratt Collection, LDS Church History Library.

[137] The growing role of Liverpool in the printing and distribution of the Saints' printed material throughout the world is discussed in David J. Whittaker, "Early Mormon Pamphleteering," (Ph.D. diss., BYU, 1982).

[138] Franklin D. Richards to Parley P. Pratt, 25 May 1855; and Richards to Pratt 6 October 1855, LDS Church History Library. Pratt had planned to call the newspaper the "Herald"; when the paper was finally launched by George Q. Cannon it was renamed the *Western Standard*.

Pratt's life to July 1840 had been copied, for which Cannon received fifty dollars and board.[139] Pratt also issued a broadside circular in August, *Repent! Ye People of California!* which proclaimed his willingness to preach wherever invited as well as advertised his bookstore on Broadway Street.[140]

Pratt had begun work on the *Key to the Science of Theology* in August 1851 and had given the manuscript to Franklin D. Richards to take with him to England in 1854. One chapter was printed in the *Deseret News* in November 1852,[141] and the entire volume was finally offered for sale in March 1855.[142] Writing to his brother Orson in May 1853, Pratt announced: "I have completed a Volume of theology which is now ready from the press. It is altogether the choicest and most perfect specimen from my pen."[143] Aware of Pratt's anxiety about the volume, Richards wrote him in May 1855 to explain the delay; the letter also provides one of the few detailed insights into the editing and publishing process in early Mormonism; hence, it is worth quoting at length:

> As regards the "Key to Theology" I can readily conceive with what anxiety you have watched for the book, and have much regretted that you should have to wait for it so long. I fully intended to have had the work out and to have forwarded your 2000 Copies to Cal. And the 500 to

[139] See Pratt to Young, 21 September 1854, LDS Church History Library. Pratt's *Autobiography* was not published until 1874. It was reprinted in Chicago in 1888 and later in Utah, and it remains in print. Pratt read portions of his history to assembled groups; for example, see Isaiah Coombs, Journal, 11 October 1856, LDS Church History Library. Pratt discussed his work in a letter to George A. Smith, 23 August 1854, LDS Church History Library. On Cannon's work, see his third and last volume of his Hawaiian mission journals, LDS Church History Library.

[140] Parley P. Pratt, *Repent! Ye People of California: for, Know Assuredly, the Kingdom of God, Has Come Nigh Among You* (San Francisco, 1854), broadside, LDS Church History Library; included in Pratt, *Autobiography*, 460–61.

[141] Chapter 16, "Man's Physical and Intellectual Progress," was reprinted from the *Deseret News* in the *Millennial Star* 15 (30 July 1853): 500–503.

[142] See *Millennial Star* 17 (31 March 1855): 208. The *Millennial Star* had earlier announced that the work was "in press" (16 [29 July 1854]: 472–74).

[143] Parley P. Pratt to Orson Pratt, 24 May 1853; also Parley Pratt to Brigham Young, 18 May 1853, LDS Church History Library. Seven editions in English of *Key to the Science of Theology* were published between 1855 and 1915, with significant changes made to later editions after Pratt's death, much of it in the chapters on the Holy Ghost and plural marriage.

Utah last fall, but such was prevented by circumstances which I could not control. The manuscript was put into the printers hands directly after my arrival in this country, but he was very unfortunate in having the plates go astray and with the type on its return from London where the stereotyping had to be done, there being no place in Liverpool where such business is done at all fit for our purpose. This I believe was several times repeated, and to make matters worse he became embarrassed. These untoward and unlooked for circumstances drove the work into our Emigrating Season when it necessarily became a some what secondary matter for the reasons I need not inform you of. Furthermore I was quite unwilling to have the work hurried thro the press without the opportunity of giving it that careful attention which I felt assured you expected of me. The book is not before the public, and when it meets your eye I trust it will also meet your approval. The sale is rapid and I think another edition will shortly be wanted. In the meantime I am having the Stereo. Plates corrected in such things as most generally escape detection in first editions. I allude to uniformity, orthography, punctuation, etc. In addition to what corrections I may make there may still be some which you would wish to introduce after reading the work. If so, I would submit that it would be very advantageous if they could be introduced before the plates leave for America.[144]

When it appeared, *Key to the Science of Theology* was a publishing event. It was among the earliest comprehensive treatments of Mormonism's doctrines.[145] The publication did not contain the dogmatism that sometimes characterized his brother Orson's writings; rather, Pratt surveyed the broad spectrum of Mormon thought in a style that invited further contemplation. He discussed the nature of the Godhead, the origin and destiny of the universe, the restoration of the gospel, the proper channel for mankind's regaining the presence of God, the resurrection, the three degrees of glory, and

[144] Franklin D. Richards to Parley P. Pratt, 25 May 1855, Pratt Collection. Richards was also preparing the eighth edition of Pratt's popular *Voice of Warning*, and both works were issued in editions of five thousand copies. See invoice, 29 August 1854, Pratt Collection. Richards charged a twenty percent commission for editing and publishing the *Key to the Science of Theology* and a ten percent commission for the same work on the eighth edition of *Voice of Warning.*

[145] Another such work was Orson Spencer's *Letters Exhibiting the Most Prominent Doctrines of the Church of Jesus Christ of Latter-day Saints* (Liverpool, England: Published by Orson Spencer, 1848). This work includes fourteen letters Spencer wrote to Rev. W. Crowel in 1847, many of which had been first issued as separate tracts. In 1853 Spencer added a fifteenth letter addressing the topic of the *Patriarchal Order, or Plurality of Wives!*

the great destiny of exalted men and women as procreative beings in the eternities. Many of these topics he had written on earlier, but this work allowed him to pull all these thoughts together into one volume, and it suggests the same process of gathering and assembling that he was using in composing his *Autobiography*. It would be his last book and his greatest work.

Pratt left California in June 1855, returning to Utah while feeling confident that George Q. Cannon would be carrying on his foundational work there. Serving as the chaplain for the 1855–56 legislative council, he read an address to the council on December 21, and Thomas Bullock read it to the territorial legislature meeting in Fillmore ten days later; he was probably drawing upon the need to publicly address the growing criticisms of the Mormons following the public announcement of the practice of plural marriage in August 1852, a topic that had demanded much of his time during his last months in California.[146] Pratt's address, *Marriage and Morals in Utah*, was printed in the *Deseret News*, in pamphlet form in Liverpool in 1856, and was expanded by Cannon in 1857 as *Scriptural Evidences in Support of Polygamy*.[147]

[146] See David J. Whittaker, "The Bone in the Throat: Orson Pratt and the Public Announcement of Plural Marriage" *Western Historical Quarterly* 18 (July 1987): 293–314. One of Pratt's plural wives, Belinda Marden Pratt, authored the first and one of the only Mormon pamphlets on the topic written by a woman: *Defence of Polygamy by a Lady of Utah*. Dated 12 January 1854, the pamphlet had been printed in February 1854 in Salt Lake City. Pratt had received and was distributing copies by September. See Pratt to Family, 21 September 1854, Pratt Collection; and Whittaker, "Early Mormon Polygamy Defenses," *Journal of Mormon History* 11 (1984): 53–57.

[147] Pratt, *Autobiography*, 480; and *Marriage and Morals in Utah, an Address Written by P. P. Pratt, One of the Twelve Apostles of the Church of Jesus Christ of Latter-day Saints, and Chaplain to the Council of the Utah Legislature. Read in Joint Session of the Legislature in the Representatives' Hall, Fillmore City, Dec. 31, 1855, by Mr. Thomas Bullock, Chief Clerk of the House. Reprinted from the "Deseret News"* (Liverpool, England: Orson Pratt; London: L.D.S. Book and Star Depot, 1856). This work had many printings in several languages. Pratt's eight-page pamphlet was expanded to twenty-four pages when Cannon added additional references in *Scriptural Evidences in Support of Polygamy: Being an Address Entitled Marriage and Morals in Utah: By Parley P. Pratt; and a Protestant Minister's Arguments from the Bible in Favor of Polygamy: Extracted from the Work of Rev. D. O. Allen, D. D., Missionary of the American Board of Foreign Missions for Twenty-Five Years in India* (San Francisco: George Q. Cannon, 1856). For the larger context see Whittaker, "Early Mormon Polygamy Defenses."

In September 1856 Pratt was assigned to preach and publish in the eastern United States and possibly to assist John Taylor with the LDS newspaper *The Mormon* then being published in New York City.[148] He preached his farewell sermon in the Salt Lake Tabernacle on September 7 and shortly thereafter began his journey east. He wrote for *The Mormon* and conducted other church business during this mission before his murder in Arkansas.[149]

Conclusion

When Pratt died in May 1857, the first era of Mormon publishing ended. Little printed matter other than newspapers or reprints from earlier works appeared until after Brigham Young's death in 1877. From 1835 to 1855, Pratt had mapped out the contours and provided much of the content of early Mormon print culture. It is not an exaggeration to call him the literary pathfinder of early Mormonism or the father of Mormon pamphleteering. His written work helped to define and explain Mormonism to an audience that increasingly understood themselves by what they read. Pratt wrote to define himself and understood that authorship was a possible avenue for income as his correspondence to his family reveals. He was (with his brother Orson) the closest person in early Mormonism to a professional writer, but he wrote in an age when authors were generally not able to live by their pen. Nevertheless, he profoundly shaped the self-understanding of the Mormon audience who read his books and the religious faith of the founding generation of Mormonism. A much-beloved Church leader, his writings on gospel topics helped expand the worldview of new converts and offered them the expansive view of the gospel that initially few

148 First Presidency to Parley P. Pratt, 10 September 1856, LDS Church History Library.

149 On Pratt's death, see Steven Pratt, "Eleanor McLean and the Murder of Parley P. Pratt," *BYU Studies* 15 (Winter 1975): 225–56; and Patrick Q. Mason's essay in this volume (chapter 8). An "appendix" to the *Autobiography*, i–vi, reprinted extracts from various Latter-day Saint periodicals to provide readers with some of the details of Pratt's murder near Van Buren, Arkansas. Pratt's death was reported in some detail for the British Saints (many of whom had been assisted in their conversion through the reading of Pratt's writings) in the *Millennial Star*: 19 (14 July 1857): 417–32; 19 (25 July 1857): 478; and 19 (29 August 1857): 544–48.

would have learned from Joseph Smith himself. Pratt had sought the wilderness in the late 1820s to find solitude in nature, and he seldom left this Romantic world the rest of his life. Pratt shared many of the traits common to the Romantic movement, including the need for freedom of space, an optimistic view of the nature of man, a strong sense of antiquarianism and interest in the past, an emphasis on intuition or revelation as the ultimate source of truth and beauty, a strong sense of the poetic, and a cosmic sense of the future destiny of man. His *Autobiography* was the ultimate testimony to this individualistic and introspective view of the self. His 1826–27 "Walden Pond" experience in Ohio did not take him into the Transcendentalism of Emerson and Thoreau; rather it prepared him for the Restoration visions and revelations of Joseph Smith that both confirmed and then encouraged this organic and subjective understanding of the world. Pratt's Romantic outlook remained central to his character and became an important part of his contributions to early Mormon print culture.

CHAPTER 4

"'Tis Not for Crimes That I Have Done"

Parley P. Pratt's Missouri Imprisonment, 1838–1839

Alexander L. Baugh

The Missouri period of early Mormonism (1831–1839) has often been considered the darkest era in the Church's history. During these years, Latter-day Saints hoped to establish a Mormon utopia in Missouri's western region, but such efforts led to misunderstandings, jealousies, mob action, destruction of property, and killings, culminating in 1838 in regional civil conflict. Beginning in early August and continuing through November of that year, a number of civil disturbances broke out between the Missourians and Latter-day Saints living in Missouri's northwestern counties. Although the contest was perpetuated primarily by religious intolerance on the part of a significant portion of the local population against the Latter-day Saints, some culpability could also be attributed to the Mormons.

The 1838 Mormon War, as it came to be called, included the following conflicts: (1) the confrontation between Mormons and Missouri vigilantes in Daviess County, including the intercession made by regional state militia (August through mid-September);

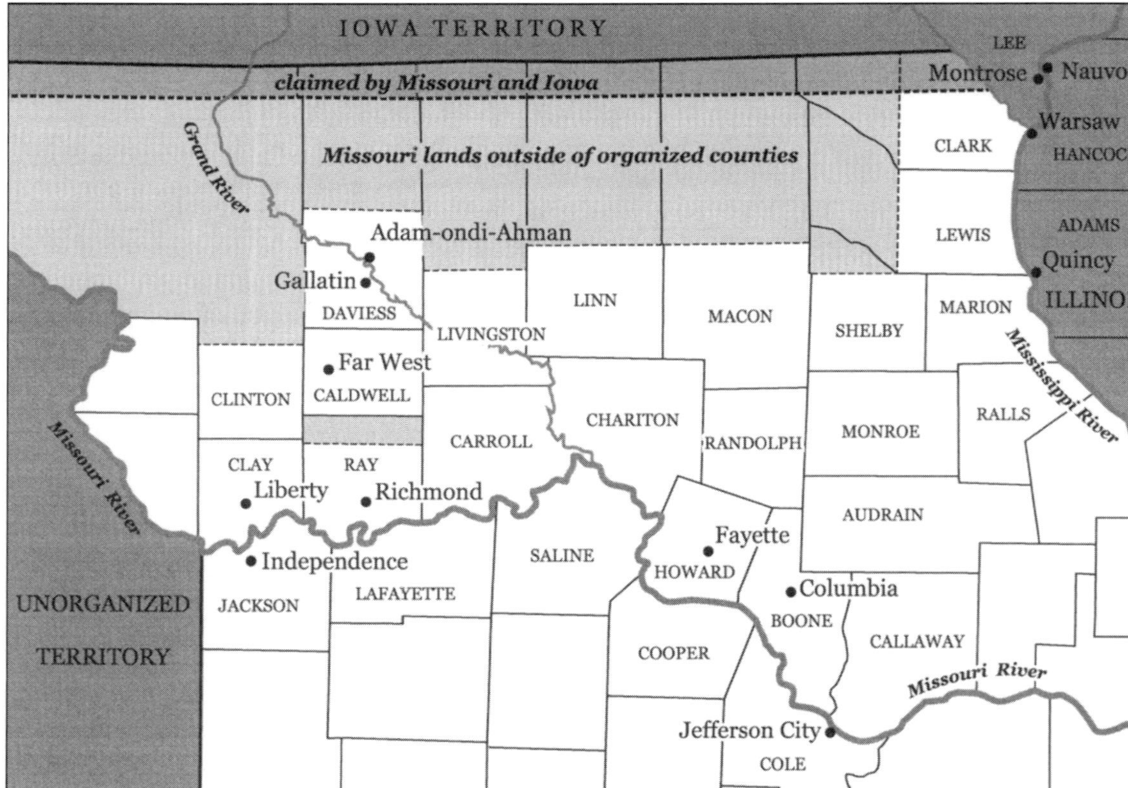

Northern Missouri counties during the Mormon period.
Courtesy of John Hamer.

(2) the Latter-day Saint defense of the Mormon population residing in De Witt, Carroll County, against county regulators and the response of the regional state militia to the disturbances (August through October 10); (3) the expulsion of the non-Mormon residents of Daviess County by Mormon militia (mid-October); (4) the encounter between Mormon and Missouri militia at Crooked River in Ray County (October 25); (5) the attack of the Mormon settlement of Hawn's/Haun's Mill by Missouri vigilantes primarily from Livingston and Daviess Counties (October 30); (6) the Mormon defense of Far West against vigilante and state militia forces (October 28–31); and (7) the Mormon surrender at Far West and the military occupation conducted by the state militia (November 1–29). These final events culminated in the expulsion of the Latter-day Saint community in early 1839 by order of the state's chief executive, Missouri governor Lilburn W. Boggs.[1]

Parley P. Pratt played a prominent role in a number of the events associated with the 1838 Mormon-Missouri conflict, particularly the Battle of Crooked River, and it was this encounter that subsequently led to his arrest and an eight-month imprisonment in Missouri's jails.[2]

Parley P. Pratt and the Battle of Crooked River

On October 23, 1838, Captain Samuel Bogart of the Ray County militia received orders from Major-General David R. Atchison, militia commander of the state's Third Division, to patrol the line running between Caldwell and Ray Counties, particularly the region known as the Buncombe Strip, a six-by-twenty-four mile sector in northern

[1] For a more comprehensive examination of the Mormon War, see Alexander L. Baugh, *A Call to Arms: The 1838 Mormon Defense of Northern Missouri* (Provo, Utah: Joseph Fielding Smith Institute for Latter-day Saint History and *BYU Studies*, Brigham Young University [hereafter BYU], 2000); and Stephen C. LeSueur, *The 1838 Mormon War in Missouri* (Columbia, University of Missouri Press, 1987).

[2] A more detailed treatise on Pratt's Missouri imprisonment is in Alexander L. Baugh, "The Final Episode of Mormonism in Missouri in the 1830s: The Incarceration of the Mormon Prisoners at Richmond and Columbia Jails, 1838–1839," *John Whitmer Historical Association Journal* 28 (2008): 1–34.

Ray County. For nearly two months, outbreaks and disturbances between the Mormons and the Missourians in northwestern Missouri had raised fears on both sides. Recent hostilities in Daviess County in mid-October led citizens living in Ray County to believe that the Mormons would strike Richmond, the county seat, next.

Upon receiving Atchison's orders, Bogart acted quickly. The following day, his company, comprising thirty-five men, appeared in the region, threatening the Latter-day Saint families and warning them to leave or suffer repercussions. Bogart also took three Mormon prisoners—Nathan Pinkham, Jr., William Seely, and Addison Green. That evening, the Ray militia set up camp in the extreme northwest corner of the county on Crooked River.

During the evening of October 24, several Mormon messengers made their way to Far West, bringing word to Church leaders about Bogart's activities and the approximate whereabouts of his company. It was also reported that Pinkham, Seely, and Green were to be tried by court-martial and would be shot the following morning. Believing the lives of the three men were in eminent danger, Mormon leaders made the decision to call out a company of Caldwell County militia to disperse the mob and rescue the men. Elias Higbee, the county judge, issued the orders. Mormon apostle David W. Patten was placed in command of the operation. Seventy-five men responded to the call-out. One of the men who volunteered was Pratt.

During the early morning hours of October 25, the Mormon militia encountered the Ray militia at Crooked River and a full-scale contest ensued. In the end, the Mormons succeeded in routing the Missourians and rescuing the prisoners, but three members of their company were killed, including Patrick Obanion, Gideon Carter, and Patten, the Mormon commander. Nine other Mormons were wounded. Bogart's company suffered one fatality—Moses Roland. Six others in the Ray militia were wounded.[3]

---

[3] For a historical examination of the Crooked River encounter, see Alexander L. Baugh, "The Battle Between Mormon and Missouri Militia at Crooked River," in Arnold K. Garr and Clark V. Johnson, eds., *Regional Studies in Latter-day Saint History: Missouri* (Provo, Utah: Department of Church History and Doctrine, BYU, 1994), 85–103; also Baugh, *A Call to Arms*, 99–113.

The battle between Bogart's Ray County militia and Patten's Caldwell County militia marked a turning point in the 1838 Mormon-Missouri conflict. Reports of the contest were immediately dispatched to the office of Missouri governor Lilburn W. Boggs. On October 27, Amos Rees and Wiley C. Williams arrived in Jefferson City where the two men met with the state's chief executive and informed him of Bogart's defeat and the alarming state of affairs in Ray County. Upon learning of the most recent events in the civil conflict, Boggs decided to take aggressive action. Based upon the report he received, the governor perceived that the Mormons had come out in open rebellion against the state of Missouri by deliberately attacking authorized militia—an act he viewed unlawful and treasonous—hence his written statement: "The Mormons [are] in the attitude of an open and avowed defiance of the laws, and of having made war upon the people of this state." The statement continued with an order: "The Mormons must be treated as enemies, and must be exterminated or driven from the state."[4]

The Mormon Surrender at Far West

By October 30, three days after the Missouri governor learned of Bogart's defeat, twenty-five hundred state troops had assembled on the outskirts of Far West to ensure that the governor's orders were carried out. The day before issuing the "Extermination Order," Boggs relieved General Atchison of his command of the state militia in the northern district.[5] Atchison's release probably stemmed from the fact that he had served as legal counsel to Joseph Smith and was at least partially sympathetic to the

[4] Lilburn W. Boggs to John B. Clark, 27 October 1838, in *Document Containing the Correspondence, Orders, &c. in Relation to the Disturbances with the Mormons; and the Evidence Given Before the Hon. Austin A. King, Judge of the Fifth Judicial Circuit of the State of Missouri, at the Court-House in Richmond, in a Criminal Court of Inquiry, Begun November 12, 1838, on the Trial of Joseph Smith, Jr., and Others, for High Treason and Other Crimes Against the State* (Fayette, Mo.: *Boonslick Democrat*, Printer, 1841), 61 (hereafter *Document*).

[5] Lilburn W. Boggs to John B. Clark, 26 October 1838, in *Document*, 62–63. Although the order was signed by B.M. Lisle, an adjutant general in the state militia, Lisle wrote by order of Boggs.

Mormons. Boggs replaced Atchison with Major-General John B. Clark of Howard County. However, because Clark was not on the scene to take charge, Samuel D. Lucas, commander of the Jackson County troops and a major-general in the Missouri militia, assumed command.

Being vastly outnumbered and fearing bloodshed, Mormon leaders recognized they had no other choice but to surrender to Missouri authorities. Significantly, it was not until October 30, the day before the Mormon surrender, when Latter-day Saint leaders learned that the battle at Crooked River was against authorized state militia, not local vigilantes. Believing that those who had taken part could face criminal charges, Mormon leaders encouraged the members of Patten's company to get out of Far West and leave the state immediately. Lorenzo D. Young, one of the Crooked River participants, later wrote: "If they [Missouri authorities] succeeded in taking the brethren who were in the Crooked River battle, they would be tried by a court martial and shot . . . [so] after counseling over the matter, it was decided that I, and others in the same situation, should start that night into the wilderness north, for the Des Moines River, in Iowa Territory."[6] One group of Crooked River boys left Far West later that day. A smaller group fled the following day. For some reason, Pratt chose not to go. Had he done so, he probably would have avoided incarceration.

Pratt's Arrest

General Lucas wasted no time in apprehending who he thought were the chief instigators behind the Mormon insurgence, namely, Joseph Smith, Sidney Rigdon, Lyman Wight, George W. Robinson,

[6] Lorenzo D. Young, "Lorenzo Dow Young's Narrative," *Fragments of Experience: Sixth Book of the Faith-Promoting Series* (Salt Lake City: *Juvenile Instructor* Office, 1882), 52; reprinted in *Four Faith Promoting Classics*, part 2 (Salt Lake City: Bookcraft, 1968), 52. Ebenezer Robinson wrote: "That night [October 31], about sixty of those who had been engaged in the Crooked River battle . . . were advised to leave, being looked upon as men who had periled their lives in defense of their brethren, and their friends wished them to escape the wrath of their persecutors" (Ebenezer Robinson, "Items of Personal History of the Editor," *The Return* 2, no. 2 [February 1890]: 209).

and Pratt. On November 1, Hyrum Smith and Amasa M. Lyman were arrested. The reasons these seven men were apprehended appears evident. Joseph Smith, Rigdon, and Hyrum Smith comprised the Church's First Presidency. George W. Robinson was the prophet's secretary. Lyman Wight was the highest-ranking Mormon militia officer in Daviess County and had played a leading role in the Mormon retaliatory strikes in Daviess County in October. Amasa Lyman was a leader of a Mormon spy company that reconnoitered throughout southern Caldwell and northern Ray Counties during the days just preceding the Mormon surrender. Finally, Pratt had been a participant in the battle at Crooked River. The fact that he was included suggests that his participation at Crooked River was known by Missouri officials. Therefore, October 31, 1838, marks the beginning of Pratt's Missouri imprisonment, a period that would last eight months and four days.

On the evening of November 1, Lucas made a rash decision to hold a military court for the seven prisoners. He believed he had to act quickly—before General Clark arrived and while he still had command of the operation—because Clark, the Howard County general, who was less familiar with the Mormon problem, might be disposed to render more lenient justice in behalf of the Church's leaders. With these considerations in mind, the Jackson County general decided to move ahead immediately with the court-martial. Details concerning the hearing are sketchy, but the evidence is clear that at the time of the hearing, Joseph Smith and his cohorts were in custody at Alexander W. Doniphan's camp and were not even allowed to be present to defend themselves.[7]

The deliberation did not last long. Upon hearing the evidence, Lucas called for a vote from officers of the court who voted three to one in favor of conviction on the charge of treason—a capital

[7] Parley P. Pratt, *Autobiography of Parley P. Pratt, One of the Twelve Apostles of the Church of Jesus Christ of Latter-day Saints, Embracing His Life, Ministry, and Travels, with Extracts, in Prose and Verse, from His Miscellaneous Writings*, ed. Parley P. Pratt, Jr. (New York: Russell Brothers, 1874), 205; and Sidney Rigdon, *An Appeal to the American People: Being an Account of the Persecutions of the Church of Latter Day Saints; and of the Barbarities Inflicted on Them by the Inhabitants of the State of Missouri* (Cincinnati: Glezen and Shepard, Stereotypers and Printers, 1840), 51.

offense.[8] Alexander W. Doniphan vehemently opposed the decision, telling his fellow officers that not one of them was familiar with military law and then left the hearing in protest.[9] Nonetheless, with the verdict rendered, Lucas drafted the execution order and dispatched it to Doniphan, expecting his compliance. The order read: "Brigadier-General Doniphan.—Sir: You will take Joseph Smith and the other prisoners into the public square of Far West, and shoot them at 9 o'clock to-morrow morning. [Signed] Samuel D. Lucas Major-General Commanding."[10] However, Doniphan was not about to be an accessory to such an order and issued a brusque response. Not only did he inform Lucas that he considered the order illegal and that he would not obey it, but he threatened legal action if the executions were carried out. The illegality of the order centered on the fact that at least three of the prisoners, namely, Joseph and Hyrum Smith, and Sidney Rigdon of the First Presidency, claimed exemption from state militia service and therefore did not come under military authority.[11]

---

[8] See *History of Clay and Platte Counties, Missouri, Written and Compiled from the Most Authentic Official and Private Sources, Including a History of Their Townships, Towns and Villages, Together with a Condensed History of Missouri; a Reliable and Detailed History of Clay and Platte Counties—Their Pioneer Record, Resources, Biographical Sketches of Prominent Citizens; General and Local Statistics of Great Value; Incidents and Reminiscences* (St. Louis: National Historical Company, 1885), 134n1.

[9] Rigdon, *An Appeal to the American People*, 51; and Rigdon petition in Clark S. Johnson, *Mormon Redress Petitions: Documents of the 1833–1838 Missouri Conflict* (Provo, Utah: Religious Studies Center, BYU, 1992), 675–76; also in Joseph Smith, Jr., *History of the Church of Jesus Christ of Latter-day Saints*, ed. B. H. Roberts, 2nd ed., rev., 7 vols. (Salt Lake City: Deseret Book, 1971), 3:460; and Parley P. Pratt, *History of the Late Persecution Inflicted by the State of Missouri upon the Mormons, in Which Ten Thousand American Citizens Were Robbed, Plundered, and Driven From the State, and Many Others Imprisoned, Martyred, &c. for Their Religion, and All This by Military Force, by Order of the Executive* (Detroit: Dawson and Bates, Printers, 1839), 40.

[10] *History of Caldwell and Livingston Counties, Missouri, Written and Compiled from the Most Authentic Official and Private Sources, Including a History of Their Townships and Villages, Together with a Condensed History of Missouri; a Reliable and Detailed History of Caldwell and Livingston Counties—Their Pioneer Record, Resources, Biographical Sketches of Prominent Citizens; General and Local Statistics of Great Value; Incidents and Reminiscences* (St. Louis: National Historical Company, 1886), 137.

[11] For statements concerning Joseph Smith's exemption from state militia duty, see Alanson Ripley, Heber C. Kimball, William Huntington, Joseph B. Noble, and Joseph Smith, Jr., petition in John P. Greene, *Facts Relative to the Expulsion of the*

This fact was clearly recognized by Doniphan, who had previously acted as Joseph Smith's legal counsel and knew firsthand of his military exemption. One of Doniphan's own brigade members reported: "These men had never belonged to any lawful military organization, and could not, therefore, have violated military law. The law of the soldier could not apply to them, as they had not been soldiers in any legal sense."[12] However, the same was not true for the other four prisoners—Lyman Wight, Parley P. Pratt, George W. Robinson, and Amasa Lyman—each of whom were commissioned or elected state militia officers. In spite of the fact that four of the seven could have come under military authority, Doniphan's dauntless refusal to carry out Lucas's order, in addition to his warning that he would pursue legal action if the executions were carried out, led Lucas to reconsider his decision, and to decide ultimately to keep all seven Mormon men in custody until they could be turned over to the appropriate civil authorities.[13]

Pratt's Incarceration at Independence

During the forenoon of November 2, a heavily guarded wagon containing the seven Mormon prisoners pulled into Far West where they were allowed to return to their homes to get some clothing and other necessities and to say good-bye to their families.[14]

Mormons or Latter Day Saints from the State of Missouri, Under the "Exterminating Order" (Cincinnati: R. P. Brooks, 1839), 32; and Lyman Wight petition in Johnson, *Mormon Redress Petitions*, 656; also in Smith, *History of the Church*, 3:441. Hyrum Smith claimed the entire First Presidency was exempt because of the ministerial status of its members, while Sidney Rigdon stated he was excluded because he was over age. See Smith and Rigdon petitions in Johnson, *Mormon Redress Petitions*, 632, 634; also in Smith, *History of the Church*, 3:417, 459.

[12] Peter H. Burnett, *An Old California Pioneer by Peter H. Burnett, First Governor of the State* (Oakland, Calif.: Biobooks, 1946), 37–38.

[13] The significance of Doniphan's intervention in behalf of the Mormon leaders cannot be overstated. Had he not blocked Lucas, Joseph Smith and the other prisoners would most assuredly have lost their lives. Missourian Peter H. Burnett wrote: "Had it not been for the efforts of Doniphan and others from Clay, I think it most probable that the prisoners would have been summarily tried, condemned, and executed" (Burnett, *An Old California Pioneer*, 38).

[14] Pratt wrote a heart-wrenching description of the scene in his *Autobiography*, 207.

After reassembling, Lucas put Brigadier General Moses Wilson in charge of three hundred men and assigned him to take the Mormon leaders to Independence while he finalized the surrender.[15] Lucas remained overnight, leaving Far West the next day in order to catch up with Wilson.

The journey from Far West to Independence took the better part of two days before the Mormon prisoners arrived on the afternoon of Sunday, November 4. The prisoners were immediately incarcerated in a vacant log house just north and across the street from Independence's public square and courthouse.[16] It was on this day that Pratt penned the first of six extant letters written to his wife Mary Ann Frost Stearns Pratt during his Missouri incarceration.[17] In the letter, Pratt noted that the militia officers were treating him and the other Mormon prisoners with kindness and civility, behavior that was certainly not anticipated:

> We arrived here to day (Sunday) about noon[—]all well; haveing been treated with every kindness and respect which we could desire. It is true I anticipated any thing but kindness and hospitality when we fell into the hands of this brigade; knowing the hostility which here existed. But we are hap[p]ily disap[p]ointed. The of[f]icers and troops of Jackson County have behaved with that respect, honor and kindness towards us, which are around here expected from Brethren, and which has in a great measure attoned for their former trespasses, and have restored the

[15] See Samuel D. Lucas to Lilburn W. Boggs, 2 November 1838, in *Document*, 75; also Samuel D. Lucas to Lilburn W. Boggs, 5 November 1838 in *Document*, 71. See also Lyman Wight, Journal, in Joseph Smith III and Heman C. Smith, *History of the Reorganized Church of Jesus Christ of Latter Day Saints*, 8 vols. (Independence, Mo.: Herald House, 1967), 2:295; and Wight petition in Johnson, *Mormon Redress Petitions*, 662; also in Smith, *History of the Church*, 3:447.

[16] Wight, Journal, 295–96; Pratt, *Autobiography*, 212; and Smith, *History of the Church*, 3:201. In his journal, Wight incorrectly indicated that the prisoners arrived in Independence on November 3, whereas the *History of the Church* and Pratt's chronology place the date as November 4. November 4 was a Sunday (as noted by Pratt) and is the correct date.

[17] Mary Ann Frost Stearns Pratt was Parley's second wife. Pratt's first marriage was to Thankful Halsey on September 9, 1827. She died in Kirtland, Ohio, on March 24, 1837. Six weeks after her death Pratt married Mary Ann Frost Stearns on May 9, 1837. Previous to her marriage to Pratt, Mary Ann had married Nathan Stearns on April 1, 1832. Nathan died on August 25, 1833.

best of feelings between us and them. We fared even better on the way than their own troops. Our meals were served to us in the best manner with plenty of coffee and shugar. We had the privilege of sleeping in a tent with the officers while many of the troops slept in the open air. No person was suffered to insult us and treat us with disrespect in the least. Crowds of gentlemen and ladys thronged the way to be [able] to see us, and General Wilson often halted the troops to introduce us to them. Thay of both sexes shack [shake] us warmly by the hand, and when we arrived in Independence we were provided with a comfortable house and a . . . fire, as the storm was very severe. There we spent the time in conversation with the throngs who flocked to see us until supper, when we were guarded to a hotel and a splendid supper was set before us. After refreshing ourselves we were guarded back to our house and provided with paper and writing materials and candles. And Br. [Joseph] Smith, Br[.] Robinson, and myself were set at the same stand, scribbleing each [a letter] to our respective families while Brs[.] Wight, Rigdon, Hiram Smith, and Br[.] Lyman are in conversation with the visitors and guards; and indeed were it not for the absence of our families we should allmost forget that we were prisoners. . . . Our greatest pain is for our families and the Church, knowing that you are exposed to danger[,] to famine, and perhaps to death. But we can only pray for you, and leave you in the hand of God, and pray the Lord God [will] bless and preserve you and us and speedily restore us to the bosom of our families. . . . Be assured that whether we meet again in this life or not, I trust in the living God whether in life or in death, and I feel resigned to his will. . . . It is for you and the little ones, that I still desire to live. And my prayer to God is that he will preserve me and my family and let us live in each others embraces. . . . I must now close as the conversation in the room is so much, it disturbs, and draws my attention till it is very difficult to write home.[18]

In consideration of their hospitable treatment, on November 5—the second day of their confinement in Independence—the Mormon prisoners drafted a card expressing their appreciation to the militia officers (Lucas and Wilson) and their subordinates for the kindness and civility shown to them since their apprehension: "It

[18] Parley P. Pratt to Mary Ann Frost Stearns Pratt, 4 November 1838, Church History Library, the Church of Jesus Christ of Latter-day Saints, Salt Lake City, Utah (hereafter LDS Church History Library). Joseph Smith also penned a letter to his wife Emma. See Joseph Smith, Jr., to Emma Smith, 4 November 1838, Community of Christ Library Archives, Independence, Missouri; also published in Dean C. Jessee, ed., *Personal Writings of Joseph Smith* (Salt Lake City: Deseret Book, 2002), 399–401.

is with feelings of no ordinary kind that the undersigned take this method of tendering their most unfeigned gratitude to you for the kind treatment and great attention they have received at your hands since they were committed to your charge as prisoners," a portion of the statement reads, "having received every degree of kindness that could be expected at the hands of a magnanimous and honorable people." It then concludes, "We have not received the first insult from any individual." Apparently, Lucas and Wilson were so pleased by the prisoners' expression of appreciation that they mailed the card to the newspaper offices of the *Boonslick Democrat*, published in Fayette, Howard County, Missouri, requesting it be printed. Although the card bears the names of each of the seven prisoners, the likelihood exists, given Pratt's literary talents, that he may have been the one selected to compose the message.[19]

On November 6, following two days of confinement in the log house, the seven prisoners were moved a short distance east to the Noland House (hotel) situated on the northwest corner of Main and Maple. Here they waited for word regarding where their hearing would be held; they were treated hospitably and permitted to come and go as they pleased.[20]

---

[19] Joseph Smith, Jr., Hiram [*sic*] Smith, P. P. Pratt, Amasa Lyman, George W. Robbinson [*sic*], Lyman Wight, and Sidney Rigdon, "A Card to the Citizens of Jackson County," Independence, Missouri, 5 November 1838, printed in the *Boonslick Democrat* (Fayette, Mo.), 10 November 1838. The article was subsequently picked up and printed on 28 November 1838, in the *Ohio Statesman*, published in Columbus. No extant copy of the *Boonslick Democrat* for the date of 10 November 1838 could be found, so the *Statesman* version is the one cited here.

[20] Lyman Wight indicated the prisoners' move from the log house to the Noland House occurred on November 6. See Wight, Journal, 296. Pratt recorded: "[After our arrival in Independence] the troops were then disbanded. In the meantime we were kept under a small guard, and were treated with some degree of humanity, while hundreds flocked to see us day after day. We spent most of our time in preaching and conversation, explanatory of our doctrines and practice. Much prejudice was removed, and the feelings of the populace began to be in our favor. . . . In a day or two we were at liberty to walk the streets without a guard. We were finally removed from our house of confinement to a hotel, where we boarded at the public table, and lodged on the floor, with a block of wood for a pillow. We no longer had any guard; we went out and came in when we pleased—a certain keeper being appointed merely to watch over us, and look to our wants" (Pratt, *Autobiography*, 213).

On November 4, the same day that Lucas and Wilson arrived in Independence with the seven Mormon prisoners, General Clark arrived at Far West where he supervised the final activities of the Mormon surrender and conducted a number of additional arrests—forty-six total.[21] On November 5, Clark dispatched Colonel Sterling G. Price and two companies of state militia to travel to Richmond to meet up with General Lucas and secure Joseph Smith and the other six Mormon prisoners. However, at the time, Clark and Price were not aware that Lucas had not gone to Richmond but had proceeded to Independence. When Clark learned that Lucas had taken the seven prisoners to Jackson County, he sent a small detachment to Independence with orders for Lucas to turn over the prisoners so they could be taken to Richmond for examination.[22] On November 7, Clark's men arrived in Independence and took charge of the prisoners. Accordingly, the next day (November 8), accompanied by a small military escort, they proceeded fifteen miles, crossed the Missouri River, and lodged that evening in an old frame house. The following day, November 9, while en route to Richmond, they were met by a strong guard commanded by Colonel Price who conducted them the rest of the way. Upon their arrival that evening at the Ray County seat, Joseph and Hyrum Smith, Sidney Rigdon, George W. Robinson, Lyman Wight, Amasa Lyman, and Pratt were put into an old log house situated twenty rods (330 feet), about one block north, of Richmond's public square and courthouse where they were placed under a guard and chained together in heavy irons.[23] For three weeks (November 9–29) the log house served as the ad hoc jail for the seven Mormon

[21] See John B. Clark to Lilburn W. Boggs, 10, 29 November 1838, in *Document*, 66, 90.

[22] Ibid.

[23] Smith, *History of the Church*, 3:205–206; and Pratt, *Autobiography*, 216; Wight, Journal, 296–98. Pratt indicated that immediately upon their arrival in Richmond, the prisoners were confined in chains. Wight noted that they were not put into chains until the following day, November 10. For a general location of the old log house, see LaMar C. Berrett and Max H. Parkin, *Sacred Places, Missouri: A Comprehensive Guide to Early LDS Historical Sites*, vol. 4 (Salt Lake City: Deseret Book, 2004), 238; and John Craig, "Richmond, Missouri, Update on Location of 'Old Vacant Log House,'" *Missouri Mormon Frontier Foundation Newsletter*, nos. 41–42 (July 2007 to May 2008): 1–7.

leaders. Athalia R. Robinson, Rigdon's seventeen-year-old daughter and wife of George Robinson, also lodged with the prisoners for a time. Because of Rigdon's tenuous health, Athalia was permitted to take care of her ailing father and to be with her husband.[24]

Pratt's Incarceration at Richmond

At the time the Mormon defendants were brought to Richmond for the preliminary hearing, Major-General John B. Clark was still uncertain whether the case surrounding the Mormons should come under civil or military laws. Although Mormon sources indicate he clearly believed the military statutes should have taken precedence in the case, he immediately addressed a letter to the governor's office requesting a ruling. To be sure, Clark dispatched an aide to Ft. Leavenworth to secure a copy of the military code.[25] In the meantime, however, much to Clark's disappointment, fifth district circuit court judge Austin A. King ruled that the civil courts had jurisdiction, and on November 12, the Richmond Court of Inquiry convened to examine the charges levied against the Mormons and to determine if there was probable cause to bind the defendants over for trial. Thomas Burch and William Wood prosecuted in behalf of the state. The Mormon prisoners were represented by Alexander Doniphan and Amos Rees.[26]

[24] Pratt, *Autobiography*, 228.

[25] John B. Clark to Lilburn W. Boggs, 10, 29 November 1838, in *Document*, 67, 91; also Smith, *History of the Church*, 3:206. Clark also wrote Boggs requesting that a decision concerning jurisdiction be made from the office of the state attorney general. On November 19, the governor sent a reply wherein he told Clark that the case should be determined in the civil court. It would have then taken several days for the governor's letter to reach Clark in Richmond, but by this time the hearing in King's court was well under way. See Lilburn W. Boggs to John B. Clark, 19 November 1838, in *Document*, 81.

[26] *Document*, 97; and Smith, *History of the Church*, 3:209, 212. For an examination of the Richmond hearing, see Stephen C. LeSueur, "'High Treason and Murder': The Examination of Mormon Prisoners at Richmond, Missouri, in November 1838," BYU *Studies* 26, no. 2 (Spring 1986): 3–30; and H. Michael Marquardt, "Judge Austin A. King's Preliminary Hearing: Joseph Smith and the Mormons on Trial," *John Whitmer Historical Association Journal* 24 (2004): 41–55.

When the preliminary hearing in Richmond began, fifty-three Mormons were in state custody. During the course of the hearing, eleven more were subsequently arrested, bringing the total number of Mormon defendants to sixty-four. Whereas Pratt and the six other Mormon leaders were held in an old log house north of the courthouse, the remaining fifty-seven Mormon defendants were housed in the courthouse itself, which was under construction. The Richmond preliminary hearing began on November 12 and continued through November 29 (with the likely exception of November 18 and 25, which were Sundays).[27] Each day court was held, Joseph and Hyrum Smith, Sidney Rigdon, George Robinson, Lyman Wight, Amasa Lyman, and Pratt were escorted by a small contingent of militia guards under the command of Sterling Price from the log house, which served as their place of confinement, to the Ray County Courthouse where they joined the other Mormon prisoners to hear the evidence presented against them. When the hearing recessed at the end of each day, Pratt and his prison companions were conducted back to the log house for the night while the remaining Mormon prisoners spent the evening confined in the unfinished courthouse. Pratt later reported that one evening during their confinement in the log house Joseph Smith issued a scathing rebuke of the militia guards, an event that has been memorialized in Mormon history.[28]

At the conclusion of the Richmond hearing, the court released twenty-nine of the sixty-four Mormon defendants. However, Judge

[27] Pratt incorrectly dated that the hearing was held from November 11 to 28. See Pratt, *Autobiography*, 228.

[28] See Pratt, *Autobiography*, 229–30. In a March 1839 letter to the Church in Quincy, Illinois, Joseph Smith may have eluded to the event of his rebuking the guards when he wrote: "And although their influance shall cast the[e] into trouble and into barrs and walls thou shalt be had in honor and but for a small moment and thy voice shall be more terible in the midst of thine enemies than the fierce Lion because of thy ritiousness [righteousness] and thy God shall stand by the[e] forever" (Joseph Smith, Jr., to the Church at Quincy, 20 March 1839, LDS Church History Library; also in Jessee, *Personal Writings of Joseph Smith*, 441). The passage has been canonized in the LDS Church's scripture as Doctrine and Covenants of the Church of Jesus Christ of Latter-day Saints: Carefully Selected from the Revelations of God (Salt Lake City: The Church of Jesus Christ of Latter-day Saints, 1981), 122: 4.

King determined that sufficient evidence existed to bind thirty-five over for trial. Hence, twenty-four Mormons were bound over for trial for crimes committed in Daviess County. These defendants were charged with arson, burglary, larceny, and robbery—all bailable offenses—and ordered to appear at the circuit court in Daviess County on March 28.[29] Probable cause was also found against Joseph Smith, Sidney Rigdon, Hyrum Smith, Lyman Wight, Alexander McCrae, and Caleb Baldwin on the charge of treason, a non-bailable offense. Their trial was set to begin on March 7, 1839, in Daviess County. However, because there was no jail in Daviess, King ordered the men be taken to Liberty Jail in Clay County to await their court appearance.[30] These six Mormon leaders were immediately transferred to Liberty where they arrived on December 1 to begin their confinement.[31] Finally, King ruled that there was sufficient evidence to charge five men—Pratt, Norman Shearer, Darwin Chase, Luman Gibbs, and Morris Phelps—in the death of Moses Rowland, which occurred during the attack at Crooked River. Because the charge of murder was non-bailable, these five men were ordered to remain confined in the Richmond Jail until March 11, 1839, when the circuit trial would convene there.[32]

Ebenezer Robinson reported that immediately after the Richmond hearing, eighteen Mormon defendants were transferred from the unfinished Ray County Courthouse (which had also been their place of confinement) to the Richmond Jail, which was also unfinished and still under construction, but far enough along

[29] *Document*, 150. By the time the Daviess trial was to begin, most of the defendants had left the state, thus they did not appear and the case was eventually dismissed.

[30] Ibid.; and Smith, *History of the Church*, 3:212. Joseph and Hyrum Smith, McRae, Baldwin, and Wight were all charged with the crime of treason in Daviess County, while Rigdon was charged with treason in Caldwell.

[31] For an examination of the Liberty Jail experience, see Dean C. Jessee, "'Walls, Grates, and Screeking Iron Doors': The Prison Experience of Mormon Leaders in Missouri, 1838–1839," in Davis Bitton and Maureen Ursenbach Beecher, eds., *New Views in Mormon History: A Collection of Essays in Honor of Leonard J. Arrington* (Salt Lake City: University of Utah Press, 1987), 19–42.

[32] *Document*, 150; and Smith, *History of the Church*, 3:212.

that prisoners could be housed there.[33] Robinson's figure of eighteen men indicates that eleven of the remaining twenty-nine prisoners charged by King must have posted bail immediately or were released soon after the hearing. Pratt was one of the eighteen who remained incarcerated. Initially, the jail was extremely crowded. However, most of the men were soon released on bail. As Pratt predicted, within a few days, thirteen of the prisoners secured bail and were released, leaving only the five who had participated in the Crooked River battle: Luman Gibbs (the oldest who was described by Pratt as being in his fifties), Morris Phelps (age thirty-two), Pratt (age thirty-one), Darwin Chase (age twenty-two), and the youngest, Norman B. Shearer (age seventeen).

Pratt's transfer from the unfinished vacant log house to the unfinished jail probably occurred on November 30, or possibly December 1, for he noted in letter written to his wife Mary Ann on December 1 that he had been moved to the jail. Here he would spend the next six months. In the letter to Mary Ann, Pratt explained the circumstances: "Our situation is decided for the present," he wrote. "Joseph and Sidney and 4 others have gone to Liberty where they will be kept in jail till ferther trial." Next he described the unfinished jail as "somewhat open and cold," probably due to the building not having been chinked or daubed. Fortunately, the sheriff had supplied them with plenty of food and drink and assured them he would provide them with a good stove and an ample supply of wood. Finally, Pratt requested that Mary Ann come live with him in the jail, a practice sometimes allowed in those days, depending on the character of the defendant, the severity of the crime, and the disposition of the judge, sheriff, and prison officers. "It is now at your own choice to come and spend the winter with me; or to live a lonely widow on a desolate prairiee, where you are not secured of a living, or protection," a lonely Pratt wrote. He instructed her to bring a bed, bedding, clothing, a table, plates, basins, books, pens, and paper. "You will have nothing to do but to sit down and study with me and keep your little one," he

[33] Robinson, "Items of Personal History of the Editor," 236.

reasoned, "and as oft[en] as you want to wash our clothing you can go out to some of the neibours and do our washing." He concluded by telling her: "You need not be afraid of the old jail for it is better than the hut where you now live.[34]

True to his instructions in the December 1 letter, Pratt's wife Mary Ann, in addition to a daughter also named Mary Ann, and an infant son, Nathan, came to Richmond and moved into the jail with him and the other prisoners.[35] Luman Gibbs's wife Phila was also permitted to live in the jail. She was not accompanied by any children (Luman and Phila were both in their fifties). Morris Phelps's wife Laura visited the jail regularly and on occasion stayed a few days. The couple had four young children, so Laura did not remain for any great length of time. Neither Chase nor Shearer appears to have been married. Mary Ann and the two children stayed with Pratt in the jail until March 17, 1839, a period of just over three months. She arrived sometime before December 9, 1839, because on that day both she and Pratt penned a letter to her parents, Aaron and Susannah (sometimes Susan) Frost, who were living in Bethel, Maine.

Seven letters and a legal petition that Pratt wrote during his six-month Richmond incarceration have survived. As noted, the first (dated December 1, 1838) instructed Mary Ann to bring herself and the children to the jail to board with Pratt. The second letter, also noted previously (December 9, 1838), was addressed to Mary Ann's parents. In this second letter, Pratt reported on the health conditions of the family, then rehearsed some of the persecutions acted against the Latter-day Saints by the state militia during the final stages of the Mormon War, noting his own arrest and

[34] Parley P. Pratt to Mary Ann Frost Stearns Pratt, 1 December 1838, LDS Church History Library.

[35] The daughter mentioned here was Mary Ann Stearns, born April 6, 1833, to Mary Ann Frost Stearns and her first husband, Nathan Stearns, and therefore would have been Pratt's stepdaughter. Nathan Pratt, born August 31, 1838, would have been only three months old. Pratt's oldest child, Parley P. Pratt, Jr., was born on March 25, 1837, to Pratt's first wife, Thankful Halsey, who died three hours after giving birth. Following Thankful's death, Parley, Jr., was placed in the care and keeping of a woman by the name of Allen who had lost a son. See Pratt, *Autobiography*, 182. The fact that Parley makes no mention of Parley, Jr., suggests the boy was still being taken care of by the woman.

Mary Ann Frost Stearns Pratt, Parley P. Pratt's second wife. *From Jas. T. Jakeman,* Daughters of Utah Pioneers and Their Mothers *(1915).*

imprisonment. At the time, the Frosts were not Mormons (they later converted), and Pratt was never one to be hesitant to bear his personal witness. "I feel firm In the faith of the fullness of the Gospel," he wrote. "For Me to live is Christ and to dye is gain; and I fear none but God. I have thus far kept the faith; faught the good fight And I Intend to finish my Course with Joy." Mary Ann's brief letter parallels Pratt's. She talked about her own condition and the health of her children and then expressed hope that Aaron and Susannah would embrace Mormonism. "O how I long to hear that my Father and the rest of the family have embraced the fullness of the Gospel. [D]o not reject it but Obay it, it is the work of God [and if] you do not believe it in time you will in eternity."[36]

The same day Pratt and Mary Ann wrote the letter to the Frosts, Pratt also wrote a letter to Nancy Haven Rockwood, wife

[36] Parley P. Pratt and Mary Ann Frost Pratt to Aaron and Susannah (Susan) Frost, 9 December 1838, LDS Church History Library. Mary Ann's letter appears at the end of Pratt's.

of Albert Perry Rockwood. The Rockwoods were Mormons living in Far West and were close friends of the Pratts. As noted, Mary Ann had just come from Far West to live with her husband in the jail and probably delivered the letter from Nancy. Pratt's response suggests that the persecution against the Church and the imprisonment of the Mormon leaders had shaken Nancy's faith and he sought to reassure her: "Brother Joseph is in full fellowship & the Church has more confidence in him . . . than ever before—Our troubles are sufficient to unite us firmer in the bonds of Union," he wrote. He then explained to Nancy that persecution against the Saints was a sign that the work was true, for the early Christians also suffered for Christ's sake. "The Blood of the Latterday . . . Saints is now mingled with the Blood of Former Day Saints, in cries to heave for vengeance upon an Ungodly World." Pratt ended the letter in melancholy prose:

> As dawn a long Dungeon with darkness are spread
> In silence and sorrow I made my lone bead [bed]
> Far[,] far from the scenes of confusion retired
> While hope from this bosom had almost expired.
>
> From all that is lovely constrained far to part
> From the friends of my bosom so dear to my heart
> While Jesus exulting, and friends far away
> In half broken slumbers all pensive I lay
>
> A light from Heaven on sud[den] appeared.
> And a voice as of Angels stole soft on my ear
> A theme full of Glory, inspired their tongue
> Of Zion's Redemption most sweetly they sung.[37]

One can only imagine the monotony that comes with imprisonment—passing away the time, hour upon hour, day after day, week after week. Yet in the case of Pratt, he found good use of his time. During the three months Mary Ann shared the jail with her husband, Pratt wrote the majority of the manuscript for what became the book *History of the Late Persecution Inflicted by the State of Missouri Upon the Mormons*. The officers and guards were well aware

[37] Parley P. Pratt to Nancy Haven Rockwood, 9 December 1839, Albert Perry Rockwood letter book, 30–34, LDS Church History Library.

that Pratt was drafting some sort of manuscript and assured him that whatever he had written would be confiscated. When word came that the sheriff was coming to seize the papers, Pratt and Mary Ann had already conceived a plan for her to take the writings out of the jail by attaching a pillowcase containing his papers to her underclothing. About the same time the sheriff arrived at the jail, the Pratts' six-year-old daughter was ascending the ladder to the main floor when the trap door accidently came down, injuring her head and arm. The accident created enough of a distraction that Mary Ann was able to carry the little girl outside without being searched by the guards. She then took the papers to the home of Sylvester B. Stoddard, a friend of the Pratts who lived a half mile from the jail, and left the writings with him. Fortunately, the daughter's injuries were not serious and all ended well.[38] In late August 1839, nearly two months after securing his freedom, Pratt (accompanied by his family), his brother Orson, and Hiram Clark left Nauvoo for an extended mission to Great Britain. En route, the party stopped in Detroit where Pratt made arrangements to publish the manuscript. The book appeared in print in October.[39] Pratt's letters written while he was incarcerated in Richmond include a number of poems that were later published in his book *The Millennium, and Other Poems*, printed in New York in 1840.[40]

On March 12, 1839, King Follett (age fifty-one), one of the Mormon defendants tried during the November hearings but released, was indicted by a Caldwell County grand jury for robbery. Two days later (March 14), he was put in the Richmond Jail with the other Mormon prisoners, bringing the number of inmates to six.[41] For some unknown reason, Follett was arrested a second time; this

[38] See Pratt, *History of the Late Persecution*, 66–68.

[39] See Peter Crawley, *A Descriptive Bibliography of the Mormon Church*, vol. 1 (Provo, Utah: Religious Studies Center, BYU, 1997), 90.

[40] See Parley P. Pratt, *The Millennium, and Other Poems: To Which Is Annexed a Treatise on the Regeneration and Eternal Duration of Matter* (New York: W. Molineux, 1840), 62–100.

[41] Morris Phelps, Reminiscences and Journal, typescript, item 3, 21, LDS Church History Library. Pratt stated in his autobiography that Follett was put in Richmond Jail about the middle of April (Pratt, *Autobiography*, 246). However, the fact that Phelps gives the exact date, March 14, suggests his knowledge of the facts was correct.

time he was bound over for trial. On March 17, three days after Follett was brought to the jail, Mary Ann Pratt and her children left the jail and returned to Far West to make preparations to leave the state.[42]

On March 20, 1839, three days after Mary Ann and the children left the jail, Pratt penned another letter to Mary Ann's father, Aaron Frost. In the letter he indicated that he had been sick for four weeks but had since recovered. He noted that Mary Ann and the children had spent most of the winter in jail with him but left for Quincy, Illinois, where the main body of the Church had gathered. He then expressed his hope that the Frosts would come west: "I most earnestly wish that [you] . . . would come to the west and live with us . . . [and] choose to suffer affliction with the people of God rather than enjoy the pleasures of the Gentiles." Pratt then opened his heart to his father-in-law, whom he had met only once, expressing his deep gratitude for the privilege of being married to Mary Ann. "My kindhearted and affectionate Mary endears you forever to my heart I feel assured that none but a kind and virtuous man one posses[s]ed of noble and generous principles could have reared a daughter such as your Mary proves to be." He continued: "[I have] heard her talk of all her father['s] family and how she sat upon her father[']s knees and learned to sing and how often she conversed concerning her dear tender mother and her sister Olive and all her brothers and sisters whil[e] the tear[s] stole down her cheeks." Although Mary Ann had only left him three days earlier, Pratt was already missing her terribly. She was "an angel of mercy," he wrote. "She was there to comfort me and administer to me in my sickness and blessed [me] with her presence." He concluded that with Mary Ann, his prison "was a palace of comfort" and his "hours passed swiftly away."[43]

April 12, 1839, marked the anniversary of Pratt's birth. He was thirty-two and he took the occasion of writing his beloved wife, beginning the letter with the following poem:

---

[42] See Pratt, *History of the Late Persecution*, 58.

[43] Parley P. Pratt to Aaron and Susannah Frost, 20–27 March 1839, LDS Church History Library.

This is the day that gave me birth
In Eighteen hundred seven
From worlds unseen I came to Earth
Far from my native Heav[e]n

Thirty and two long years have passed
To grief and sorrow given
And now to crown my woes at last
I am confin[e]d in prison

'Tis not for crimes that I have done
That to my foes I'm given
But to the world I am unKnown
And my reward in Heaven

What troubled scenes may yet ensue
To strew my path with sorrow
Is not for me to Know 'tis trew
I boast not of tomorrow

One thing is sure this life at best
Is like a troubled Ocean
I often wish myself at rest
From all its dire Commotions

But let its troubled bosom heave
It surges but around me
To truth—Eternal truth I cleave
Its floods will never drown me[44]

Pratt failed to finish the letter, and did not pick up the pen again until April 21, twelve days later. By this time, word had reached Richmond that Joseph and Hyrum Smith, Lyman Wight, Caleb Baldwin, and Alexander McRae had escaped. The following day, April 22, Pratt confirmed the reports. "The news is certain here, that the others prisenors are all Escapted. . . . Every Boddy seems glad they are gone. . . . No Exertions will be made to retake them."[45]

On April 22, a hearing was held before Judge Austin King at which time Darwin Chase and Norman Shearer were released,

[44] Parley P. Pratt to Mary Ann Frost Stearns Pratt, 12–22 April 1839, LDS Church History Library.

[45] Ibid.

having spent nearly five months in the Richmond Jail.[46] The two men left immediately and traveled to Far West where they were present on the occasion of the resetting of the southwest cornerstone of the Far West temple by seven members of the Twelve during the early morning hours of April 26.[47] In piecing together Pratt's narrative, it was shortly after Chase and Shearer's release, probably the last week in April, when Pratt experienced a remarkable vision of his departed first wife Thankful Halsey from whom he learned that he would eventually be released.[48]

On May 12, Pratt received a letter from Mary (dated April 26) that prompted him to send a letter in return. His words clearly reveal his loneliness and desire for her companionship: "I generally go to sleep with my thoughts draw[n] out in prair [prayer] for you and the children; and In my night visions I often See you and my little babes, but it is allways at a distance . . . which forever disappoints me in my dreams. O Mary, why do you forever fly from my visionary persuit, But nevermind, dreams are nothing; it is your own dear self, in Open day that I wish to see."[49]

The following day, May 13, Pratt wrote an outspoken letter to circuit court judge Austin A. King. In the letter, Pratt lashed out regarding the treatment and injustices he and the Mormon people had received from Missouri's citizens, the militia, the judges (including King), the state legislature, and governors Dunklin and Boggs. Pratt seemed perturbed that he and his three other prison companions were the only Mormons still incarcerated.[50] By this time, even Joseph Smith, Sidney Rigdon, and Hyrum Smith—the

[46] Pratt reported that the hearing was held on April 24. See Pratt, *History of the Late Persecution*, 58; also Pratt, *Autobiography*, 246. However, in a letter written by Laura Clark Phelps, wife of Morris Phelps, she stated she "[at]tended the Co[u]rt at richman [Richmond] April 22" (Laura Clark Phelps to John Cooper, June 1839, LDS Church History Library; see also Boone County, Missouri, Circuit Court Records, Miscellaneous, Case No. 1379, fld. 11, Ellis Library, Columbia, Missouri).

[47] See Scott G. Kenney, ed., *Wilford Woodruff's Journal, 1833–1898*, 9 vols. (Midvale, Utah: Signature Books, 1983–1984), 1:326–27.

[48] See Pratt, *Autobiography*, 261–62.

[49] Parley P. Pratt to Mary Ann Frost Stearns, 12 May 1839, LDS Church History Library.

[50] Parley P. Pratt to Austin A. King, 13 May 1839, in Pratt, *History of the Late Persecution*, 80–83.

First Presidency—were no longer in custody. Clearly, his patience with the law and the courts was growing thin. Pratt requested that he either be banished from the state or be allowed a hearing before a federal judge. Four days later (May 17), the four Mormon prisoners met personally with King, presenting him with a formal request for a change of venue because the citizens were "so much prejudiced against them . . . that they cannot have a fair and impartial trial."[51] The judge complied with their request and ordered the prisoners be taken to Columbia, Boone County, for their final hearing.[52]

Pratt's Incarceration at Columbia

On May 22, 1839, Benjamin Brown, the Ray County sheriff, and four guards chained Pratt, Phelps, Follett, and Gibbs together, two to two, loaded them into a carriage, and started for Boone County.[53] Inclement weather and swollen rivers delayed their journey, causing it to take five days to travel the 120 miles to Columbia. The party arrived in Columbia on Sunday, May 26. Four days after their arrival, Pratt wrote Mary Ann, who by this time had relocated in Quincy, Illinois. The letter contains a lengthy description of the journey from Richmond and a short description of their new surroundings. Believing this too might be a lengthy confinement, Pratt encouraged Mary to come to Columbia and live at the jail: "If I Stay here Long I shall want to see you here," he wrote. "I hardly know which I want to See most, My dear wife, My Lovely daughter, or my little babes. I Cannot ask you to part with either of them for my sake for they all need a mothers care and attention.

[51] Petition of Parley P. Pratt, Morris Phelps, and Luman Gibbs to Austin A. King, 17 May 1839, in Boone County, Missouri, Circuit Court Records, Miscellaneous, Case No. 1379, fld. 10. The petition appears to be in the handwriting of Pratt. A separate petition was prepared in the case of King Follett. See Boone County, Missouri, Circuit Court Records, Miscellaneous, Case No. 1380, fld. 20.

[52] Austin A. King, Statement, 17 May 1839, in Boone County, Missouri, Circuit Court Records, Miscellaneous, Case No. 1379, fld. 15. Austin King issued a separate statement in the case of King Follett.

[53] Pratt, *Autobiography*, 262.

But however you must act [on] your own judgement."[54] Mary Ann must have been preoccupied with trying to establish a temporary household in Quincy, as she chose to remain there.

Shortly after their arrival in Columbia, the prisoners learned that the next session of the district court was not scheduled to be held until September 23, nearly four months away. Anxious to have the date moved up, the prisoners petitioned for a special session, which was granted.[55] On June 7, Thomas Reynolds, of Howard County, and judge of Missouri's second judicial district, scheduled a special term of the court for Monday, July 1.[56] The next day, June 8, filled with optimism, Pratt wrote Mary Ann to inform her that a date had finally been set for their case to be heard, then noted the compassionate and civilized treatment exhibited to them by the jailor and the sheriff: "We are treated with every kindness here," Pratt wrote. "The Jailor boards us as well as we can ask and does every thing in his power to make us comfortable. . . . The sheriff . . . brings us new[s]papers and enquires after our comfort and the cleanliness of the prison." The local citizenry also appeared to be more well-mannered than those in northern Missouri. "We have not recieved a single Impolite word from any boddy Since we have been here," he continued. "The people in the streets always appear Civil, there is no noisy profaneity. And Such a thing as a pistol or any weapon to guard us we have never seen Since we bid farewcll to our Savage nabours of the upper Country." In the Richmond Jail, Pratt had continually feared that his writings would be confiscated by the authorities, but this was not the case in the Columbia Jail: "We

[54] Parley P. Pratt to Mary Ann Stearns Pratt, 30 May to 1 June 1838, LDS Church History Library. Pratt provided additional descriptive narratives of the journey from Richmond to Columbia in Pratt, *History of the Late Persecution*, 61–63; and Pratt, *Autobiography*, 263–64.

[55] Pratt, *History of the Late Persecution*, 65.

[56] Th. [Thomas] Reynolds, Judge of the Second Judicial Circuit, and Roger N. Todd, Clerk of the Second Judicial Court to the State of Missouri, 7–8 June 1839, in Boone County, Missouri, Circuit Court Records, Miscellaneous, Case No. 1379, fld. 10. Coincidentally, this was the same Thomas Reynolds, who the following year (1840) was elected governor of Missouri, succeeding Lilburn W. Boggs. Later, as governor, he tried on two occasions to extradite Joseph Smith from Illinois back to Missouri.

write and send out what we please, and recieve in what we please without any examination . . . [and] enjoy the Liberty to Speak and write, a privilege which relieves my full heart Like the Steem blowing from an over charged boiler. It will take a number of months at least to give full vent and exercise to the Smuthered feelings of Liberty and patriotism which have so Long Slept in my bosom."[57]

Pratt's final Missouri imprisonment letter was written from Columbia Jail on June 17 and was addressed once again to Mary Ann's parents, Aaron and Susannah Frost. The letter parallels in many ways the December 9, 1838, letter. Much of it is written in the form of testimony. "Dear friends," he began:

> I Know, and am a witness, that God has sent forth the Book of Mormon and raised up his Church, in order to gather his sheep into [one] fold that they may be prepared for his coming.—And I ferther Know that [the] modern sistems of Religion partake much of mans inventions [an]d [tr]aditions, wherein many points of the doctrine of Jesus Christ is neglected or pe[r]vorted, and those sistems will not stand the test of that coming day when nothing but truth will stand. [N]ow those who fight against this [work] fight against God And those who neglect this work, neglect the things that belong to their own enternal welf[are]. The persecutions that are [heaped] upon us are enough to prove much in our favour [a]s being the C[hristian] Church, for there is not a single sect in American who are [called] to endure the like.[58]

Pratt also clearly believed in the moving power of poetic prose and verse. As evidence of this, in his letter to the Frosts, he attached seven poems that he had written during his confinement.

Whatever optimism Pratt and the other prisoners felt during the month of June was relatively short-lived. When the court convened on July 1, a number of prosecution witnesses were present, but none of the witnesses for the defendants appeared. With no witnesses, the attorneys for the Mormons recommended that they not go ahead with the hearing at that time and requested the hearing be rescheduled for September 23, the date for the regular term

[57] Parley P. Pratt to Mary Ann Frost Stearns Pratt, 8 June 1839, LDS Church History Library.

[58] Parley P. Pratt to Aaron and Susannah Frost, 18 June 1839, LDS Church History Library.

of the court.[59] The postponement and the prospects of spending three more months in jail were too much for Pratt and his prison companions. Convinced justice was not on their side, and feeling divinely directed, Pratt, Phelps, and Follett made immediate plans to attempt a jail break. By this time, the fourth prisoner, Luman Gibbs, had turned apostate and was excluded in the get-away scheme.[60] With the help of Orson Pratt (Parley's younger brother), Laura Clark Phelps (wife of Morris Phelps), and John Wesley Clark (Laura's brother), each of whom had traveled to Columbia to be present for the July 1 court hearing, plans were put into place for an escape on July 4.

Thursday, July 4, 1839, marked the sixty-third anniversary of America's independence, and the Mormon prisoners commemorated the event with their own expectation of deliverance. The day previous, with the help of Orson and John, the prisoners secured a few items to make a "Liberty flag," which they proudly hung from one of the jail's windows. Little did the citizens of Boone County realize that the Mormons were proclaiming that this day would be their own day of liberty.

As evening approached, final preparations were put in place for the escape. Orson and John had saddled three horses and secluded them in a thicket located about a half mile from the jail where they awaited the arrival of the escapees. Near sunset, when the jailor, John Martin, came with the evening victuals, after unlocking the main jail door to pass the coffee pot through, King Follett flung the door open, Morris Phelps grabbed hold of Martin, and the escape was on. All three men made a sprint to the thicket. Unfortunately Follett, who was the oldest and probably the slowest of the three, was recaptured almost immediately, but Pratt and Phelps were successful in mounting the horses and getting away. After six adventuresome days and several close calls, both

[59] Phelps, Reminiscences and Journal, 3.

[60] Concerning Gibbs's disaffection, Pratt reported that he turned apostate, "denied the faith and turned traitor . . . in order to save his life and gain his liberty . . . [and was] kept in prison . . . [to] spy upon us" (Pratt, *Autobiography*, 257).

men made their way independent of each other to Quincy, Illinois, where they were reunited with family and friends.[61] Follett remained in the Columbia Jail until September 25, 1839, when his case was heard and he was acquitted and released.[62] The apostate, Luman Gibbs, remained incarcerated until November 4, 1839.[63]

Conclusion

Parley P. Pratt believed the charges issued against him by Missouri's authorities were not because of any illegal activity on his part but centered on religious persecution, therefore any criminal allegations against him were unwarranted. Believing he was innocent, he also felt justice would be on his side and he would eventually be acquitted in the courts. However, after several failed attempts to obtain an impartial hearing, Pratt felt justified in securing his personal freedom by flight rather than submitting to what he believed was an inequitable justice system.

No attempt was ever made by Missouri authorities to extradite the two escapees, Pratt and Phelps, from Illinois, although a Missouri court document shows that papers were filed on October 6, 1839, in Boone County to have the two men appear before the Adams County, Illinois, circuit court. It appears likely that the papers were never even executed. That Follett was acquitted and Gibbs was subsequently released suggests that by late 1839, Missouri officials were content to drop everything in connection with charges made against Pratt and the others.

[61] For Pratt's account of the flight to freedom see Pratt, *Autobiography*, 271–310. He also provided a less detailed account in a letter to his in-laws. See Parley P. Pratt to Aaron and Susannah Frost, 21 July 1839, LDS Church History Library. For Phelps's account, see Phelps, Reminiscences and Journal, 5–11.

[62] See Boone County, Missouri, Circuit Court Records, Miscellaneous, Case No. 1380, fld. 21.

[63] Ibid., 15.

Parley P. Pratt's Missouri Imprisonment Letters and Documents

Date	*Document*	*Written From*	*Addressed To*	*Document Location*
November 4, 1838	Letter	Independence (vacant log house)	Mary Ann Frost Stearns Pratt	LDS Church History Library
November 5, 1838	Card	Independence (vacant log house)	To the Citizens of Jackson County *Note:* The document was co-signed by Joseph Smith, Hyrum Smith, Amasa Lyman, George W. Robinson, Lyman Wight, and Sidney Rigdon.	Printed in the *Boonslick Democrat* (Fayette, Missouri), November 10, 1838; reprinted in the *Ohio Statesman* (Columbus), November 28, 1838
December 1, 1838	Letter	Richmond Jail	Mary Ann Frost Stearns Pratt	LDS Church History Library
December 9, 1838	Letter	Richmond Jail	Aaron and Susannah (Susan) Frost *Note:* The letter also includes a letter by Mary Ann Frost Stearns Pratt to her parents Aaron and Susannah Frost.	LDS Church History Library
December 9, 1838	Letter	Richmond Jail	Nancy Haven Rockwood	LDS Church History Library

Date	*Document*	*Written From*	*Addressed To*	*Document Location*
March 20–27, 1839	Letter	Richmond Jail	Aaron and Susannah (Susan) Frost	LDS Church History Library
April 12–22, 1839	Letter	Richmond Jail	Mary Ann Frost Stearns Pratt	LDS Church History Library
May 12, 1839	Letter	Richmond Jail	Mary Ann Frost Stearns Pratt	LDS Church History Library
May 13, 1839	Letter	Richmond Jail	Austin A. King	Printed in Pratt, *History of the Late Persecution*, 80–83; and Pratt, *Autobiography of Parley P. Pratt*, 197–99
May 17, 1839	Petition	Richmond Jail	Austin A. King *Note:* The petition includes the names of Parley P. Pratt, Morris Phelps, and Luman Gibbs and appears to be in the handwriting of Pratt.	Boone County, Missouri, Circuit Court Records, Miscellaneous, Case No. 1379, fld. 10, Ellis Library, Columbia, Missouri
May 30 to June 1, 1839	Letter	Columbia Jail	Mary Ann Frost Stearns Pratt	LDS Church History Library
June 8, 1839	Letter	Columbia Jail	Mary Ann Frost Stearns Pratt	LDS Church History Library
June 17, 1839	Letter	Columbia Jail	Aaron and Susanna (Susan) Frost	LDS Church History Library

CHAPTER 5

"We Glory in Tribulations"

Parley P. Pratt, Martyrology, and the Memory of Persecution

David W. Grua

Parley Parker Pratt celebrated his thirty-second birthday in a Missouri prison on April 12, 1839, by writing a poem to his wife Mary Ann Frost. In the poem he remarked:

> What troubled scenes may yet ensue
> To strew my path with sorrow,
> Is not for me to know 'tis true,
> I boast not of to-morrow.
>
> One thing is sure, this life at best
> Is like a troubled ocean;
> I often wish myself at rest
> From all its dire commotions.[1]

Pratt's reflections in prison came at perhaps the nadir of his sojourn in Missouri during the 1830s, an experience he would later describe

---

This essay is an outgrowth of the author's "Memoirs of the Persecuted: Persecution, Memory, and the West as a Mormon Refuge" (master's thesis, Brigham Young University [hereafter BYU], 2008).

[1] "Birthday in Prison," in Parley P. Pratt, *The Millennium, and Other Poems: To Which Is Annexed a Treatise on the Regeneration and Eternal Duration of Matter* (New York: W. Molineux, 1840), 71; see also Parley P. Pratt to Mary Ann Frost Pratt, 12 April 1839, Parley P. Pratt Collection, L. Tom Perry Special Collections, BYU, Provo, Utah.

as an "awful tale of woe and suffering."[2] During the decade, Pratt and other members of the Church of Jesus Christ of Latter-day Saints were expelled from three Missouri counties, leaving behind a great deal of property and perhaps forty Latter-day Saints who had been killed in the clashes.

For much of Christian history, religious persecution was a state-sponsored affair. Roman officials tried and executed early Christians, and European magistrates arrested, tortured, and killed those accused of divergent religious beliefs in early modern Europe.[3] In response, Christians from the New Testament times developed martyrological rhetoric to define themselves in opposition to their oppressors. With the exception of Massachusetts officials who executed Quakers for their religion in seventeenth-century Massachusetts, early America by contrast was characterized by a remarkable absence of state-backed religious violence.[4] Despite lacking officially condemned martyrs, early Americans were adept at using the language of martyrdom and persecution to describe their own sufferings, from captivity narratives to political combatants. American Protestants used martyr tales from Europe such as those published in John Foxe's *Book of Martyrs* to promote devotion and form identities as God's people.[5] In Susan Juster's words, "the image of the martyr continued to exert a powerful pull on the colonial mind."[6] This fascination with martyrdom among

[2] Parley P. Pratt, *The Autobiography of Parley Parker Pratt, One of the Twelve Apostles of the Church of Jesus Christ of Latter-day Saints, Embracing His Life, Ministry, and Travels, with Extracts, in Prose and Verse, from His Miscellaneous Writings*, ed. Parley P. Pratt, Jr. (New York: Russell Brothers, 1874), 322.

[3] See Elizabeth A. Castelli, *Martyrdom and Memory: Early Christian Culture Making* (New York: Columbia University Press, 2004); and Brad S. Gregory, *Salvation at Stake: Christian Martyrdom in Early Modern Europe* (Cambridge, Mass: Harvard University Press, 1999).

[4] Jonathan M. Chu, *Neighbors, Friends, or Madmen: The Puritan Adjustment to Quakerism in Seventeenth-Century Massachusetts Bay* (Westport, Conn.: Greenwood Press, 1985).

[5] Stephen Cattley, ed., *The Acts and Monuments of John Foxe*, 8 vols. (London: R. B. Seeley and W. Burnside, 1837–1841).

[6] Susan Juster, "What's 'Sacred' about Violence in Early America?" *Common-Place* 6, no. 1 (October 2005), http://common-place.org/vol-06/no-01/juster/, accessed June 18, 2008.

Americans continued during the early years of the republic and the antebellum period. Abolitionists, itinerant missionaries, and Latter-day Saints such as Pratt articulated their own sufferings through martyrological imagery.[7]

Despite the prevalence of martyrological themes in early Mormon thought, there is a paucity of scholarly literature on the subject. Historian R. Laurence Moore argues that Latter-day Saints remembered persecution to create a sense of difference and apartness from other Americans and to form their identity as outsiders in the American religious landscape.[8] In addition, Kenneth Winn has argued persuasively that early Mormons utilized republican discourses to describe their persecutions as a means to claim Americanness and seek redress for losses suffered in Missouri and Illinois.[9]

Throughout the nineteenth century, and to a lesser degree during the twentieth and twenty-first centuries, Latter-day Saints have fashioned their identities as a persecuted people, basing their self-understanding on the collective memory of persecutions suffered in Missouri and Illinois. By using the language of martyrology, marginalized Mormons recast their experience in the United States during the 1830s and 1840s not as a series of failures and setbacks but rather as triumphs. For Latter-day Saints, remembering their sufferings in martyrological terms was not simply a means to construct themselves as outsiders or to seek sympathy and redress

[7] On John Brown presenting himself as a Christian martyr, see Richard Slotkin, *The Fatal Environment: The Myth of the Frontier in the Age of Industrialization, 1800–1890*, paperback edition (1985; Norman: University of Oklahoma Press, 1994), 276. On itinerant Nancy Towle's use of martyrology, see Nancy Towle, *Vicissitudes Illustrated: In the Experience of Nancy Towle, in Europe and America* (Charleston, S.C.: James L. Burges, 1832), 198–99. I am indebted to Samuel Brown for the latter reference.

[8] R. Laurence Moore, *Religious Outsiders and the Making of Americans* (New York: Oxford University Press, 1986), 34, 35. For a study of rhetorical forms employed by Mormon orators Sidney Rigdon, Joseph Smith, and Brigham Young in persecution narratives, see also Zachary L. Largey, "The Rhetoric of Persecution: Mormon Crisis Rhetoric from 1838–1871" (master's thesis, BYU, 2006). Largey's thesis, while useful, is limited due to the lack of emphasis on how Mormons used these rhetorical forms in constructing identity and difference from others.

[9] Kenneth H. Winn, *Exiles in a Land of Liberty: Mormons in America, 1830–1844* (Chapel Hill: University of North Carolina Press, 1989).

but also to exercise ideological resistance against their opponents.[10] Early Mormons lacked access to legal power structures that could be used to punish their enemies and obtain restitution for losses. Therefore, Latter-day Saints used memory as a site of resistance to challenge narratives that portrayed the Mormons as religious fanatics who deserved their fate. Latter-day Saints thus sought to influence how their readers remembered and understood the persecutions in Missouri and Illinois in an effort to control not only the past but also the present and future.

Beginning in the 1830s, Pratt produced a tremendous amount of literature describing his people's persecutions. He wrote for his fellow religionists as well as to inform other Americans of the Mormon plight and seek redress.[11] Of the hundreds of pages of his prose, among the most significant included his first published writing, the February 1834 extra of the Mormon newspaper *The Evening and the Morning Star*, entitled "'Mormons,' So Called," which is perhaps the most comprehensive description of the 1833–34 Jackson County expulsion.[12] Pratt included this extra as part of his eighty-four-page history of the Missouri persecutions that he published in 1839, which became a principal document in the creation of the Mormon memory of persecution.[13] In turn, this history later formed the basis of parts of Pratt's autobiography written in the mid-1850s.[14] Beyond his narrative contributions, Pratt also wrote several poems describing his people's sufferings that he published in 1840 in *The Millennium, and Other Poems.* Indeed, persecution and the memory of suffering ran through many of Pratt's writings

[10] See Castelli, *Martyrdom and Memory*, 25.

[11] For example, in his *History of the Late Persecution*, Pratt wrote: "Awake, O Americans—Arise, O sons and daughters of freedom, restore a persecuted and injured people to their rights as citizens of a free Republic. Down with tyranny and oppression, and rescue your liberties from the brink of ruin" (Parley P. Pratt, *History of the Late Persecution Inflicted by the State of Missouri upon the Mormons, in Which Ten Thousand American Citizens Were Robbed, Plundered, and Driven from the State, and Many Others Murdered, Martyred, &c. for Their Religion, and All This by Military Force, by Order of the Executive* [Detroit: Dawson and Bates, Printers, 1839], 69).

[12] Parley P. Pratt and others, "'Mormons,' So Called," Extra, *The Evening and the Morning Star*, February 1834.

[13] Pratt, *History of the Late Persecution.*

[14] Pratt, *Autobiography.*

throughout his life and career.[15] Kenneth Winn has described Pratt as the leading Mormon commentator on the persecutions.[16]

Indeed, no other Mormon author during Pratt's lifetime could claim a comparable corpus of writings on the persecutions. Sidney Rigdon wrote a descriptive pamphlet in 1840 that coincidentally also contained eighty-four pages, but he wrote little else on the subject.[17] In terms of poetry describing the persecutions, Eliza R. Snow was the only Latter-day Saint who rivaled Pratt's production.[18] Assessing Pratt's literary output and comparing it to others is a simple task, but understanding how his contemporaries read, interpreted, and used his writings is more difficult. Information concerning the circulation of Pratt's writings is limited, and it was not uncommon for writers at the time to "borrow" the writings of others without acknowledging their debt, making it difficult to determine Pratt's direct influence on other authors.[19] Nevertheless, some clues exist as to how ordinary Mormons and non-Mormons perceived Pratt's work. Printers thought enough of Pratt's

---

[15] Pratt, *The Millennium, and Other Poems.*

[16] Winn, *Exiles in a Land of Liberty*, 147.

[17] Sidney Rigdon, *An Appeal to the American People: Being an Account of the Persecutions of the Church of Latter Day Saints; and the Barbarities Inflicted on Them by the Inhabitants of the State of Missouri* (Cincinnati: Glezen and Shephard, 1840). John P. Greene published a forty-three-page compilation of documents on Missouri (John P. Greene, *Facts Relative to the Expulsion of the Mormons or Latter Day Saints, from the State of Missouri, Under the "Exterminating Order"* [Cincinnati: R.P. Brooks, 1839]). Hundreds of Latter-day Saints wrote short redress petitions that were presented to Congress on multiple occasions during the 1840s. Most of these petitions were transcribed and published in Clark V. Johnson, ed., *Mormon Redress Petitions: Documents of the 1833–1838 Missouri Conflict* (Provo, Utah: Religious Studies Center, 1992). The *Times and Seasons* throughout the 1840s also published dozens of short persecution narratives and poems by different authors. In terms of total pages, the only publication that compares to Pratt's output was the serialized "History of Joseph Smith," a multiauthor hybrid autobiography/biography of the prophet published in the *Times and Seasons*, *Deseret News*, and *Latter-day Saints' Millennial Star* (see Howard C. Searle, "Early Mormon Historiography: Writing the History of the Mormons, 1830–1858" [Ph.D. diss., University of California–Los Angeles, 1979]).

[18] Many of Snow's poems describing persecution were published in *Poems, Religious, Historical, and Political*, vol. 1 (Liverpool, England: F.D. Richards, 1856).

[19] See Peter Crawley, *A Descriptive Bibliography of the Mormon Church, 1830–1847* (Provo, Utah: Brigham Young University Press, 1997), 42–43, 89–90, 98–100; and Crawley's foreword to *The Essential Parley P. Pratt* (Salt Lake City: Signature Books, 1990), xx–xxiii.

1839 history to reprint it two additional times in 1840;[20] the editors of the *Times and Seasons* found it worthwhile to not only advertise the work but also reprint portions of it and print several of Pratt's poems;[21] Mormon John Pulsipher felt justified in "borrowing" one

[20] Parley P. Pratt, *Late Persecution of the Church of Jesus Christ, of Latter Day Saints: Ten Thousand American Citizens Robbed, Plundered, and Banished; Others Imprisoned, and Others Martyred for Their Religion. With a Sketch of Their Rise, Progress and Doctrine* (New York: J. W. Harrison, 1840) reproduced the original pamphlet with few revisions but with the additions of a new historical and doctrinal introduction and several historical documents and newspaper clippings. Parley P. Pratt, *History of the Late Persecution Inflicted by the State of Missouri upon the Mormons, in Which Ten Thousand American Citizens Were Robbed, Plundered, and Driven from the State, and Many Others Murdered, Martyred, &c. for Their Religion, and All This by Military Force, by Order of the Executive* (Mexico, N.Y.: Oswego County Democrat, 1840) reproduced the original pamphlet with few if any revisions or additions.

[21] The editors of the *Times and Seasons* described the Pratt's history upon receipt in late 1839 or early 1840, providing some clue of its reception history:

> We have received a copy of the history of the late persecution in Missouri, written by P.P. Pratt, while imprisoned in that State; published at Detroit, Michigan. It contains 84 pages written in a concise and comprehensive manner; beginning with the outrages of Jackson county, he exhibits the most conspicuous characters, in their unhallowed conduct from that time, until the whole society of the saints were driven from the State. It contains an account of his miraculous escape from prison, also the escape of Elder Morris Phelps, at the same time. We could say much in favor of the style and boldness of the writer, but this is not our object; the plain unvarnished statement of facts, which can be demonstrated by thousands; is what pleases us, though it's but a small pamphlet, yet we would that all ears were made to hear it, and that every true Republican would awake from the slumber that has so long pervaded this Republic, and no longer suffer innocence to groan under the lash of murderers and tyrants, and would raise the standard of "equal rights," and bring to condign punishment, those that have trampled with impunity upon our wholesome constitution, and made laws and Justice a mere *by-word*. ("New Years Address," *Times and Seasons* [January 1840], 43)

For the advertisement, see "Books! Books! Books!" *Times and Seasons* (2 August 1841): 502. For the reprinted excerpts of Pratt's narrative describing the 1838 persecutions, see "A History, of the Persecution, of the Church of Jesus Christ, of Latter Day Saints in Missouri," *Times and Seasons* (April 1840): 81–82; and "A History, of the Persecution, of the Church of Jesus Christ, of Latter Day Saints in Missouri," *Times and Seasons* (June 1840): 113–16. For his poems that appeared in the *Times and Seasons*, see Parley P. Pratt, "Pratt's Defense," *Times and Seasons* (January 1840): 48; Parley P. Pratt, "Zion in Captivity: A Lamentation," *Times and Seasons* (February 1840): 64; and Parley P. Pratt, "Cry of the Martyrs," *Times and Seasons* (2 September 1844): 639.

of Pratt's poems and claiming it as his own;[22] and at least one non-Mormon, government surveyor, John Gunnison, relied on Pratt to reconstruct "a picture of horrors and inhumanity toward his people which would surpass our belief."[23] As a producer of the Mormon memory of persecution, Pratt therefore spoke to themes that printers and writers believed would appeal to readers.[24]

Historical Summary

Before analyzing Pratt's use of memory, it will be useful to provide an overview of anti-Mormon persecutions in Missouri and Illinois.[25] Latter-day Saints began settling in northwestern Missouri in the early 1830s, primarily in Jackson County. Although relations with non-Mormons were at first friendly, by the winter of 1833–34 vigilantes demanded that the Latter-day Saints leave the county. There were multiple causes of the friction. The rapid increase in the Mormon population led many to assume that the Latter-day Saints would gain political and economic control of the county. Anti-Mormons also complained of the poverty of the Latter-day Saints and accused the Mormons of thievery. Missourians filtered these fears through the frame of fanaticism, constructing the new religious group as deluded, un-republican, and, like American Indians and African Americans, outside the bounds of citizenship.

[22] On his twenty-first birthday, Pulsipher adapted Pratt's poem "Birthday in Prison," quoted in part at the opening of this chapter. Not knowing the true origin of the poem, Wallace Stegner opined that Pulsipher's "jingle is a compendium of Mormon self-righteousness and long-suffering expressed in ladies' magazine clichés" (Wallace Stegner, *The Gathering of Zion: The Story of the Mormon Trail* [1964; Lincoln: University of Nebraska Press, 1992], 200–201). For the text of the poem, with insertions and deletions, see http:// juvenileinstructor.org/parley-p-pratt-writing-and-the-history-of-reading/#comment-9778, comment 1, accessed June 1, 2010. See Pratt, "Birthday in Prison," *The Millennium, and Other Poems*, 70–71.

[23] J.W. Gunnison, *The Mormons, or Latter-Day Saints, in the Valley of the Great Salt Lake: A History of Their Rise and Progress, Peculiar Doctrines, Present Condition, and Prospects, Derived from Personal Observation, During a Residence Among Them*, ed. Robert Kent Fielding (1852; Brookline, Mass.: Paradigm Publications, 1993), 110.

[24] On the role of producers in the construction of myths, see Slotkin, *The Fatal Environment*, 26–32.

[25] For additional context, see Alex Baugh's essay in this volume (chapter 4).

By late 1833, Pratt and a thousand Mormon residents from Jackson County were expelled, and the Latter-day Saints resettled in adjoining Clay County from 1833 to 1836.[26] Non-Mormon residents in Clay County expressed many of the same concerns as the Jackson County vigilantes, though they generally opposed the violent removal of the Latter-day Saints.

In 1836, the Missouri legislature created Caldwell County in northern Missouri as a place for Latter-day Saints to settle in semi-isolation.[27] Within a few years, however, anti-Mormon vigilantes threatened to expel Latter-day Saint settlers from Caldwell and surrounding counties. As with the Jackson County expulsion, various causes spurred the conflict. Some of these paralleled reasons for the earlier violence, including rapid population growth and non-Mormon perceptions of Latter-day Saints as fanatics. In addition, in June 1838 some Mormons formed the Danites, an ultra-loyalist vigilante group dedicated to stopping internal dissent and opposing external persecution, which further aroused non-Mormon suspicions. Also, remembering the 1833 violent expulsion from Jackson County, the Latter-day Saints declared they would resist future persecutions.[28] In August and September 1838, Mormon and anti-Mormon vigilantes both committed scattered acts of violence, culminating in a Mormon raid of Daviess County in October 1838 that resulted in the sacking and burning of several buildings and the theft of non-Mormon property as war appropriations.[29]

---

[26] Warren A. Jennings, "Zion Is Fled: The Expulsion of the Mormons from Jackson County, Missouri" (Ph.D. diss., University of Florida, 1962); and J. Spencer Fluhman, "Anti-Mormonism and the Making of Religion in Antebellum America" (Ph.D. diss., University of Wisconsin–Madison, 2006).

[27] Max H. Parkin, "A History of the Latter-day Saints in Clay County, Missouri, from 1833 to 1837" (Ph.D. diss., BYU, 1976); and Stephen C. LeSueur, "Missouri's Failed Compromise: The Creation of Caldwell County for the Mormons," *Journal of Mormon History* 31, no. 3 (Fall 2005): 113–44.

[28] Stephen C. LeSueur, *The 1838 Mormon War in Missouri* (Columbia: University of Missouri Press, 1987), 28–53.

[29] Ibid., 54–130; and Alexander L. Baugh, *A Call to Arms: The 1838 Mormon Defense of Northern Missouri* (Provo, Utah: Joseph Fielding Smith Institute for Latter-day Saint History and *BYU Studies*, BYU, 2000), 47–98.

On October 25, Pratt joined Mormon forces acting as a unit of the state militia in an effort to liberate three captured Mormon scouts by engaging non-Mormon militiamen at Crooked River near the Caldwell and Ray County border. Although the Latter-day Saints routed the Missourians, anti-Mormons killed three Mormons, including Apostle David W. Patten, while one Missourian died.[30] Rumors that the Mormons had massacred the militia led Missouri governor Lilburn W. Boggs to issue an order authorizing his militia commanders to exterminate or drive the Mormons from Missouri.[31] While the state militia marched to Far West in Caldwell County, rogue Missouri militiamen attacked the Mormons at Haun's Mill, killing seventeen Mormon men and boys, apparently to avenge earlier Mormon depredations in Daviess County.[32] On November 1, reports of the massacre reached Joseph Smith, convincing him to surrender to the governor's militia force at Far West.[33] During November 1838, the state charged Smith and other Mormon leaders with treason and other crimes, while Pratt was charged with murder for his participation in the Battle at Crooked River.[34] Meanwhile, the main body of perhaps eight thousand Latter-day Saints made preparations to leave the state for Illinois.[35] From November 1838 until July 1839, Pratt was incarcerated in various Missouri prisons. On July 4, Pratt celebrated the national holiday by escaping from his Missouri prison and fleeing to Nauvoo, Illinois, where he joined a burgeoning Mormon population.

---

[30] Baugh, *A Call to Arms*, 99–114; and LeSueur, *The 1838 Mormon War*, 131–42.

[31] LeSueur, *The 1838 Mormon War*, 143–53.

[32] Baugh, *A Call to Arms*, 115–34; and LeSueur, *The 1838 Mormon War*, 162–68.

[33] Baugh, *A Call to Arms*, 135–70; and LeSueur, *The 1838 Mormon War*, 161–79.

[34] *Document Containing the Correspondence, Orders, &c., In Relation to the Disturbances with the Mormons; and the Evidence Given Before the Hon. Austin A. King, Judge of the Fifth Judicial Circuit of the State of Missouri, at the Court-House in Richmond, in a Criminal Court of Inquiry, Begun November 12, 1838, on the Trial of Joseph Smith, Jr., and Others for High Treason and Other Crimes Against the State* (Fayette, Mo.: *Boonslick Democrat*, Printer, 1841), 150 (hereafter *Document*). See also Gordon A. Madsen, "Joseph Smith and the Missouri Court of Inquiry: Austin A. King's Quest for Hostages," *BYU Studies* 23, no. 4 (2004): 92–136.

[35] William J. Hartley, "'Almost Too Intolerable a Burthen': The Winter Exodus from Missouri, 1838–39," *Journal of Mormon History* 18 (Fall 1992): 6–40.

Nauvoo grew to be a city of over ten thousand inhabitants. As in Missouri, tensions with non-Mormons accompanied growth. Not only were non-Mormons suspicious of the Mormons' expanding economic and political power, they were also alarmed by the militarism exhibited by the Mormon militia, known as the Nauvoo Legion. Rumors ran rampant in the surrounding areas that Mormons were practicing polygamy, which Smith had secretly introduced among his most trusted followers including Pratt in the early 1840s. Internal dissent led Smith, acting as mayor of the city, to order the suppression of a dissident newspaper in 1844 and to institute martial law in Nauvoo, resulting in his incarceration on charges of riot and treason. Before Smith's case came to trial, anti-Mormon vigilantes from Illinois and Missouri murdered him while he was in prison.[36] Pratt immediately returned to Nauvoo from a mission in the eastern states to mourn with the Latter-day Saints.[37] In the confusion following Smith's death, Pratt supported Brigham Young as Smith's successor.[38] Young, facing continued threats of violence, decided to move the Latter-day Saints out of the United States and into the West.[39]

Mormons: Deluded Fanatics or Weak and Designing Knaves

Pratt's martyrology and memory of persecution subverted and contested the narratives that Missourians and Illinoisans used to explain and rationalize the violence perpetrated against the Mormons. While not all of his writings were direct responses to his tormentors, he did rebut explicitly accusations made by vigilantes

[36] See Robert Bruce Flanders, *Nauvoo: Kingdom on the Mississippi* (Urbana: University of Illinois Press, 1965) and Glen M. Leonard, *Nauvoo: A Place of Peace, A People of Promise* (Salt Lake City and Provo, Utah: Deseret Book and Brigham Young University Press, 2002).

[37] Pratt, *Autobiography*, 370–73.

[38] D. Michael Quinn, "The Mormon Succession Crisis of 1844," BYU *Studies* 16 (Winter 1979): 187–233.

[39] Richard E. Bennett, *We'll Find the Place: The Mormon Exodus 1846–1848* (Salt Lake City: Deseret Book, 1997).

and government officials in Jackson County as well as in northern Missouri. Jackson County vigilantes articulated the points of contention between themselves and the Latter-day Saints by calling the Mormons "fanatics or knaves (for one or the other they undoubtedly are)," justifying their vigilante activities by portraying Mormons as either deluded fanatics or thieves and criminals, or both.[40]

As Spencer Fluhman has argued, antebellum Protestants denied that Mormonism (along with Islam and other marginalized religions) was, by proper sensibilities, a religion. This strategy allowed Protestants to discursively organize the American religious landscape with themselves at the center and all other groups outside of the boundaries of authentic religion. Persecution of these groups was not seen as evidence that God was with them (as He was with the early Christians and early modern martyrs), for they were not part of God's people.[41] For instance, in an 1833 declaration, the Jackson County vigilantes described Mormons as adhering to a "pretended religious sect."[42] The authors of the declaration justified their forcible removal of the Mormons from the county by arguing that they were beset by a host of evils stemming from Mormon settlements in the county. These evils included Mormon beliefs in continuing revelations, healing the sick, replicating the miracles performed by the apostles and prophets of old, speaking in tongues, and openly declaring that God had given them Jackson County.[43]

Allegations of religious fanaticism again surfaced in Missourian explanations for prosecuting and imprisoning Smith and other

---

[40] Pratt, *History of the Late Persecution Inflicted by the State of Missouri upon the Mormons, in Which Ten Thousand American Citizens Were Robbed, Plundered, and Driven from the State, and Many Others Murdered, Martyred, &c. for Their Religion, and All This by Military Force, by Order of the Executive* (Detroit: Dawson and Bates, Printers, 1839), 7.

[41] Fluhman, "Anti-Mormonism and the Making of Religion," 2, 6–9. For more on the use of fanaticism to explain divergent religions, see Ann Taves, *Fits, Trances, and Visions: Experiencing Religion and Explaining Religion from Wesley to James* (Princeton: Princeton University Press, 1999).

[42] Pratt, *History of the Late Persecution*, 7.

[43] Ibid., 8–9.

Mormon leaders during the November 1838 hearing. The prosecuting attorney pointed to the fanaticism of the Latter-day Saints in presenting evidence of religious deviance in his argument that Mormon leaders were guilty of treason against the state of Missouri. In Pratt's portrayal of the hearing, he described the inquiries by the state into Mormon interpretations of the seventh chapter of the book of Daniel thusly: "Our Church organization was converted by such testimony into a temporal kingdom, which was to fill the whole earth and subdue all other kingdoms. This Court of Inquisition inquired diligently into our belief of the seventh chapter of Daniel concerning the kingdom of God, which should subdue all other kingdoms and stand forever." Judge Austin A. King responded to the testimony by instructing his clerk to record the evidence as a "'strong point for treason.'"[44] Pratt also described the court's interest in the Church's international proselytizing missions, concluding that along with the Mormon interpretation of the Bible, there were sufficient grounds to charge the Latter-day Saint leaders with treason.[45]

Additionally, Pratt summarized Missourian charges against the Latter-day Saints of being knaves. Claiming that most Latter-day Saints had entered the county with little or no property, the vigilantes suspected that these individuals had only attached themselves to "the Mormon car" because they had nothing to lose, either in heaven or earth, by converting. Likewise, the vigilantes charged that Mormon leaders, if they had not embraced the religion, would be convicted criminals. The vigilantes also accused the Mormons of encouraging rebellion among the local slave population and of inviting free blacks to the territory (which was illegal).[46] Likewise, the state presented allegations in the November 1838 hearing that the Mormons had committed treason, murder, and other crimes.[47]

Pratt challenged these allegations, arguing that the Latter-day Saints were neither fanatics nor knaves and therefore had been

[44] Pratt, *Autobiography*, 230.

[45] Ibid., 231.

[46] Pratt, *History of the Late Persecution*, 9.

[47] Pratt, *Autobiography*, 233.

expelled from their homes unlawfully. To the charges that the Mormons were fanatics because they believed they were replicating New Testament religion, Pratt rhetorically asked: "I would enquire whether our belief as set forth in this declaration, as to gifts, miracles, Revelations, and tongues, is not the same that all the Apostles and disciples taught, believed and practiced, and the doctrine of the New Testament?" Further, he queried: "I would enquire when the New Testament religion ceased, and a law revealed or instituted, which made blaspheme of the belief and practise of it? or what holy religion the Jackson mob was speaking of, which was thrown into contempt by the revival of the New Testament religion?"[48] In so doing, Pratt reversed the Missourian narrative by placing Mormonism as the true embodiment of authentic religion and heir to primitive Christianity and recasting the Protestantism of the Jackson County vigilantes as inauthentic. Pratt likewise challenged the allegations proffered by the state in the November 1838 hearing by describing the proceedings as "a mock Court of Inquiry" and a "Court of Inquisition," invoking an image of the horrors and injustices of the Spanish Inquisition, thereby invalidating the proceedings and the charges against Mormon leaders.[49]

To the charges that the Mormons were impoverished criminals, Pratt again turned the accusations around and recast the image of the Latter-day Saints in relation to the Missourians. He asked if the vigilantes had "never read in the New Testament that God had chosen the poor of this world, rich in faith, and heirs of the Kingdom of God? And when did poverty become a crime known to law?"[50] The Saints' poverty therefore became a sign of their chosenness before God. Pratt further denied that any Latter-day Saint had broken the law by tampering with the slave population or inviting free blacks to the state, and he challenged the vigilantes to find in the records of the Jackson County Circuit Court any indictments that named a Mormon as a defendant.[51] To the

[48] Pratt, *History of the Late Persecution*, 10.
[49] Pratt, *Autobiography*, 230.
[50] Pratt, *History of the Late Persecution*, 10.
[51] Ibid., 10–11.

charges presented in the November 1838 hearing that he had committed murder, Pratt insisted repeatedly that he was being prosecuted for defending himself against the mob. To his father-in-law, Pratt wrote from prison that he and his fellow prisoners were "to be tried for the crime of self-defense when attacked by a band of mobbers."[52] Therefore, as he had contested the Missourian allegations that his religion gave the vigilantes just cause to remove the Latter-day Saints from their homes, he reversed accusations that his people were poor and consisted of criminals.

Persecuted for the Cause of Christ

Pratt and other Mormon authors were determined not to lose the battle over how the atrocities against their people were to be remembered and understood by the American public as well as by the Mormon people. In contrast to anti-Mormon narratives that portrayed the Latter-day Saints as dangerous fanatics or criminals and the persecutions as evidence that God was not with them, Pratt argued that his people had been persecuted *because* God was with them and that they suffered for the cause of Christ. In this manner, Pratt drew upon martyrological discourse to construct his narratives of persecution and in doing so challenged alternative understandings of why the Latter-day Saints had suffered their fate.

Pratt believed that the Latter-day Saints had been persecuted not only for their testimonies of Christ but also for being adherents of God's true church on the earth. He used the persecutions to certify the truth of the new church, concluding his 1839 *History of the Late Persecution* by stating: "I now bear witness to small and great, that the system of religion for which we are persecuted, is true; and that God has committed unto us a dispensation of the Gospel in its fulness."[53] It was a privilege for the Latter-day Saints

[52] Parley P. Pratt to Aaron Frost, 17 June 1839, Pratt Collection, L. Tom Perry Special Collections. See also Pratt, *History of the Late Persecution*, 55; and Pratt, *Autobiography*, 214–15, 233.

[53] Pratt, *History of the Late Persecution*, 79.

to suffer persecution "for the sake of laying the foundation of the kingdom of God."[54] Rather than agreeing with his ideological opponents that claimed that Mormon suffering was proof of folly, Pratt interpreted his anguish as evidence that his ministry was indeed of God.

Not only was it a privilege to be persecuted, but some Latter-day Saints were also called to lay down their lives as martyrs in the work of God. While in his Missouri prison, Pratt related to his father-in-law Aaron Frost that "some 30 of the Saints died[,] were murdered, or martyred for their religion."[55] He explained in his 1839 history that David W. Patten, killed at the Battle of Crooked River with two others, "died that evening in the triumphs of faith: having laid down his life as a martyr in the cause of his country and his God."[56] In his autobiography, Pratt further explicated the impact of the deaths of Patten and his compatriots on the Latter-day Saint community: "[A] whole people, as it were followed them to the grave. All wept whose feelings were not too intense to find vent in tears. He was the only member of the Quorum of the Twelve who had as yet found a martyr's grave."[57] In addition to Patten and his fellow Crooked River victims, Pratt remembered the seventeen Mormon men and boys killed at Haun's Mill as martyrs.[58]

The central figure in Pratt's martyrology was Joseph Smith. For Pratt, Smith was "the chosen vessel honored of God," a man "whose innocent blood is now dripping fresh, as it were, from the hands of assassins and their accessories."[59] Smith's death demanded an

[54] [Parley P. Pratt], *Proclamation of the Twelve Apostles of the Church of Jesus Christ of Latter-day Saints. To All the Kings of the World; to the President of the United States of America; to the Governors of the Several States; and to the Rulers and People of All Nations: Greeting* (New York: *The Prophet*, Printer, 1845), 4.

[55] Pratt to Aaron Frost, 17 June 1839.

[56] Pratt, *History of the Late Persecution*, 36.

[57] Pratt, *Autobiography*, 197–98.

[58] Pratt, *History of the Late Persecution*, 39.

[59] Parley P. Pratt, *Key to the Science of Theology: Designed as an Introduction to the First Principles of Spiritual Philosophy; Religion; Law and Government; as Delivered by the Ancients, and as Restored in This Age, for the Final Development of Universal Peace, Truth and Knowledge* (Liverpool, England: F. D. Richards, 1855), 76.

explanation, given the common belief that Providence determined everything that occurred in this life.[60] How could God have allowed his chosen and honored vessel to be murdered? Pratt's explanation was simple. Smith's death while defending the cause of truth was necessary and had sealed his testimony with his own blood.[61] Less than three weeks after Smith's murder, Pratt and other Mormon leaders wrote to the devastated Latter-day Saints that Smith's death should not be interpreted as a sign that God had failed in his promises. Instead of hindering Smith in his mission, his death had simply prepared him "to enter upon a greater and more effectual work," that of bringing about the restoration of all things.[62] The Latter-day Saints were not to falter despite the loss of their leader, but rather they were to continue in the work.[63]

This sense of purpose in the face of failure was shaped by the biblical martyrology that informed Pratt's thinking about persecution. Martyrology served as the lens through which Pratt constructed Mormon identities in his writings.[64] In particular, he drew upon the writings of Paul for frameworks in which to situate Mormon suffering. For example, in a short passage in *History of the Late Persecution*, Pratt alluded to at least three New Testament verses: "And having this ministry to fulfil we glory in tribulation, in persecution, in imprisonment, in banishment, in reproaches for Christ's sake and the Gospel; yea, we take joyfully the spoiling of our goods, and even count our lives not dear to us, if it so be that we may finish our course with joy, and the ministry we have received of the Lord Jesus."[65] Drawing on this biblical language to

[60] On the culture of Providence, see Lewis O. Saum, *The Popular Mood of Pre–Civil War America* (Westport, Conn.: Greenwood Press, 1980), 3–26.

[61] [Pratt], *Proclamation of the Twelve Apostles*, 4.

[62] Parley P. Pratt and others to the Saints Abroad, *Times and Seasons* (15 July 1844): 586.

[63] Pratt, *Autobiography*, 371.

[64] On the relationship between identity and history, see Étienne Balibar, *The Nation Form: History and Ideology*, quoted in Michael Rossington and Anne Whitehead, eds., *Theories of Memory: A Reader* (Baltimore: Johns Hopkins University Press, 2007), 254.

[65] Pratt, *History of the Late Persecution*, 80. Pratt alluded to 2 Corinthians 12:10, Hebrews 10:34, and Acts 20:24. Likewise in a letter written to his parents-in-law from prison, Pratt alluded to Hebrews 11:25, Hebrews 10:34, 2 Corinthians 12:10, and Matt. 26:64 (Pratt to Aaron Frost, 20 March 1839).

narrate the persecution of his people, Pratt placed the Mormons within a biblical story of suffering for Christ's sake.

This use of language was part of a larger effort to establish continuity between the Mormons of the nineteenth century and the early Christians. Establishing a link to a past civilization is a crucial element of constructing group identity as well as being a boundary-maintenance device.[66] Establishing this continuity allowed Latter-day Saints to imagine a history that extended through the time of Christ and even into the Old Testament era. Latter-day Saints constructed the Old Testament prophets and early Christians as proto-Mormons, adherents to the same gospel, and compatriots in the cause of Zion. By implication, non-Mormons stood outside of this history and therefore did not have claim to being part of God's true church on earth. Latter-day Saints thus interpreted their persecutions within this framework and contested alternate narratives that attributed Mormon suffering to other causes.

On various occasions Pratt commented on the similitude and even communion between ancient martyrs and modern ones. In his 1840 poem "Farewell," Pratt asked if Latter-day Saints should "spend [their] lives as pilgrims here, / Or lose them for the gospel's sake? / When Jesus Christ has done the same."[67] The audacity of such a statement was not so much in its content (Christians had sought to imitate Christ's sufferings for centuries) but in its context—that Pratt, a Mormon, would claim in Protestant America that his fellow Latter-day Saints had died for the gospel's sake as had Christ. In his *History of the Late Persecution*, Pratt went further by arguing that "[t]he spirits of the ancient martyrs will hail their brethren of the Church of latter-day Saints [*sic*], as greater sufferers than themselves."[68] Because Protestants largely regarded Mormons as residing outside the pale of authentic religion, such a claim to communion with and even superiority to ancient Christian martyrs no doubt furthered the distance between the groups.[69]

---

[66] See Benedict Anderson, *Imagined Communities: Reflections on the Origin and Spread of Nationalism*, rev. ed. (London: Verso, 1991), 195–96.

[67] Pratt, "Farewell," *The Millennium, and Other Poems*, 61.

[68] Pratt, *History of the Late Persecution*, 56.

[69] Fluhman, "Anti-Mormonism and the Making of Religion in Antebellum America."

When describing the martyrdom of Joseph Smith, Pratt imagined continuity between Smith's death and the deaths of the ancient Saints. He saw especially compelling parallels between Smith's life, mission, and death and John the Baptist: "Like John, who filled a similar mission preparatory to the first advent of the Son of God . . . he [Smith] was imprisoned; and like him [John], his [Smith's] life was taken from the earth."[70] This parallel not only assured Latter-day Saints of Smith's place in the history of martyrdom but also contested anti-Mormon narratives describing his death. In his autobiography, Pratt described returning to Nauvoo in 1844 following the martyrdom and being taunted by a crowd of non-Mormons who asked how the Latter-day Saints would continue without their prophet: "To these taunts and questions I replied . . . that nearly all the prophets and Apostles who were before him had been killed, and also the Saviour of the world, and yet their death did not alter the truth nor hinder its final triumph."[71]

Just as Pratt contradicted the scoffers, he consistently challenged narratives that suggested that suffering was harmful and disastrous by framing the persecutions as positive and redemptive events. Despite the Mormons' great losses in Missouri and Illinois, Pratt primarily saw God's deliverances. In an 1841 public letter to the Latter-day Saints, he recounted Mormon suffering in Missouri, concluding: "Out of all these things the Lord has delivered us, and has caused the nations of the proud to tremble before us, and the meek of the earth to hail us as the messengers of salvation."[72] What could have been seen as God's abandonment of the Latter-day Saints was interpreted by Pratt to be the ultimate sign of Mormon chosenness. Pratt attributed his escape from prison to the hand of Providence, which he described poetically:

> I mount—I fly—I haste away,
> Buoyed, as it were, on angel's wings;
> O home! O friends! O liberty!—
> O God of strength, thy praise I'll sing.

---

[70] Pratt, *Key to the Science of Theology*, 76–77.

[71] Pratt, *Autobiography*, 359.

[72] Parley P. Pratt to the Authorities and the Members, 12 August 1841, *Times and Seasons* (14 December 1841): 624.

Hosanna now in highest strains,
Glory to God and to the Lamb.[73]

After Pratt's harrowing escape from Missouri, Latter-day Saints in Illinois embraced him as one miraculously delivered from bondage and death.[74]

Pratt believed that persecution would actually strengthen the Latter-day Saints rather than impede them. Writing to his parents-in-law from prison, Pratt assured them that "[t]his persecution so far from discouraging the Saints or hindering the work of God from rolling on will increase and spread it with tenfold [speed?] the Saints endure all these things cheerfully and help each other in removing to the dividing of their last mite with each others."[75] On another occasion Pratt expanded this metaphor by describing the Church as a mountain that would crush obstacles on its way toward filling the whole earth prior to the millennium: "Although obstacles may interpose to retard its progress for a moment, yet as if strengthened by this very opposition, it moves forward in its awful majesty, crushing all things beneath its weight, or blowing them away like the chaff of the summer threshing floors, until becoming a great mountain, it fills the whole earth, and ushers in the reign of eternal peace."[76] Persecution, rather than leading to a decrease in membership, would instead increase conversions by tens of thousands.[77] In this way Pratt turned what could have been seen as a massive blow to the Mormon people into a temporary setback that would ultimately be for their benefit.

Part of this optimism doubtless stemmed from Pratt's belief that ancient and modern prophets had predicted that in the last days the Saints of God would suffer persecution. In his poem "The Millennium," Pratt answered critics who argued that persecution proved Mormonism was false.

All parties cry at once, the saints are wrong;
For if they were the chosen of the Lord,

[73] Pratt, "Pratt's Deliverance," *The Millennium, and Other Poems*, 100.

[74] Pratt, *Autobiography*, 323.

[75] Pratt to Aaron Frost, 20 March 1839.

[76] Pratt, *History of the Late Persecution*, v.

[77] Pratt, "The Millennium," *The Millennium, and Other Poems*, 20.

He would protect them and fulfil his word.
O fools, and slow of heart to understand
The prophecies concerning Zion's land.
Have ye not read the words of them of old?
When wrapt in vision clear they have foretold
The wicked deeds that you of late fulfill'd.[78]

In this way Pratt subverted the narrative put forward by Protestants that cast the persecutions as evidence of Mormon delusion; he in fact reordered the narrative, placing Protestants in the role of prophesied persecutors of the Saints of the last days. Pratt had also received personal assurances in a blessing that he would face persecution and even imprisonment in his lifetime. When Pratt was chosen and ordained an apostle in 1835, Oliver Cowdery told him: "You will be dragged before the authorities for the religion you profess; and it were better not to set out than to start, look back or shrink when dangers thicken upon or appalling death stares you in the face. I have spoken these things, dear brother, because I have seen them in visions. There are strong dungeons and gloomy prisons for you."[79] Pratt believed that his course had been foreseen by God's servants, and that his persecutions were of divine design.

For Pratt and other Latter-day Saints, being called to suffer and even die for the truth was preferable to the alternative of remaining unscathed in Babylon. Writing in 1840 from New York, Pratt related that "[t]he spirit that prevails is 'west ward Ho!' to suffer, to live, or to die with the saints their brethren. There is scarce a saint here who would stay another month if they had means to go west. It is the bad times here and not the good times which keeps them from emigrating."[80] While in prison Pratt wrote to his parents-in-law in Maine, encouraging them to join the main body of the Saints then leaving Missouri: "I most earnestly wish that our friends in Maine would come to the west and live with us[;] that is if they choose to suffer affliction with the people of God rather than enjoy the pleasures of the Gentiles for a season."[81] This desire

[78] Ibid., 18. See also Pratt, *History of the Late Persecution*, 54.

[79] Pratt, *Autobiography*, 129–30, also 128, 133–35.

[80] Parley Pratt and others to the Church of Jesus Christ of Latter Day Saints, 19 February 1840, *Times and Seasons* (March 1840): 71.

[81] Pratt to Aaron Frost, 20 March 1839. Pratt's language echoes Hebrews 11:25.

to suffer therefore reversed the definition of affliction as something to be avoided and reinvented it in positive terms. Pratt's construction of the Mormons as the suffering people of God served as a means by which to maintain a boundary between true believers and their opponents. In the broader American culture, notions of suffering underwent significant change during the nineteenth century, shifting from a view of pain as beneficial to something that should be avoided. Pratt harkened back to the older views.[82]

Constructing Missourians and Illinoisans as "Others"

Pratt drew upon several frameworks from biblical and American culture to cast the Mormons' tormentors in opposition to the Latter-day Saints, defining the Mormons by what they were not. He portrayed his persecutors and their actions as inhuman, barbarous, and cruel.[83] For example, he referred to "a lawless banditti, who were utter strangers to humanity."[84] Because Pratt envisioned the Latter-day Saints as God's chosen people, he in turn represented his persecutors as emissaries of Satan. This portrayal fit the Missourians and Illinoisans within a cosmic scene in which the children of darkness fought against the children of light. Pratt explicitly cast his opponents as demons, referring to "fiends in human form" and a "gang of demons in human shape."[85] In perhaps his most famous example, Pratt in his autobiography described Joseph Smith's rebuke of his Missouri prison guards who were vulgarly bragging of their crimes against the Mormons. Pratt recalled that Smith majestically arose in his chains and proclaimed: "*SILENCE, ye fiends of the infernal pit. In the name of Jesus Christ I rebuke you and command you to be still; I will not live another minute and hear*

[82] Matthew J. Grow, "The Suffering Saints: Thomas L. Kane, Democratic Reform, and the Mormon Question in Antebellum America," *Journal of the Early Republic* 29, no. 4 (Winter 2009): 681–710.

[83] Pratt, *History of the Late Persecution*, 81, 82; and Pratt and others, "'Mormons,' So Called."

[84] Pratt, *History of the Late Persecution*, 43; and Pratt, *Autobiography*, 207.

[85] Pratt, *History of the Late Persecution*, iii; and Pratt, *Autobiography*, 324.

such language. Cease such talk, or you or I die this INSTANT*!*"[86] When describing his own arrest and entering the Missouri militia camp on October 31, 1838, Pratt indicated: "If the vision of the infernal regions could suddenly open to the mind, with thousands of malicious fiends all clamoring, exulting, deriding, blaspheming, mocking, railing, raging and foaming like a troubled sea, then could some idea be formed of the hell which we had entered."[87] By demonizing his tormentors, Pratt explained their motivations and situated the Mormons as God's people opposed by Satan's minions.

Illustrating his sense of being an outsider in the American religious landscape, Pratt contended that the primary movers behind the persecutions were Protestant ministers.[88] In his poem "The Millennium," Pratt wrote: "The hireling priests against the truth engage, / While hell beneath stands trembling with rage."[89] According to Pratt, these priests feared the rapid increase in conversions to Mormonism. In his autobiography, Pratt argued: "Religious priests and bigots felt that we were powerful rivals, and about to excel all other societies in the state in numbers and in power and influence."[90] In accounts written in the 1850s, Pratt widened his condemnation beyond merely ministers to include all of the Protestant people in the United States. In one speech given not long before his death, Pratt contended that Americans persecuted the Latter-day Saints out of fear that Mormonism was true, hoping that persecution would stop the Church's progress.[91] In

[86] Pratt, *Autobiography*, 229 (italics and capitalization in original).

[87] Ibid., 204.

[88] Pratt, *History of the Late Persecution*, 84; see also Pratt, "Pratt's Defence," *The Millennium, and Other Poems*, 97–98. He mentioned three Protestants ministers by name: Isaac McCoy (Baptist), Sashel Woods (Methodist), and Samuel Bogart (Baptist). On McCoy, see Pratt, *History of the Late Persecution*, 21; Pratt and others, "'Mormons,' So Called"; and Pratt, *Autobiography*, 108. On Woods, see Pratt, *History of the Late Persecution*, 29; Pratt, *Autobiography*, 191; and Pratt, "The Mormon Prisoners," Pratt Collection, L. Tom Perry Special Collections. On Bogart, see Pratt, *Autobiography*, 197.

[89] Pratt, "The Millennium," *The Millennium, and Other Poems*, 17.

[90] Pratt, *Autobiography*, 102–103.

[91] Parley P. Pratt, "Reminiscences," 7 September 1856, *Journal of Discourses of Brigham Young, President of the Church of Jesus Christ of Latter-day Saints, His Two Counselors, the Twelve Apostles, and Others*, 26 vols. (Liverpool, England: F.D. Richards and S.W. Richards, 1854–1886), 5:199.

another speech, Pratt vilified Americans for priding themselves in living in a "Protestant" nation while tolerating very un-Christian treatment of American citizens.[92]

Pratt not only condemned Protestants for perpetrating and condoning the persecutions, he also expressed his ire for government officials who participated in the violence. In particular, Missouri governor Lilburn W. Boggs became for Pratt (and other early Mormons) the embodiment of government complicity, and the governor was often portrayed in Pratt's prose with images associated with government persecutors of the ancient Christians. In a letter to his wife written from prison on April 12, 1839, Pratt referred to the governor as "his Missouri Magesty, Emperor Boggs" and on other occasions condemned Boggs as "the modern Herod" as well as "a Nero or a Nicholas."[93] Just as Pratt imagined a community of persecuted Saints between the Mormons and the early Christians, he also saw continuity between the oppressions of Boggs and those of earlier rulers who opposed God's people. He argued in his *History of the Late Persecution* that "tyranny itself will blush to hear her [Missouri's] deeds mentioned in the annals of history; and the most cruel persecutors of the christians [*sic*] or reformers, in Pagan or Papal Rome, will startle with astonishment from their long slumbers, and with a shudder of the deepest horror, and a frown of the most indignant contempt, they will look upon her unheard of deeds of blind infatuation, and inconscienable [*sic*] absurdity."[94] When Pratt revised this passage for his autobiography, he altered the image by having the ancient persecutors react to Missouri's persecutions "with a mixture of envy and admiration, yield[ing] to her the palm."[95] Pratt, however, was not willing to yield to his tormentors the palm, preferring instead to show his readers that although his persecutors had temporarily won the upper hand, the Latter-day Saints would ultimately have power over them.

---

92 Parley P. Pratt, "Christianity," ca. 1850s, Pratt Collection, L. Tom Perry Special Collections.

93 Parley P. Pratt to Mary Ann Frost Pratt, 12 April 1839; Pratt, *History of the Late Persecution*, 54; and Pratt, *Autobiography*, 217–18, 230–31.

94 Pratt, *History of the Late Persecution*, 56.

95 Pratt, *Autobiography*, 237.

Power Over His Enemies

The language of martyrdom and persecution provided Pratt the linguistic tools to reverse the power relations as they had been defined by the Missourians. Mormon opponents were successful in expelling the Latter-day Saints from both Missouri and Illinois, prosecuting and imprisoning Mormon leaders for crimes, all while avoiding legal repercussions for their own actions. Well aware of these inequalities, Pratt imagined a time when God would vindicate his people. While in prison in Missouri, he prayed:

How long, O Lord! will thou forsake
The saints, who tremble at thy word?
Awake, O arm of God, awake—
And teach the nations thou art God.
Descend with all thy holy throng,
The year of thy redeemed bring near,
Haste—haste, the day of vengeance on—
Bid Zion's children dry their tears.
Deliver Lord, thy captive saints,
And comfort those who long have mourn'd;
Bid Zion cease her dire complaints,
And all creation cease to mourn.[96]

Pleading for "the day of vengeance" allowed Pratt and other Mormons to contest and contradict their tormentors' narratives of what had happened in Missouri and Illinois. Rather than being fanatics punished for their crimes, as anti-Mormons conceived of them, the Mormons reversed those power relations by constructing themselves as God's people, waiting for a future day when the Lord would rescue His people and punish their enemies.

Latter-day Saints constructed their notions of vengeance through the lens provided in Revelation 6:9–11, which described John the Revelator's vision of the martyrs under the altar: "I saw under the altar the souls of them that were slain for the word of God, and for the testimony which they held: And they cried with a loud voice, saying, How long, O Lord, holy and true, dost thou

[96] Pratt, "Zion in Captivity," *The Millennium, and Other Poems*, 73. See also Pratt, "Reflections," in ibid., 62.

not judge and avenge our blood on them that dwell on the earth? And white robes were given unto every one of them; and it was said unto them, that they should rest yet for a little season, until their fellowservants also and their brethren, that should be killed as they *were*, should be fulfilled." These verses, among the most frequently cited in early Mormon martyrological writings, shaped how Latter-day Saints understood the workings of vengeance and functioned as a means by which Mormons defined their relationships with God, ancient martyrs, and other Americans.

As Mormons saw continuity between themselves and persecuted peoples of ancient times, Latter-day Saints imagined their own martyrs as being under the altar with martyrs from earlier ages pleading with God to bring vengeance upon their tormentors. Pratt imagined this community with the former-day Saints by claiming that "the blood of ancient and modern Saints, will mingle together in cries of vengeance, upon those who are drunken with their blood, till justice will delay no longer to excuse his long suspended mission of vengeance upon the earth."[97] Pratt also argued that those who had not been resurrected at the time of Christ must wait to be raised from the dead until the Lord would bring "vengeance on all those who have shed the innocent blood whether of Latter-day Saints or Former-day Saints."[98] After Joseph Smith's death, Pratt penned a poem entitled "Cry of the Martyrs" that described the ancient martyrs under the heavenly altar pleading to God for vengeance, with a voice answering that they must wait until the Mormons have bled in Missouri and Illinois:

> "How long, O Lord! holy and true, dost thou
> Not judge and avenge our blood on them that
> Dwell on the earth?"
> Are these the awful words? And what reply
> Is given by the avenging heavens?
> BE PATIENT O ye martyred souls and wait
> Till your fellow servants who are to be
> Killed in like manner shall be fulfilled.

[97] Pratt, *History of the Late Persecution*, 56.

[98] Pratt, "Literal Fulfillment of Prophecy," 7 October 1855, *Journal of Discourses*, 3:137.

> WAIT—till Missouri's plains are soaked in blood
> Of innocence, and the souls of Latter day Saints
> Mingle their cries with yours for vengeance on
> The earth. Wait, till the plains of Illinois,
> And the walls of Carthage, are soaked with
> The blood of martyred prophets, whose cries
> Ascend to heaven for vengeance on a mob.[99]

By linking Mormon martyrs with ancient martyrs, Pratt established authenticity for the Latter-day Saint gospel.

For Pratt, vengeance would be brought by God himself upon the persecutors of the Latter-day Saints. In a prison letter to his father-in-law, Pratt angrily wrote that rather than he being tried in a Missouri court of law, his captors should be hung for their crimes, "but vengeance belongs to the Lord, and he will repay."[100] Pratt imagined a future time when God would scourge Missouri, thereby preparing for the return of the Latter-day Saints. He told his parents-in-law: "It is wisdom for us to step out from among them [the Missourians] for a little season untill the indignation of a just God has disencumbered the land and made room for the rights of man and the laws of the land to be restored."[101] In these imaginings, God himself brought vengeance to the earth, not Latter-day Saints taking justice into their own hands.

Pratt used this vengeance discourse to explain the demise of the Latter-day Saints' enemies. In his autobiography, Pratt described an incident in 1834 during Zion's Camp when a rainstorm impeded a mob from attacking a small body of Latter-day Saints. When word came that several of the mobbers had drowned when their boat sank in the rainstorm, Pratt recalled Joseph Smith saying that "it was the angel of the Lord who sank the boat."[102] Such lurid descriptions of the fate of the persecutors had cultural precedents reaching back centuries in the writings of Christians. Drawing on this tradition, Pratt included in his autobiography excerpts

[99] Pratt, "Cry of the Martyrs," *Times and Seasons* (2 September 1844): 639.
[100] Pratt to Aaron Frost, 17 June 1839. Pratt was alluding to Romans 12:19.
[101] Ibid., 20 March 1839.
[102] Pratt, *Autobiography*, 125.

describing the gruesome ends of individuals who had persecuted the Mormons in Missouri and Illinois.[103] Some rotted alive, one was continually haunted by a vision of Joseph Smith, and a Missourian was eaten alive by worms and maggots. One man who had participated in Smith's murder admitted in agony: "'*I know he was a prophet of God!* And, oh, that I had stayed at home and minded my own business, and then I would not have lost my life and been tormented with a guilty conscience, and with this dreadful wound, which none can heal!'"[104] Such stories circulated widely among Mormons during the nineteenth century. Whether there is any truth behind such stories matters less than the role they played in Mormon discourse.[105] They reassured the Latter-day Saints that God would ultimately bring the vengeance upon their persecutors.

These stories of God's vengeance functioned as a means of social differentiation between Latter-day Saints and others. God punished Mormon persecutors while He blessed the Latter-day Saints. Pratt wrote in his autobiography: "Lilburn W. Boggs is dragging out a remnant of existence in California, with the mark of Cain upon his brow, and the fear of Cain within his heart, lest he that findeth him shall slay him. He is a living stink, and will go down to posterity with the credit of a wholesale murderer."[106] This assessment of Boggs's degraded life in California was immediately preceded by Pratt's description of Mormon life in Utah Territory: "The Saints are growing into power amid the strongholds of the mountains of Deseret, and will sure take the Kingdom, and the greatness of the Kingdom, under the whole Heaven."[107]

---

[103] This tradition was perhaps most readily available to Pratt in the form of Cattley, *The Acts and Monuments of John Foxe*, 7:656–57; and Charles Buck, *A Theological Dictionary: Containing Definitions of all Religious Terms* (Philadelphia: J.J. Woodward, 1837), 282. I am indebted to Samuel Brown for these references.

[104] Pratt, *Autobiography*, 475–77, quote on p. 476.

[105] For an analysis of these stories within the context of American folklore, see Richard C. Poulsen, "Fate of the Persecutors of Joseph Smith: Transmutations of an American Myth," *Dialogue: A Journal of Mormon Thought* 11, no. 4 (Winter 1978): 63–70.

[106] Pratt, *Autobiography*, 231.

[107] Ibid.

Pratt warned the American people that if they did not address and correct the wrongs perpetrated against the Latter-day Saints in Missouri and Illinois, God would punish the nation as a whole. He wrote: "But, so long as they [the American people] remain indifferent and ignorant on these subjects, and so long as they continue to breathe out slanders, lies, hatred and murder against the Saints and against the remnants of Israel, and to speak evil of and oppose the things which they understand not, so long the blood of the Saints and of the martyrs of Jesus must continue to flow, and the souls to cry from under the altar for vengeance on a guilty land, till the great Messiah shall execute judgment for the Saints, and give them the dominion."[108] All Americans, by virtue of the ties of citizenship, were for Pratt under condemnation for not helping the Latter-day Saints. He wrote: "The blood of innocence is crying from the ground against, not only the perpetrators of these crimes, but against the protestants, catholics, clergy, rulers and people, because they were bound by the common ties of humanity, by the common bonds of citizenship, by the laws of God, and by the most sacred obligations of their laws and constitution, to have protected persons and property, and punished crime."[109] The day of vengeance therefore lay ahead of all Americans that did not come to the aid of the Latter-day Saints.

Pratt was quick to clarify that the Latter-day Saints themselves did not seek to act out their violent fantasies. Vengeance was not the only discourse that shaped Mormon interactions with others. At the moment when vengeance was most readily in their grasp, in the aftermath of the murder of Joseph Smith, the Nauvoo Legion could have exacted their revenge on the perpetrators, Pratt wrote. "The legion sprang to arms, and would have desolated the whole rebel counties, now left unprotected, had not their judgments balanced the burning attribute of justice which swelled their

---

[108] [Pratt], *Proclamation of the Twelve Apostles*, 12–13.

[109] Parley P. Pratt, *Proclamation Extraordinary*, in *Writings of Parley Parker Pratt: One of the First Missionaries and a Member of the First Quorum of the Twelve Apostles of the Church of Jesus Christ of Latter-day Saints*, ed. Parker Pratt Robison (Salt Lake City: Deseret News Press, 1952), 158.

bosoms."[110] In Pratt's narrative, sound reason overrode the desire to avenge the death of the Mormon prophet. Pity for their oppressors was another attribute that Pratt appealed to in the aftermath of the martyrdom to dispel any notion that the Latter-day Saints should take justice into their own hands. He wrote: "As to our country and nation, we have more reason to weep for them, than for those they have murdered; for they are destroying themselves and their institutions and there is no remedy; and as to feelings of revenge, let them not have place for one moment in our bosoms, for God's vengeance will speedily consume to that degree that we would fain be hid away and not endure the sight."[111] The urge for vengeance was therefore tempered by reason, pity, and patience that God would at some future date right their wrongs.

These conceptions of a future time of bliss were often applied to Pratt's imaginings of an afterlife where the Latter-day Saints would have power over, and be safe from, mobs. In the instructions given to his family concerning his funeral, Pratt asked that they read this message: "Know assuredly that I am only sleeping a few short years where the wicked cease from troubling and the weary are at rest," as well as to write this in his epitaph: "The rod of the Tyrant shall reach thee no more."[112] In his short story "One Hundred Years Hence. 1945," Pratt presented a fictional account of himself going forward one hundred years, when the millennium had already commenced. He recounted that while traveling in this future place, he "discovered the fragment of a hewn stone, of a lightish blue colour, with an abbreviated word 'Mo.' and the figures '1838' upon it. To which the 'Lion of the Lord' exclaimed:—'*The wicked are turned into hell*, and are forgotten, but the righteous reign with God in glory,' and it seemed as if the echo came from a redeemed world—'*glory*.'"[113] Although Pratt for much of his life

[110] Pratt, *Key to the Science of Theology*, 89–90.

[111] Pratt and others to the Saints Abroad, *Times and Seasons* (15 July 1844): 586.

[112] Parley P. Pratt, "Directions for my Funeral and Epitaph," Pratt Collection, L. Tom Perry Special Collections.

[113] [Parley P. Pratt], "One Hundred Years Hence. 1945," *The Latter-day Saints' Millennial Star* (15 October 1845): 141.

was powerless to reverse the social relations that had produced the persecutions, he exercised some power by articulating his vision of the world to come, a world free from persecution and mobs.

Conclusion

In 1854, three years prior to his death, Pratt was living in California directing the Church's missionary efforts in the Pacific Basin. While there, he engaged in several polemical exchanges in California newspapers with Protestant ministers who attacked Mormonism and the Church's practice of polygamy. In a public debate held at the Mercantile Library Debating Society of San Francisco in December 1854, Pratt responded to an accusation made by Methodist minister M. C. Briggs that the Mormons had committed "theft, robbery, murder, etc.," but that he and the Mormons did not consider these acts crimes "provided these crimes were committed on the Gentiles, and in favor of the Church treasury, etc."[114] Pratt compared Briggs's allegations to a Quaker man who wanted a dog to be killed. The Quaker told the dog that he [the

[114] These allegations were first articulated in Missouri during the 1830s. In the November 1838 hearing, witnesses testified that during the October 1838 offensive on Daviess County, Mormon soldiers took goods from the non-Mormon dwellings and "consecrated" them to the Church. For example, witness George M. Hinckle testified: "It was taught, that the time had come when the riches of the Gentiles were to be consecrated to the true Israel." This probably referred to an 1831 Joseph Smith revelation: "And it shall come to pass, that he that sinneth and repenteth not shall be cast out, and shall not receive again that which he has consecrated unto me: For it shall come to pass, that which I spake by the mouths of my prophets shall be fulfilled; for I will consecrate the riches of the Gentiles unto my People which are of the House of Israel" (*A Book of Commandments, for the Government of the Church of Christ, Organized According to Law, on the 6th of April, 1830* [Zion (Independence, Mo.: W. W. Phelps & Co., 1833), 44:31–32]). Although this passage was edited for the 1835 Doctrine and Covenants of the Church of Jesus Christ of Latter-day Saints: Carefully Selected from the Revelations of God to clarify that the Lord would "consecrate the riches of those who embrace my gospel among the Gentiles," apparently some Latter-day Saints during the 1838 Missouri conflict preferred the 1833 printed version over the 1835 version and interpreted "Gentiles" to mean non-Mormons rather than converted Gentiles who had left the Church ([Kirtland, Ohio: F. G. Williams & Co., 1835], 13:11).

Quaker] would not kill him, but he would give him a bad name. By crying out that the dog was mad, "the people soon despatched the poor animal."[115]

Pratt concluded that Briggs was attempting to do the same thing by falsely accusing the Mormons: "Perhaps my friend [Reverend Briggs] thinks to get the Mormons killed off in the same pious and Christian-like manner. Even should he succeed in his peaceful, pious purposes, it would not be the first time that the blood of martyrs has stained our soil through the influence of such Christian benevolence."[116] This exchange illustrates many of the themes introduced in this chapter. It shows that Pratt was engaged in a contest with other Americans over how to understand and remember the past. In Pratt's response to Briggs, the Mormons in the 1850s were not criminals, as Briggs contended, but rather they were being maligned, persecuted, and martyred in the same manner as those Latter-day Saints who had passed through Missouri and Illinois. Just as in those states, Pratt saw his enemy primarily as Protestant ministers, and by identifying them as such he discursively constructed cultural distance between himself as a true disciple of Christ and American Protestants as hypocritical opponents to God's people. Although Pratt resided on the margins of the Americans religious landscape, thereby lacking access to the power structures available to his opponents, his writings gave him power to shape how the past was understood and therefore claim legitimacy for himself and his people. Perhaps as a fitting irony, Pratt's death in 1857 would become part of the martyrological tradition that he helped forge in life.[117]

[115] Pratt, *Autobiography*, 466.

[116] Ibid. On Pratt's debate with Briggs, see Matthew J. Grow, "'A Providential Means of Agitating Mormonism': Parley P. Pratt and the San Francisco Press in the 1850s," *Journal of Mormon History* 29, no. 2 (Fall 2003): 173–74.

[117] See Matthew J. Grow's essay in this volume (chapter 9).

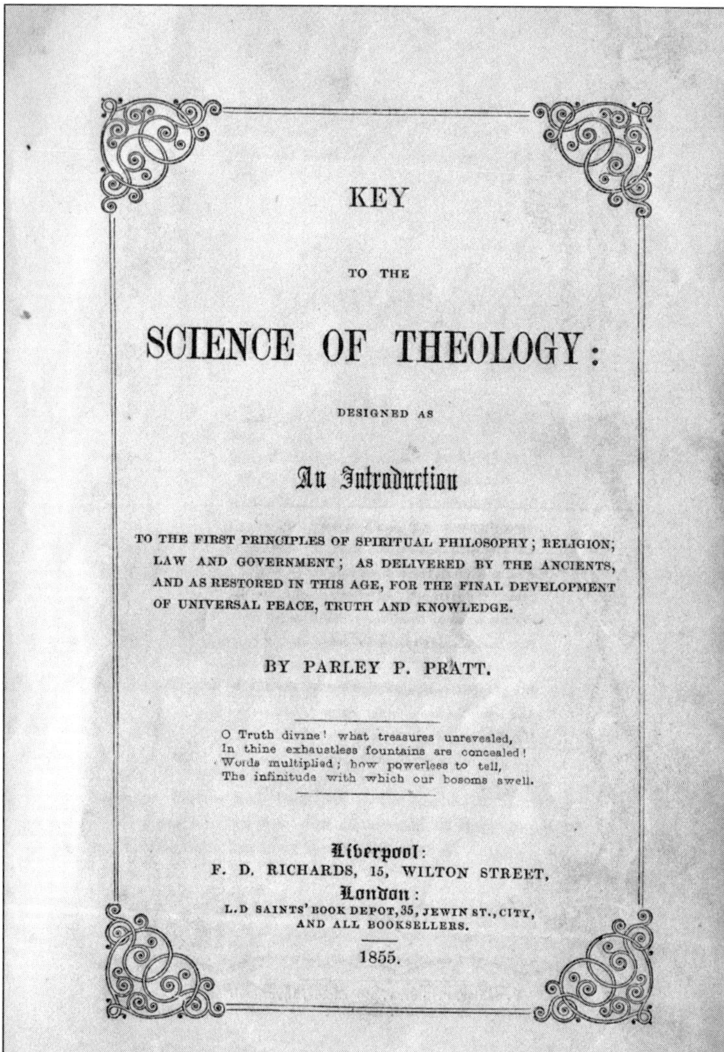

KEY

TO THE

SCIENCE OF THEOLOGY:

DESIGNED AS

An Introduction

TO THE FIRST PRINCIPLES OF SPIRITUAL PHILOSOPHY; RELIGION; LAW AND GOVERNMENT; AS DELIVERED BY THE ANCIENTS, AND AS RESTORED IN THIS AGE, FOR THE FINAL DEVELOPMENT OF UNIVERSAL PEACE, TRUTH AND KNOWLEDGE.

BY PARLEY P. PRATT.

O Truth divine! what treasures unrevealed,
In thine exhaustless fountains are concealed!
Words multiplied; how powerless to tell,
The infinitude with which our bosoms swell.

Liverpool:
F. D. RICHARDS, 15, WILTON STREET,
London:
L.D SAINTS' BOOK DEPOT, 35, JEWIN ST., CITY,
AND ALL BOOKSELLERS.

1855.

Title page, *Key to the Science of Theology*, 1855.
Courtesy of the L. Tom Perry Special Collections, Harold B. Lee Library, Brigham Young University, Provo, Utah.

CHAPTER 6

"All of One Species"

Parley P. Pratt and the Dialectical Development of Early Mormon Conceptions of Theosis

Jordan Watkins

In *Key to the Science of Theology* (1855), the first published synthesis of early Mormon thought, Parley P. Pratt asserted that "Gods, angels and men are all of one species." This radical affirmation of man's ontological equality with God contributed to Pratt's unique formulation of human divinization.[1] "Man is a candidate for a series of progressive changes," he explained, and thus he can "become like [the Father and the Son] in every respect, physically and in intellect, attributes or powers."[2] Pratt's mature conception of theosis (the process by which humans become divine) constituted the culmination of early Mormons' engagement with ideas of deification. Pratt derived much of his thought on theosis from the revelations and teachings of Mormonism's founder, Joseph

[1] Parley P. Pratt, *Key to the Science of Theology: Designed as an Introduction to the First Principles of Spiritual Philosophy; Religion; Law and Government; as Delivered by the Ancients, and as Restored in This Age, for the Final Development of Universal Peace, Truth and Knowledge* (Liverpool, England: F.D. Richards, 1855), 33. In this essay, "ontology" and "ontological" refer to the nature of being, or the study of the nature of being.

[2] Ibid., 32, 149.

Smith, but Pratt's work also contributed to this discourse. His writings display the evolution of theosis in early Mormon thought.

Theosis is also referred to as apotheosis, human divinization, or deification.[3] Proponents of many belief systems, both ancient and modern, have promoted various forms of theosis.[4] Nineteenth-century America exhibited extreme versions of divinization. In the early nineteenth century, Alexis de Tocqueville observed that American equality "gave [perfectibility] a new quality," opining that "democratic nations stretch [the bounds of human perfectibility] sometimes to excess."[5] Such excesses took a variety of shapes,

[3] Though not always synonymous with one another and all employed in a number of ways, the terms "theosis," "divinization," and "deification" are used interchangeably within this essay.

[4] For example, a recent study outlines various views of theosis throughout Christian history, describing and analyzing deification in Classical and Late Antiquity, Patristic thought, the Medieval and Reformation periods, and modern Christianity (Michael J. Christensen and Jeffrey A. Wittung, eds., *Partakers of the Divine Nature: The History and Development of Deification in the Christian Traditions* [Grand Rapids, Mich.: Baker Academic, 2007]). Mormon scholars have pointed to early Christians' beliefs in theosis and have offered insightful comparisons between Mormon views of exaltation and Christian conceptions of deification (see Keith Norman, "Divinization: The Forgotten Teaching of Early Christianity," *Sunstone* 1 [Winter 1975]: 15–19; Philip Barlow, "Unorthodox Orthodoxy: The Idea of Deification in Christian History," *Sunstone* 8 [September–October, 1983]: 13–18; and Grant Underwood, "Justification, Theosis, and Grace in Early Christian, Lutheran, and Mormon Discourse," *International Journal of Mormon Studies* 2 [Spring 2009]: 206–23). For a study comparing Patristic and Mormon ideas of divinization, see Jordan Vajda, "'Partakers of the Divine Nature': A Comparative Analysis of Patristic and Mormon Doctrines of Divinization," *FARMS Occasional Papers*, no. 3 (Provo, Utah: Foundation for Ancient Research and Mormon Studies, Brigham Young University [hereafter BYU], 2002), which is a revised version of Vajda's master's thesis. In a study on the development of early Mormon doctrine, Thomas G. Alexander compares early Mormon notions of perfection with the doctrines of human perfectionism advocated by nineteenth-century religious groups, including the Methodists and the Disciples of Christ (Alexander, "The Reconstruction of Mormon Doctrine," in *Line Upon Line: Essays on Mormon Doctrine*, ed. Gary J. Bergera [Salt Lake City: Signature Books, 1989], 56).

[5] Alexis de Tocqueville, *Democracy in America* (London: Penguin Books, 2003), 522. The spread of the idea of human perfectability may be representative of an American ideological shift from a theocentric to an anthropocentric focus. This shift has been traced in Mormonism. See J. Frederic Voros, Jr., "Moving Gracefully Toward Godhood: Was the Book of Mormon Buried with King Follett?" *Sunstone* 11 (March 1987): 15–18.

including the Wesleyan-based holiness movement, John Humphrey Noyes's social theory of perfectionism, and the early optimism of Ralph Waldo Emerson, who, in *Nature* (1836), famously cited a certain poet, stating that "a man is a god in ruins."[6] Early Mormon formulations of theosis, culminating in one of America's most radical forms of human perfectibility, evolved through dialogues within Mormonism but also between Mormons and non-Mormons. This essay traces the development of theosis in the writings of Parley P. Pratt as an example of the way in which early Mormon theology developed through dialectics.

As one of the new movement's earliest converts, Pratt occupied an important place in the Latter-day Saint Church. With the publication of *Voice of Warning* (1837), he became the preeminent public promoter and defender of Mormonism.[7] In 1837 the Church was in its formative years, and given the emphasis upon continuing revelation, many concepts remained undeveloped.[8]

---

[6] See John Leland Peters, *Christian Perfection and American Methodism* (New York: Abingdon Press, 1956), 90–132; Ira L. Mandelker, *Religion, Society, and Utopia in Nineteenth-Century America* (Amherst: University of Massachusetts Press, 1984), 93–133; and Ralph Waldo Emerson, "Nature," in *The Complete Works of Ralph Waldo Emerson*, ed. Edward Waldo Emerson, 12 vols., Centenary Edition (Boston: Houghton Mifflin, 1903–1904), 1: 71.

[7] Peter Crawley notes that Pratt "all but single-handedly invented Mormon book writing" (Crawley, "Parley P. Pratt: Father of Mormon Pamphleteering," *Dialogue: A Journal of Mormon Thought* 15 [Autumn 1982]: 13–26). See also David J. Whittaker, "Early Mormon Pamphleteering" (master's thesis, BYU, 1982), 58–63; and Whittaker's essay in this volume (chapter 3). Crawley explains that Pratt's *Voice of Warning* "was the first [missionary tract] to emphasize the differences between Mormonism and orthodox Christianity." He continues: "It established a formula for describing the Church's basic doctrines, and it included biblical proof-texts, arguments, and examples which would be used by Mormon pamphleteers for a hundred years" (Crawley, *A Descriptive Bibliography of the Mormon Church*, vol. 1 [Provo, Utah: Religious Studies Center, BYU, 1997], 71).

[8] On the development of Mormon theology before this point, see Robert J. Matthews, "The New Translation of the Bible, 1830–1833: Doctrinal Development During the Kirtland Era," *BYU Studies* 11, no. 4 (1971): 400–22; Dan Vogel, "The Earliest Mormon Concept of God," in Bergera, *Line Upon Line*, 17–29; Alexander, "The Reconstruction of Mormon Doctrine," 53–64; and Kurt Widmer, *Mormonism and the Nature of God: A Theological Evolution, 1830–1915* (Jefferson, N.C.: McFarland & Company, 2000). For a critique of Widmer's book, see Ari D. Bruening and David L. Paulsen, "The Development of the Mormon Understanding of God: Early Mormon Modalism and Other Myths," *FARMS Review of Books* 13, no. 2 (2001): 109–69.

Pratt contributed to the development of Mormon thought as he explained and defended Latter-day Saint beliefs. The translations, revelations, and teachings of Joseph Smith served as Pratt's most important primary sources, but while Smith's works contained profound theological assertions, they left some ideas ambiguous and undeveloped, including beliefs about the nature of God and man. Though early Mormons likely discussed many of these ideas orally, an examination of the concepts in Pratt's publications suggests that an indirect and text-based conversation—an intertextual dialogue—among Mormons and between Mormon and non-Mormon authors also contributed to the development of Mormon theology. Smith's writings and teachings largely shaped the content of Pratt's ideas on theosis, but Pratt's publications possibly contributed to Smith's thought and certainly helped clarify and popularize early Mormon views of God and man.

Another dialectic, aside from the one within Mormonism, also contributed to early Mormon formulations of theosis. Mormon critics struck early and often during the first decades of the Latter-day Saint Church's existence. The earliest anti-Mormon pamphlets attacked Smith's character and discredited his spectacular claims, but they rarely critiqued Mormon theology.[9] Beginning in the late 1830s, while maintaining an emphasis on Smith and the Book of Mormon, a few anti-Mormon publications began highlighting perceived blasphemous beliefs. Mormon writers, including Pratt, often engaged and responded to anti-Mormon writings, and at times the anti-Mormon publications seem to have led Pratt to reinterpret Smith's works and may have even influenced him to develop teachings he might have otherwise ignored. An analysis of extant texts suggests that dialogues among early Mormons influenced the development of Mormon thought to a greater extent than did the polemics between anti-Mormons and Latter-day Saints, but both dialectics remain important in explaining the evolution of early Mormon conceptions of theosis. Pratt's publications

[9] See J. Spencer Fluhman, "An 'American Mahomet': Joseph Smith, Muhammad, and the Problem of Prophets in Antebellum America," *Journal of Mormon History* 35, no. 3 (Summer 2008): 23–45.

demonstrate that influences both inside and outside of Mormonism shaped his formulation of theosis.

The Impact of Pratt's Doctrine of Equality

Pratt's *Voice of Warning*, early Mormonism's most important non-canonical book, contains little information with respect to what would become unique Mormon theological and anthropological claims, but one anti-Mormon picked up on a phrase that became central to Pratt's early conception of theosis.[10] In *Voice of Warning*'s last section, "The Contrast Between the Doctrine of Christ and the False Doctrines of the Nineteenth Century," Pratt displayed a belief in human perfectionism. He stated that while Latter-day Saints interpreted literally the scripture, "Be ye therefore perfect, even as your Father who is in heaven is perfect," the contemporary doctrines of men warned, "Do not think to be perfect, for it is impossible to live without sin."[11] Perhaps because this understanding compared closely with some contemporary Methodist views of the perfectibility of man, it did not trouble most anti-Mormon writers. But lurking behind a fairly commonplace idea of perfectionism, anti-Mormons discovered one of Mormonism's most blasphemous teachings: the doctrine of equality with Christ.

In *Voice of Warning*, Pratt cited a portion of a revelation Smith

[10] Most American newspapers did not review *Voice of Warning*, but in November 1838, *The Christian Examiner and General Review* offered a short analysis. *The Examiner*, a leading Unitarian periodical, provided brief reviews of eight publications, including negative reviews of Emerson's recently delivered "Divinity School Address" and Pratt's *Voice of Warning*. The reviewer warned against Emerson's depersonalizing of God and his desire to attribute divinity beyond Christ. The author, though even more damning in his review of Pratt's work, expressed no problems with Pratt's theology, including his view of God or man, in part because such a description is absent from *Voice of Warning* ("Notices and Intelligence," *Christian Examiner and General Review* 25, no. 2 [November 1838]: 261–73, in American Periodical Series [hereafter APS] [database online], UMI-Proquest, http://proquest.umi.com, accessed May 26, 2008).

[11] Parley P. Pratt, *A Voice of Warning and Instruction to All People, Containing a Declaration of the Faith and Doctrine of the Church of the Latter Day Saints, Commonly Called Mormons* (New York: W. Sandford, 1837), 213.

had dictated to Frederick G. Williams in late December 1832, which includes the phrase, "The saints shall be filled with [Christ's] glory, and receive their inheritance and be made equal with him."[12] Pratt did not explain the phrase's meaning, as he had situated the scripture within a multipage quotation warning the wicked of imminent destruction. Pratt had not intended to outline a Mormon belief in theosis, and based upon a search of contemporary documents, it is unlikely that early Mormons discussed the meaning of this phrase to any great extent, much less employed it to explain human divinization. However, though the phrase was buried and unexamined in Pratt's book, it was targeted by one of the book's critics. In 1838, LaRoy Sunderland, a prominent antislavery advocate, responded to Pratt's *Voice of Warning* in an eight-part series in his New York City Methodist newspaper, *Zion's Watchman*.[13] Sunderland quoted this phrase in his February 1838 editorial, "Mormonism," under the heading, "The Writings of the Mormonites Are Replete with Nonsense and Blasphemy."[14] Sunderland provided no explanation as to the nonsensical and blasphemous nature of the statement, but Pratt, instead of ignoring the quotation or offering a mitigating interpretation, responded with an explicit affirmation of theosis.

In *Mormonism Unveiled* (1838), a response to Sunderland, Pratt outlined what he labeled as the "doctrine of equality," a teaching that some anti-Mormons would highlight, embellish, and use to

[12] Doctrine and Covenants of the Church of Jesus Christ of Latter-day Saints: Carefully Selected from the Revelations of God (hereafter Doctrine and Covenants) (Kirtland, Ohio: F G. Williams & Co., 1835), 7:24–35, especially 33; Doctrine and Covenants (1981), 88: 87–116, especially 107; and Pratt, *Voice of Warning*, 142–46, pertinent citation on p. 145.

[13] Craig L. Foster, *Penny Tracts and Polemics: A Critical Analysis of Anti-Mormon Pamphleteering in Great Britain, 1837–1860* (Salt Lake City: Greg Kofford Books, 2002), 16.

[14] LaRoy Sunderland, "Mormonism," *Zion's Watchman*, 10 February 1838. Sunderland reprinted his periodical series in a pamphlet entitled *Mormonism Exposed and Refuted* (New York: Piercy & Reed, 1838). Sunderland again cited this scripture in his 1842 exposé on Mormonism, which contained much of the same information as his 1838 series (Sunderland, *Mormonism Exposed. In Which Is Shown the Monstrous Imposture, the Blasphemy, and the Wicked Tendency, of That Enormous Delusion, Advocated by a Professedly Religious Sect, Calling Themselves "Latter Day Saints"* [New York: Office of N.Y. Watchman, 1842], 36, 56.

discredit the Mormons.[15] Pratt quoted the scripture Sunderland had cited and explained that Christ and his apostles had taught the same doctrine, as demonstrated in the New Testament.[16] He included the scripture from John, where Christ teaches that the Spirit "will guide you into all truth."[17] In explicating these scriptures, Pratt explained that God possessed all truth and thus contained all knowledge, which made him the all-powerful God.[18] According to Pratt, through the Spirit, God's followers could also obtain all truth and become equal with God in knowledge and power. Pratt wrote that through this process "the redeemed return to the fountain, and become *part* of the great *all*, from which they eminated." He continued, quoting from Smith's February 1832 revelation, "Hence, the propriety of calling them 'GODS, even the *sons of God*.'"[19]

[15] Parley P. Pratt, *Mormonism Unveiled: Zion's Watchman Unmasked, and Its Editor, Mr. L. R. Sunderland, Exposed: Truth Vindicated: The Devil Mad, and Priestcraft in Danger!* 3rd. ed. (New York: O. Pratt & E. Fordham, 1838), 27. While Pratt's American contemporaries often used the phrase "doctrine of equality" in reference to democratic ideals, religious figures only rarely appropriated the phrase. The phrase, as Pratt used it, did not take hold within Mormon rhetoric. See n24 below for anti-Mormon sources attacking the claim that the Saints would be made equal with Christ.

[16] Specifically, Pratt noted Christ's prayer for his disciples to become one with him and his Father, the reference to becoming joint heirs with Christ and the scripture explaining that those who overcome will sit with Christ, as Christ overcame and sits with the Father.

[17] John 16:13.

[18] Some of Smith's early revelations and translations emphasize knowledge as the key to power, and this idea became a central component of his thought during the Nauvoo period. See Joseph Smith, *The Words of Joseph Smith*, ed. Andrew F. Ehat and Lyndon W. Cook (Provo, Utah: Religious Studies Center, BYU, 1980), 113–14, 202.

[19] Pratt, *Mormonism Unveiled*, 27. See Document and Covenants (1835), 95:5; and Document and Covenants (1981), 76:58. This wording can be traced to John in the New Testament and Psalms in the Old Testament (John 10:34; Psalms 82:6). Peter Crawley suggests that in describing this doctrine of equality, Pratt anticipated "the dramatic ideas outlined by Joseph Smith in the King Follett discourse" (Crawley, *A Descriptive Bibliography of the Mormon Church*, 1:78). The phrase, "the redeemed return to the fountain, and become *part* of the great *all*, from which they eminated," reminds one of some hermetic, mystic, Gnostic, and Neoplatonic teachings. In 1832, Joseph Smith dictated a revelation demonstrating his persistent quest to uncover a prelapsarian "pure language." The revelation states that Sons Ahman "are the greatest of all the parts of God excepting Son Ahman and Ahman." In 1855, Orson Pratt cited this revelation and, with respect to Sons Ahman, concluded that "these intelligent beings (*continued, next page*)

Pratt based his doctrine of equality on Smith's revelation, now known as Section 76 of the Doctrine and Covenants, but Pratt interpreted the 1832 statement in new ways. He may have heard Smith or another Latter-day Saint explain this scripture or, alternatively, he may have independently interpreted the phrase in this way before 1838. But it seems that Sunderland's citation of the scripture led Pratt to contemplate the revelation's meaning and then offer a new interpretation. Pratt, instead of hiding the idea of deification, felt that Smith's revelations, backed by the Bible, justified him in articulating a kind of theosis. During the next few years, anti-Mormon pamphlets mischaracterized the Mormon doctrine of equality, but they pointed to *Mormonism Unveiled* as the source of the teaching, and indeed, Pratt's 1838 pamphlet seems to be the first noncanonical Church publication containing an idea of theosis, which, at this stage, was not much different from contemporary views of human perfectionism.

While anti-Mormon pamphlets went beyond what Pratt had stated, his brother Orson borrowed from *Mormonism Unveiled* in outlining a similar doctrine, though he downplayed some of the implications. It seems probable that *Mormonism Unveiled*, which Orson helped distribute after Parley left New York for England in 1839, became the principal source for Orson's discussion of the Saints becoming like Christ in his *Interesting Account of Several Remarkable Visions* (1840).[20] Similar to Parley, Orson reasoned that Christ's disciples had potential to become like God, explaining:

---

are all parts of God, and that those who have the most of the parts of God are the greatest . . . [and] wherever a great amount of this intelligent Spirit exists, there is a great amount or proportion of God, which may grow and increase until there is a fulness of this Spirit, and then there is a fulness of God." By this point Orson had equated the Holy Spirit, which he conceived of as an inexhaustible amount of intelligent particles existing throughout the universe, with the Great God. Ahman, for Orson, was the Great God, and consequently, intelligences had achieved or could achieve godhood only by interacting with, and allowing the indwelling presence of, the Holy Spirit (Orson Pratt, "The Holy Spirit and the Godhead," in *The Essential Orson Pratt* [Salt Lake City: Signature Books, 1991], 357). The manuscript for this revelation has recently been published in Robin Scott Jensen, Robert C. Woodford, and Steven C. Harper, eds., *The Joseph Smith Papers: Revelations and Translations*, vol. 1, *Manuscript Revelation Books*, eds. Dean C. Jessee, Ronald K. Esplin, and Richard Lyman Bushman (Salt Lake City: Church Historian's Press, 2008), 265.

[20] Crawley, *A Descriptive Bibliography of the Mormon Church*, 1:76–79.

"We believe that God will continue to give revelations . . . until [the Saints] come in possession of all the truth there is in existence, and are made perfect in knowledge." Orson further noted: "When in their immortal and perfect state . . . when they are made perfect in one, and become like their Saviour, then [the Saints] will be in possession of all knowledge, wisdom, and intelligence: then all things will be theirs, whether principalities or powers, thrones or dominions, and, in short, then they will be filled with all the fulness of God."[21] Orson, like his brother, equated omniscience with godhood and expressed the Saints' potential to reach such a state, but Orson tempered his claim—that the Saints would "become *like* their Saviour"—and expounded upon the meaning of equality—"then all things will be theirs . . . principalities, powers, thrones or dominions." Perhaps the Pratts drew their understanding of the revelation from Smith's own exegesis, but whatever the ultimate source of these ideas, in this instance Orson's wording suggests his reliance upon Parley. Whereas Orson, as with many early Mormon writers, often failed to cite both outside and inside sources, including his own brother's writings, anti-Mormons quickly pointed to Parley's publications as the foundational source for a radical Mormon belief in equality.

The 1841 pamphlet *Mormonism Portrayed*, ghostwritten by the Nauvoo period's most active anti-Mormon, Thomas C. Sharp, contains the phrase "the saints shall be made equal with Christ" (from Doctrine and Covenants) and cites the whole of Pratt's commentary on the scripture from *Mormonism Unveiled*.[22] However, Sharp went well beyond Pratt. He wrote that Mormons "believe that they will have power to create worlds, and that those worlds

[21] Orson Pratt, *A [sic] Interesting Account of Several Remarkable Visions, and the Late Discovery of Ancient American Records* (Edinburgh, Scotland: Ballantyne and Hughes, 1840), 30–31.

[22] William Harris, *Mormonism Portrayed; Its Errors and Absurdities Exposed, and the Spirit and Designs of Its Authors Made Manifest* (Warsaw, Ill.: Sharp & Gamble, 1841), 22–23. In 1844, *The Warsaw Signal*, edited by Thomas C. Sharp, accused Captain Frederick Marryat, an English novelist whose *Narrative of the Travels and Adventures of Monsieur Violet* (1843) contains information on the Mormons, of plagiarizing from *Mormonism Portrayed*, which, according to the front-page editorial, "was written by the editor [Sharp] of this paper, from materials furnished by Mr. Harris" ("Monsieur Violet and the Mormons," *The Warsaw Signal* 29, no. 145 [11 September 1844].

will transgress the law given, consequently they will become saviors to those worlds, and redeem them; never, until this is accomplished, will their glory be complete; and then there will be 'Lords many, and Gods many.' "[23] During the next few years, other prominent anti-Mormon writers attacked this seemingly exaggerated belief, using *Mormonism Portrayed* or *Mormonism Unveiled* as their source.[24] According to extant documents, nowhere had Pratt or any other Mormon published the claim that exalted Saints would create worlds and inhabit those worlds with humans, much less become saviors and redeem them. However, given that these views show up in later Mormon texts, anti-Mormons such as Sharp probably received their information from credible sources.[25] Pratt,

[23] Harris, *Mormonism Portrayed*, 23.

[24] On this point, Origen Bacheler (in 1841) and John C. Bennett (in 1842) both quoted *Mormonism Portrayed.* Jonathan B. Turner (in 1842), cited Pratt's *Mormonism Unveiled*. Henry Caswall described a personal anecdote and in a later work cited Turner and *Mormonism Unveiled* (O. Bacheler, "Miscellaneous," *Christian Secretary* 4, no. 42 [31 December 1841]: 4, in APS [database online], UMI-Proquest, http://proquest.umi.com, accessed May 30, 2009; John C. Bennett, *The History of the Saints; or, an Expose of Joe Smith and Mormonism* [Boston: Leland & Whiting, 1842], 130; Jonathan B. Turner, *Mormonism in All Ages: or the Rise, Progress, and Causes of Mormonism; with the Biography of Its Author and Founder, Joseph Smith, Junior* [New York: Platt & Peters, 1842], 240–41; Henry Caswall, *The City of the Mormons; or Three Days at Nauvoo in 1842* [London: J.G.F. & J. Rivington, 1842], 34; and Henry Caswall, *The Prophet of the Nineteenth Century; or, the Rise, Progress, and Present State of the Mormons, or the Latter-day Saints: To Which Is Appended, an Analysis of the Book of Mormon* [London: J.G.F. & J. Rivington, 1843], 94–95).

[25] As will be seen, Pratt's *Key to the Science of Theology* expresses the idea that exalted humans will create and people worlds. Orson also advocated this idea. See Orson Pratt, "Celestial Marriage," 1, no. 2 (February 1853): 25, in *The Seer*, photo-reprint (Salt Lake City: Eborn Books, 2000; Washington, D.C., and Liverpool, England: 1853–1854); Orson Pratt, "Celestial Marriage," 1, no. 3 (March 1853): 47, in *The Seer*; Orson Pratt, "Celestial Marriage," 1, no. 10 (October 1853): 157, in *The Seer*; and Orson Pratt, "The Redemption of the Earth—Pre-Existence—Marriage," in *Journal of Discourses of Brigham Young, President of the Church of Jesus Christ of Latter-day Saints, His Two Counselors, the Twelve Apostles, and Others*, 26 vols. (Liverpool, England: F.D. Richards and S.W. Richards, 1854–1886), 14:242 (20 August 1871). On January 11, 1846, Brigham Young received his second anointing from Heber C. Kimball, in which Kimball stated: "Thou shalt attain unto [the] Eternal Godhead, and receive a fulness of joy, and glory, and power; and that thou mayest do all things whatsoever is wisdom that thou shouldest do, even if it be *to create worlds and redeem them*" (Devery S. Anderson and Gary James Bergera, eds., *The Nauvoo Endowment Companies, 1845–1846: A Documentary History* [Salt Lake City: Signature Books, 2005], 397) (emphasis added).

based on his writings, had not conceived of theosis in this way, but in the years between *Mormonism Unveiled* and *Key to the Science of Theology*, he reformulated his views about God's nature, the nature of man, and godhood, which led him to understand equality with Christ and God to mean something similar to the view characterized by Sharp in *Mormonism Portrayed*.

The Collapse of the Divine Distance

As Pratt's understanding of God's ontology developed, so did his view of godhood and theosis. In *Mormonism Unveiled*, he presented his first printed explanation on God's ontology, attacking the unembodied God of Methodism and describing the "true God" as anthropomorphic.[26] In his early 1840s pamphlets, Pratt again denounced the Methodist idea of the Godhead and defended a God with parts. But while he held that Christ had "flesh and bones," Pratt noted that the Father was "not composed of such gross materials."[27] By the early 1840s, Pratt seemed to have grasped Smith's dictations on materialism and eternalism, which significantly revised the ontological distinction between God and man.

In his essay "The Regeneration and Eternal Duration of Matter" (1840), Pratt seems to have relied upon Smith's May 6, 1833, revelation in formulating his discussion on the eternality of matter and intelligence. Smith's revelation, now known as Section 93 of the Doctrine and Covenants, reads: "Man was also in the beginning with God. Intelligence, or the light of truth, was not created

[26] Pratt, *Mormonism Unveiled*, 31.

[27] Parley P. Pratt, *A Reply to Mr. Thomas Taylor's "Complete Failure," &c. and Mr. Richard Livesey's "Mormonism Exposed"* (Manchester, England: W. R. Thomas, 1840), 9–10; and Parley P. Pratt, *An Answer to Mr. William Hewitt's Tract Against the Latter-day Saints* (Manchester, England: W. R. Thomas, 1840), 9. Pratt's 1844 essay "Immortality and Eternal Life of the Material Body" again attacked churches that worshipped a God without body or parts. However, based on his description of the Godhead, it is difficult to know, at this point, whether Pratt believed the Father was made of flesh and bones (Parley P. Pratt, *An Appeal to the Inhabitants of the State of New York, Letter to Queen Victoria (Reprinted from the Tenth European Edition) the Fountain of Knowledge; Immortality of the Body, and Intelligence and Affection* [Nauvoo, Ill.: John Taylor, 1844], 25–26, 31–32).

or made, neither indeed can be. . . . For man is spirit. The elements are eternal, and spirit and element, inseparably connected, receive a fulness of joy."[28] According to the revelation, intelligence, or man's spirit, and matter are eternal. In his 1840 essay, Pratt also distinguished between matter and spirit and explained that both are eternal. "Matter and Spirit are the two great principles of all existence," he noted. "Every thing animate and inanimate is composed of one or the other, or both of these eternal principles."[29] In August 1839, according to Willard Richards, Joseph Smith stated that "the Spirit of Man is not a created being; it existed from Eternity & will exist to eternity."[30]

Five years later, in the essay "Immortality and Eternal Life of the Material Body" (1844), Pratt explained that "man's body is as

---

[28] Doctrine and Covenants (1835), 82:5; and Doctrine and Covenants (1981), 93:29, 33.

[29] "Matter and spirit," Pratt wrote, "are of equal duration; both are self-existent,—they never began to exist, and they never can be annihilated" (Parley P. Pratt, *Millennium, and Other Poems: To Which Is Annexed, a Treatise on the Regeneration and Eternal Duration of Matter* [New York: W. Molineux, 1840], 105). Though Pratt did not describe spirit as refined matter, his views, suggesting a materialistic monism, relate to a statement made by Smith in the summer of 1843. Perhaps Smith drew upon Pratt's work in clarifying his materialistic ontology. According to William Clayton, on May 17, 1843, Smith heard a Methodist preacher speak in Ramus and following the lecture he offered a few corrections. Clayton noted that Smith responded: "Speaking of eternal duration of matter, he I [*sic*] said. There is no such thing as immaterial matter. All spirit is matter but is more fine or pure and can only be discerned by purer eyes" (Smith, *The Words of Joseph Smith*, 203; Doctrine and Covenants [1981], 131:7). Based on the texts, Smith's borrowing from Pratt seems minimal, but Smith's language (if it is indeed his) suggests he had read Pratt's essay, which likely caused him to further question and develop his ideas on the matter. Though the phrase "eternal duration of matter" did not originate with Pratt, it does not appear to have been commonplace in nineteenth-century American rhetoric. Previously, in April 1842, Smith, or someone expressing his ideas, had stated that "spirit is a substance; that it is material, but that it is more pure, elastic, and refined matter than the body" (Joseph Smith, "Try the Spirits," *Times and Seasons* 3, no. 11 [1 April 1842]: 745). In 1844, Pratt drew upon the language of Smith's 1833 revelation in stating that material substance is "*inseparably connected* with all organized existence in all worlds, past, present, and to come" (Pratt, *An Appeal*, 26 [emphasis added]). In Pratt's "Intelligence and Affection" (1844), he again relied upon Smith's 1833 revelation in stating that intelligence and affection, "like material things, have their origin in eternal, uncreated elements" (Pratt, *An Appeal*, 36).

[30] Smith, *The Words of Joseph Smith*, 9.

eternal as his soul, or his spirit."[31] From the early to mid-1840s, Pratt, building from Smith's 1832 and 1833 revelations and with his Nauvoo teachings in mind, concluded that God, Christ, and humans exist as eternal material beings, and thus, in a radical move away from Christian conceptions of deification, asserted that no significant ontological barrier lay between man and deity. In a recent study on various traditions of Christian deification, Michael J. Christensen points out the persistence of ontological differentiations in each belief system.[32] In the few cases where Christian traditions, including forms of Eastern Christianity, propose an ontological view of human deification, advocates maintain important distinctions between Creator and divinized creation.[33] Pratt's formulations, based on Smith's teachings, uniquely closed the ontological gap between deity and mankind.

In Pratt's 1844 pamphlets, he began to focus on the qualities God possessed and especially God's use of those qualities. Pratt explained that man would possess the same attributes, and, as a matter of course, do the same things as God. In his pamphlet "Intelligence and Affection" (1844), he emphasized God's attributes, linking knowledge with affection. "The reason why [God] loves," Pratt stated, "is because he is light and truth. Or in other words, he loves because he knows." Pratt asserted that the human mind, as with God's mind, "is capable of a constant and gradual expansion to an unlimited extent." "Having discovered and set forth in plainness the origin, purpose, and destiny of man's physical organization and the powers, attributes, energies, affections and capabilities of his intellect," Pratt stated, "we must now inquire into the nature of his employment in that eternal world

[31] Pratt, *An Appeal*, 21.

[32] Christensen notes that in the Christian tradition, "what has been commonly agreed upon is that human beings are creatures, called, in some way, to be God." "Theologically," Christensen states, "human deification understood ontologically is objectionable in most Western Christian traditions" (Christensen, "The Promise, Process, and Problem of *Theosis*" in Christensen and Wittung, *Partakers of the Divine Nature*, 27, 28).

[33] See, for example, Andrew Louth, "The Place of *Theosis* in Orthodox Theology" in Christensen and Wittung, eds., *Partakers of the Divine Nature*, 39–40.

of joy and bliss." As the Godhead reigns over their kingdoms in love, so mankind could eventually rule as kings and priests and ultimately "occupy an exalted station among the councils of the sons of God." In a contemporary publication, Pratt explained that postmortal man would be made "a king and a priest unto God" and "by the acquisition of new creations, form a sufficient field for the exercise of his priestly and kingly powers," which would fulfill Isaiah's prophecy concerning the endless increase of Christ's kingdom and government. In 1844, and in the years to follow, Mormons began to openly teach and freely publish that equality with Christ meant, in part, something similar to what anti-Mormons had claimed. Mormon leaders went in different directions with this, as most plainly evidenced by Brigham Young's Adam-God theory and Orson Pratt's view of the Holy Spirit as the Great God.[34] Parley's 1845 essay "Materiality" represents his early understanding of Smith's 1844 teachings and contains elements that became central to Pratt's conception of theosis in *Key to the Science of Theology*, published a decade later. "Materiality" teaches a doctrine of theosis similar to that which *Mormonism Portrayed* had attributed to the Latter-day Saints just four years earlier.[35]

Raising Gods

Joseph Smith's April 7, 1844, sermon, known as the King Follett Discourse, represents the apogee of his thinking with respect to

[34] According to extant texts, Brigham Young first publicly taught his Adam-God doctrine on April 9, 1852, during the Church's spring general conference (Young, "Self-Government—Mysteries—Recreation and Amusements, Not in Themselves Sinful—Tithing—Adam, Our Father and Our God," in *Journal of Discourses* 1:46–53). See David Buerger, "The Adam-God Doctrine," *Dialogue* 15, no. 1 (Spring 1982): 14–58. Though in 1845, for the first time in print, Orson Pratt began developing his intelligent-matter theory, he forcefully articulated his idea of the Great God in "Great First Cause, or the Self-Moving Forces of the Universe" (1851), in *The Essential Orson Pratt* (Salt Lake City: Signature Books, 1991), 173–97. The different interpretations advanced by Young and Pratt contributed to their contentious relationship. See Gary J. Bergera, *Conflict in the Quorum: Orson Pratt, Brigham Young, Joseph Smith* (Salt Lake City: Signature Books, 2002).

[35] Pratt, *An Appeal*, 35–40, quotes on pp. 35, 37, 36, 39, and 40.

God, man, and godhood, and it contains teachings that Mormon thinkers, Pratt included, employed in outlining later conceptions of theosis.[36] In the sermon, Smith asserted that God was a man who had experienced mortality. He also stated that both God and man possessed self-existent spirits. Having projected the human species into the heavens and having proclaimed the co-existence of man with God, Smith urged the Saints to become Gods and receive the same exaltation as all Gods had done, which, in turn, would glorify the Father.[37] These radical ideas significantly influenced Pratt's view of theosis, as evidenced in his essay "Materiality," an editorial published in the Mormon New York periodical *The Prophet*.

In "Materiality," Pratt built upon his previous writings in shaping a Mormon monism, which he summarized in the statement, "Nothing exists which is not material." Pratt separated atheistic non-materialists from believing materialists, declaring that the spiritualized sectarian God and heaven do not exist. Taking his cue from Smith's 1844 teachings on God's nature and man's potential, Pratt questioned, "What is God?" and responded, "He is material, organized intelligence, possessing both body and parts. He is in the form of man, and is in fact of the same species; and is a moddle [*sic*], or standard of perfection which man is destined to attain." Christ, Pratt explained, "is every way like his father . . . possessing [immortal flesh and bones and] the same power and atributes [*sic*]." In outlining a Mormon version of the Great Chain of Being, Pratt further described the makeup of angels, spirits, and men, and provided an advanced Mormon conception of theosis.[38]

In answering the question "What are men?" Pratt asserted man's ontological equality with God and outlined an *Imitatio Christi* that exceeded previous Mormon conceptions of theosis. Men "are the offspring of God the father, and brother of Jesus Christ," Pratt

[36] On the doctrinal importance of the King Follett Discourse, see Van Hale, "The Doctrinal Impact of the King Follett Discourse," *BYU Studies* 18, no. 2 (Winter 1978): 209–25.

[37] For the extant manuscripts of the King Follett Discourse, see Smith, *The Words of Joseph Smith*, 340–62; and Stan Larson, "The King Follett Discourse: A Newly Amalgamated Text," *BYU Studies* 18, no. 2 (Winter 1978): 193–208.

[38] Parley P. Pratt, "Materiality," *The Prophet* 1, no. 52 (24 May 1845), no pagination.

explained. "They were once intelligent spirits in the presence of God, and were with him before the earth was formed." Fit for "several changes," he continued, humans are "capable of receiving intelligence and exaltation to such a degree, as to be raised from the dead with a body like that of Jesus Christ, and to possess immortal flesh and bones, in which they will eat, drink, converse, love, walk, sing, play on musical instruments, go on missions from planet or from system to system: being Gods, or sons of God, endowed with the same powers, atributes [*sic*], and capacities that their heavenly father and Jesus Christ possess." Pratt's 1845 definition of godhood, like the contemporary rhetoric of Manifest Destiny, emphasized mobility and land acquisition. "Thus perfected," he wrote, "the whole family will possess the material universe, that is, the earth, and all other planets and worlds." By 1845, Pratt conceived of theosis as achieving the same divine status as Christ and his Father. But by the time Pratt wrote *Key to the Science of Theology*, he believed that perfected humans' co-existence with God meant more than ontological equivalence.[39]

Key to the Science of Theology, written between 1851 and 1855, contains a well-developed conception of theosis and serves as the culmination of Pratt's writings about godhood and man's potential. Though these late teachings on theosis depend heavily upon Smith's Nauvoo instructions, including his King Follett Discourse, and build upon Pratt's own 1840s writings, the particular conception of theosis that Pratt outlined in *Key to the Science of Theology* went beyond Smith's public explanations of deification and exceeded Pratt's previous explorations. In chapter 5, Pratt outlined his understanding of the nature of God and man and in some ways collapsed the two ideas. Over four years prior to the King Follett Discourse, William Clayton recorded Joseph Smith as having stated: "That which is without body or parts is nothing. There is no other God in heaven but that God who has flesh and bones. . . . God the father took life unto himself precisely as Jesus did."[40] In April 1843 Smith reaffirmed, "The Father has a body of

[39] Ibid.

[40] Smith, *The Words of Joseph Smith*, 60.

flesh & bones as tangible as mans, the Son also."[41] In *Key to the Science of Theology*, Pratt explained that God, like Christ, possessed a body of "flesh and bones and sinews, and all the attributes, organs, senses, and affections of a perfect man." Pratt worked this anthropological emphasis into his definition of godhood: "An immortal man, possessing a perfect organization of spirit, flesh and bones, and perfected in his attributes, in all the fullness of celestial glory, is called God." Pratt explained that Christ had obtained a fullness: Christ "claims affinity and equality . . . with His Father," he wrote, and "claims, on the other hand, affinity and equality with His brethren." Those humans who receive a fullness of celestial glory, Pratt noted, "will become like [the Father and the Son] in every respect, physically and in intellect, attributes or powers." Pratt, in line with Smith's King Follett Discourse, emphasized the kinship between God and man, but he further concluded that exalted humans would participate in the creative and governing processes that defined godhood.[42]

Pratt emphasized God's creating and governing powers, including the procreation of "pure, holy, incorruptible and eternal beings," but he also attributed these godly activities to exalted Saints. Pratt noted, "Any one of these Gods may create, organize, people, govern, control, exalt, glorify and enjoy worlds on worlds." The only difference between God and man, he explained, "consists in the varied grades of intelligence and purity, and also in the variety of spheres occupied by each." As Christ is subordinate to the Father "because of age and authority," so man is subordinate to the Son. In Pratt's last chapter, he added Smith's teachings on (plural) marriage and procreation into the equation and summed up his theory of theosis in a question: "Would you, like your heavenly Father, prompted by eternal benevolence and charity, wish to fill countless millions of worlds with our begotten sons and daughters, and to bring them through all the gradations or progressive being,

[41] Ibid., 173. As early as 1832 and 1833, Smith dictated revelations suggesting that man's "fulness of joy" depended upon the possession of a body. Perhaps this idea informed later views on God's possession of a body (Doctrine and Covenants [1835], 7:3, 6; 82:5; and Doctrine and Covenants [1981], 88:15, 28; 93:33–34).

[42] Pratt, *Key to the Science of Theology*, 31, 32, 33.

to inherit immortal bodies and eternal mansions in your several dominions?" As one would expect, Pratt's conception of theosis depended on a particular understanding of the nature of God, and once he had accepted the idea that "Gods . . . and men are all of one species, one race, one great family," then human divinization meant becoming all that God was and doing all that God did.[43]

Pratt's idea of man's evolution toward godhood evolved through engaging Smith's teachings and responding to anti-Mormon attacks. In these dialogues Pratt formed his views of God and man, which determined how he understood and explained exaltation. His 1838 conception of theosis centered on a godly attribute, omniscience, but as Pratt's subsequent exegesis of Smith's early revelations led to his understanding of man's co-eternal and co-material existence with God, human divinization came to mean that exalted Saints would be, ontologically, qualitatively, and experientially the same being as God. The development of theosis within Pratt's publications evidences the dialectical nature and evolving process involved in shaping early Mormon theological concepts.

[43] Ibid., 31–32, 33, 35, 171, quotes on pp. 31 and 162.

CHAPTER 7

Parley P. Pratt, Mormonism, and Latin America

A Mission's Contribution to Latter-day Saint Growth

DAVID CLARK KNOWLTON

Parley P. Pratt's voyage to Chile in 1851 is generally cited as the beginning of Latter-day Saint missionary work in Latin America, despite the fact that Pratt was unable to gain converts and decided to cut his trip short.[1] On board the ship *Dracut*, returning to San Francisco, Pratt penned a letter to Church president Brigham Young describing his mission and the future of Mormon missionary work in South America.[2]

> [W]e embarked on this ship bound for San Francisco, without a sufficiency of the language to turn the keys of the Gospel as yet to these nations. We staid till all our means were exhausted and sought and prayed diligently for our way to open; but we could neither speak the language sufficiently to preach the Gospel nor find any way to earn our

[1] F. LaMond Tullis, *Mormons in Mexico: The Dynamics of Faith and Culture* (Logan: Utah State University Press, 1987), 6; Nestor Curbelo, *The History of Mormons in Argentina* (Salt Lake City: Greg Kofford Books, 2008); Rodolfo Acevedo, *Los Mormones en Chile* (Santiago, Chile: Cumora, 1991).

[2] Scot Facer Proctor and Maurine Jensen Proctor, eds., *Autobiography of Parley P. Pratt* (Salt Lake City: Deseret Book, 2000), 501–502.

living, so we found it necessary to return to California while we still study the language on board.

Although Pratt was frustrated, he felt there was a future for Mormonism in South America and had plans to ensure that future was obtained. However, decades passed before a permanent Mormon missionary presence was established in South America, Central America, or Mexico. Nevertheless, Pratt's mission to the Pacific, which included Chile, and the larger context in which he and other Mormon missionaries labored, built the base for the future success of the church in Spanish- and Portuguese-speaking America.

Mormonism and California

Five years before Pratt's travels to Chile, Mormons made an earlier foray into Latin America, when the ship *Brooklyn* docked in what its passengers thought was Mexican San Francisco in July 1846. The 238 Latter-day Saints on board were part of a migration of Mormons to what was then northern Mexico. They had sailed around the tip of South America to reach California while the main body of Saints went overland.[3] The Mexican-American War broke out while the Saints were traveling, and the Mormons on the *Brooklyn* arrived that July day in what they thought was Mexican California, only to find a U.S. flag flying. Nevertheless, the culture and institutions of California remained Hispanic.[4]

When the Saints disembarked from the *Brooklyn*, they doubled or more the population of Yerba Buena, as San Francisco was then

[3] Michael Van Wagenen, *The Texas Republic and the Mormon Kingdom of God* (College Station: Texas A&M University Press, 2002), details the important discussions of the Nauvoo leadership around settling in Texas, on the Mexican frontier, an area where Lyman Wight and followers would later settle, while Brigham Young went west to Mexico with the larger body of the Church. See also Melvin C. Johnson, *Polygamy on the Pedernales: Lyman Wight's Mormon Villages in Antebellum Texas 1845–1858* (Logan: Utah State University Press, 2006).

[4] I depart from the view that sees Latin America as an assemblage of countries and looks at it instead as an area strongly impacted by Spanish (and Portuguese) language and institutions. As a result, in this point of view, Latin America arguably includes California and the southwest United States.

known.[5] For a brief period, the Anglo population of San Francisco was predominantly Mormon.[6] However, this picture of Anglos overwhelming Hispanic California and quickly transforming it is deceptive. San Francisco was already a predominantly Anglo settlement near the Mission Dolores and military fort, the Presidio.[7] Although Hispanics also were drawn to the community, San Francisco had eight hundred inhabitants, mostly Anglos, just before the discovery of gold.

The Hispanic population of the area provides critical background for understanding Pratt's later mission to Chile and its travails. In the last years of the 1840s, the heart of Spanish-Mexican settlement in Northern California was at the south end of the San Francisco Bay, in the Villa of San José near the missions of Santa Clara and San José. With seven hundred Spanish inhabitants, and three thousand to four thousand "ex-neophyte Indians" who had been resident on the missions and adapted to Spanish and Mexican culture, San José, and not San Francisco, was the largest town in Northern California.[8] San José remains a center of Latino population and culture to this day. In 1846, Mormons arrived in a world that, though flying a U.S. flag, was still heavily Latin American.

A Spanish-speaking population was scattered throughout this part of Northern California, organized by the institutions of colonial Spain and, briefly, Mexico. There were three bases to this system: 1) the Spanish towns and forts, such as San José, 2) the missions, such as Dolores, Santa Clara, and San José, which brought Indians into Spanish society, and 3) the ranches, which organized

[5] See Ted J. Warner, "Pioneer Settlements in California," in Daniel H. Ludlow, ed., *Encyclopedia of Mormonism*, vol. 1. (New York: Macmillan, 1992), 246–48.

[6] Hubert H. Bancroft, *The History of California*, vol. 5, *1846–1849* (San Francisco: The History Company Publishers, 1886), 551, quoted in B.H. Roberts, *A Comprehensive History of the Church of Jesus Christ of Latter-day Saints* (Provo, Utah: Brigham Young University Press, 1965), 3:31.

[7] Martha Ortega Soto holds that Yerba Buena was founded in 1836 by Anglo immigrants to Alta California near the Mission Dolores, and that Hispanic settlers joined them shortly afterward. See Ortega Soto, *Alta California: Una frontera olvidada del Noroeste de México, 1769–1846* (Mexico, D.F.: Plaza y Valdés, 2001), 347.

[8] Bancroft, *History of California*, vol. 5, 3.

rural society under the direction of land grantees. This society was racially and socially complex, similar to other parts of Latin America during the same period.[9]

After the discovery of gold, Anglo Mormons found themselves joined by the first rush of miners who came from Mexico, Chile, and elsewhere in Latin America. F. LaMond Tullis writes that more than fifty thousand Chilenos arrived by 1852.[10] Add to this the large numbers of Mexicans and people from other Latin American countries, and California experienced an immigration that strengthened the region's Hispanic cultural base as Anglo dominance began to increase. Furthermore, San Francisco, because of the economy of the gold rush, was a center of Hispanic settlement and became ever more tightly connected with Pacific South America and Polynesia. Chile provided not only miners and people knowledgeable about mining, it also provisioned the mines. In addition, the sea-lanes centered in San Francisco opened to the entire Pacific, connecting San Francisco to the ports of South America as well as Australia, Polynesia, the Spanish Philippines, and China. The city was a good place from which to communicate with the entire Pacific, and Latin America in both senses of the term was an important part of Pratt's Pacific.

Not only did Latter-day Saints, under the direction of Samuel Brannan, begin holding services in San Francisco, they also spread into the other major areas of Northern California, following economic possibilities.[11] John Horner, one of the celebrated travelers on the *Brooklyn*, settled near San José, becoming one of the first Anglos to reside in the heavily Hispanic area.[12] He built in 1850 what has been described as "the first Mormon Chapel in

---

[9] Soto, *Alta California*, 377, holds that the largest number of mestizos—culturally and racially mixed populations—was in northern California and Los Angeles. Soto also writes that the San Francisco area had the largest number of large ranches established, in part as a means of halting the Anglo advance.

[10] F. LaMond Tullis, "California and Chile in 1851 as Experienced by the Mormon Apostle Parley P. Pratt," *Southern California Quarterly* 67 (Fall 1985): 291–307.

[11] On the Mormon experience in early California, see Kenneth N. Owens, *Gold Rush Saints: California Mormons and the Great Rush for Riches* (Norman: University of Oklahoma Press, 2005).

[12] Bancroft, *History of California*, vol. 5, 9.

California."[13] Horner made a fortune as a farmer during the gold rush and also was president of the San José branch of the Church. Orgin Mowry, another Latter-day Saint who settled near San José, earned a fortune by traveling to Chile in 1848, after the discovery of gold but before Pratt's journey, to buy produce that he re-sold to the miners.[14] He also made money farming and operating ship transport, as did Horner, between the South Bay and San Francisco.

Other Mormons, such as Moses Meder and John Sirrine, resided in Santa Cruz, where they built businesses such as the lumbering firm Stout, Sirrine and Meder. Santa Cruz was the site of a Spanish mission and a town that was once the third largest in Mexican California. According to Hubert Howe Bancroft, Santa Cruz's natural resources "fostered mills and factories, and for a long time placed the county next to San Francisco as a manufacturing field."[15]

Other Latter-day Saints settled close to the Swiss colony of New Helvetia near present-day Sacramento. Johan August Sutter established the Swiss colony in 1839, building it into an enclave of foreigners resistant to Spanish-speaking California. New Helvetia also established a center for trade with Indians in the area.[16] Near there, on the Stanislaus River by the San Joaquin Valley, Latter-day Saints led by William Stout built the ill-fated colony of New Hope. With its demise by 1848, many of the Mormons moved near New Helvetia.[17] Even though Latin Americans did not settle this region as thickly as the San José area, it was still part of Latin American society, evident even in the name of the Stanislaus River, which was named after a Yokuts Indian, Estanislao. Estanislao had been a mission Indian in San José. After obtaining prestige there, he rebelled and took many other mission Indians with him to the San Joaquin valley.[18] Although the Spanish

---

[13] Leo J. Muir, *A Century of Mormon Activities in California*, vol. 1 (Salt Lake City: Deseret News, 1951), 24.

[14] Philip Holmes and Jill M. Singleton, *Irvington, Freemont* (Charleston, S.C.: Arcadia Publishing, 2005), 7.

[15] Bancroft, *History of California*, 525.

[16] Soto, *Alta California*, 347–48.

[17] See Warner, "Pioneer Settlements in California."

[18] Thorne B. Gray, *The Stanislaus Indian Wars* (Modesto, Calif.: McHenry Museum Press, 1993); Jack Holterman, "The Revolt of Estanislao," *Indian Historian* 3 (Winter 1970): 43–54.

defeated Estanislao in 1829, his story indicates how important mission life and Spanish culture had become in the lives of native people even in the region near New Hope. Moreover, the area around New Hope was not only home to Hispanicized Indians, it also contained Mexican settlers and was the subject of Mexican land grants in the 1840s. Although separated by Anglo administrators from the Spanish and Mexicans, the native people who lived there were culturally part of a Latin American–style society that joined Spanish and Indian together. Furthermore, once gold was discovered, this area filled with Latino miners, especially before the forty-niners arrived and violent ethnic conflict broke out as Anglos attempted to drive out Latinos.

The Anglo Mormons were like most other Anglo immigrants to California in their unwillingness to assimilate to the norms of Hispanic California, although some did learn Spanish and interact with Hispanic Californians.[19] Nevertheless, it is easy for historians to overlook the Saints in Northern California because, as Paul Bailey wrote concerning Addison Pratt's 1847 to 1848 experience there, "his zealous soul quickly discerned all was not right with the Church."[20] Northern California Mormons existed in a certain ambivalence vis-à-vis the Church in Utah, given the main body of the Church's decision to people Utah, and the pressures it placed on Mormons elsewhere to join them. Nevertheless, that ambivalence, which was felt both by California Mormons for Utah and Utah Mormons for those in California, is less important than the residence of these members in Latin American California and

[19] Armand Mauss, *All Abraham's Children: Changing Mormon Conceptions of Race and Lineage* (Urbana: University of Illinois Press, 2003). Mauss discusses the cultural project of Anglo Saxon dominance that was and still is to some degree common among Latter-day Saints.

[20] William Glover, *The Mormons in California* (Los Angeles: G. Dawson, 1954), 77. Addison Pratt was called to do missionary work in Tahiti in 1843. He was in Tahiti when the prophet Joseph Smith was martyred. Addison Pratt decided to travel to Utah see if the news was true. After finding Brigham Young in Salt Lake City and consulting with the new church leadership there, he was called to return to California in 1849. See S. George Ellsworth, ed., *The Journals of Addison Pratt* (Salt Lake City: University of Utah Press, 1990).

their importance, in turn, for the future LDS Church throughout Latin America.

In 1849, Parley P. Pratt was called to preside over a mission to the Pacific and, as a result, entered this context of early Mormon life in California. Pratt's mission was not just to Chile, but to the entire Pacific. He wrote from San Francisco in 1851 to Addison Pratt, who was then in Tahiti (the Society Islands), "I hold the presidency of all the islands and coasts of the Pacific, under the direction of the First Presidency of the Church—to open the door to every nation and tongue, as fast as the way is prepared and the Lord directs, for the preaching of the gospel of salvation."[21] This area his presidency encompassed included California, and Pratt actively took charge of the Northern California Saints prior to traveling to Chile, and after his return from there.

Pratt in California

Although he had been called in 1849, Pratt began his journey from Salt Lake City to California and on to Chile in March 1851. He arrived in Los Angeles in June. After three weeks of preaching in English in a very Spanish Los Angeles, Pratt embarked on the four-day voyage to San Francisco. He arrived on July 11, and met with apostles Amasa Lyman and Charles Rich. Lyman had been the president of the California mission since April 1849. Lyman's presidency "resulted in establishing something like discipline among the scattered church members on the Pacific slope," according to B.H. Roberts.[22] Pratt, his wives, and missionaries accompanied the two apostles and their company first to the area where the Mormon colony of San Bernardino would be established in Southern California and then on to San Francisco.

[21] Proctor and Proctor, *Autobiography*, 486.

[22] Roberts, *Comprehensive History of the Church*, 3:385. For the 1849 call, see A. Delbert Palmer and Mark L. Grover, "Hoping to Establish a Presence: Parley P. Pratt's 1851 Mission to Chile," *BYU Studies* 38 (1999): 132, citing "Journal History of the Church," May 27, 1849.

In San Francisco, Pratt began preaching. There, he was named president of the San Francisco branch; wrote "A Proclamation to the Peoples of the Coasts and Islands of the Pacific," which was published in Australia;[23] began his work *A Key to the Science of Theology*; sent missionaries to Hawaii; and directed correspondence to other parts of the Pacific. He re-baptized New Hope colonist William Stout on August 19 and then traveled to San José and branch president John Horner's home.[24] Pratt also excommunicated Samuel Brannan, the former leader of the Mormons who had arrived on the *Brooklyn* and become an increasingly prominent Californian. Pratt removed him for "a general course of unchristianlike conduct, neglect of duty, and for combining with lawless elements to commit murder and other crime."[25]

This action likely referred to Brannan's relationship to the Vigilance Committee that had brought vigilante "justice" to the chaos of San Francisco.[26] The Committee had been organized in Brannan's office on June 9, 1851, almost a month before Pratt's arrival in town, and contained 716 citizens on its rolls.[27] As Will Bagley points out, part of the work of the Vigilance Committee involved the protection of Latino miners and merchants from nativist attacks by Anglos,[28] who were provoked in part by the governor of California, Persifer Smith. According to Bagley and Tullis, Brannan recognized that Anglo Californians depended on Chile's exports

[23] David J. Whittaker, "Parley P. Pratt and the Pacific Mission: Mormon Publishing in 'That Very Questionable Part of the Civilized World'," in Davis Bitton and John L. Sorenson, eds., *Mormons, Scripture, and the Ancient World: Studies in Honor of John L. Sorenson* (Provo, Utah: FARMS, 1998).

[24] Reva H. Stanley and Charles L. Camp, eds., "A Mormon Mission to California in 1851: From the Diary of Parley Parker Pratt," *California Historical Society Quarterly* 14, no. 2 (March 1935): 175.

[25] Stanley and Camp, "Mormon Mission," 176.

[26] Ibid.

[27] "California's Vigilantes; Hubert Howe Bancroft on 'Popular Tribunals.' The Organization and Work of the First Vigilance Committee in San Francisco, 1851–52," *New York Times*, July 24, 1887, 10.

[28] Will Bagley, *Scoundrel's Tale: The Samuel Brannan Papers* (Logan: Utah State University Press, 1999), 312; Jay Monaghan, *Chile, Peru, and the California Gold Rush of 1849* (Berkeley: University of California Press, 1973).

for their bread.[29] Nevertheless, despite his plans to travel to Chile, Pratt felt the activities of the Vigilance Committee and Brannan's role were not appropriate for a member of the Church. Pratt seems to have been disgusted by the Committee's lack of proper law and order. But the issue of Brannan, the Vigilance Committee, and Pratt's Chilean plans is something that needs further research if one hopes to establish what Pratt knew or did not know about Chile as he planned his missionary trip there.

These events that occupied Pratt's time in San Francisco and before he went to Chile are significant. Anglo American nativism has been a common American strategy in times of conflict over resources. As Tullis points out, nativism in California was accompanied by the appropriation of homes, farms, and enterprises of Latino Californians as well as Latino immigrants, in the face of a perceived Anglo right to California and its produce. An Anglo resistance to the learning of other languages and cultures has often accompanied nativism. Nevertheless, not all Anglo Mormons fit in with this trend, and this proved important for Pratt's efforts. One crucial example is William Stout, who did not follow the general Anglo resistance to assimilation in Hispanic Californian society. He arrived on the *Brooklyn* in 1846, was the leader of the New Hope settlement on the Stanislaus River, learned Spanish, and was a partner in a lumbering business in Santa Cruz. Apostles Lyman and Rich relied on his expertise to translate the documents of purchase in Spanish of San Bernardino from the very powerful and well-connected Lugo family.[30] People like Stout who avoided the dominant Anglo reluctance to assimilate became important for the future growth of the Church, as were Pratt's efforts to foment Spanish language skills.

Pratt's efforts to encourage Spanish language learning took place after his return from Chile. He tarried in San Bernardino, California, on his way back to Utah to make his report. While there,

[29] Tullis, "California and Chile," 294–95.

[30] Edward Leo Lyman, *San Bernardino: The Rise and Fall of a California Community* (Salt Lake City: Signature Books, 1996).

Pratt, along with apostles Lyman and Rich, "met and appointed Certain Young men to Study the Spanish Language with a view to a mission hereafter, and Br. Stout to teach a Class in Spanish in the place, to Consist of such young men as we now have, or may hereafter select."[31] Pratt felt that his mission to Chile suffered because neither he nor fellow missionary Rufus Allen spoke Spanish adequately. Pratt's missionary work depended on the technique of publishing broadsides, pamphlets, and books in order to circulate them to a broad audience and obtain an opening for potential conversions. Yet in this dependence one can also see some of the difficulties that beset his missionary endeavors when language was a barrier. As a result, Pratt took steps, such as the establishment of the Spanish classes in San Bernardino, to use the language skills available among Latter-day Saints who broke the dominant pattern of cultural closure and learned Spanish. John Henry Evans, in his book on Apostle Rich, writes, "[T]his class succeeded so well that a number of the pupils presently went to Mexico and converted many."[32]

It is significant that the classes were organized in San Bernardino. This colony of Latter-day Saints was on land that had been part of a Spanish mission, and Hispanicized mission Indians lived nearby. It was near the Spanish-speaking New Mexican settlement of Agua Mansa, which was home to thirty families, or 130 inhabitants, in 1850.[33] In San Bernardino the students could study Spanish and practice it in their daily lives.

After announcing the formation of the Spanish classes in San Bernardino, Pratt described a harvest festival he attended:

> S. Burnardino Sept 4th Atended a Harvest feast in the Bowery or Meeting house. The entire people made this feast, and assembled to enjoy it.

---

[31] Stanley and Camp, "Mormon Mission," 180.

[32] John Henry Evans, *Charles Coulson Rich, Pioneer Builder of the West* (Whitefish, Mont.: Kessinger Publishing, 2006), 219.

[33] Harold A. Whelan, "Eden in Jurupa Valley: The Story of Agua Mansa," *Southern California Quarterly* 55.4 (1973): 413–29, cited in R. Bruce Harley, "Agua Mansa: An Outpost of San Gabriel 1842–1850," *California Mission Studies Association Newsletter*, www.ca-missions.org/harleyagua.html, last accessed July 26, 2008.

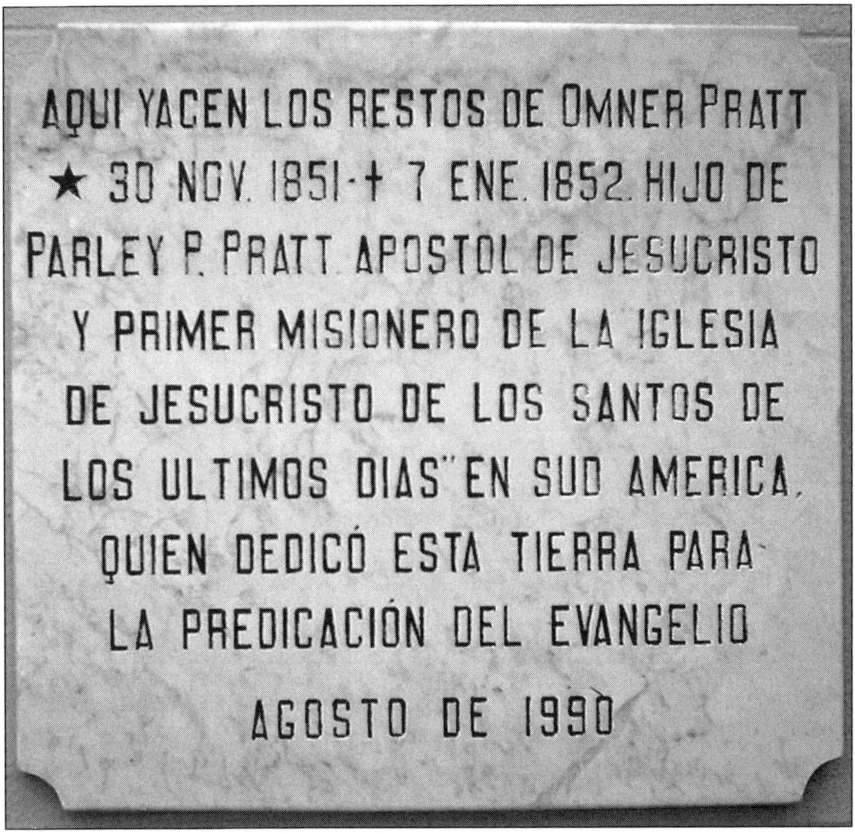

The language barrier was not the only difficulty Pratt faced in Chile. His wife Phoebe Soper gave birth there to a son, Omner, but the baby died five weeks later. This plaque commemorates his grave: "Here lie the remains of Omner Pratt, 30 November 1851–7 January 1852, son of Apostle of Jesus Christ, Parley P. Pratt, first missionary of the Church of Jesus Christ of Latter-day Saints in South America, who dedicated this land for the preaching of the Gospel."
Courtesy of the Church History Library, the Church of Jesus Christ of Latter-day Saints.

> The Room was highly and tastfully ornimented, and set off with evergreens, specimens of Grains, vegitables etc. While above the Stand was written in Large Letters HOLINESS TO THE LORD. Meeting opened by prayer and singing and a few Remarks from myself and others, after which the entire day and evening was spent in feasting dancing etc. Every variety almost which the earth produces, or Skill could prepare, was spread out in profusion, and partaken of by all citizens, Strangers, Spaniards or Indians, with that freedom and good order which is characterestic [of] the Saints. The dances were conducted with decorum and propriety, Old and young, Married and Single, Grandsire and child all mingling in the dance So far as they Chose with out a Jaring Spirit to Mar their peace. An address from A. Liman and a few words from C C Rich and myself, and a prayer and benediction closed, at about 9 o Clock P.M. one of the most interesting assemblies ever witnessed in this age.[34]

If for nothing else, the assembly was interesting because it joined Indians, Spanish Californians, and Mormons, along with people of different generations. This, along with the "decorum and propriety," modeled a future Pratt desired as the Church grew among Latin Americans.

Pratt not only organized Spanish classes in San Bernardino, he personally showed a pattern of studying Spanish in preparation for some unfulfilled future return to South America. After leaving Chile and arriving in San Francisco, before traveling to San Bernardino, Pratt wrote, "[M]y time was again devoted to the ministry in the Church at San Francisco and San Jose, and in visiting, studying language, writing to the other missionaries, and in the preparations for our homeward journey."[35] It is not known if he availed himself of the Spanish-speaking communities in San Francisco and San José, but in both places Pratt could easily have found interlocutors, including some of his fellow Mormons, to aid him in strengthening his command of the language.[36] Once back in Salt Lake City, Pratt continued studying Spanish, even though

[34] Stanley and Camp, "Mormon Mission," 180.

[35] Proctor and Proctor, *Autobiography*, 509.

[36] Tullis, "California and Chile," 299, argues that Pratt had no native speakers to help him learn Spanish. Yet native speakers abounded in California. Whether there were Latino members of the Church and to what degree Pratt may or may not have relied on them is an important issue that requires more research.

his time was occupied with legislative duties. In 1854, before his return to California on his second mission, he taught a Spanish class in Salt Lake, perhaps at the University of Deseret.[37]

Pratt was called to a second mission to California in 1854, after his return from Chile. He stayed in California this second time for more than a year and dedicated himself to the affairs of the Church in Northern California, to writing, and, most significantly, to efforts to establish a press for the publishing of Mormon materials, in order, in part, to avoid dependency on outsiders. The press probably had the purpose, as well, to enable the publication of works in languages such as Spanish. Pratt wrote a broadside while in Chile, which he partially translated into Spanish. Yet he could not get it published in Chile, in part because of limits on the press. Once he returned to California, he published a bilingual edition entitled "Proclamation Extraordinary." Although Pratt did not accomplish his dream of establishing a Mormon press—he had run out of time at the end of his California mission—his successor, George Q. Cannon, did accomplish the task. According to Whittaker, this press would contribute to what later became Deseret Book, the most significant Latter-day Saint publishing house.[38]

In 1857, the year of Pratt's death, the Church called the California Saints to leave their homes and to come to Utah because of hostilities between the federal government and the Church in the Utah War. Nevertheless, the Church continued to build on the language and cultural skills developed among particular Latter-day Saints in the engagement with Latin America. Parley P. Pratt's ongoing influence is evident there, though it must be understood in context.

Daniel Jones and Nathan Tenney

Although the Church of Jesus Christ of Latter-day Saints closed the San Bernardino colony as part of the general events of 1857 and recalled the Saints to Utah, Brigham Young continued to suggest

[37] Proctor and Proctor, *Autobiography*, 511.
[38] Whittaker, "Pratt and the Pacific Mission."

and sponsor interaction with Latin America. The focus narrowed, however, to the immediate environs of Utah and its neighboring states, though Mexico and other countries were still of interest to the Church. The Church's engagement with Latin American society in the Southwest had many purposes, including the exploration of land for future settlement as well as missionary work. Pratt's influence on the mission work in these places was developed through other people, and occasionally indirectly.

One of the people who continued Pratt's work with Latin America was Daniel Jones, who arrived in New Mexico during the Mexican-American War. After the war, the New Mexico territory, as well as Utah, was transferred to the United States. Originally from Missouri, Jones stayed among Spanish-speakers in New Mexico for three years and became an intermediary between Anglos and Mexicans. He wrote in his autobiography, "While in Mexico I formed a kindly feeling toward many of the Mexican people, studied the Spanish language so as to read and write it and act as an interpreter."[39] He traveled to Utah on the Old Spanish Trail in 1850 with a company that was taking sheep to sell in the mines of California. Jones wrote that the guide was a man named Thomas Chacón, "a Mexican Indian."[40] Chacón had traveled prior to this "as an assistant guide" with the Mormon Battalion, a military unit of Church members during the Mexican-American War, and had spent the winter of 1847–48 with the Mormons in Salt Lake City. Jones stated that he "was much under the influence of the guide, being conversant with his language. I was in the habit of riding along with him and listening to his talk about the Indians. He often told me how he succeeded in making peace with them."[41] Of importance for Jones, Chacón had knowledge and skills that enabled the party to pass through Ute country. Chacón also recommended that Jones travel to the Mormons and stay with them

---

[39] Daniel W. Jones, *Forty Years among the Indians: A True yet Thrilling Narrative of the Author's Experiences among the Natives* (Salt Lake City: Juvenile Instructor Office, 1890), 19.

[40] Ibid., 23.

[41] Ibid., 24.

to heal from a gunshot wound. Following this advice, Jones played on Chacón's influence with the Mormons and was able to stay. As a result, Jones subsequently joined the Mormon Church and played an important role in missionary work in Latin America.

Building on his knowledge of Spanish and his increasing acquaintance with Indian languages and customs, Jones became an Indian trader. Spanish was a useful tongue for engaging southwest Indians. At the time, because of the centuries of Spanish colonization, the language was a kind of lingua franca in the region. Importantly for Utah, some of the Utes spoke Spanish. They had learned the language because of their historic role on the northern frontier of the Spanish empire and their historic trade with Spanish and Mexican towns and villages, and now with Mormons.[42] Brigham Young and other authorities drew on Jones's skills as an interpreter, such as in negotiations with Mexican merchants to have them cease purchasing captive children from the Utes.[43] Both Jones's knowledge of Spanish and his experience with Indians were useful to the Church over the coming years in its attempts to missionize in Latin America.

Jones developed his language and cultural skills without the influence of Parley P. Pratt. They came from the broader circumstances of interaction between Anglos and Mexicans. Nevertheless, they contributed, indirectly, to expanding Pratt's influence in Latin America. Jones's experience also illuminates the Spanish-speaking, Latin American world that was part of Mormon life in the West, though underrepresented in Mormon history.

Another intermediary between Mormons, Mexicans, and Indians was Ammon Tenney, whose work also shows the influence of

---

[42] See Ned Blackhawk, *Violence over the Land: Indians and Empires in the Early American West* (Cambridge, Mass.: Harvard University Press, 2006).

[43] Jones, *Forty Years*. On the slave trade, see Sondra Jones, *The Trial of Don Pedro León Luján: The Attack against Indian Slavery and Mexican Traders in Utah* (Salt Lake City: University of Utah Press, 2000), as well as Forrest Cuch, ed., *A History of Utah's American Indians* (Salt Lake City: Utah Division of Ethnic Affairs and the Utah State Historical Society, 2004), and Carling Malouf and A. Arline Malouf, "The Effects of Spanish Slavery on the Indians of the Intermountain West," *Southwestern Journal of Anthropology* 1.3 (Autumn 1945), 378–91.

Parley P. Pratt's attitudes toward Spanish. Born in 1844 in Iowa, Tenney lived much of his childhood in the Mormon colony of San Bernardino, California. He was one of the young men called to study Spanish by Pratt. Tenney's father, Nathan, was the bishop in San Bernardino, and his mother taught school for Anglos and Mexicans in San Bernardino. The school was located in one room of the Estancia building, now called Asistencia, which was the Spanish center of the rancho of the San Gabriel Mission.

Before his participation in the language classes, Tenney likely already had some small knowledge of Spanish given his and his family's interactions with the Spanish-speaking community in and near San Bernardino. However, the focus of the Spanish classes must have helped give impetus for and encouraged more interaction with local Spanish speakers over the next five years. As noted earlier, Hispanicized Indians lived in and near San Bernardino, and there was a substantial Spanish-speaking New Mexican settlement, called Agua Mansa, near the colony on land that had belonged to the secularized mission.

Shortly after leaving California to move to Utah in 1858, Ammon Tenney, only fifteen years old, served as an interpreter for Jacob Hamblin's 1858 expedition to the Hopi mesas.[44] William Stout, whom Pratt and the other apostles had called to teach the San Bernardino Spanish classes, stayed in California. A teacher and local politician in San Bernardino, he became an opponent to continued Church authority in political affairs.[45] He did not migrate to Utah; his will was probated in 1886 in San Bernardino.[46] In contrast, after they left San Bernardino, Tenney and his family settled in Washington County, Utah, an area still on the Old Spanish Trail, whose terminus had been in San Bernardino. Tenney's abilities as an interpreter made him continually useful in the Church's expansion.

The twin issues of colonization and missionary work motivated Brigham Young to call missionaries to Mexico and New Mexico

[44] James H. McClintock, *Mormon Settlement in Arizona* (Whitefish, Mont.: Kessinger Publishing, 2004), 57.

[45] Lyman, *San Bernardino,* 154–55.

[46] "Ship Brooklyn Passengers," www.shipbrooklyn.org/graves4.html, accessed July 27, 2008.

in 1874, among them Ammon Tenney and Daniel Jones. Given the more than twenty years of interaction between Mormons and Mexican Americans in the Southwest, it is notable that Mormons did not rely at this time on native speakers of Spanish to aid the missionary effort. Instead, President Young relied on people with experience exploring and settling southern Utah, people who had a background of work with Indians, and people who spoke Spanish.

Mission to Mexico

Why Young waited until 1874 to send missionaries to Mexico is an important question. Part of the answer stems from a problem that made Parley P. Pratt's 1851 trip to Chile difficult, an issue that he communicated at length in his letters to Brigham Young: the lack of religious freedom. It is probable that Pratt had thought the liberals would win the civil conflict there and open the door to religious pluralism. Unfortunately, that was not the case. He arrived in the midst of a civil war won by the pro-clerical conservatives. Pratt wrote:

> The constitution [of Chile] establishes the Roman Catholic religion, supports it out of the treasury, and prohibits all others. . . .
>
> The revolution which raged so violently this season in Chili professed to be in favor of universal suffrage, and of absolute liberty of conscience, of speech, and of the press. The masses, so far as I am able to judge, are warm revolutionists, but they don't like to fight. The revolution cost some 5,000 lives, and ended in a general amnesty, without any alteration of the Government. But the people are sanguine in their hope—they think to accomplish their liberties in a few years.
>
> In the provinces of Buenos Ayres a long civil war has raged, which is now about terminating in favor of the more liberal party, aided by Brazil.
>
> Peru is tranquil. . . . Should Peru sustain her liberties, a field is opened in the heart of Spanish America, and in the largest, best informed and most influential city and nation of South America, for the Bible, the Book of Mormon, and the fullness of the Gospel to be introduced.[47]

Mexican society also was closed to religious pluralism in 1852, when Pratt wrote. Five years later, the liberals established a

[47] Proctor and Proctor, *Autobiography*, 502–503.

constitution guaranteeing religious freedom. However, the liberal republic was overthrown and a conservative monarchy established in 1864. In 1867, when Mormons had garnered ten more years of experience in the U.S. Southwest since the evacuation of California in 1857, and at a time of increasing demand for expansion due to Mormon population growth, the liberals won once again and restored the Mexican republic. Religious pluralism again became possible. By 1873, the liberal reforms were incorporated into the constitution.[48] Furthermore, United States business interests were increasingly active in northern Mexico, and other efforts were afoot to settle Anglo Americans there.[49] As a result, the LDS Church could consider sending missionaries.

In 1874, Brigham Young called Daniel W. Jones as well as Henry Brizzee, who spoke Spanish, to prepare for a mission to Mexico.[50] Brizzee had been a member of the Mormon Battalion and had stayed in California as part of a smaller company after the main Battalion returned home. Jones wrote about the dread he felt when first informed he was to be called to Mexico: "My dread was owing to the power of Catholicism that I had seen prevail in that land while living there from 1847-1850. . . . That the country had been revolutionized and religious freedom declared I had not learned."[51]

Young instructed Jones and Brizzee to begin translating extracts of the Book of Mormon, something Pratt had hoped to accomplish. The translation effort advanced once an educated, native speaker of Spanish, Meliton G. Trejo, joined the effort. Trejo was a Spaniard of social standing who learned of the Church while in the Philippines and came to Utah, where he was baptized. Two decades earlier, Pratt had hoped that a young, educated Chilean—a native Spanish-speaker—would accompany him, his wife, and Rufus Allen on their return to California on the *Dracut* and help

[48] See Michael C. Meyer, William L Sherman, and Susan M. Deeds, *The Course of Mexican History* (Oxford: Oxford University Press, 2006), for a treatment of the Mexican political history of this period.

[49] John Mason Hart, *Empire and Revolution: The Americans in Mexico since the Civil War* (Berkeley: University of California Press, 2002).

[50] Tullis, *Mormons in Mexico*, 17.

[51] Jones, *Forty Years*, 221.

in the efforts of translation. But it was the Spaniard Trejo, twenty years later, who provided that assistance.[52]

The effort had to face the challenge of raising independent money for publication, since the Church did not take that responsibility but delegated it to the missionaries and their friends and contacts. This was one of Pratt's concerns, and one that motivated him, in his second mission to California, to attempt to establish a Latter-day Saints press.[53]

Once the selections of the Book of Mormon were in press with money raised by Jones and the others, an expedition was put together in 1875 to explore Arizona and northern Mexico as well as to proselytize along the way. Jones wrote that "[a]t this time there was but little known by our people of Arizona. Even Salt River valley was not known by the head men."[54] Helaman Pratt, Parley Pratt's son who was raised in the Salt Lake valley and pioneered along the Muddy River in what is now southern Nevada, related that his brother Parley P. Pratt, Jr., wrote him that "Bro. D. W. Jones wanted one of Father's boys to accompany him on a mission to Old Mexico. Parley asked me how I would like to go. I answered that if called by the proper authority I was willing to go as the spirit had seemed to impress me with a desire to for some time."[55] Helaman Pratt was called to be part of this mission and his participation set the stage for descendants of Parley P. Pratt to have continuing influence on the affairs of the Church in Latin America.

[52] Another Spaniard, Olivas Villanueva Aoy, may also have helped in the translation of the Book of Mormon selections. He joined the Church in 1873 in Utah and evidently assisted with the translation. He subsequently was important as a schoolteacher and in building the Church in El Paso, Texas. See Conrey Bryson, "A Man Named Aoy," *Password* 35 (Summer 1990); Mario T. García, *Desert Immigrants: The Mexicans of El Paso, 1880–1920* (New Haven, Conn.: Yale University Press, 1981); and Teresa Terrazas, Monica Guillen, and Christine Ansalmo, "Enigmatic Olivas Aoy Began School for Mexican Children," *Borderlands*, www.epcc.edu/ftp/homes/monicaw/borderlands/19_olivas_aoy.htm, accessed July 23, 2008.

[53] Whittaker, "Pratt and the Pacific Mission," 51–84.

[54] Jones, *Forty Years*, 263.

[55] "Helaman Pratt's Journal. While traveling from Salt Lake City on a Mission to Old Mexico [1875–1878]," original at LDS Church History Library, transcript on http://jared.pratt-family.org/parley_family_histories/helaman-pratt-journal-1875.html, accessed July 27, 2008.

The mission also included James Z. Stewart, who from 1873 to 1875 was principal of the Logan Seminary,[56] Wiley C. Jones (Daniel Jones's son), Robert H. Smith, and, significantly, Ammon Tenney, as well as Anthony Ivins. At the time both Tenney and Ivins resided in southern Utah, although Ivins would later become a General Authority of the Church, specifically an apostle and counselor in the Church's First Presidency. The expedition explored southward from Utah into the Salt River Valley, then to the old Spanish town of Tucson, and finally eastward to El Paso, Texas. Along the way the group distributed copies of the selections from the Book of Mormon to Mexicans and Indians.[57]

While the main body of missionaries traveled in northern Mexico, distributing their literature, scouting out possible settlement sites, and proselytizing, Ammon Tenney and Robert Smith returned to New Mexico and converted many people at Zuni, through the medium of Spanish.[58] Other missionaries to the southwest Indians joined them.

After the return of the main party from Mexico, another group was organized to go there. It included Helaman Pratt, James Z. Stewart, Isaac Z. Stewart, George Terry, Lewis Garff, and Meliton Trejo. Upon reaching Mexico, this group split into three sets of two to travel distinctive paths into Mexico. Brigham Young was interested in the possibility of settling in Yaqui country, which was part of Helaman Pratt's responsibility to search out. In 1879, Apostle Moses Thatcher, James Z. Stewart, and Meliton Trejo returned to central Mexico, this time to Mexico City, where the Church became established.[59] In subsequent years, many of those

---

[56] Rodney J. Sorenson, "Establishment of Brigham Young College," MendonUtah.Net, www.mendonutah.net/history/cache_county/26.htm, accessed July 23, 2008.

[57] Jones, *Forty Years*, 251.

[58] Tullis overstates the case when he writes, "Robert H. Smith and Ammon M. Tenney associated themselves with the affair until the travelers reached El Paso del Norte (Ciudad Juarez), where their difficulties with Daniel W. Jones occasioned their leaving the group and returning home." F. LaMond Tullis, "Early Mormon Exploration and Missionary Activities in Mexico," *BYU Studies* 22, no. 3 (1982): n. 2.

[59] Intriguingly, Moses Thatcher grew up in the intercultural mix of the California gold fields. He was born in 1842 and lived in California from 1849 to 1857, his key growing-up years.

who had been in Mexico would serve multiple missions there, and many would reside in Mexico and the U.S. Southwest, lands also occupied by Mexican Americans.

As a result of the base laid by these missionaries, Anglo Latter-day Saints colonized northern Mexico at the same time people in central Mexico became dedicated to the Church.[60] Their work also led to Mormon colonization in northern Arizona, New Mexico, and southern Colorado. These latter cases of colonization should not be separated from the work in Latin America, because they are historically of a piece and because the establishment of colonies became part of the reality of Spanish-speaking peoples as they engaged with Mormonism.

Ammon Tenney, following his mission to the Zuni, purchased land in San Juan, Arizona, which became the important Mormon settlement of St. Johns. A Spanish settlement grew up around the ford there. Following Tenney's purchase, Anglo Mormons settled the area and developed a relationship with the Spanish-speaking residents of the area.[61] After his second mission to Mexico, James Z. Stewart in 1878 was assigned by Church president John Taylor to help a group of Saints migrating from Alabama to southern Colorado by train. Stewart purchased land for them in the San Luis Valley, already inhabited by Spanish Americans, some of whom were favorable to Mormonism.[62]

The selections from the Book of Mormon that Jones, Helaman Pratt, and James Z. Stewart distributed on their first mission to Mexico circulated to Mexico City and to the hands of Plotino Rhodakanaty, who wrote letters of inquiry to the Church in Salt Lake City and, once a member, became president of the first branch in Mexico City.[63] John Taylor called veteran Mexican missionary

---

[60] Thomas Cottam Romney, *Mormon Colonies in Mexico* (Salt Lake City: University of Utah Press, 2005); Tullis, "California and Chile."

[61] McClintock, *Mormon Settlement in Arizona*, 146.

[62] Camille G. West, "Antonio's Book," *Ensign* (March 1991), 29. West cites James Z. Stewart, "Settling the San Luis Valley," San Luis Stake Manuscript History, 1878.

[63] See Raymundo Gómez González and Sergío Pagaza Castillo, *"El Aguila Mormón o el Anarquista Cristiano": Plotino Constantino Rhodakanaty, Primer Miembro de la Iglesia de Jesucristo de los Santos de los Ultimos Días en México* (México, D.F.: Museo de Historia del Mormonismo en México, 1997).

James Z. Stewart, Meliton Trejo, and newly called Apostle Moses Thatcher to a mission in Mexico to meet with Rhodakanaty. As a result of their efforts, not only was a branch established in Mexico City, but also the Church took hold among rural peoples in central Mexico who with their descendants have proven key to the Church's expansion in the country. Furthermore, they translated and published Parley P. Pratt's "A Voice of Warning" as the initial LDS missionary tract.[64]

Mormon Colonies and Parley Pratt's Descendants

The last decade of the nineteenth century found Parley P. Pratt's son Helaman residing in the Mormon Colonia Dublán, in the Mexican state of Chihuahua. While serving first as a missionary and then as the president of the Mexican mission from 1883 to 1887, Helaman Pratt helped locate and negotiate the purchase of land on which LDS colonists from the United States could settle. At the end of his mission he was called to be one of the colonists, and his family traveled from the United States to join him in Chihuahua. The Mormon settlements in Mexico mark the culmination of the period of Mormon settlement in lands occupied by Spanish-speakers. Not only were these colonies a refuge for polygamists such as Pratt from U.S. prosecution, they also produced generations of committed, loyal Anglo Mormons, many connected by close kinship to the central families of the Church, who developed native language and cultural skills in both English and Spanish as Anglo Mexicans.

The colonists have played a key role in the expansion of the Church in Latin America, along with other Americans from the Southwest who have had some Spanish language and cultural abilities. From their ranks have come many missionaries, mission presidents, and temple presidents in Latin America. Among them have been the descendants of Parley P. Pratt, especially through Helaman's line. Perhaps the most significant of Pratt's descendants

[64] Tullis, "Early Mormon Exploration and Missionary Activities in Mexico."

to serve in Latin America—and one of the most important leaders there historically in his own right—was Rey Lucero Pratt, Parley P. Pratt's grandson and Helaman's son.

Although born in Salt Lake City, Rey Lucero Pratt moved to the Mexican colonies at the age of nine. At the age of twenty-seven, he was called as a missionary and traveled to Mexico City, where a strong center of growth of Mormonism had been established in villages and towns of the Valley of Mexico and the neighboring state of Puebla. A year later, Rey Lucero Pratt was named president of the Mexican mission. He was withdrawn to the United States with the outbreak of the Mexican Revolution in 1913. While in the United States, he continued to supervise the affairs of the members in Mexico and initiated missionary work in Spanish in the United States. For much of this period his mission was headquartered in El Paso, Texas.

In 1925 Rey Lucero Pratt accompanied Apostle Melvin Ballard and Elder Rulon Wells, a member of the Quorum of the Seventy, to Buenos Aires to open the Argentine mission. Pratt was the only Spanish speaker to go. The Church had arrived in Argentina in the hearts of members from Germany who had immigrated there. As a result, Wells's German proved useful. However, Rey Lucero Pratt's cultural skills enabled the Church to begin growing outside the German ethnic enclave, a key to future growth. From Argentina, the Church subsequently expanded to the other countries in South America. In this effort, both people from the Mexican colonies and "Los Ches," those who served missions in Argentina, provided a key body of personnel. Rey Lucero Pratt was also named a member of the Seventy.

Since he spoke Spanish fluently, Rey Lucero Pratt accomplished something that eluded his grandfather, Parley P. Pratt: the translation of gospel material into Spanish. The translation effort became professionalized, however, in the hands of Eduardo Balderas. Balderas was born in Mexico City in 1907, the year Rey Lucero Pratt became mission president. Balderas's family moved to El Paso, Texas, where they joined the Church in 1918. In 1930, Balderas was asked to help translate the Doctrine and Covenants. Since then, a solid, professional force of Spanish translators has grown within the LDS Church. The material they have translated can now be published by the Church's own press. Translators and missionaries no longer have to seek independent means of publishing.

Balderas is but one of an army of Latter-day Saint missionaries and leaders who have developed the Church's work in Latin America. They have fulfilled part of what Parley P. Pratt felt was missing in his own efforts to spread the gospel in Chile. The descendants of Parley P. Pratt who have served the Church in Latin America are legion. They include Waldo Pratt Call, who was sustained in 1984 as the first Mexican-born general authority, and Carl Barton Pratt, who was named to the First Quorum of the Seventy in 1997. A great-great grandson of Parley P. Pratt, Carl B. Pratt was born in the industrial city of Monterrey, Mexico, where his father worked for American Smelting and Refining Company. Although Carl B. Pratt grew up in Arizona, from age six on, he was raised to be bilingual. Carl B. Pratt made a career as an attorney for the Church in Latin America. He also filled numerous Church callings, including regional representative, 1985–88, president of the Spain Seville Mission 1988–91, and area authority and counselor in the South America North Area, 1995–97.[65]

Conclusion

At present, more than a century and a half after Parley P. Pratt's voyage to Chile, almost forty percent of the Church's total membership is found in Spanish- and Portuguese-speaking countries, and Latino Mormons form an ever more important segment of the Church in the United States. Pratt's mission has borne much fruit. But its path was not direct.

Pratt was hampered in Chile by the difficulty of learning to communicate successfully and convincingly in a foreign language

[65] John L. Hart, "Elder Pratt Follows Five Generations of Family Footsteps," *Church News*, April 19, 1997.

as an adult, as well as by the lack of religious freedom that made his efforts to preach and publish impossible. In California, Pratt began the effort to build a Church press that could publish materials written in foreign languages, such as Spanish, and he drew together Anglos who broke with the dominant anti-assimilation attitudes, in order to prepare a cadre of young men with the language and cultural skills to proselyte Latin Americans. Because of the slow change in political affairs, it was not until the 1870s, almost twenty years after Pratt's death, that the Church sent missionaries to Mexico and to Mexican American and Spanish-speaking Indian communities in the Southwest, away from the Utah fringe. Among those missionaries was one of the pupils from the language school Pratt established in San Bernardino, as well as his son Helaman Pratt.

Parley P. Pratt's Spanish-speaking grandson, Rey Lucero Pratt, was a much-beloved leader among Latin American members of the Mormon church, and he contributed greatly to the growth of the Church in Mexico and the Southwest, as well as its beginning in Argentina. He also accomplished much of his grandfather's dream of translating materials into Spanish. The work of producing a corpus of Spanish literature, though, fell to members such as Eduardo Balderas, who created a professional group of translators, at the same time the Church's own press flourished. Although the baton of translation has passed to others, Parley P. Pratt's descendants continue to occupy roles in the Church's efforts. The Church has blossomed like a rose in Latin America. Pratt's dream has been fulfilled.

Crawford County Courthouse, Van Buren, Arkansas, where Pratt was tried and where in 2008 his descendants obtained permission to remove his remains. Photo by Ernie Deane of E. S. Burch's artwork, which was first published in *The Arkansas Valley* in 1910 by the Missouri Pacific-Iron Mountain Railway. *From the Collections of the Arkansas History Commission.*

CHAPTER 8

Honor, the Unwritten Law, and Extralegal Violence

Contextualizing Parley Pratt's Murder

PATRICK Q. MASON

"The whole country is being overwhelmed with the most abominable lying, mockery, and hatred of the Saints, and with all manner of corruption." So wrote Parley P. Pratt, an apostle of the Church of Jesus Christ of Latter-day Saints (LDS Church), reflecting on his missionary service in the eastern United States during the fall and winter of 1856–57. Having had less than miraculous results in his preaching engagements in cities including St. Louis, Cincinnati, Philadelphia, and New York, Pratt complained of the "ignorant, blind, and impenetrable" state of the people who rejected his message of salvation.[1] Though often given to hyperbole, Pratt's ruminations on the "hatred" facing him and his fellow believers became both real and personal when he discovered in St. Louis in March 1857 that Hector McLean was in hot pursuit with a vow to kill him.

Pratt and McLean had met three years earlier while Pratt was in San Francisco to preside over the LDS Church's Pacific mission. McLean's wife, Eleanor, had embraced the principles of

[1] Parley P. Pratt, *Autobiography of Parley P. Pratt*, ed. Parley P. Pratt, Jr. (Salt Lake City, Deseret Book, 1985), 402, 409.

Mormonism in 1851 and joined the Church through baptism three years later with the permission of her husband. However, Hector's displeasure with the Mormon faith steadily intensified, driving an unbridgeable wedge into a marriage already troubled by his alcoholism and occasional physical abuse. Eleanor distanced herself from her husband even as she grew closer to the Church and to Pratt, whose home she visited frequently to assist him and his ailing wife, Elizabeth Brotherton. In 1855, after Hector sent their children—without her knowledge—to live with Eleanor's parents in New Orleans so as to shield them from further indoctrination in Mormonism, Eleanor decided to leave her husband and San Francisco. She traveled first to New Orleans, where she made an unsuccessful attempt to recover her children. Empty-handed, Eleanor made her way to Salt Lake City, where in November 1855, in a ceremony officiated by Brigham Young in the Endowment House, she was sealed to Pratt as his twelfth wife, despite the fact that she was never legally divorced from Hector.

Informed about the apostle's whereabouts, perhaps by Mormon apostates, McLean followed Pratt's trail until he nearly caught him in St. Louis. With the help of other Church members, Pratt narrowly escaped to Indian Territory (modern-day Oklahoma), where he hoped to meet up with Eleanor, who had, under false pretenses, retrieved her children in New Orleans and was taking them to Utah by wagon train. With the help of numerous informers along the way, on May 6, 1857, McLean finally tracked down Eleanor a little west of Arkansas, rode up to her wagon, grabbed the children, and galloped off. Three hours later, a man identified as a "state marshal" arrested Eleanor on the charge of stealing ten dollars' worth of clothing belonging to her parents. A military escort led by an army captain apprehended Pratt the same day, and after rendezvousing with Eleanor and her captors, the entire party rode first to Fort Gibson and then to Van Buren, Arkansas, arriving on May 11.

Pratt languished in jail as Eleanor was first brought before U.S. commissioner judge John Ogden. After hearing her impassioned and forthright narration of McLean's abusive behavior toward her,

Ogden released Eleanor without further charges, although the lawyers did ask several questions about the condition of women in Utah before dismissing her. When Pratt entered the overcrowded courtroom for his hearing, McLean pulled his gun and threatened to kill the Mormon elder on the spot. Restrained by court officials, McLean put down his firearm and read a litany of charges against Pratt, successfully riling up the onlookers but having no effect on the judge, who apparently had lost sympathy for Hector after hearing Eleanor's story. The judge postponed the trial until the next day, a ruse meant to put off McLean while Pratt could be secretly released, the court finding no prosecutable charges against him.

Pratt was kept overnight in jail for his own protection. The following morning, Wednesday, May 13, 1857, Judge Ogden woke Pratt, delivered his horse, and offered him a knife and pistol for his protection, which Pratt refused before riding away. McLean soon discovered that Pratt had escaped and immediately commenced in chase, along with two other men he had assembled to assist in his manhunt. The small posse caught up with Pratt about twelve miles north of Van Buren, and McLean started shooting but missed. He then closed in on the exhausted Pratt, stabbed him twice in the chest, and rode away. Several minutes later McLean returned, dismounted, and fired his gun point blank into Pratt's neck. The local resident who witnessed the episode gathered together some of his neighbors, then listened as Pratt gave his final testimony before dying.[2]

[2] The details of Pratt's murder appear in multiple sources, the most complete of which is Steven Pratt, "Eleanor McLean and the Murder of Parley P. Pratt," *BYU Studies* 15 (1975): 1–27. The most extensive single primary source on the murder is from Pratt's wife Eleanor, who either witnessed the events firsthand or had them immediately related to her. Her sixty-two-page handwritten testimonial is Eleanor J. McComb, "Account of the Death of Parley P. Pratt," ca. 1857–1860, Church History Library, the Church of Jesus Christ of Latter-day Saints, Salt Lake City, Utah (hereafter LDS Church History Library). Eleanor's account is particularly important, not only for its eyewitness character but also because it shows her as a bold and active participant in the events leading up to Pratt's death, rather than the passive object of stronger (male) forces as she was commonly depicted in other highly gendered, male-produced nineteenth-century sources. A profitable area of future research would be to apply a more thorough gender analysis to compare various accounts of Pratt's murder.

For months, the cloak of impending martyrdom had seemed to settle upon Pratt's mind. Letters written in the months before his death took on a morbid tone. He told his brother Orson in January 1857, "Our pilgrimage will soon be over." In another letter, he expressed love to his family, wanting them to know how he felt "should I never return." He informed them that he was nearly finished compiling his personal history, and that "the word *finis*" would "soon be added to the end."[3] Before being marched to Van Buren for the trial, Latter-day Saint missionary George Higginson recounted that Pratt privately told him: "I am perfectly reconciled to my fate. I am in the hands of the Lord and he can do just as he likes with me. I had rather die than live. I have no desire to live except to do good and my way appears to be hedged up on every hand." He requested that Higginson accompany him so that "if he was murdered" a report could be made to Brigham Young "of the true circumstances, of his death and trial."[4] Martyrdom filled Pratt's closing thoughts. In his final words, uttered as he lay on the ground dying, he left his testimony of the gospel of Jesus Christ and the prophetic mission of Joseph Smith, and then gasped, "I am dying a martyr to the faith."[5] Latter-day Saints readily echoed Pratt's self-assessment.[6]

Historians are ill equipped to evaluate whether or not the powers of darkness conspired to silence Pratt through the murderous machinations of Hector McLean. We are forced instead to consider the proximate causes of Pratt's death, which are easily enough ascertained, and then situate them within his broader social and cultural milieu. Other authors, from contemporary journalists to modern historians, most notably Steven Pratt, have explored in

[3] Letters quoted in Pratt, *Autobiography*, 409–10, 420.

[4] George Bouncer Higginson, "Account of the Assassination of Parley P. Pratt," n.d., LDS Church History Library (spelling modernized). Higginson later referred to Pratt being "Martyred for the Gospel Sake" (Letter to Andrew Kimball, March 1892, LDS Church History Library).

[5] John A. Peel, "Dying Remarks of Parley P. Pratt," LDS Church History Library, quoted in Pratt, "Eleanor McLean," 16.

[6] See Matthew J. Grow's essay in this volume (chapter 9).

depth the details surrounding Pratt's relationship with Eleanor McLean, which sparked Hector McLean's homicidal rage. Less understood is the wider context in which the events occurred. This essay therefore seeks to understand, but not condone, McLean's actions as part of and responding to particular elements of his culture. Three key aspects of antebellum society that are more or less foreign to early twenty-first-century America—honor, "the unwritten law," and extralegal violence—intersected with the controversial Mormon practice of plural marriage to motivate McLean to kill Pratt and to cause most Americans to approve of the murder.

The Cultural Context

As southerners, Hector and Eleanor McLean were deeply rooted in the system of beliefs, attitudes, behaviors, and relationships that scholars refer to in shorthand as "honor." In the 1850s, honor was a defining concept for most Americans, holding particular sway in the South and West. Bertram Wyatt-Brown, a historian who wrote the definitive study on the culture of honor in the antebellum South, defines honor as "the cluster of ethical rules, most readily found in societies of small communities, by which judgments of behavior are ratified by community consensus."[7] According to Wyatt-Brown, honor, by definition, is a communally constructed characteristic, as opposed to virtue or integrity, which can be possessed by an individual regardless of social opinion. In the mid-nineteenth-century South, a person could not have honor outside of the bounds of his or her community, whose collective estimation dictated the social reputation of each individual. Thus, acting honorably was dependent on understanding local values and mores and behaving in accordance with them. Honor, unlike personal integrity, was not gained by adhering to abstract concepts of law or righteousness, although in most (but certainly not all) cases, being law-abiding and devout were considered positive assets.

[7] Bertram Wyatt-Brown, *Southern Honor: Ethics and Behavior in the Old South* (New York: Oxford University Press, 1982), xv.

Indeed, honor was not just the sum total of what one did but rather an indication of who and what one was being inextricably bound up with ascribed characteristics and the standing of one's family, both present and past generations. While the happenstance of one's fate at birth could be mitigated somewhat through upward socioeconomic mobility, the reputation of a man's family followed him even if his immediate circumstances changed. This arrangement created in the antebellum South numerous situations of "great" families who were actually quite poor, or the nouveaux riche who were treated with a bit of disdain in the most respectable circles for not having proper pedigree or breeding, despite their enormous fortunes. The cultural concept of honor impacted all members of a community, not just the white male planter elite. Blacks were generally considered to be without honor, and women had additional standards (such as domesticity) by which they were judged; thus, the meaning and application of honor would be dependent on one's race, gender, class, or social standing. In many ways, honor was the cultural glue that held together antebellum southern society.

Honor did not appear per se on the law books, largely because, as Wyatt-Brown points out, "it was commonly understood that there should be a division between the workings of the law and the stalwart defense of a man's sense of self." When a man's honor was impugned, it was imperative that he confront the transgressor in order to save face (turning the other cheek is not typically a compelling value in honor-bound societies). In particularly severe cases, only violence against the offending party could restore lost honor. This applied not only to the South but also the American West in the nineteenth century, as honor was "the key factor in regard to western violence and western values," according to historian Richard Maxwell Brown. By the mid-nineteenth century, the United States had transitioned from the English common law, "in which threatening situations of individual combat required flight or retreat, to the American and western idea of no duty to retreat." The English prescription to retreat in the face of danger came to be perceived by Americans as cowardice. As Justice Oliver Wendell

Holmes remarked in regard to the violent West, "a man is not born to run away."[8]

No insult to a man's honor was more egregious—and thus more deserving of a violent response—than an imputation on the character of a close female relative, including mothers and sisters, but most especially wives and daughters. Sexual deviance involving a man's wife, whether via consensual adultery or coercive rape, required swift and thorough retribution, as it undermined the man's mastery over the most sacred aspect of his household. In such a case, as Wyatt-Brown observed: "Unpleasant though violence was, the most socially approved course for a husband with a wayward mate was to take the law into his own hands. Even judicial experts all but suggested that physical retort was the proper means of restoring lost honor." This violence was not technically sanctioned by the law, but most states and juries were loath to convict an aggrieved husband in a case where orthodox sexual mores had been transgressed.[9]

The violent enforcement of honor was a powerful means of social control in which the family, particularly the wife and her sexuality, became the exclusive preserve of the male head of the household. Law in the antebellum South underscored the ideal of absolute patriarchal authority and strictly upheld the dependency of all domestics (including wives, children, and slaves) on the husband and father. "The law," according to historian Laura Edwards, "presumed that heads of household always acted in the interests of their dependents and the public." Virtually any act of resistance by a dependent constituted wicked defiance to proper authority, which in turn provided sufficient grounds for the dominant man to punish the deviant transgressor. Husbands had the legal right to physically discipline their wives; thus, "the law turned violent

[8] Richard Maxwell Brown, "Western Violence: Structure, Values, Myth," *Western Historical Quarterly* 24 (February 1993): 14–15. See also Richard Maxwell Brown, *No Duty to Retreat: Violence and Values in American History and Society* (New York: Oxford University Press, 1991); Daniel Justin Herman, *Hell on the Range: A Story of Honor, Conscience, and the American West* (New Haven, Conn.: Yale University Press, 2010).

[9] Wyatt-Brown, *Southern Honor*, 305–306.

acts committed against dependents into regrettable but necessary means to keep subordinates in their place."[10]

A husband's violent prerogative over his wife was not reserved to cases of infidelity, and wife beating was a pervasive though not unchallenged practice in antebellum America. A close study of wife beating in late nineteenth-century Oregon, which is suggestive of broader trends, shows that men did beat their wives, although abusive husbands "were somewhat restrained in their violence" and generally resorted to physical force only infrequently and rarely as a first response. Battered women sometimes sought and were granted divorce, demonstrating that the victims did not find such violence necessary or appropriate and that community opinion and the law were not entirely allied with the abuser. Nevertheless, violence was only one tool in an elaborate system of patriarchal domination, as "husbands could be extremely abusive without using overt, physical force." Furthermore, "men's overwhelming social and economic advantages" meant that nearly all nineteenth-century marriages had at least some element of coercive male power.[11] The power of family patriarchs did not go uncontested and was more absolute in theory than practice, but the fact remained that women and children were viewed as dependents of the husband or father, with little or no individual standing before the law. This relationship was moderated somewhat in cases in which the husband's actions "went beyond accepted discipline and disturbed the peace of the community," but the occasional legal and cultural privileging of dependents over heads of household was very much the rare exception.[12]

A husband's right to use violence in his home was not unlimited, with boundaries typically drawn at severe injury and especially death. Nevertheless, even homicide—not of the wife but of her seducer—became excusable in certain circumstances under what

[10] Laura F. Edwards, "Law, Domestic Violence, and the Limits of Patriarchal Authority in the Antebellum South," *Journal of Southern History* 65 (November 1999): 733–70, quotes on pp. 759 and 767.

[11] David Peterson, "Wife Beating: An American Tradition," *Journal of Interdisciplinary History* 23 (Summer 1992): 97–118, quotes on pp. 105 and 117.

[12] Edwards, "Law, Domestic Violence, the Limits of Patriarchal Authority," 750.

came to be known as "the unwritten law." Put simply, the unwritten law dictated that "an outraged husband, father, or brother could justifiably kill the alleged libertine who had been sexually intimate with the defendant's wife, daughter, or sister."[13] This rule did not provide a blank check for vengeful violence, however. Legal historian Hendrik Hartog has observed that the unwritten law only applied when the husband "found his wife and her lover together, in a seriously and unquestionably compromising position. And only if he had acted immediately. Time was of the essence." This unwritten (and therefore uncertain) law was rooted in the aforementioned notions of honor and dependency. When homicidal husbands went to trial for murdering their wives' lovers, as they were in a handful of high-profile cases in the nineteenth century, defense lawyers trotted out the traditional images of dependent wives and patriarchal husbands, with wives sometimes even referred to as the property of their husbands.[14]

Men appeared as the key figures in such cases, with the dutiful, loving, and wronged husband pitted against the scheming, opportunistic, even satanic libertine. The seducer's "only goal was the destruction of domestic peace," and he achieved his aim by violating "the sanctity of the 'marriage bed'" and thus "remaking," or rather destroying, "the holy institution of marriage." The struggle was only partly over the woman in question. In fact, as Hartog observed, "wives were barely relevant." Women, weak and vulnerable by nature and in constant need of their husband's protection, were simply objects in the contest between male actors. Their sexual purity was an issue, particularly in an age obsessed with the virtue of women, but the real crime lay not in what was done to the woman but rather to the man: a seducer stole not only a woman's virtue but also a man's honor and his rightful, monopolistic possession of his wife's sexuality.[15]

---

[13] Robert M. Ireland, "The Libertine Must Die: Sexual Dishonor and the Unwritten Law in the Nineteenth-Century United States," *Journal of Social History* 23 (Autumn 1989): 27.

[14] Hendrik Hartog, "Lawyering, Husbands' Rights, and 'the Unwritten Law' in Nineteenth-Century America," *Journal of American History* 84, no. 1 (June 1997): 67, 90.

[15] Ibid., 75, 79. See also Ireland, "The Libertine Must Die," 29, 33.

If the morality underlying the unwritten law was based on the concepts of honor and dependency, its rationale was predicated on the notion that the formal mechanisms of the law sometimes failed to satisfy the higher cause of justice. Defenders of the unwritten law argued that the permissiveness of the U.S. legal structure, which in the mid-nineteenth century increasingly refused to punish the crime of adultery, "encouraged some outraged husbands to exercise private vengeance against adulterers."[16] If the courts would not uphold the honor of men—all men, not just the aggrieved husband in question—then honor dictated that men take matters into their own hands. In the trials of husbands who killed their wives' lovers, defense lawyers frequently asked the jurors to go against (or beyond) the letter of the law—which would find the men guilty of at least manslaughter—in order to answer a higher law, namely the protection of home and hearth from the invasion of ravenous libertines.[17] Each seduction was a threat not only to the individual home in question but also to the entire institution of marriage and the mastery of every husband over his own household. Honor demanded punishment of the seducer, and if the courts failed in their duty, then it was up to individual citizens to uphold justice by meting out their own chastisement.

This logic motivated the wave of extralegal violence that swept over America, particularly the South and West, in the nineteenth century. Vigilantes knew they were working outside the restraints of the law; that was precisely the point. They considered their extralegal actions to be justified—and therefore not illegal in the higher sense—in maintaining social order, preserving true democracy, and purging their communities of unwanted elements. In antebellum America, and continuing well beyond the Civil War in the frontier West and much of the South, it was possible for the voice of the people to manifest itself in violent extralegal action that superseded regularly constituted law and government on behalf of the perceived common good. One of the McLeans' contemporaries in San

[16] Ireland, "The Libertine Must Die," 27.

[17] Ibid., 36.

Francisco, a Yale-educated lawyer named Henry Haight, justified vigilantism because the "inefficiency of the Courts, the imperfections of the laws and the corruption of public officers" had "rendered the punishment of crime very uncertain and infrequent."[18]

Indeed, 1850s San Francisco in many ways represented the climax of American vigilantism, with a Committee of Vigilance essentially taking over the city in 1851 and then again five years later in what became the largest vigilante movement in American history.[19] Historian David Johnson noted that in an era that celebrated the virtue and wisdom of the common man, "the vigilantism of the people's court enjoyed a broad cultural sanction" based largely on notions of "the moral authority of popular action" as opposed to what was deemed to be the corrupt, inefficient, and coercive power of the state. As another 1850s Californian argued, "The system without civil law, but with summary justice is . . . incomparably better than the system with such law, but without such justice." The people believed themselves to be possessors of "an unerring, natural sense of justice," and when due process failed to sate them, they considered it their right—even duty—to engage in vigilantism. Such extralegal violence represented, in the words of the *Alta California*, "a transcendancy [*sic*] of the law rather than a violation of it."[20]

---

[18] Quoted in Christian G. Fritz, "Popular Sovereignty, Vigilantism, and the Constitutional Right of Revolution," *Pacific Historical Review* 63, no. 1 (February 1994): 56.

[19] On the San Francisco Vigilance Committee of 1856, which Richard Maxwell Brown calls the "pivot of American vigilantism," see Brown, *Strain of Violence: Historical Studies of American Violence and Vigilantism* (New York: Oxford University Press, 1975), 134–43. See also Mary P. Ryan, *Civic Wars: Democracy and Public Life in the American City During the Nineteenth Century* (Berkeley: University of California Press, 1997), 139–45; and Robert M. Senkewicz, *Vigilantes in Gold Rush San Francisco* (Stanford, Calif.: Stanford University Press, 1985).

[20] David A. Johnson, "Vigilance and the Law: The Moral Authority of Popular Justice in the Far West," *American Quarterly* 33, no. 5 (Winter 1981): 558–86, quotes on pp. 562–66. In his study of antebellum mob violence in the South, David Grimsted expresses somewhat greater skepticism about vigilantes' motives: "Mob activity, like personal violence, was less an attack on legality than an alternative system to which Southerners could resort when it offered securer promise of gaining 'justice,' revenge, power, or property. It was often justified in terms of weaknesses in the formal legal system in ways that were dubious but telling about its alternative status" (Grimsted, *American Mobbing, 1828–1861: Toward Civil War* [New York: Oxford University Press, 1998], 110).

Richard Maxwell Brown rightly emphasized: "The typical frontier vigilante movement was socially conservative. It was dedicated to the defense of traditional structure and values of the local community against the threatening presence of the criminal and disorderly." In the mid-nineteenth century, many Americans viewed vigilantes who organized extralegally to take the law into their own hands not as criminals but rather as anti-criminals, preserving society from those who would endanger it and reifying the traditional values of law, social order, and property. Vigilante groups did often include men with violent streaks, but that was and is still true of legally authorized groups, such as the police and army, who use violence as a primary means of accomplishing their mission. Rather than being socially marginal, vigilante movements often formed under the direction of leading citizens of the community, including politicians, judges, lawyers, and businessmen. As a result of being controlled by community elites, vigilante violence worked to strengthen, not alter or overthrow, the existing norms and values of society in which the elites maintained their power. The raison d'être of a typical vigilante movement was not revolution but rather reinforcement of the status quo.[21]

Nineteenth-century vigilante groups targeted those perceived to be criminals, social deviants, and ne'er-do-wells, including horse thieves, adulterers, murderers, and of course American Indians and insurrectionary slaves. Extralegal violence was also directed against those guilty of "religious unconventionality," a category under which Latter-day Saints indubitably fell.[22] Many Americans regarded Mormons, alongside other undesirables such as Catholics and Masons, as members of a "subversive group" that embodied "those traits that were precise antitheses of American ideals."[23] Terryl Givens showed in his analysis of nineteenth-century

[21] Quotes from Brown, *Strain of Violence*, vii, 5. The summary of vigilantism in this paragraph is taken broadly from Brown's general observations.

[22] Wyatt-Brown, *Southern Honor*, 306.

[23] David Brion Davis, "Some Themes of Counter-Subversion: An Analysis of Anti-Masonic, Anti-Catholic, and Anti-Mormon Literature," in *From Homicide to Slavery: Studies in American Culture* (New York: Oxford University Press, 1986), 140.

anti-Mormon rhetoric and literature that because the founding principles of the nation sheltered religious diversity, those who opposed Mormonism necessarily transmuted their objections into social, cultural, and political arguments rather than focusing on mere theological differences that were (presumably) protected under the First Amendment.[24] Indeed, religious historian William Hutchison contended that even in the religiously explosive antebellum period, Americans typically tolerated radical beliefs but not radical behavior, that "manner" meant more than "matter."[25]

Polygamy, of course, provided more than enough objectionable "manner" as well as "matter" to inspire the transformation of anti-Mormonism from a relatively localized (if sometimes highly violent) phenomenon into a veritable national pastime. Mormonism may have been a heresy to traditional Christians in the 1830s and 1840s and a threat to the power of non-Mormon settlers in certain Ohio, Missouri, and Illinois communities, but it barely registered on the national radar during the Joseph Smith era. The establishment of a Mormon theocracy in the state of Deseret in the late 1840s and in the 1852 public announcement of plural marriage, combined with the annexation of the intermountain and Pacific West into the United States after the Mexican-American War, made Mormonism a national concern, as it now seemed to challenge fundamental American institutions of republican government, the rule of law, and Christian monogamous marriage. National scrutiny of Mormon particularity continued when the Republican Party made the eradication of polygamy part of its 1856 platform, and furthermore when the U.S. Army marched against the Mormons in the so-called Utah War of 1857–58. Anti-Mormonism had become so intense and so popular that by June 1857,

---

[24] Terryl L. Givens, *The Viper on the Hearth: Mormons, Myths, and the Construction of Heresy* (New York: Oxford University Press, 1997). While recognizing the importance of nonreligious factors and the necessity for anti-Mormons to frame their principal objections in those terms, Givens still privileges theology as the "inescapable" and "constant feature in anti-Mormon antagonisms" (8).

[25] William R. Hutchison, *Religious Pluralism in America: The Contentious History of a Founding Ideal* (New Haven, Conn.: Yale University Press, 2003), 32.

shortly after Pratt's murder, Pratt's younger brother, Latter-day Saint apostle Orson Pratt, described it from his vantage point in Liverpool, England, as a truly international phenomenon: "The old Missouri mob spirit seems to be reviving in the States. . . . The same spirit has found its way across the Atlantic, and the journals of the day are filled with the most barefaced & malicious lies, that wicked men, with the help of the Devil can invent—and so violent is their hatred, and great is their prejudice, that we cannot get a single word in one of them in self defence."[26]

Polygamy doomed Mormons—who earlier in their history had garnered widespread sympathy as an oppressed and downtrodden people—to the basest representations in the popular imagination. Moralists and voyeuristic commentators nationwide derided Mormon plural marriage as "an institution founded in the lustful and unbridled passions of men, devised by Satan himself to destroy purity and authorize whoredom." Critics dubbed the LDS Church a "society for the seduction of young virgins" and called Salt Lake City "the biggest whorehouse in the world."[27] Latter-day Saints proved remarkably perseverant, even defiant, in the face of such sustained opposition from virtually every segment of American government and society, but placing themselves so far outside the religious, cultural, and political mainstream had its costs. Not the least of these costs was the assassination of Pratt, whose killing was a symptom of the broader cultural trends of honor, the unwritten law, and extralegal violence, all filtered through a national anti-Mormon movement galvanized by the Saints' practice of polygamy.

---

[26] Orson Pratt to Brigham Young, 27 June 1857, Brigham Young Collection, LDS Church History Library.

[27] Gregory Pingree, "'The Biggest Whorehouse in the World': Representations of Plural Marriage in Nineteenth-Century America," *Western Humanities Review* 50 (Fall 1996): 213–14, 226. See also Craig L. Foster, "Victorian Pornographic Imagery in Anti-Mormon Literature," *Journal of Mormon History* 19 (Spring 1993): 115–32. On the national anti-polygamy campaign, especially in its more formal legal forms in the 1870s and 1880s, see Sarah Barringer Gordon, *The Mormon Question: Polygamy and Constitutional Conflict in Nineteenth-Century America* (Chapel Hill: University of North Carolina Press, 2002). See also Patrick Q. Mason, *The Mormon Menace: Violence and Anti-Mormonism in the Postbellum South* (New York: Oxford University Press, 2011).

The Pratt Murder in Cultural Context

When the *Daily Missouri Republican* reported Pratt's death nearly two weeks after the fact, it claimed that Hector and Eleanor McLean "were happy and prosperous until she made the acquaintance of Pratt, and embraced the Mormon faith."[28] Such was also the assumption of Judge Ogden when he questioned Eleanor regarding the charge of larceny that had been brought against her as a means of stopping her flight from New Orleans to Utah. "Well Madam," he queried, "I suppose you will not deny that you were happy with Mr. McLean until this man Pratt and Mormonism crossed your pathway?"[29] This view reflected the Victorian tendency to tolerate or ignore even violent abuse by husbands as part of the fantasy of universally successful and blissful matrimony. Men were faithful husbands, women were good wives, and marriages were holy: this was an essential construction if the trope of the libertine preying upon a defenseless wife and shattering the sanctity of home and hearth was to hold sway. In reality, of course, most marriages allegedly broken by "seducers" such as Pratt "had soured long before the libertines made their appearance."[30]

Eleanor shattered the myth of marital happiness in her testimony in the Arkansas courtroom. She asserted that alcohol and abuse, not religion or seduction, had destroyed her marriage. Hector "drove happiness from our home by imbibing that spirit that comes in bottles," she claimed. While she conscientiously strove to do her "duty as a virtuous wife and faithful mother," he abandoned his responsibilities and "had learned to love wine more than he loved the happiness of the wife of his bosom."[31] In Eleanor's testimony, it was Hector, not her, who had betrayed their marital vows. Later she declared: "It has been said and written that my Mormonism drove McLean to drinking. But he knows to the contrary, and I have evidence."[32] Indeed, within the first three years

[28] "Tragical," *Daily Missouri Republican*, 25 May 1857.

[29] McComb, "Account," 11–12.

[30] Ireland, "The Libertine Must Die," 35.

[31] McComb, "Account," 12 (capitalization modernized).

[32] Ibid., 60.

of their marriage, Hector's drinking had become severe enough that it caused the couple to separate. Eleanor sent him an ultimatum, and Hector expressed penitence and the desire to "be saved and reformed," although claiming it would be impossible in New Orleans among his established drinking associates.[33]

Their decision to move to San Francisco in the late 1840s to accomplish his rehabilitation is a strange one in hindsight, for the city, as the commercial heart of the gold rush, was notorious for getting men immersed in, not saved from, the vices of alcohol, gambling, and prostitution. Conditions in the frontier municipality had degenerated to the point that in 1851, upwards of three thousand citizens convened to form a vigilance committee to deal with the city's epidemic of "robbers and murderers." By the time the extralegal tribunal had disbanded in 1853, ninety-one prisoners had been taken, about one-third of whom were expelled from the city, one whipped, and four hung.[34] The vigilantes had apparently not been thorough enough in cleansing their fair city, however, as continuing crime, social disorder, and ethnic and political rivalries sparked the even larger (and more violent) vigilante movement of 1856. In short, of all the places in the United States for an alcoholic with violent tendencies to relocate his family in hopes of recovery and reform, San Francisco was one of the worst possible choices. Not surprisingly, Hector's problems with the bottle continued unabated, and his marriage with Eleanor grew ever more fragile. Eleanor recounted that during the late 1840s and early 1850s she silently suffered and even covered up Hector's alcoholism. In the 1857 trial, she reflected with pathos on those days in which she alone knew and grieved the extent of her husband's usually unsuccessful battle with the bottle: "Who but a wife knows bedroom scenes? . . . The wife might shed a million tears of untold bitterness between the setting and rising of the sun, and who could know it?"[35]

---

[33] Pratt, "Eleanor McLean," 1–2.

[34] Ryan, *Civic Wars*, 139–40. The exact timing of the McLeans' move to San Francisco is not clear, but it could not have preceded the gold rush, because their youngest child was born in New Orleans in 1847 (see Pratt, "Eleanor McLean," 22n4).

[35] McComb, "Account," 13–14.

One might expect that Eleanor would try to challenge the culture of domesticity that had bound her for over a decade to a violent drunk. To the contrary, Eleanor's testimony, rather than being subversive in the least, fully wielded the rhetoric of domesticity, though in a strategic manner that worked to her favor. By invoking the sanctity of the bedroom, the most private and hallowed of all spaces, and by showing how Hector's vice had corrupted it through neglect and abuse, she persuasively established the incontrovertible brokenness of the marriage even while asserting her own wifely fidelity and declaring that her conscience in the matter was "clear as the morning's dew."[36] She had faithfully performed her prescribed role, but her husband had fallen down in his duties as protector of his dependents; the guilt and dishonor were entirely his to bear. That her narrative was compelling to contemporary sensibilities is demonstrated by her immediate release and the subsequent courtesy offered her by the judge and marshal who only moments earlier had been implicated in McLean's plot to label her a criminal. Eleanor had proven herself a true woman.

Eleanor's statement starkly contrasted her two husbands, McLean and Pratt. In her words, McLean was a "raging beast," "the unrelenting tyrant," "that Demon," "the child of hell," "my arch enemy," who possessed "no mercy" and had "torn my children . . . from me." Pratt, on the other hand, was "the man of God," a true apostle and holy man who had visions, healed the sick, cast out demons, and liberated the oppressed (including herself).[37] Of course, her portraits of the two men were strongly disputed. The *Daily Missouri Republican* closed its account of Pratt's murder by emphasizing how "deeply do we sympathize with McLean in the unfortunate condition in which Mormon villainy and fanaticism," namely Pratt's seduction of his wife, "has placed him."[38] At stake lay who was victimized by whom, and most importantly, whose honor was preserved. Was Parley Pratt a sincere and upright man of God who acted chivalrously in freeing an innocent woman from

[36] Ibid., 15.
[37] On McLean, see ibid., 1, 5, 43, 54; on Pratt, see ibid., 3, 4, 10, 30, 33–36.
[38] "Tragical," *Daily Missouri Republican*.

the clutches of an abusive husband? Or was he a lecherous libertine who destroyed a marriage, seduced another man's wife, and placed her in his polygamous harem, thus proffering the ultimate disrespect and challenge to her husband's honor? Was Hector McLean a quintessentially honorable and heroic figure who removed his children from threat and literally traveled the breadth and length of the country to rescue his deluded wife from the clutches of the sexually depraved minister of a theocratic cult? Or was he an unregenerate alcoholic with a violent streak who neglected his family and abused his wife, then went on a murderous rampage when she chose to leave him for her own protection?

From the start, Hector believed he acted well within his prerogatives as a husband. He was shaped by an antebellum southern worldview established upon the foundation of personal and family honor and which upheld the unwritten law to protect husbands whose mastery of their household had been challenged by seducers. Typical of husbands in a patriarchal culture, he asserted control over even the private affairs of the members of his family, including his wife's religious affiliation. He attended the meeting where Eleanor was first attracted to Mormonism and allowed her, after initial opposition, to be baptized, but he forbade any religious display of Mormonism within his home. Eleanor covertly practiced her faith and held morning devotionals with her children in secret, but when Hector discovered her singing from a Saints' hymnbook, he threw her into the street and locked the door. At one point Hector tried to commit his wife to an insane asylum to keep her from the influence of Mormonism, thus suggesting how the coercive power of the state could be mobilized to reinforce a husband's control over his wife and family. When this plan failed, Hector exercised his mastery over the household by sending their children to New Orleans without Eleanor's knowledge or permission.[39]

It is not entirely clear why Hector was so vehement in his objection to Mormonism. An LDS Church missionary who worked for nearly a month as a cook in the McLean home without disclosing

[39] Pratt, "Eleanor McLean," 2–5.

his true identity recalled the nearly deadly encounter when Hector discovered he had housed a Mormon unknowingly. When the missionary asked him what he found so noxious about Mormonism, Hector reportedly exclaimed, "You are teaching the false doctrines of Joseph Smith," specifically complaining that Mormons "claimed to confer the Holy Ghost by the laying on of hands, while the scriptures declare that it has been done away and is not needed in this day."[40] It is difficult to know how accurately this represented the source of McLean's hostility toward the faith, as nineteenth-century Mormons commonly ascribed to theological differences and a cosmic battle between good and evil, what non-Mormons saw as political, cultural, and social conflict.[41] Admittedly, even unchurched nineteenth-century Americans were remarkably religiously literate, and ordinary churchgoers often participated in tense debates over theological fine points that seem like meaningless minutiae to modern sensibilities.[42] Still, it stretches the imagination to believe that McLean was so passionate about the proper mechanisms of conferring the Holy Ghost that he was willing to throw his wife out of the house and threaten a missionary's life over it. Eleanor gave a clue that perhaps helps to unravel the mystery when she testified that her belief in Mormonism—an unpopular, culturally marginal religion even before polygamy was publicly disclosed—simply provided her already abusive husband with a "pretext" so that "upon this ground he might treat his family with personal violence."[43] In other words, McLean's dispute with Mormonism may have been simply a cover to justify his own preferred method of laying on of hands.

When, upon Eleanor's invitation, Parley entered the McLean home to reconcile the feuding spouses in 1854, such a strategy could only be seen by Hector as a direct challenge to his honor. To bring in an outsider was to diminish the authority of the husband

---

[40] "Autobiography of John R. Young," LDS Church History Library, quoted in ibid., p. 4.

[41] See Givens, *Viper on the Hearth*, 45–46; Mason, *The Mormon Menace*, 152–63.

[42] See Stephen Prothero, *Religious Literacy: What Every American Needs to Know—and Doesn't* (San Francisco: HarperSanFrancisco, 2007), esp. chapter 3.

[43] McComb, "Account," 12.

and to imply his loss of mastery over the household. That the mediator in this case was a prominent Mormon elder who had gained notoriety in the local and national press for his polygamous marriages only fueled Hector's ire. His fierce anger at this point is understandable in its cultural context, even if it does not excuse his prior abusive behavior or if his subsequent transcontinental manhunt ending in Pratt's murder was excessive. From McLean's perspective, his wife had defied his patriarchal authority, joining a heretical and dangerous sect. She had his children baptized into the Church without his permission, forcing him to send them to New Orleans so that she would not steal them away to Utah, as he believed was clearly her intent. The privacy of his marital relationship had been violated on numerous occasions, both by a Mormon missionary who essentially acted as a spy in his home and through the repeated offer of marriage counseling by a polygamous Mormon apostle. Furthermore, his wife fled from him into the arms of said polygamist and was wed to him in a secret ceremony performed by a theocratic prophet who was one of the most notorious Americans of the day. In McLean's view, his home had been invaded, his marriage broken, his wife's chastity corrupted, his children brainwashed, his control over his family questioned and then destroyed, his reputation bruised, and his honor shamed, all through the instrumentality of Mormonism. Pratt personified this series of insults and abuses, not only as the hated religion's leading authority in California but also as the seducer of his wife.

Eleanor's parents took Hector's side rather than hers, suggesting both the general cultural antipathy toward Mormonism and the solidarity felt among family patriarchs when their authority was challenged. They offered to shelter the children rather than have them accompany their mother to Utah. When Eleanor traveled to New Orleans in 1857 and retrieved the children by subterfuge, her father, James McComb, immediately notified Hector. To the McComb and McLean men, Eleanor's conversion to Mormonism constituted nothing less than a defection from the family and reflected willful defiance of their rightful patriarchal authority.

Family relationships were famously strong in the antebellum South, but they could be severed when a member deeply offended the family's honor and failed to repent or even show remorse. By sealing herself to Pratt and Mormonism, Eleanor cut the ties that bound her to family members and rejected the cultural norms that shaped their world. Leaving her husband was a shame and joining Mormonism was dishonorable, but becoming a polygamist was unforgivable. In late May of that year, shortly after Parley's murder, her father sent Eleanor a letter saying she was cut off and that he would never see her again, as she had consciously opted for Mormonism over her own flesh and blood: "As you have chosen *the saints*!!! for your companions, I advise you to go to the Saints. . . . The moment you accepted the name of Mr. Pratt *you* cut the last cord of sympathy that bound me to you."[44] Eleanor's mother concurred with her husband, writing, "Eleanor [my] own loved daughter—hard as it is I never wish to see your face while you call yourself a mormon."[45]

Eleanor, though sorrowful at the separation from her parents, reciprocated their feelings, seeing it as an unfortunate but necessary sacrifice for the kingdom of God. She noted that her "real kindred" were "in the midst of the rocky Mountains," not San Francisco or New Orleans. Furthermore, she told her mother, "If my earthly father and mother cannot see me, without I deny my faith—Lo I turn to those who are willing to be my father, mother, sister, brother son daughter &c."[46] In Eleanor's eyes, Hector destroyed their marriage through his pathological reliance on alcohol and abuse, and her parents had unrighteously abandoned her by joining forces with her persecutor. Mormonism provided her not only temporal relief but also spiritual salvation connected to an eternal family. From the McComb and McLean perspective, it seemed equally clear that Mormonism had stolen their daughter and wife and thus destroyed their family here on earth.

[44] Quoted in McComb, "Account," 49–50 (emphasis and spelling in original).
[45] Ibid., 51 (capitalization original).
[46] Ibid., 37, 48.

The antebellum code of southern honor not only allowed but encouraged a violent response to such a deep insult to the family. McLean's decision to kill Pratt was a conscious, premeditated strategy. The night before the murder, when Judge Ogden talked long into the night attempting to sway him from his vengeful aim, McLean coolly said that "he did not wish any [other] man to touch [Pratt]," because "that was a privilege he wished to reserve to himself."[47] McLean's cross-country hunt for Pratt did not fully satisfy the technical requirements of the unwritten law, which was meant to protect a husband who caught his wife and her seducer in the act, a transgression so unspeakable and shocking that it was understandable that he would become homicidal in the moment. Hector never actually discovered Parley and Eleanor in a compromising situation, but the fact that she had become Pratt's plural wife in Salt Lake provided fairly compelling evidence of the nature of their relationship. Hector's rage was largely explained by the fact that he still considered Eleanor his wife—which in fact she legally was. Eleanor recognized that the courts would not grant her a divorce without her husband's consent, which he refused to give, but her understanding of the Mormon doctrine of celestial marriage led her to believe that her broken marriage with Hector was null and void in God's eyes and had been replaced with something more holy and eternal when she was sealed to Pratt in the Endowment House.[48] It was an odd twist for an alleged seducer to marry his "prey," but the unique circumstances of the case still fulfilled the spirit if not the letter of the unwritten law, and it showed how the practical application of husbands' rights, in a context of patriarchal honor, assumed the logic of extralegal violence.

Vigilantism can operate successfully only where a community consensus deems certain people to be threats to social order and then supports the notion of ordinary citizens pursuing justice outside the bounds of legally constituted mechanisms. McLean's pursuit of Pratt fulfilled both requirements, as the Van Buren

---

[47] Ibid., 40.

[48] See Pratt, "Eleanor McLean," 24n26.

court failed to convict Pratt, even as citizens from New Orleans to St. Louis were outraged at the story of a Mormon elder stealing away a man's wife. In mid-March 1857, two months before the murder, Mormon apostle Erastus Snow reported to Brigham Young from St. Louis on the heightened tension in the region and the animosity felt toward Pratt:

> Elder Parley P Pratt spent one Sabbath with us since he returned from the East, but he has had to flee for his life, and hide away from his enemies, who are hunting him as bloodhounds would a hare.
>
> A story was published in the newspapers about a Woman stealing away her children from New Orleans to take them among the Mormons, and it is said that her Husband is searching for them in this City, and blames Elder Pratt in some way about the matter. And that he has the sympathies of the Mayor, Police and the Apostates of this City who contribute their aid in searching the Saints Houses and keeping up a general watch.[49]

A day later, another apostle in St. Louis, George A. Smith, confirmed Snow's assessment in a letter to Young: "There is an unusually bitter state of feeling against us throughout the states. The people are full of hatred, and they believe every lie that is published concerning us. Elder P. P. P. [Pratt] has been hunted by the Police of this city for some time. . . . It is said, that he is to be charged with adultery, and that two women in this city will swear that he introduced a certain California Gentleman's wife as Mrs. P. . . . It is probable that all this is a mere ruse to renew the old Missouri persecution on him. . . . There is a general excitement against him in the country."[50]

It was no secret that community opinion had been mobilized in favor of McLean and against Pratt, who was fully aware of the danger to his life. Indeed, the case had been public at least since a New Orleans newspaper ran the story in December 1856, naturally sympathizing with the plight of the aggrieved McLean and McComb

[49] Erastus Snow to Brigham Young, 14 March 1857, Brigham Young Collection, LDS Church History Library.

[50] George A. Smith to Brigham Young, 15 March 1857, Brigham Young Collection, LDS Church History Library.

men versus the Mormon polygamist.[51] As Elders Snow and Smith reported, McLean had not only the general public but also the police and city authorities on his side. The hunt for Pratt was thus a classic example of antebellum law enforcement in the South or West in which private citizens acted alongside formal officers of the law in searching for criminals, showing how the boundaries between legal and extralegal were often blurred. Pratt was lawfully apprehended and tried in a formal court, but when the court did not fulfill its duty in punishing this publicly perceived danger, the processes of vigilantism went into action. The general consensus held that McLean was well within his rights in killing Pratt. A *Daily Missouri Republican* article written a fortnight after the murder was representative: "There being no law in that country by which the arch fiend [Pratt] could be brought to justice, McLean had only the alternative left him of being exposed to his tormentings the remainder of his life, or of administering justice to him in a summary way."[52] McLean had two choices: permanently suffer a loss of honor as Pratt laughed in the face of justice or restore his honor by exacting true justice on his own. When a regularly constituted court failed to bring an offender to justice—especially one who represented such a dire threat to male honor, female purity, and community morality—this was precisely the kind of situation that called for extralegal action. Although a warrant was issued for McLean's arrest after he killed Pratt, it was clear that the court of public opinion had already ruled in his favor. The newspaper reported that "the public and the press of the country in which McLean put an end to the tormenter of his life, unanimously sustained him in the act," and a correspondent on the scene asserted that "no jail could have held him in Arkansas, had he been arrested."[53]

Support for McLean was not universal, however. A handful of the law enforcement officials involved in Pratt's arrest and trial knew that McLean planned on taking matters into his own hands, and they repeatedly tried to resist his vigilante impulses.

[51] "An Illustration of Mormonism," *New Orleans Bulletin*, 19 December 1856, quoted in "The Mormon Tragedy in Arkansas," *Daily Missouri Republican*, 26 May 1857.

[52] "The Mormon Tragedy in Arkansas."

[53] Ibid.

The marshal who accompanied Eleanor informed her, "They have arrested Pratt, and McLean is determined to kill him, but he shall not do it while he is a prisoner!" When McLean drew his pistol on Pratt in the courtroom, officers held his arm and prevented him from shooting. Judge Ogden stayed with McLean late into the night, trying to dissuade him from exacting revenge on Pratt, and scheduled a false court time the next day to give Pratt a head start on his pursuers after releasing him from jail, where he had been held overnight for his safety.[54] Although vigilante justice enjoyed widespread support, especially in a cause so inflammatory to the public conscience as the Pratt-McLean affair, there were usually at least some civil officers who opposed the action as a threat to law and order. And even though it was generally acknowledged after the murder that McLean himself would go free, the populace did not support the local men McLean had convinced to help him in his hunt. As the marshal told Eleanor, "Many of the people feel that McLean was deeply wronged, and perchance they would clear him, but popular sentiment is against our citizens, who have aided in bringing this man's blood upon our soil."[55] Certain allowances were thus made for a wronged husband, in this version of the unwritten law, that were not extended to the other men whose honor was not directly harmed but who participated nevertheless in the revenge killing. Extralegal violence, though operating outside of or parallel to the written law, was not lawless, and had its own code agreed upon, if informally, by public consensus. The people were rarely if ever unanimous or absolutely consistent in formulating or applying community standards, but the pursuit of justice outside the courts was tolerated, within bounds, if a clear moral outrage had occurred and formal law enforcement failed to sufficiently address it.

Conclusion

The problem with vigilante justice, as many law enforcement officers and politicians pointed out throughout the nineteenth century,

[54] McComb, "Account," 3, 22, 24, 40.

[55] Ibid., 27.

was that it could take on a life of its own and extinguish the fragile flame of democracy that initially sparked it. Twenty years before Parley Pratt's murder, a young Illinois lawyer named Abraham Lincoln gave a speech following the mob murder of antislavery newspaper editor Elijah Lovejoy entitled "The Perpetuation of Our Political Institutions." Lincoln warned: "There is even now something of ill-omen amongst us. I mean the increasing disregard for law which pervades the country; the growing disposition to substitute the wild and furious passions, in lieu of the sober judgments of the courts; and the worse than savage mobs, for the executive ministers of justice."[56] In its celebration of democracy and the common man, Jacksonian and antebellum American culture virtually sanctified the vox populi, raising the question of whether the new nation was governed by the people or by law. In the name of the ascendant will of the people, as historian Michael Feldberg observed, majorities "used extralegal violence or intimidation to compel acquiescence from weak or unpopular minorities, or to punish them for their beliefs or their behavior," especially when the courts and public authorities did not fulfill the desire of the general populace to suppress those minorities.[57] As historian David Grimsted shrewdly argued in his study of Jacksonian riots, extralegal violence in the redressing of perceived threats to the community "is not antithetical to, or abnormal in, a democracy but a result of very basic tendencies and tensions within it." Riots and vigilantism thus pose "in stark form many of the deepest dilemmas a democracy faces."[58]

Latter-day Saints and scholarly observers alike have frequently noted how the rise of Mormonism was nurtured in the soil of early

[56] Abraham Lincoln, "The Perpetuation of Our Political Institutions: Address to the Young Men's Lyceum of Springfield, Illinois," in Lincoln, *Speeches and Writings, 1832–1858: Speeches, Letters, and Miscellaneous Writings, the Lincoln-Douglas Debates* (New York: Literary Classics of the United States, distributed by Viking Press, 1989), 29.

[57] Michael Feldberg, *The Turbulent Era: Riot and Disorder in Jacksonian America* (New York: Oxford University Press, 1980), 90–91.

[58] David Grimsted, "Rioting in Its Jacksonian Setting," *American Historical Review* 77 (April 1972): 397. See also Brown, *Strain of Violence*, 62.

America, in which constitutional protections of religious freedom and the lack of strong religious establishments fostered the emergence of new religious movements. At the same time, the middle decades of the nineteenth century witnessed the highest incidence of extralegal violence in American history, as popular tribunals and vigilante movements sprouted up across the country to preserve social order in dozens of rapidly changing and thus disconcertingly unstable communities. Political theorists such as John Adams, James Madison, and Alexis de Tocqueville warned about the "tyranny of the majority," in which democracy would mutate into mobocracy, thus violating the protection of minority rights that liberal democracy is founded upon. Mormons experienced such violent tyranny repeatedly in their early years, particularly in Missouri and Illinois. Yet in the moments when they achieved a democratic majority, they too were not immune to wielding power for their own self-preservation at the expense of the minorities among them. In short, vigilantism does not so much violate the rule of the people as fulfill it, and the challenge of aspiring democratic societies is to establish and respect the rule of law and thereby avoid the temptation of prejudicial majoritarianism.

The central issue, the sine qua non, behind Parley Pratt's murder was not Mormonism per se but rather its doctrine and practice of plural marriage. Just as it is difficult to think of a more fertile climate than Jacksonian America for Mormonism to have been born in, there could hardly be a less opportune moment for the announcement of plural marriage than the 1850s (though, to be fair, one would be hard pressed to discern any historical moment, at least in modern Europe and America, in which polygamy would be widely accepted and given the sanction of law). In the mid-nineteenth century the United States was dominated by a broad evangelical Protestant coalition that was not afraid to use the coercive power of the state to enforce its morality on any number of issues ranging from temperance to slavery to marriage. Furthermore, a cultural revolution was well under way in which American culture was being "feminized," and Victorian standards of morality were concretized, which celebrated—and virtually worshipped—absolute female purity and the sanctity of the Christian home.[59] This dovetailed with southern, and then western, notions of honor, which gave rise to the unwritten law, allowing for the violent defense of home and hearth against libertines. Even rough-and-tumble San Francisco witnessed a "domestic revolution" in the mid-1850s, "in which the middle-class values of home and hearth attained hegemony over the male-dominated gold rush society."[60] From a historical and cultural perspective, it is not difficult to see why Hector McLean, a southerner living in mid-1850s San Francisco, believed he was within his rights to kill the polygamist who took his wife.

Parley Pratt's murder represents a kind of perfect storm, in which a number of powerful forces that shaped antebellum America intersected and reinforced one another. Victorian morality combined with a southern culture of honor and patriarchy to create an idealized nation of peaceful homes and loving marriages, with pure women entirely and gratefully dependent on the strong protection of their husbands. A man's honor was inextricably bound up with community perceptions of the honor of his family and his ability to demonstrate utter mastery over his household. Any breaches to the sanctity of the home, and especially the marriage bed, constituted an assault on the man's reputation and the very moral foundations of society. The legal machinery of the state was mobilized to uphold the interconnected myths of male honor, female purity, and domestic harmony. In addition, the unwritten law allowed for an aggrieved husband to immediately eliminate corruption and restore lost honor when a seducer was caught working his wiles with his wife. Where the unwritten law was not applied and the law failed to deliver swift and full justice, community norms established by the voice of the people could be upheld through the means of extralegal violence. Vigilantism

[59] The literature on this subject is vast. The seminal historical work is Ann Douglas, *The Feminization of American Culture* (New York: Knopf, 1977).

[60] Johnson, "Vigilance and the Law," 578.

served as the ultimate check on deviant behavior and guaranteed that the will of the people—or at least some of them—would reign supreme. The theocratic elements of Mormonism that had posed a threat in Missouri and Illinois had been effectively dealt with by vigilantism. Polygamy was even more dangerous, as it imperiled the Christian home that formed the bedrock of Victorian America. Federal action would be taken throughout the last half of the nineteenth century to address the problem of plural marriage writ large. But for Hector McLean, the menace of polygamy had already swallowed up his wife and threatened his children, and only decisive, violent action against the agent of Eleanor's fall, Parley Pratt, could restore lost honor and preserve social order. Whether justice was done is only a matter of definition.

CHAPTER 9

Martyred Apostle or Un-Saintly Seducer?

Narratives on the Death of Parley P. Pratt

Matthew J. Grow

On May 13, 1857, twelve miles outside of Van Buren, Arkansas, Hector McLean—the estranged husband of Eleanor McComb, then the twelfth wife of Mormon apostle Parley P. Pratt—shot, stabbed, and killed Pratt.[1] News of the event soon splashed across newspapers throughout the nation. Pratt's murder had everything a sensational story needed: violence, sex, and religion. Moreover, the tumultuous debate over Mormonism (especially in the context of the oncoming Utah War) and the extralegal tradition that sanctioned a husband's right to kill his wife's seducer intensified the national reaction. The national press cast Parley in the role of an un-Saintly seducer who had used the wiles of Mormonism to deceive Eleanor and victimize Hector. Eleanor, however, argued in numerous venues that Parley had acted heroically in an attempt to save her and her children from Hector's abuse. News of Pratt's death stunned the Latter-day Saints, and Pratt entered the top echelon of the pantheon of Mormon martyrs. The competing narratives of Pratt as seducer and Pratt as

[1] Steven Pratt, "Eleanor McLean and the Murder of Parley P. Pratt," *BYU Studies* 15, no. 2 (1975): 225–56.

martyr illuminate the American reaction to Mormons and other radical religious outsiders.

Before the Murder

Even before Pratt's death, two vastly different narratives of his relationship to Eleanor had been argued in the press by partisans of Hector and Parley himself. In December 1856, the *New Orleans Bulletin*, McLean's hometown newspaper, in a widely reprinted story titled a "Sad Story of Mormonism: The Mother and Children," first framed the relationship of Parley, Hector, and Eleanor for a national audience. Although the *New Orleans Bulletin* did not name these people, it clearly referred to them. The article narrated how Hector, a "gentleman," and Eleanor, a lady of "more than an ordinary share of intellect," had moved to the "golden shores of the Pacific" and attended a Mormon meeting along with Eleanor's brother. "Fatal curiosity! Inconspicious day!" the paper roared. Eleanor soon converted and was convinced to abandon Hector if he refused to join the "grand rendezvous of the Latter Day Saints" in Utah. Hector "resolved to save the children" by sending them to Eleanor's parents in New Orleans.[2]

Eleanor immediately followed, "chafing like an enraged tigress, whose young had been taken from her," but her parents were determined "she should not drag her innocent babes down into the foul abyss with her." Eleanor's character could be determined by her choice not to "relinquish joining the wild horde which contaminate the air of Great Salt Lake by their abominations" but to leave her children behind and travel alone to Utah. However, Eleanor soon returned to New Orleans and told her parents that "she had been mad, had now left the Mormons and had come to live with her parents and children, and to do what she could to make them happy," though she did not renounce Mormonism itself. After

[2] "Sad Story of Mormonism: The Mother and Children," *New Orleans Bulletin*, republished in *The Mormon* (New York City), 14 March 1857. The article was also republished in other newspapers. See, for instance, "Recapture of Children Stolen by Mormons—Elder Pratt in Custody," *St. Louis Evening News*, 19 May 1857.

requesting "permission to take her children into town" to shop, Eleanor and the children disappeared.[3]

The *New Orleans Bulletin* implicitly integrated its portrayal of Parley and Eleanor into the well-established public narrative of the evils of Mormonism, which portrayed the movement as a threat to evangelical religion and American republicanism, a product of fraud and fanaticism.[4] Authors also emphasized the sexual and economic exploitation of women in polygamy (which the year before Pratt's murder had been condemned as one of the "twin relics of barbarism" by the infant Republican Party). Depictions of Mormonism generally rested on a sharp dichotomy between unscrupulous leaders (like Parley) and the deceived rank-and-file members (like Eleanor), who, though innocent, would unquestioningly obey their evil superiors. Thus, the *New Orleans Bulletin* concluded that Eleanor intended to take her children to Utah "to be thrust into the opening throat of the grim visaged and horrible monster, who sits midway upon the Rocky Mountains, lapping his repulsive jaws, and eager to devour new victims as they become

[3] Ibid.

[4] The past several years have seen the publication of several important works on Mormon public image, including Terryl L. Givens, *The Viper on the Hearth: Mormons, Myths, and the Construction of Heresy* (New York: Oxford University Press, 1997); Jan Shipps, "From Satyr to Saint: American Perceptions of the Mormons, 1860–1960," in *Sojourner in the Promised Land*; and Sarah Barringer Gordon, *The Mormon Question: Polygamy and Constitutional Conflict in Nineteenth Century America* (Chapel Hill: University of North Carolina Press, 2002). Older studies include: David Brion Davis, "Some Themes of Counter-Subversion: An Analysis of Anti-Masonic, Anti-Catholic, and Anti-Mormon Literature," *Mississippi Valley Historical Review* 47 (September 1960): 205–24; Leonard Arrington and Jon Haupt, "Intolerable Zion: The Image of Mormonism in Nineteenth Century American Literature," *Western Humanities Review* 22 (Summer 1968): 243–60; Charles A. Cannon, "The Awesome Power of Sex: The Polemical Campaign Against Mormon Polygamy," *Pacific Historical Quarterly* 43 (February 1974): 61–82; Lester E. Bush, "A Peculiar People: The Physiological Aspects of Mormonism, 1850–1975," *Dialogue* 12 (Fall 1979): 61–83; Gary L. Bunker and Davis Bitton, *The Mormon Graphic Image, 1834–1914: Cartoons, Caricatures, and Illustrations* (Salt Lake City: University of Utah Press, 1983); and Gregory Pingree, "'The Biggest Whorehouse in the World': Representations of Plural Marriage in Nineteenth-Century America," *Western Humanities Review* 50 (Fall 1996): 213–32.

entangled in his foul, his leprous coils."[5] The *New Orleans Bulletin*'s portrayal reached a wide audience and assisted Hector McLean in his search for Pratt.[6]

McLean's hunt and the widespread attention given the article from the *New Orleans Bulletin* prompted Pratt to respond. Writing under the pseudonym "A Friend of the Oppressed," he wrote his own narrative of his relationship with Eleanor and Hector in *The Mormon*, a New York City newspaper edited by Apostle John Taylor, in an article titled "Sad Story of Presbyterianism: The Mother and Children." Parley reframed the history of Eleanor and Hector to blame religious intolerance, not Mormonism, for the breakup of the family (which had already been marred by abuse and alcohol). Following Eleanor's conversion, her brother and husband "raged, foamed, cursed, railed, stormed," and even held a "large *sword cane*" over her head, threatening to kill her "and the minister who dare[d] baptize her." Nevertheless, Eleanor (before she met Parley) obtained her husband's consent to be baptized and "remained a faithful and obedient wife and mother," though he remained "harsh and tyrannical." The McLeans continued in an uneasy truce for a few years, with Eleanor "utterly forbidden to mention any point in her religion in [the] presence of her husband." One day, after she sang two lines of a Mormon hymn, Hector flew into a "violent rage" and threw her out of the house at night. Hector then sent their children away to punish her, rather than to save them.[7]

Parley placed Eleanor's experience within the larger Mormon narrative of persecution for religion's sake, which the Latter-day Saints had honed since their expulsions from Missouri in the 1830s. His own writings, particularly his *History of the Late Persecution*

---

[5] "Sad Story of Mormonism: The Mother and Children."

[6] Erastus Snow to Brigham Young, 14 March 1857, Brigham Young Collection, Church History Library, the Church of Jesus Christ of Latter-day Saints, Salt Lake City, Utah (hereafter LDS Church History Library); and George A. Smith to Young, 15 March 1857, Young Collection, LDS Church History Library.

[7] "A Friend of the Oppressed" [Parley P. Pratt] to *The Mormon*, 20 February 1857, published as "Sad Story of Presbyterianism: The Mother and Children," *The Mormon*, 14 March 1857.

Inflicted by the State of Missouri Upon the Mormons (1839), had been instrumental in establishing a Mormon narrative of suffering and martyrdom in which the Saints portrayed themselves as sincere devotees of religious truth who had endured violent persecutions and been driven into exile in a land of supposed religious liberty.[8] Parley exclaimed, "Talk not of Rome, of Nero, of the dark ages, or of the Spanish Inquisition. All these combined could scarce form a parallel worthy to compare with the heartless, unfeeling, inhuman, savage and worse than fiendish tyranny of the nineteenth century. And all this enacted by Protestants in a land of freedom!" When Eleanor arrived in New Orleans, she "found her bigoted and hard-hearted Presbyterian parents and brothers and sisters in the same plot" and only traveled to Utah after she found herself "sinking under the accumulated wrongs and oppressions of those who should have been her friends." Only then did she leave her children "for a season . . . promising to return to them in due time." After teaching school in Salt Lake City for a year, she then traveled back to her children. The latest news about Eleanor, as reported in the *New Orleans Bulletin*, "opens up another chapter in her somewhat romantic and heroic life." If intolerant Christians had reacted to Mormonism differently, Parley concluded, or if Eleanor had "had a kind and dutiful husband, instead of an unfeeling tyrant, religious differences would not have separated the family."[9]

Initial Reactions to Pratt's Murder

Less than three months after Pratt wrote this article in February 1857, McLean brutally murdered him. In widely reprinted articles, local newspapers set the national tone by portraying McLean as Pratt's victim. The *Fort Smith Herald* trumpeted: "One Mormon

[8] See David W. Grua's essay in this volume (chapter 5); Richard Bushman, *Joseph Smith: Rough Stone Rolling* (New York: Knopf, 1995), 402; and Matthew J. Grow, *"Liberty to the Downtrodden": Thomas L. Kane, Romantic Reformer* (New Haven, Conn.: Yale University Press, 2009), chapter 5.

[9] "Sad Story of Presbyterianism: The Mother and Children."

Less! Nine More Widows!! Alas for the Mormon Prophet!!! If thou hast power to raise the dead, Parley, raise thyself!!!!" In the *Herald*'s version of events, McLean, "an abused and aggravated husband," had justifiably killed Pratt. The paper exulted: "We are pleased to see that such men, not men, demons, pursuing such a course cannot, with impunity, come into our midst, in Arkansas, and advocate their unholy, diabolical doctrine, and go away unpunished." Better to kill a Mormon apostle than to allow him to cause "the ruin of hundreds, and perhaps, thousands of his fellow beings by leading them astray and getting them under the clutches of Mormonism, there to practice crime in its every shape."[10]

The *Arkansas Intelligencer*, published in Van Buren, wrote that while it regretted Pratt's killing, "more than all" did it "deplore the melancholy affair that lead [*sic*] to its commission." The *Intelligencer* depicted the McLeans' marriage as "happy and prosperous until she made the acquaintance of Pratt." Thus, the paper continued, "deeply do we sympathize with McLean in the unfortunate condition in which Mormon villainy and fanaticism has placed him."[11] The *New Orleans Bulletin*, in a widely reprinted article, repeated the same basic narrative as the Arkansas papers, presenting McLean as "stung to phrenzy, maddened beyond the power of endurance, under the grievous outrages he had endured, leaped upon a charger and as with the wings of the wind, overtook the destroyer of his peace, and slew him." The *New Orleans Bulletin* likewise condoned McLean's actions by noting the "mountain weight of wrong and insult" Pratt had "heaped upon [his] head."[12]

In response, Eleanor moved quickly to shape the news. On May 18, she wrote a lengthy letter to the *Arkansas Intelligencer*, and a local judge, John B. Ogden—who had dismissed legal charges against

---

[10] As quoted in "Tragic End of a Mormon Patriarch," *Farmer's Cabinet*, 4 June 1857.

[11] "Another Startling Tragedy," *New York Times*, 28 May 1857, reprinted an article from the *St. Louis Democrat*, 25 May 1857, which had reprinted the article from the *Arkansas Intelligencer*.

[12] *New Orleans Bulletin*, reprinted in "Terrible Tragedy: The Second Head of the Mormon Church Killed by an Injured Husband," *Texas State Gazette* (Austin), 6 June 1857.

Parley and Eleanor and allowed him to escape the night before his murder—arranged for its publication.[13] In an account that echoed Parley's article in *The Mormon*, Eleanor focused on Hector's abuse, her own choice to convert, and Parley's righteousness. She wrote that Hector had "by his own acts blighted and consigned to eternal death all the delicate ties that existed between us, and that before Mormonism crossed our pathway." Furthermore, Parley had not "induced" her to convert to Mormonism; rather, she was baptized in San Francisco before his arrival, though he did baptize her two sons. Like Parley's explanation in *The Mormon*, she made no mention of their marriage. But she did not deny the rumored marriage, conceded that she had boarded with Parley's family, and wrote that "whatever relation existed between us was of my own seeking." Eleanor characterized Parley as "a fountain of light and intelligence, at which thousands might drink, and yet the stream flowed, *clear, pure, and free*."[14] Her article was reprinted throughout the country, often accompanied by biting commentary.[15] Eleanor later overheard a group of her pursuers in St. Louis who concluded on the basis of this article: "She's smart" and "so full of her tricks there is no telling what she will do. . . . I doubt whether there is two equal to her in the U.S."[16]

[13] Eleanor McComb Pratt, "Account of the Death of Parley P. Pratt," ca. 1857–1860, LDS Church History Library.

[14] "Another Article by Mrs. McLean," *Arkansas Intelligencer*, in Reva Stanley, *A Biography of Parley P. Pratt: The Archer of Paradise* (Caldwell, Idaho: Caxton Printers, 1937), 317–24.

[15] "More About the Murder of Parley Pratt, the Mormon Elder by McLean," *New York Herald*, 9 June 1857; "The McLean and Pratt Mormon Tragedy," *North American and United States Gazette* (Philadelphia), 1 June 1857; "The Murder of Parley Pratt," *Daily Chronicle and Sentinel* (Augusta, Georgia), 13 June 1857; and "The Death of the Mormon Elder Pratt," *The Weekly Raleigh Register* (Raleigh, North Carolina), 17 June 1857. While some of these newspapers published Eleanor's article without comment, most used the occasion to celebrate Pratt's death. A sympathetic paper, the *Chicago Weekly Ledger*, noted that Eleanor's statement had "been quite generally published, by the leading papers of the country, but everywhere with a sneer, a cold voice of insult and bitter insinuation" ("The Woman's Story—Mrs. McLean," *Chicago Weekly Ledger*, 13 June 1857, in "Journal History of the Church of Jesus Christ of Latter-day Saints," 13 May 1857, 20).

[16] Eleanor Pratt, "Account," 55.

Eleanor also influenced the coverage of Parley's murder in the Mormon press by writing similar accounts for *The Mormon* and for the *Latter-day Saints' Millennial Star*, a British periodical under the editorship of Parley's brother Orson. The Mormon press also republished Eleanor's account to the *Intelligencer* as well as her poem "The Orphans' Lamentation, on Hearing of the Martyrdom of Their Father." The poem's narrator "heard a wail from out a distant mountain home":

> It was the voice of wives and children wild with grief,
> Who sought to heaven, with prayers and tears, for kind relief;
> For they'd learned, by a paper from a distant place,
> The news that they no more could see a father's face.[17]

Their cry soon "reach'd the throne of God," who promised to avenge the "blood of Parley." God's wrath would fall not only on the perpetrators, but "that nation shall atone / For every widow's tear, and every orphan's moan."[18] Eleanor's emphases on Parley's martyrdom and God's vengeance upon the wicked set part of the tone for the Mormon response.

A similar focus can be seen in a letter that also made the rounds of the Mormon press. It was written by missionaries George Higginson (who had been arrested with Pratt) and George Crouch. They alleged that after McLean murdered Pratt, he boasted of his deed and was allowed to walk "the streets [of Van Buren] with impunity" before leaving. Placing Pratt's death in the context of past Mormon persecution, they compared the "church-going citizens of Van Buren" with the "blood-thirsty mobocrats of Missouri and Illinois." Significantly, *The Mormon* refused to issue a blanket condemnation of the local residents. Rather, it noted that some had sympathized with and assisted Eleanor; the "respectable inhabitants" had shown no "disrespect" to either Parley or Eleanor, and the local authorities had arrested two men who had helped Hector McLean in the murder.[19]

---

[17] *Latter-day Saints' Millennial Star*, 19:417, in "Journal History," 13 May 1857, 5.

[18] Ibid.

[19] *The Mormon*, 20 June 1857, in "Journal History," 13 May 1857, 18–19. The fate of McLean's two associates remains unclear.

In a letter published in San Francisco's *Daily Alta California*, McLean, by contrast, cited widespread public approval for his action. Recounting Pratt's trial in Arkansas before "about five hundred spectators," McLean declared that he implicated "the scoundrel in court, Parley P. Pratt as the principal cause" of all his "sorrows." An "intense excitement" ensued and McLean "really thought the crowd were about making a move to lay hold of him and tear him to pieces" before the judicial authorities intervened. He matter-of-factly stated that following Pratt's release the following morning, he "overtook Pratt, and . . . *killed him*." Regarding the murder, McLean concluded, "I am not able to say how you will view the act but I look upon it as the best act of my life. And the people of West Arkansas agree with me in this view of the commission of the deed."[20]

National Contexts

Most Americans were sympathetic with McLean as well. While the national debate over the "Mormon Question" simmered throughout the nineteenth century, it was probably never more volatile than at this moment. President James Buchanan, inaugurated two months before Pratt's death, immediately faced a crisis in Utah, as federal territorial officials charged Mormon leaders with disloyalty to the nation. As the complaints of these officials captured the attention of the press and public, politicians of both parties flocked to the anti-Mormon standard. For instance, Democratic senator Stephen Douglas from Illinois, a former ally of the Mormons, called for Congress to "apply the knife and cut out this loathsome, disgusting ulcer."[21] William Appleby, an experienced Mormon observer of eastern perceptions of the Saints, commented that public opinion had never been worse: "I have never perceived such an acrimonious spirit prevailing against the Mormons, as appears to be gathering at present."[22] By the time of Pratt's murder,

[20] *Daily Alta California*, 9 July 1857, in Stanley, *Archer of Paradise*, 330–31.

[21] Quoted in Will Bagley, *Blood of the Prophets: Brigham Young and the Massacre at Mountain Meadows* (Norman: University of Oklahoma Press, 2002), 79.

[22] William Appleby to Young, 1 April 1857, Young Collection, LDS Church History Library.

Buchanan had decided to dispatch an army that would install an outsider to replace Brigham Young as governor of Utah and compel the Saints' submission to national power.[23] (One newspaper helpfully suggested that Buchanan appoint McLean as Utah's governor because he would bring the "old Brigand" [Young] to "have a sudden weakness in his knees.")[24]

News of Pratt's murder fit easily with stories of other Mormon horrors, another example of the depravity of the Latter-day Saints in general and the evils of the polygamous hierarchy in particular. For the *St. Louis Democrat*, it was "another painful narrative of Mormon iniquity, seduction and villainy."[25] The *Daily Alta California* used the incident to argue that "Mormonism is ripe for dissolution—ripe and ready to fall and putrefy with its own innate rottenness."[26] Any charge seemed believable. The *New-Hampshire Patriot* asserted, "Pratt was one of the greatest rascals among that great army of great rascals who inhabit Utah." As proof, it claimed that he had sold "two or three" of his wives "to the Indians in exchange for a pair of horses!"[27] The reactions to Pratt's death deepened the narrative of Mormon crimes in the American consciousness.

---

[23] On the Utah War, see Norman F. Furniss, *The Mormon Conflict, 1850–1859* (New Haven, Conn: Yale University Press, 1960); William P. MacKinnon, *At Sword's Point: A Documentary History of the Utah War to 1858* (Norman, Okla.: Arthur H. Clark, 2008); and Grow, *"Liberty to the Downtrodden,"* chapters 9 and 10.

[24] "Hector H. McLean, the Man Who Killed the Seducer of his Wife," *Jeffersonian Democrat* (Chardon, Ohio), 8 July 1857 (article copied from the *New Orleans Bulletin*).

[25] Reprinted as "Another Startling Tragedy," *New York Times*, 28 May 1857, 5.

[26] "The Beginning of the End," *Daily Alta California*, 15 July 1857, in Roger Robin Ekins, ed., *Defending Zion: George Q. Cannon and the California Mormon Newspaper Wars of 1856–1857* (Spokane, Wash.: Arthur H. Clark, 2002), 319–24.

[27] "A Mormon Elder Killed," *New-Hampshire Patriot*, 3 June 1857. This charge was repeated by other authors who alleged specifically that Pratt had sold his plural wife Martha Monks to the American Indian chief Wakara in the early 1850s. In reality, Monks had abandoned Pratt, Utah, and plural marriage for the California goldfields in that era. See Mrs. Benjamin G. Ferris [Elizabeth Cornelia Woodcock Ferris], *The Mormons at Home: with Some Incidents of Travel from Missouri to California, 1852–3, in a Series of Letters* (New York: Dix & Edwards, 1856); Austin N. Ward, *Husband in Utah; or, Sights and Scenes Among the Mormons: with Remarks on their Moral and Social Economy*, ed. Maria Ward (New York: Derby & Jackson, 1859), 281; and Parley P. Pratt, Family Record, LDS Church History Library.

An extralegal tradition that asserted the right of a husband to kill the seducer of his wife, explained by Patrick Mason in chapter 8 of this volume, also shaped the national response.[28] In general, the American South had a much higher tolerance for extralegal, socially sanctioned violence such as dueling and rioting than the rest of the nation.[29] (In the coming decades, the penchant for extralegal violence combined with the region's virulent anti-Mormonism led to hundreds of incidents of threats or actual violence against Latter-day Saints and their property in the South.)[30] But most northerners—generally less favorable to other forms of extralegal violence—also accepted this tradition. In Pratt's Utah, the territorial legislature had codified it (known there as "mountain common law") after two incidents in 1851.[31]

Nearly all of the national newspapers blamed Parley Pratt for his own death by asserting that he had "seduced" Eleanor and thus invited the wrath of her husband. According to the narrative of seduction, Hector McLean had justifiably invoked the "unwritten law" by killing Parley. The *Daily Alta California*, for instance, repeatedly referred to Pratt as "that hoary-headed seducer" and asked, "Who of us shall blame [McLean], or say that, under the circumstances, we would have acted otherwise?"[32] Pratt's polygamy

---

[28] Hendrik Hartog, "Lawyering, Husbands' Rights, and 'The Unwritten Law' in Nineteenth-Century America," *Journal of American History* 84, no. 1 (1997): 67–96; and Patrick Q. Mason's essay in this volume (chapter 8).

[29] David Grimsted, *American Mobbing, 1828–1861: Toward Civil War* (New York: Oxford University Press, 1998); and Bertram Wyatt-Brown, *Honor and Violence in the Old South* (New York: Oxford University Press, 1986).

[30] Patrick Q. Mason, *The Mormon Menace: Violence and Anti-Mormonism in the Postbellum South* (New York: Oxford University Press, 2011).

[31] The most notorious event occurred when Howard Egan, a prominent Saint, killed a non-Mormon, James Monroe, who had impregnated Egan's wife while Egan was in California. As Monroe fled Salt Lake a year after the affair, Egan tracked him down and killed him near the Utah border. Defended in court by W. W. Phelps and George A. Smith, who justified the killing by appeals to "mountain common law" ("the man who seduces his neighbor's wife must die, and her nearest relative must kill him," according to Smith), Egan was acquitted. See Kenneth L. Cannon II, "'Mountain Common Law': The Extralegal Punishment of Seducers in Early Utah," *Utah Historical Quarterly* 51, no. 4 (1983): 308–27.

[32] "The Beginning of the End," *Alta California*, 15 July 1857, in Ekins, *Defending Zion*, 319–24.

powerfully reinforced the tale of seduction. Mormon missionaries of the era were often accused of being seducers, and the actions of Pratt appeared to confirm this suspicion. According to the newspapers, Parley had not only seduced Eleanor, but he intended to take her and her children "into the valley of moral death—Utah!"[33]

This extralegal tradition assumed that women had no will of their own, that they were always the victims of seduction rather than active participants. In Eleanor's case, this assumption was heightened—notwithstanding her protests—by the common notion that a woman would not freely choose polygamy and Mormonism. She must have been duped, forced, coerced, or even mesmerized, a belief constantly reinforced in the popular anti-Mormon literature of the era.[34] The national press erased Eleanor's agency by emphasizing Parley's powers of seduction. The *New Orleans Bulletin* presented her as the "victim of this extraordinary imposture."[35] The *Farmer's Cabinet* asserted that Pratt had "succeeded in converting Mrs. McLean to his beastly faith and then to his own beastly uses."[36] Other papers obliterated Eleanor's choice by charging her with insanity.[37] San Francisco's *Daily Evening Bulletin* charged that her "incoherent raving" in support of Pratt established without doubt "the necessity of her confinement in an asylum."[38] The *Galveston News* wrote that the "lecherous Pratt" had preyed upon the "insane" Eleanor. Though McLean had "rid the world of his pestilential presence," the "effect of the Elder's bad deeds" lived after him: "a family destroyed—children more than orphaned—gray hairs brought with sorrow to the grave. Such is the hellish fruit of Mormonism."[39]

[33] "Violent Death of Parley P. Pratt," *Daily Cleveland Herald*, 27 May 1857.

[34] See Givens, *Viper on the Hearth*.

[35] *New Orleans Bulletin*, reprinted in "Terrible Tragedy: The Second Head of the Mormon Church Killed by an Injured Husband," *Texas State Gazette* (Austin), 6 June 1857.

[36] "Tragic End of a Mormon Patriarch," *Farmer's Cabinet*, 4 June 1857.

[37] "The Mormon Pratt's Last Victim," *Galveston News*, reprinted in the *New York Times*, 11 June 1857, 3.

[38] "Frightful Effects of Mormonism," *Daily Evening Bulletin*, 18 July 1857.

[39] "The Mormon Pratt's Last Victim," *Galveston News*, reprinted in the *New York Times*, 11 June 1857, 3.

At least one newspaper dissented from this chorus by both recognizing Eleanor's agency and using her story to rail against abusive husbands and the hypocrisy of anti-polygamy rhetoric in a land of prostitution and sexual abuse of slaves. The *Chicago Weekly Ledger* criticized the national coverage: "McLean is almost canonized as a hero for the deed. Pratt is treated as would be the death of a beast of prey. Mrs. McLean is looked upon as the denizen of a brothel." The *Chicago Weekly Ledger* came to Eleanor's defense—not because of any affinity to Mormonism, which it clearly repudiated—but to protect womanhood. Indeed, the paper viewed polygamy, which it disdained, as a "great deal better" than "the licensed brothelism" of America's "Christian cities" and a "million times better than the open, shameless, ravishing all over the land of slavery." Referring to Hector's abuse, the paper described Eleanor as "persecuted in the most tender ties of womanhood and motherhood" and asked, "Where is the instinctive woman who will turn cold from her and with smiling complacency upon McLean?"[40] The *Chicago Weekly Ledger* demonstrated that, depending on a newspaper's own agenda, Eleanor's plight could be used as a critique of American morality, tolerance of domestic abuse, and the violence of the "unwritten law," which elevated a husband's rage over a wife's suffering.

Martyred Apostle

While most of the nation cheered and jeered, the Saints mourned Pratt's death. Reports from Mormon leaders in the Midwest had apprised Brigham Young of McLean's pursuit of Pratt in the months preceding his murder. In late April, Erastus Snow informed Young that since early March, "McLean and his friends . . . had the Police of Saint Louis Cincinnati and Boston on the look out for Elder P. P. Pratt; and Railroad conductors and every public conveyance posted." Because of their association with Pratt, even Snow and George A. Smith "could not move without being watched." Perhaps fearing that his letter might be intercepted (a common concern among Mormons in the era), Snow added in

[40] "The Woman's Story—Mrs. McLean," *Chicago Weekly Ledger*, 13 June 1857.

code language that Parley had escaped and that Eleanor was on her way to Utah with her children, indicating that Young knew of Parley's assistance to Eleanor. Snow wrote: "The Hare however escaped narrowly but silently by a way they knew not and the blood hounds have lost every scent of his trail. The Bird with her Young had flown over the Gulf and her beak headed towards the high places of the Mountains. *Selah!*"[41]

Snow's premature optimism proved ill-founded. A month later from St. Louis, another Mormon leader, Horace S. Eldredge, wrote to Young: "It is currently reported & generally believed by Saint & Sinner that Parley P. Pratt has been taken while enroute to Utah by McLean, his wife's former husband. . . . We sincerely trust it is a hoax, but fear it is true, or at least something in it." Before sending the letter, Eldredge added a postscript noting that the St. Louis newspaper, the *Daily Republican*, had published confirmation of Pratt's death that day.[42] Before the news arrived in Salt Lake City, Mormons on the trail west learned of Pratt's death. Philip Margetts, along the Missouri River with a group of handcart missionaries in June 1857, wrote that his associates "felt like young lions and almost as savage in consequence of hearing of the assassination" of their "beloved P.P. Pratt."[43] When news of Pratt's death arrived in Salt Lake City on June 23, Apostle Wilford Woodruff recorded: "This was painful news to his family. The papers of the United States are filled with bitter revileings against us. The devil is exceding mad."[44]

Brigham Young asked Apostle George A. Smith, who had returned to Utah, "if it was not hard to acknowledge the hand of God in the death of Parley P. Pratt by as wicked a man as McLain." For Young, the lesson of Pratt's death was: "If we live our religion we shall have all the world upon us." Indeed, he continued, "the

[41] Erastus Snow to Young, 25 April 1857, Young Collection, LDS Church History Library.

[42] Horace S. Eldredge to Young, 25 May 1857, Young Collection, LDS Church History Library.

[43] Quoted in Bagley, *Blood of the Prophets*, 71. See also Juanita Brooks, *The Mountain Meadows Massacre* (Norman: University of Oklahoma Press, 1979), 57–58.

[44] Scott G. Kenney, ed., *Wilford Woodruff's Journal, 1833–1898* (Midvale, Utah: Signature Books, 1983–1984), 5:61, entry for 23 June 1857; and "Journal History," 23 June 1857, 1.

day has come when the Elders have got to take care of themselves, for the people will publish a lie and shoot them if they are not careful."[45] In informing other Saints, Young wrote of the "lamented death of our old friend and true and faithful Brother."[46] He added that Pratt's mission had not ended with his death. Referring to Joseph Smith and his brother Hyrum who had been killed by a mob thirteen years earlier, Young wrote, "One more good man has gone to assist brothers Joseph [and] Hyrum . . . in another sphere."[47] The news quickly raced around Mormon country. One Saint wrote, "I cannot yet believe that bror Parley P. Pratt is dead," an event that reminded him "of the power of the destroyer, and the fatal effects of fiendish enmity."[48]

In the context of the impending Utah War, the Latter-day Saints easily incorporated Pratt's assassination into their narrative of persecution. William Appleby wrote from New York City, "Editors, Priests, and people are rejoicing over the murder of Br. Parley. Their joy will be turned into mourning before long."[49] A crowd in London, after listening to Apostle Ezra Taft Benson "expose their abominations," taunted him: "Where's your brother Parley and where's Joe. Smith? We'll serve you the same as they were served." Benson asked, "How long, oh Lord, wilt thou withhold thine hand from vengeance?"[50] In the Mormon colony of San Bernardino, California, one woman recorded that the Saints "met in

[45] Kenney, *Woodruff's Journal*, 5:62, entry for 25 June 1857.

[46] Brigham Young to Henry G. Boyle, 4 July 1857, Young Collection, LDS Church History Library; see also Young to George Q. Cannon, 4 July 1857, Young Collection, LDS Church History Library.

[47] Brigham Young to Orson Pratt and Ezra T. Benson, 30 June 1857, *Millennial Star*, 19:556.

[48] Thomas D. Brown to Brigham Young, 27 June 1857, Young Collection, LDS Church History Library.

[49] William I. Appleby to Brigham Young, 11 June 1857, Young Collection, LDS Church History Library.

[50] "Correspondence. Letter from Elder E. T. Benson to His Family," dated 23 June 1857 from London, *Deseret News*, 28 October 1857, 7; and "Correspondence," letter from Ezra Taft Benson dated 24 June 1857 from London, *Deseret News*, 30 September 1857, 5. See also Orson Pratt to Brigham Young, 27 June 1857, Young Collection, LDS Church History Library.

groups" and "talked of how much [Pratt] had preached and written! How many hearts had been made to rejoice at the sound of his voice, souls redeemed, which had it not been for his indefatigable labors, might have remained in darkness forever. We rejoiced that though gone from our sight he yet lived in his writings!"[51]

The Mormon press immediately cast Pratt in the role of martyr. The *Deseret News* said little on the matter (probably because the Utah War crisis diverted its attention and resources) and more far-flung newspapers took the lead. In the *Millennial Star*, Orson Pratt cast his brother as a martyr who "fell in a righteous cause . . . in the defense of suffering innocence, while endeavouring to aid by his letters a helpless female with her little children, to escape the fury of her savage persecutors." Following his brother's lead, Orson recounted the story of the marriage of Hector McLean (the "unfeeling, brutal monster") to Eleanor, her sufferings, and their later separation, without mentioning Eleanor's marriage to Parley. The reluctance of the Pratt brothers and Eleanor herself to publicly refer to the marriage between Parley and Eleanor in eastern and British newspapers illustrated that they recognized the potential public relations damage this fact could cause. For most Americans, acknowledgment of the polygamous marriage would only confirm the narrative of Parley as seducer. In the *Millennial Star*, Orson thus portrayed his brother as a "great philanthropist, and good man" who sympathized with Eleanor's plight and "sought to advise her, by letters through the post, of the pursuits of her old enemy," which led McLean to murder him.[52] This "last great and magnanimous act," Orson predicted, "will be handed down to unborn generations, as an imperishable monument to his praise; while his wicked brutal murderers, and all that gave countenance to the diabolical deed shall gnaw their tongues for pain, and perish, and be forgotten."[53]

Other Mormon newspapers echoed Orson Pratt's declaration.

---

[51] S. George Ellsworth, ed., *The History of Louisa Barnes Pratt: The Autobiography of a Mormon Missionary Widow and Pioneer* (Logan: Utah State University Press, 1998), 256.

[52] "Murder of Parley P. Pratt, One of the Twelve Apostles of the Church of Jesus Christ of Latter-day Saints," *Millennial Star* 19, no. 27 (4 July 1857), 417.

[53] "Biographical Sketch of Parley P. Pratt," *Millennial Star* 19, no. 27 (4 July 1857), 423–24.

The Mormon had similarly proclaimed that Pratt was "revered by thousands and tens of thousands" and would "be honored by millions yet unborn, when that of his cowardly assassin and those who . . . cheered him on to his damning deed, and who . . . rejoice over their crime" would "be loathsome and a stink in the nostrils of God and good men."[54] A writer in the San Francisco-based *Western Standard* stated, "Parley's name will be embalmed in the hearts of millions and will be handed down to posterity as that of a noble philanthropist and a martyr to the cause of truth."[55] In the immediate aftermath, the Latter-day Saints thus lamented Pratt's death and remembered him as a martyr for conscience sake. However, the events surrounding Pratt's death gave at least some other leaders pause before integrating him into the larger Mormon martyrology narrative. In January 1858, a group of Church leaders discussed Pratt's death at a prayer meeting. Apostle Woodruff recorded that while Pratt was in St. Louis in March 1857, George A. Smith told him "not to go to Arkansaw but to go diret to Salt Lake & take care of himself. He told Parly if he went to try to protet Eleanor & her Children He would loose his life. But He did not take Care of himself or take G. A. Smith Council But went to Arkansas & was murdered by Mr McLain."[56] Pratt likely believed that Smith, however well-intentioned, was suggesting that he abandon his responsibility toward one of his wives. Nevertheless, the belief that Pratt had ignored Smith's advice and had foolishly provoked his own murder long caused controversy over how to interpret his death among some Mormons.

Seven years later, Brigham Young stated in a meeting of missionaries that Pratt was killed "for adultery." He continued: "I was glad of it for it paid the debt he owed, for he whored. He felt the law was made for the rest of the elders of Israel but not for him."[57]

[54] As quoted in "Mormonism in New-York," *New York Daily Times*, 1 June 1857.

[55] William Shearman, "Assassination of President P. P. Pratt," *Western Standard*, 3 July 1857 and George Q. Cannon, "Assassination of President P. P. Pratt," *Western Standard*, 17 July 1857, both in Ekins, *Defending Zion*, 316–18, 324–27.

[56] Kenney, *Woodruff's Journal*, 3 January 1858, 5:153.

[57] Ibid., 1 May 1865; and General Minutes, Missionary Meeting, 1 May 1865, LDS Church History Library.

Led by Brigham Young, nineteenth-century Mormons believed that, as Mormon Joseph West explained to a national audience, "There are mortal sins which deprive the doers of the expiation wrought by Jesus; and the shedding of their own blood is the only sacrifice which can save such guilty ones from an outer darkness which shall endure forever."[58] In 1851, Pratt had written about adultery: "While every man who stoops from his Godlike majesty to a level with the brute creation so far as to trifle with the fountain of life, (female virtue) will atone for the same with his blood."[59] In his accusation of adultery, Young referred not to Parley's relationship with Eleanor but to his unauthorized (in Young's eyes) plural marriages to Phoebe Soper, Ann Agatha Walker, and Martha Monks in 1846 and 1847.[60] Following Joseph Smith's death in 1844, members of the Quorum of the Twelve Apostles clashed over who could authorize new polygamous marriages. Young believed that only he, as the most senior apostle, possessed this authority, while Pratt and John Taylor argued that when Young was absent, other apostles possessed such authority. Young's viewpoint eventually prevailed but not until Pratt and Taylor had entered into plural marriages unauthorized by him. In 1847, he censured Pratt and Taylor, declaring that they had "committed an insult on the Holy Priesthood."[61] As a result, Young remarried Parley to Phoebe and Agatha in the Endowment House in 1851 (Martha had previously left Parley).[62]

Furthermore, the association of Pratt's death with the Mountain Meadows Massacre complicated Mormon efforts to recognize

[58] Joseph A. West, "Mormon Blood-Atonement," *North American Review* 143 (December 1886): 643–46.

[59] Pratt, "'Mormonism!' 'Plurality of Wives!' An Especial Chapter, for the Especial Edification of Certain Inquisitive News Editors, Etc.," broadside published in San Francisco on 13 July 1852, republished in Charles L. Camp and Reva Holdaway Stanley, "A Mormon Mission to California in 1851: From the Diary of Parley Parker Pratt," *California Historical Society Quarterly* 14, no. 1 (March 1935): 59–73.

[60] For context on these marriages, see R. Steven Pratt's essay in this volume (chapter 2).

[61] Gary James Bergera, *Conflict in the Quorum: Orson Pratt, Brigham Young, Joseph Smith* (Salt Lake City: Signature Books, 2002), 57–58.

[62] Endowment House Records, February 26, 1851, LDS Church History Library (reference courtesy of R. Steven Pratt).

him as a martyr. Did the Saints' anger over Pratt's martyrdom lead some Mormons to commit a horrific crime?[63] The bare facts are certainly suggestive, and commentators at the time linked Pratt's murder in Arkansas with the massacre of Arkansans in Utah four months later. When news of the Mountain Meadows Massacre arrived in California in October 1857, the California press attributed the bloodshed to retribution for the death of, in the words of the *Daily Alta California*, the "Sainted Parley."[64] In the wake of John D. Lee's execution for his participation at Mountain Meadows in 1877, a new round of national news stories asserted that Pratt's murder had been a primary cause of the massacre.[65] Certainly, the Saints' reaction to Pratt's death demonstrates their intense bitterness over the crime, its celebration in the national press, and the lack of McLean's prosecution. Nevertheless, as Richard Turley demonstrates in chapter 10 of this volume, Pratt's murder ranks low in the causes of the Mountain Meadows Massacre, a conclusion Juanita Brooks reached in her classic history nearly sixty years ago.[66]

Nevertheless, for the most part, Latter-day Saints integrated Pratt into the pantheon of martyrs. A memorial from the Utah territorial legislature to the U.S. Congress in January 1858 cited the lack of punishment of Pratt's assassins who slew him "beneath

[63] On the Mountain Meadows Massacre, see Ronald W. Walker, Richard E. Turley Jr., and Glen M. Leonard, *Massacre at Mountain Meadows* (New York: Oxford University Press, 2008); Bagley, *Blood of the Prophets*; and Brooks, *Mountain Meadows Massacre*.

[64] "The Killing of Pratt—Letter from McLean," *Alta California*, 9 July 1857; "The Beginning of the End," *Alta California*, 15 July 1857; and John Nugent, "Topics of the Day," *San Francisco Herald*, 12 October 1857, all reproduced in Ekins, *Defending Zion*, 319–24, 368. See also Bagley, *Blood of the Prophets*, 190.

[65] "The Death of Parley P. Pratt," *Daily Evening Bulletin* (San Francisco) (26 March 1877); "The Former Residence of Hector H. McLean Is Still Standing on the Corner of Jones and Filbert Streets, San Francisco," *Idaho Avalanche* (Silver City) 7 April 1877; "McLean and Mountain Meadows: Reminiscences of the McComb Family in Port Gibson," *Hinds County Gazette* (Raymond, Mississippi), 16 May 1877; and "Elder Pratt: The Tragedy That Led to the Mountain Meadow Massacre, Described by an Eye-Witness—A Mother's Life Ended in Lunacy," *St. Louis Globe-Democrat* (reprinted from the *New York Sun*), 20 September 1875.

[66] Brooks, *Mountain Meadows Massacre*, 57–58. See also Richard Turley's essay in this volume (chapter 10).

the portals of the court which had pronounced him guiltless" as among the country's actions against the Latter-day Saints.[67] A mass meeting in Lehi, Utah, in February 1858 designed to demonstrate support for Young and other leaders during the Utah War crisis, passed resolutions asserting that the Saints had "been cruelly persecuted, mobbed, driven many times," their "females ravished," their "children butchered," and some of their "best men murdered in cold blood," including Joseph and Hyrum Smith, David Patten, and Parley P. Pratt.[68] In 1869, Woodruff stated in his journal that Pratt had been "Martered."[69] In 1888, the *Deseret News* listed Pratt among about forty "martyrs to the truth of this dispensation" whose "blood has been shed for the testimony of Jesus," including victims of battles and the Haun's Mill Massacre in Missouri in the 1830s, Joseph and Hyrum Smith, and various members and missionaries killed by mobs.[70] Long after the rest of the nation forgot Pratt, Mormon authors and leaders continued to hail him as a martyr. In 2001, Church president Gordon B. Hinckley stated that Pratt "died a martyr to this great work and kingdom."[71]

The drama of Pratt's death, combined with the contemporaneous furor over the Utah War, ensured that it would cheer, perhaps even amuse and titillate, the general American public. But what does the reaction say about the place of Mormonism in nineteenth-century America? As the most despised religion of nineteenth-century America, Mormonism tested the boundaries of tolerable religious dissent. The mainstream narrative of Pratt as evil seducer thoroughly trumped the alternative narratives of Pratt as victim or Pratt as martyr in the American press and mind. Likewise, the dominant narrative of Latter-day Saints as malicious fanatics

---

[67] "Memorial," *Deseret News*, 13 January 1858, 4. See also Robert Glass Cleland and Juanita Brooks, eds., *A Mormon Chronicle: The Diaries of John D. Lee, 1848–1876* (Salt Lake City: University of Utah, 1983), 1:142, entry for 6 January 1858.

[68] "Mass Meetings," *Deseret News*, 10 March 1858, 5. See also "Mass Meeting. Harmony," *Deseret News*, 24 March 1858, 4.

[69] Kenney, *Woodruff's Journal*, 6:489, entry for 4 September 1869.

[70] "Martyrs to the Truth," *Deseret News*, 29 December 1888, 16. See also "A Roll of Honor," *Deseret News*, 19 November 1892, 20.

[71] Gordon B. Hinckley, "The Miracle of Faith," *Ensign* (May 2001): 67.

easily beat back the Mormon counternarrative of themselves as the objects of religious persecution.

The nearly unanimous voice of the American press in either condoning or celebrating Pratt's murder demonstrates the profound depths to which American opinion of Mormonism had plummeted in the wake of plural marriage and the tumult over governance in Utah in the 1850s. While Mormonism had inspired heated opposition since its beginning, sympathetic voices could be found in the national press following the death of Joseph Smith in 1844 and the murders of Mormon missionaries in the South in the last decades of the nineteenth century. The near-unanimous praise for Pratt's murder resulted both from the heated historical atmosphere against Mormonism in 1857 and because he, with his "seduction" of Eleanor, appeared to confirm the worst stereotypes about the Mormon hierarchy. The coverage—both by the national and Mormon press—suggests how thoroughly both sides considered the Latter-day Saints as outsiders in America. The definition of their marginal status, of course, differed—were they outsiders by their embrace of heretical religious doctrines and behaviors or because they had been persecuted and martyred by a nation that gave only lip service to religious liberty?

CHAPTER 10

The Murder of Parley P. Pratt and the Mountain Meadows Massacre

RICHARD E. TURLEY JR.

On September 11, 1857, in a verdant highland valley in southern Utah known as the Mountain Meadows, dozens of Mormon settlers and some Paiute Indians massacred more than a hundred California-bound emigrants, most of whom hailed from northwest Arkansas. It was arguably the darkest day in Utah and Latter-day Saint history, as well as in the antebellum history of the Ozarks. For more than a hundred and fifty years, people have speculated on the causes of the Mountain Meadows Massacre. This essay examines the theory that the killers wanted to avenge the murder of Parley P. Pratt, which had occurred four months earlier in Arkansas.

Pratt was a Mormon apostle—a high official in the Church of Jesus Christ of Latter-day Saints. He was also much admired by fellow Church members. While in San Francisco in 1854, he met Eleanor McLean, a Mormon convert whose husband, Hector, opposed the baptism of their children into her church. Without

Many people contributed to this essay. In particular, I would like to thank Sarah Barringer Gordon, Barbara Jones Brown, Rebecca Taylor, Chad Foulger, Brian Reeves, Andrea Maxfield, Alison K. Gainer, Janiece Johnson, and LaJean Purcell Carruth.

consulting Eleanor, Hector sent the children to live with her parents in New Orleans. Eleanor left Hector, tried without success to regain custody of the children, then moved to Salt Lake City, where she became Pratt's polygamous wife in November 1855.[1]

In the fall of 1856 both Eleanor and Parley headed east, Eleanor to look for her children and Parley to direct Church business. Enraged at losing his wife, Hector pursued them until he finally shot and stabbed the apostle to death near Van Buren, Arkansas, in mid-May 1857. Hector was never charged with the crime—which gave rise to the notion that Parley's death was unpunished.[2]

Months later, after the Mountain Meadows Massacre, journalists in California proposed a connection between Pratt's death and the September killings at Mountain Meadows. On October 10, 1857, for example, the *Los Angeles Star* published an early account of the atrocity: "The blow fell on these emigrants from Arkansas, in retribution of the death of Parley Pratt," the story concluded.[3] Two days later, an article in the *Sacramento Daily Bee* reported, "It is generally supposed that the Indians were instigated by the Mormons, to revenge the death of Parley P. Pratt."[4]

Since then, many writers have repeated the theory. The most thorough development of it to date has been that of historian Will

---

[1] Steven Pratt, "Eleanor McLean and the Murder of Parley P. Pratt," *BYU Studies* 15 (Winter 1975): 225–34; John R. Young, *Memoirs of John R. Young: Utah Pioneer, 1847* (Salt Lake City: Deseret News, 1920), 70–71; and Ronald W. Walker, Richard E. Turley Jr., and Glen M. Leonard, *Massacre at Mountain Meadows: An American Tragedy* (New York: Oxford University Press, 2008), 30–32. When a newspaper reporter asked Eleanor if she divorced Hector before marrying Parley, she answered, "No, the sectarian priests have no power from God to marry; and as a so-called marriage ceremony performed by them is no marriage at all, no divorce was needed" (Eleanor McLean Pratt, interview, *New York World*, 23 November 1869, in Pratt, "Eleanor McLean," 233n26).

[2] Pratt, "Eleanor McLean and the Murder of Parley P. Pratt," 234–50; and Walker, Turley, and Leonard, *Massacre at Mountain Meadows*, 30–32.

[3] "Horrible Massacre of Emigrants!! Over 100 Persons Murdered!!" *Los Angeles Star*, 10 October 1857.

[4] "News from the South," *Sacramento Daily Bee*, 12 October 1857. See also "The Massacre on the Plains," *San Jose Tribune*, 16 October 1857; and "Massacre of Immigrants by the Indians," *Auburn* (California) *Placer Herald*, 17 October 1857.

Bagley in his award-winning book *Blood of the Prophets: Brigham Young and the Massacre at Mountain Meadows*, as well as in subsequent public addresses. Bagley wrote: "Several events—the murder of Parley Pratt, the arrival of his overwrought and vengeful widow in Salt Lake in July 1857 amid war hysteria, and the inflammatory exhortations of Mormon leaders—support [massacre historian Juanita] Brooks's belief that unfortunate circumstance played a part in the fate of the emigrants."[5]

Subsequent treatments have relied on Bagley's evidence and interpretations. In *Under the Banner of Heaven: A Story of Violent Faith*, best-selling author Jon Krakauer wrote that *Blood of the Prophets* "must now be considered the definitive work" on the massacre. Sally Denton, author of *American Massacre: The Tragedy at Mountain Meadows, September 1857*, expressed appreciation for Bagley and his "generous cooperation" in her work. Following Bagley's lead, both authors suggest that Latter-day Saints' desire to avenge Pratt's death led to the killing of the Arkansas emigrants.[6]

The present study examines the evidence linking Pratt's death with the massacre. Because Bagley's work cumulates other sources on this topic and has been so widely influential, this essay focuses on his data and reasoning as it addresses three key components of the theory: (1) the Mormon reaction to Pratt's death, (2) the effect of Eleanor McLean Pratt's arrival in Salt Lake City, and (3) Mormon leaders' exhortations for vengeance.

The Mormon Reaction to Pratt's Death

Parley P. Pratt's murder in 1857 was not an isolated incident: he was merely the latest in a string of Latter-day Saints killed over the previous two and a half decades. On June 27, 1844, the Church's

[5] Will Bagley, *Blood of the Prophets: Brigham Young and the Massacre at Mountain Meadows* (Norman: University of Oklahoma Press, 2002), 378.

[6] Jon Krakauer, *Under the Banner of Heaven: A Story of Violent Faith* (New York: Doubleday, 2003), 214n, 215–17; and Sally Denton, *American Massacre: The Tragedy at Mountain Meadows, September 1857* (New York: Alfred A. Knopf, 2003), 109–12, 155, 294.

founding prophet, Joseph Smith, and his brother Hyrum were gunned down by vigilantes while imprisoned at Carthage, Illinois. In 1838 Mormon apostle David W. Patten was fatally wounded in a skirmish with Missouri militiamen. Between 1833 and 1838, virtual civil war between Mormons and Missourians left other Saints dead, including seventeen men and boys killed by rogue militiamen in the Hawn's Mill Massacre of 1838.

In the years following these deaths, the Latter-day Saints migrated to Utah, where tensions developed between the local citizenry and federal officials. News of Pratt's death reached Salt Lake City in June 1857. A few weeks later the Mormons learned that U.S. president James Buchanan was sending federal troops to Utah Territory to suppress a perceived rebellion there.[7]

Bagley writes, "The party from Arkansas was probably doomed from the moment the Mormons learned of the death of Parley Pratt and the approach of an American army."[8] Bagley describes Mormon reaction to Pratt's death as follows:

> The news of the martyrdom of their most beloved apostle devastated the Saints and aroused sentiments of anger and grief. When [Utahn] Philip Margetts reached the Missouri River with a party of eastbound handcart missionaries in June 1857, his companions "felt like young lions and almost as savage in consequence of hearing of the assassination of our beloved P. P. Pratt." The *Western Standard*, the Mormon voice in California, published the melancholy and heart-sickening news of Pratt's murder on July 3. The paper . . . mourned Pratt as a martyr for the cause of truth and predicted God would come out of his hiding place: "Upon this generation shall come all the righteous blood which has been shed from the time of Jesus to the present."[9]

Bagley's logic rests on three unproven assumptions. First, showing that Philip Margetts's companions were upset by news of Pratt's death does not establish that they or anyone else planned to seek vengeance, especially since Margetts and his fellow travelers

---

[7] Walker, Turley, and Leonard, *Massacre at Mountain Meadows*, 30–40. "Hawn's" Mill Massacre is used instead of the traditional "Haun's" spelling in order to reflect the spelling at the time.

[8] Bagley, *Blood of the Prophets*, 380.

[9] Ibid., 71.

were headed east, not west, and were nowhere near Utah when the massacre occurred. Second, although the Mormon newspaper in California mourned Pratt's death and "predicted God would come out of his hiding place," it did not call for earthly revenge. On the contrary, the article proclaimed, "We are willing to rest our case in the hands of our great 'Advocate' and 'Judge,'" Jesus Christ.[10] Third, Mormons were not universally as strident as Bagley's book may lead readers to believe. Isaiah Moses Coombs, for example, reacted to news of Pratt's death with shock that left him dazed and "unfit for business." Coombs finally found peace in the realization that "others have fallen martyrs to Christ & many more have yet to follow, & all is well." He prayed "God to overrule it all for the best." He later wrote, "I sometimes feel like cursing the murderous fiends, but that would do no good for they are already cursed of *God* and in his hands I leave them."[11]

The reaction of Mormon president Brigham Young, the title figure of Bagley's book, was also restrained. On hearing the news, he said little about it publicly, and his letters belied the idea of vengeance. "The seeing of our faithful Elders slaughtered in cold blood," he wrote on July 4, 1857, is "at times almost to[o] grevious to be borne, but . . . the Spirit within me whispers, peace be still."[12] Another letter, sent to Pratt's brother Orson, offered simple condolences. "I regret very much to learn of the assassination of Bro Parley by the villain McLane," Young wrote, adding, "One more

[10] "Assassination of President P. P. Pratt," *Western Standard*, 3 July 1857.

[11] Isaiah Moses Coombs, Journal, [25]–26 May 1857, Isaiah Moses Coombs, Collection, 1835–1938, Church History Library, the Church of Jesus Christ of Latter-day Saints, Salt Lake City, Utah (hereafter LDS Church History Library) (emphasis in original). The journal entries of other Saints focused primarily on the facts of the event. Wilford Woodruff—then an apostle like Pratt—wrote on June 23, 1857, "We also are informed that Elder Parley P Pratt was Murdered By . . . MCLain who s[h]ot him in Arkansaw. This was painful news to his Family" (Wilford Woodruff, Journal, 23 June 1857, LDS Church History Library). Elias Smith wrote simply, "Elder Parley P. Pratt was killed by one McLane about the 10th of May in Arkansas the particulars of which will be published as soon as fully known" (Elias Smith, Journal, 23 June 1857, LDS Church History Library).

[12] Brigham Young to Silas Smith and the Brethren on the Sandwich Islands, 4 July 1857, Letterpress Copybook 3:698–99, Brigham Young, Office Files, LDS Church History Library.

good man has gone to assist Bro. Joseph [and] Hiram."[13] A third letter invoked providence and divine justice. "The Lord's not my will be done," it said.[14]

The Effect of Eleanor McLean Pratt's Arrival in Salt Lake City

To bridge the gap between Pratt's death in May and the massacre in September, Bagley emphasizes "the arrival of [Pratt's] overwrought and vengeful widow in Salt Lake in July 1857 amid war hysteria."[15] Bagley describes Eleanor's earlier visit to the spot in Arkansas where Parley died, using excerpts from a letter she wrote to apostle Erastus Snow: "Standing where her first husband had murdered her second, the widow Pratt prayed silently, 'Oh! God of Israel let the blood of beloved Parley come up before thee. Let it plead the cause of the innocent, and condemn the guilty!!' . . . The bereaved woman cried, 'Parley thou are not dead but sleeping. And thy innocent blood and thy wounds are before the God of Israel, to plead for the innocent, and call forth vengeance on the guilty.' "[16] This interesting piece of evidence deserves further analysis.

In her letter, Eleanor Pratt did not seek to take matters into her own hands or encourage others to break the law. Instead, as persecuted Christians have done since New Testament times, she turned her thoughts to God. Her language recalled a passage found in Revelation 6:9–10 (KJV): "And when he had opened the

[13] Brigham Young to Orson Pratt and Ezra T. Benson, 30 June 1857, Letterpress Copybook 3:658, Young Office Files. See also Brigham Young to Henry G. Boyle, 4 July 1857, Letterpress Copybook 3:694, Young Office Files.

[14] Brigham Young to George Q. Cannon, 4 July 1857, Letterpress Copybook 3:691, Young Office Files. While mourning Pratt's death, Young believed that in some ways his fellow churchman brought the consequences upon himself through his actions. See Brigham Young, Remarks, 1 May 1865, in Historian's Office, General Church Minutes, LDS Church History Library; and Woodruff, Journal, 1 May 1865 (for translation of shorthand, see Scott G. Kenney, ed., *Wilford Woodruff's Journal: 1833–1898,* 9 vols. [Midvale, Utah: Signature Books, 1983–85], 6:222).

[15] Bagley, *Blood of the Prophets*, 378.

[16] Ibid., 71.

fifth seal, I saw under the altar the souls of them that were slain for the word of God, and for the testimony which they held: And they cried with a loud voice, saying, How long, O Lord, holy and true, dost thou not judge and avenge our blood on them that dwell on the earth?"

Having portrayed Eleanor as vengeful, Bagley describes how a Mormon express party "rushed the widow Pratt from Fort Laramie to Salt Lake in an incredible five days and three hours, perhaps passing the [Arkansas] parties on the trail."[17] Bagley emphasizes that a few days later, on July 26, Brigham Young and other Mormon leaders attended a prayer meeting. He writes, "The meeting was apparently restricted to males, but they read Eleanor Pratt's impassioned letter describing her husband's murder and discussed their future plans. In his journal Brigham Young wrote, '*We prayed for our enemies*.'"[18]

In a speech given at a conference of ex-Mormons in Salt Lake City and later published online, Bagley says that when he learned of the widow's arrival in Salt Lake shortly before the prayer meeting, he concluded that the massacre "was a calculated act of vengeance—that the orders came from Brigham Young, and they originated when the apostles met on the evening of the 26th of July, 1857, at Salt Lake." Bagley asserts, "It was at that meeting that they decided to send George A. Smith south with orders to murder everyone in that party from Arkansas."[19]

Yet the sources he gives for the July 26 meeting do not mention sending George A. Smith south, nor do they name the Arkansas

[17] Ibid., 80; see also 401n32. Other Mormons were hurrying along the trail because they had been threatened in Independence, Missouri, and elsewhere. John Taylor, describing conditions in the Midwest and the treatment of the Saints, wrote, "The spirit of 'border ruffianism' is rampant in most of the western country, and 'Regulators' and mob law seem to bear rule" (John Taylor to Brother Appleby, 9 July 1857, in "Editorial Correspondence from the Plains," *The Mormon*, 8 August 1857.

[18] Bagley, *Blood of the Prophets*, 81 (emphasis in original).

[19] Will Bagley, "Blood of the Prophets: Brigham Young and the Massacre at Mountain Meadows" (speech, Annual Ex-Mormon Conference, Salt Lake City, Utah, October 5, 2002), available at http://www.salamandersociety.com/interviews/willbagley/, accessed June 1, 2010.

company or cite orders to hurt anyone.[20] In fact, the Arkansas company was not even organized yet, the two main families who would later make up the company—the Fanchers and the Bakers—being at different locations along the trail. Nor could Young have known that the yet-to-be-formed company would travel south. Many of those who later died at Mountain Meadows had not yet arrived in the Salt Lake Valley, and emigrants typically traveled north from Salt Lake City, not south.[21]

Furthermore, that Mormon leaders prayed for their enemies does not mean they ordered vengeance against them. Consistent with Christ's admonition in Matthew 5:44 (KJV) to "pray for them which despitefully use you," Mormon leaders often prayed for their enemies, expressing hope that their persecutors would repent or, if not, that God himself would punish them. A prayer reprinted in the October 16, 1852, *Deseret News*, a Latter-day Saint newspaper, followed this pattern. Joseph Smith had offered the prayer in 1836 at a temple dedication in Kirtland, Ohio. In it he referred to the Missourians who drove the Mormons from their homes in Jackson County:

> O Lord, we delight not in the destruction of our fellow men; their souls are precious before thee; but thy word must be fulfilled. . . .
>
> Have mercy, O Lord, upon that wicked mob, who have driven thy people, that they may cease to spoil, that they may repent of their sins, if repentance is to be found; but if they will not, make bare thine arm, O Lord. . . .
>
> And . . . that the cause of thy people may not fail before thee, may thine anger be kindled, and thine indignation fall upon them, that they may be wasted away, both root and branch, from under heaven; but inasmuch as they will repent, thou art gracious and merciful, and will turn away thy wrath, when thou lookest upon the face of thine anointed.[22]

Brigham Young exhibited a similar disposition. For example, on August 30, 1857—two weeks before the massacre—he urged

[20] See *Diary of Brigham Young, 1857*, ed. Everett L. Cooley (Salt Lake City: Tanner Trust Fund/University of Utah Library, 1980), 54; and *Woodruff's Journal*, 5:70.

[21] Walker, Turley, and Leonard, *Massacre at Mountain Meadows*, 82–88, 101–104.

[22] "Life of Joseph Smith," *Deseret News*, 16 October 1852.

Church members not to be angry with people who opposed them. "They are in the hands of God," he said. "Instead of feeling a spirit to punish them, or anything like wrath, live your religion."[23]

Bagley's interpretation breaks down for another reason. He claims Eleanor Pratt rushed to Salt Lake, where she told of Parley's death and incited her hearers to vengeance. Yet by the time she arrived in Salt Lake City, his death was already old news, having reached the city a month earlier. Bagley concedes that "Mormon leaders in Salt Lake barely mentioned Pratt's death over the next month."[24] They also made little mention of Pratt's death in the weeks between July 26 and September 11, the culminating day of the massacre.

Why did Eleanor Pratt rush to Salt Lake City? Contemporary sources show she was running from Hector, who threatened to commit her to an insane asylum. According to June 1857 newspaper accounts, Hector chased Eleanor through St. Louis "seeking to imprison her on the plea of insanity," but she escaped "on to the plains."[25] A July 1 California newspaper confirmed that Hector made arrangements "to send the wife to a lunatic asylum, so soon as her whereabouts [could] be ascertained."[26] Utah provided a refuge, with sympathetic friends to shelter her.

Still pursuing the reasoning that Eleanor's arrival sparked vengeance against the Arkansas emigrants, Bagley notes, "On August 1 Apostle Wilford Woodruff had called on 'Eleanor Pratt & got an account of the death & burial of Elder P. P. Pratt.'"[27] Bagley assumes that in this meeting Eleanor provided a "long narrative" that has survived to this day and included one arguably vengeful sentence: "One thing I know *McLean has to die and go to hell* for what he has done, and every man who assisted him in this deed."

---

[23] Brigham Young, sermon, August 30, 1857, in *Journal of Discourses* (London: Asa Calkin, 1858), 5:171.

[24] Bagley, *Blood of the Prophets*, 81.

[25] "Mrs. McLean," *The Mormon*, 27 June 1857, citing the *St. Louis Sunday Herald*, 16 June 1857.

[26] "The Utah Question," *San Francisco Daily Evening Bulletin*, 1 July 1857.

[27] Bagley, *Blood of the Prophets*, 98.

As Bagley tacitly acknowledges in an endnote, however, the document he cites may not have been composed until 1860, well after the massacre.[28] Even if Eleanor's 1857 recitation to Wilford Woodruff contained similar language, her desired punishment of Hector did not require human intervention.

Finally, Bagley notes a New York newspaper correspondent's interview with Eleanor in 1869, a dozen years after the massacre. Bagley acknowledges, "The reporter's tale of Pratt's murder was incorrect in almost all its sensational detail, but he apparently captured Eleanor Pratt's feelings accurately. . . . The reporter asked if Hector McLean was ever punished for killing Pratt. 'No,' she replied. 'But his death has been fearfully avenged upon the nation that has permitted the blood of the Prophets to be spilt without punishing the murderers.' The reporter did not ask what she meant."[29]

Bagley does not explain why he accepted Eleanor's statement about vengeance when he believed the rest of the interview was flawed. Assuming that the reporter quoted Eleanor accurately, did she actually claim that the massacre avenged Parley P. Pratt's death? There is another, more likely explanation for her purported statement. During the 1860s when this interview occurred, many Latter-day Saints spoke of the Civil War as divine retribution on

[28] Bagley writes: "Woodruff 'got an account of the death and burial of Elder P. P. Pratt' from Pratt's widow on August 1. The long narrative expressed her bitterness against Arkansas and her certainty that Parley Pratt's innocent blood must be avenged. A lawyer in Van Buren had asked her 'whether the Mormons would not avenge this man's blood, even if the Court did nothing.' She assured him, 'If the murderers can feel secure in any nation under heaven or upon any island of the sea they are welcome to feel so. One thing I know *McLean has to die and go to hell* for what he has done, and every man who assisted him in this deed'" (Bagley, *Blood of the Prophets*, 81 [emphasis in original]). But in n37 on p. 401 of his book, Bagley acknowledges, "Pratt read her story of the murder to Woodruff on 24 August, but the surviving version now in the LDS Church History Library may be a revised account composed in April 1860 at the request of George A. Smith."

Bagley also writes: "Years later Charles Wandell, an embittered Mormon apostate, reported that when the Fancher train passed th[r]ough Salt Lake, the widow Pratt 'recognized one or more of the party as having been present at the death of Pratt'" (ibid., 98, 269). Wandell, however, was not in Utah at the time of these events, and in another endnote Bagley himself casts doubt on Wandell's claim, writing, "If the widow Pratt actually made such a charge, it was false" (ibid., 404n18).

[29] Ibid., 265–66.

the nation for the Saints' suffering.[30] For example, one poem of that era included the lines:

> Oh! Wretched land, both North and South,
> Thy doom! Thy doom!!
> By Joseph's God has been decreed,
> For prophet's thou hast made to bleed.[31]

Because Eleanor purportedly referred to retribution "upon the nation," it seems likely the allusion was to the Civil War, not the Mountain Meadows Massacre.

Mormon Leaders' Exhortations for Vengeance

The third factor Bagley invokes to connect Pratt's death with the massacre is "the inflammatory exhortations of Mormon leaders."[32] Partly summarizing and partly quoting Brigham Young's public address of August 16, 1857, Bagley writes:

> Their ten years' peace in the mountains was the longest rest the Saints had ever enjoyed. The government had now "come out, not openly and boldly, but underhandedly, and sneekingly, raskaly—in the form of a mob—again to pour their intolerant persecution upon this people and break them up, and ruin them—to destroy and kill them." He held the United States responsible for the deaths of thousands of Saints. Joseph and Hyrum Smith had been murdered while under the protection of the state of Illinois, and the blood of the prophets continued to flow, for "they [had] killed Parley lately." The prophet vowed to lift his sword and slay those who wished to destroy his people, a promise the congregation greeted with "a unanimous shout, 'Amen.'"[33]

Note what Young did not say here. He condemned the approaching army and the country that tolerated the death of the Saints, including Pratt, and vowed to resist those seeking to destroy his

[30] See, for instance, statements in E.B. Long, *The Saints and the Union: Utah Territory During the Civil War* (Urbana: University of Illinois Press, 1981), 13–33; and Eugene E. Campbell, *Establishing Zion: The Mormon Church in the American West, 1847–1869* (Salt Lake City: Signature Books, 1988), 289–92.

[31] Martha Eleanor Waldorf Kearney, *Song for the Times—The War Cry*, broadside, ca. 1862, LDS Church History Library.

[32] Bagley, *Blood of the Prophets*, 378.

[33] Ibid., 89.

people. But resisting military aggression is not the same as seeking vengeance. Young never mentioned vengeance or Arkansas.[34]

Bagley also points to reputed statements by Young after the massacre that purportedly tie Pratt's death to the killings. He writes: "Years later an anti-Mormon pamphlet charged that a few weeks after the massacre, Young spoke in the old tabernacle before thousands of people, some of whom were still living in Salt Lake in 1884. These witnesses claimed Young said, 'The blood of these emigrants and of the whole of the people of Arkansas would not atone for the blood of Apostle P. P. Pratt.' Allegedly, the prophet repeated the statement the next spring in the Seventies Hall."[35]

Bagley cites only one source to support this claim, a pamphlet published in 1884 under the pseudonym of Vindex.[36] In another publication, he speculates that Vindex may well have been Robert N. Baskin, an attorney who helped prosecute John D. Lee, the only man convicted of a role in the massacre.[37] Baskin was not in Utah when Young purportedly gave the speech mentioned in the pamphlet.[38] If Baskin was indeed Vindex, one wonders why he never mentioned Pratt's death in his efforts to indict Church leaders during Lee's first trial.[39] Bagley acknowledges that "Vindex's assault . . . was not

---

[34] See Brigham Young, Discourse, August 16, 1857, reported by George D. Watt, in Historian's Office, Reports of Speeches, ca. 1845–85, LDS Church History Library.

[35] Bagley, *Blood of the Prophets*, 184.

[36] Ibid., 418n60, 457.

[37] Will Bagley, *Avenging Mountain Meadows, A Keepsake for the Limited Edition of Blood of the Prophets: Brigham Young and the Massacre at Mountain Meadows* (Salt Lake City: Benchmark Books/Prairie Dog Press, 2002), preface.

[38] See "Noted Jurist and Public Leader Succumbs to Age's Infirmities," *Salt Lake Tribune*, 27 August 1918; and S. A. Kenner, *Utah as It Is* (Salt Lake City: Deseret News, 1904), 409.

[39] The transcripts of Lee's two trials lack a single reference to Pratt's death. See *United States v. John D. Lee*, First and Second Trial, Adam Patterson Shorthand Notes and Jacob S. Boreman Transcript, Jacob S. Boreman Collection, Huntington Library, San Marino, California; and *United States v. John D. Lee*, First and Second Trial, Josiah Rogerson Shorthand Notes and Transcripts, Josiah Rogerson, Transcripts and Notes of John D. Lee Trials, 1875–85, LDS Church History Library. The book *Mormonism Unveiled*, which includes Lee's depiction of the massacre and his involvement in it, likewise contains no references to Pratt's death. Lee prepared the book with the assistance of his attorney, William W. Bishop. In their efforts to shift responsibility for the massacre to others, Lee and Bishop likely would have mentioned Pratt's death if Church leaders had sought to avenge it. See William W. Bishop, ed., *Mormonism Unveiled; or the Life and Confessions of the Late Mormon Bishop, John D. Lee* (St. Louis: Bryan, Brand and Co., 1877).

particularly brilliant" and that "a few of Vindex's stories contradict current knowledge." Despite these problems, Bagley is inclined to believe "stories that appear to be unique to this obscure broadside," specifically the story about Young's remarks in the tabernacle.[40]

Because the only source of this information is unattributed hearsay published under a pseudonym by someone who, as Bagley acknowledges, got other facts wrong, it remains weak evidence—especially since the tabernacle speech was supposedly given before thousands of people but is nowhere else known to be recorded in public or private records. Even if Young made the statement as alleged, however, it was after the massacre and thus not a cause of the atrocity.

Similarly problematic is Bagley's reliance on purported evidence about a private meeting held on September 1, 1857, in Young's office. Bagley writes: "Frontiersman James Gemmell . . . claimed he was in Young's office when [Jacob] Hamblin arrived and reported that the Arkansas train was near Cedar City. If he were in command of the Nauvoo Legion, Governor Young said, he 'would wipe them out.'"[41] Later in the book, Bagley reemphasizes Gemmell's assertion: "He claimed he was 'in Brigham's office when Bishop Hamlin came in and reported the Arkansas train near Cedar City' on September 1 and 'heard Brigham tell Hamlin that if he (Brigham) were in command of the Legion he would wipe them out.' Gemmell told [Joseph C.] Walker he was with Young 'when a courier came to the office with the horrible news of the Mountain Meadow massacre.'"[42]

The Gemmell story "would be easy to dismiss as more fantastic lore," Bagley observes, if it weren't for a letter Gemmell wrote fifteen years after the massacre to "Young's nephew and business partner." In it, Gemmell said that investigators had questioned him about the meeting in Young's office "between Jacob Hamblin President Young and others, in regard to the Arkansas Train then passing through the southern settlements . . . and of their boasting, of Parley been killed in their neighborhood before they left. . . . And if I knew what was the purpose of the Instructions sent South, and if I thought the massacre was in retaliation for the

[40] Bagley, *Avenging Mountain Meadows*, preface.

[41] Bagley, *Blood of the Prophets*, 114.

[42] Ibid., 285.

killing of Parley."[43] To buttress this statement, Bagley writes that "Gemmell's headstone reported he 'fled for his life with one wife' to Montana and was 'Excommunicated by Brigham Young because of what he found out about Mountain Meadow Massacre.' "[44]

This evidence merits further consideration, beginning with Bagley's statement that Gemmell was in Young's office for the important September 1 meeting. Dimick Huntington's 1857 journal, which recorded the meeting and is the main source for what happened in it, does not mention Gemmell being present.[45] In addition, Gemmell's letter does not mention the date September 1. A careful analysis suggests that the meeting Gemmell attended was in fact a September 10 meeting in Young's office, a meeting in which Jacob Hamblin was present when messenger James Haslam came from Cedar City with a letter about the Arkansas company. Even if Young did make the inflammatory statement that Gemmell claimed, it did not cause the massacre, which culminated two days before the messenger arrived back in Cedar City.[46]

In fact, the 1872 Gemmell letter seems little more than an extortion attempt by an adventurer. Young appears to have simply ignored it. Gemmell's claim that members of the train boasted about the killing of Pratt in their neighborhood before they left has little credibility because they left home before Parley was killed.[47]

[43] Ibid., 284–85; and James Gemmell to Feramorz Little, 14 October 1872, Incoming Correspondence, Young Office Files. Bagley's version of Gemmell's letter silently edits the original, which reads, "And if I knew what was the purpose of the Instructions that was sent South, and if I thought the massacree was in retaliation of the killing of Parley." In his letter, Gemmell does not say what he knows about the massacre; he mentions only that people keep asking him about it.

[44] Bagley, *Blood of the Prophets*, 286.

[45] Dimick Baker Huntington, Journal, 1 September 1857, LDS Church History Library.

[46] Gemmell to Little, 14 October 1872; William F. Wheeler, "The Late James Gemmell," *Contributions to the Historical Society of Montana* (Boston: J. S. Canner, 1966), 2:334; and "Died," *Dillon* (Montana) *Tribune*, 9 April 1881. On the September 10 meeting and the messenger, see Walker, Turley, and Leonard, *Massacre at Mountain Meadows*, 182–86, 225, 226.

[47] Mary Baker's October 22, 1860, deposition stated that her husband, Jack Baker, "left the county of Carroll and state of Arkansas in the month of April A.D. 1857." Her son John H. Baker said the same thing in his October 22, 1860, deposition (Papers Pertaining to the Territory of Utah, 1849–70, 36th Cong., Records of the Senate, RG 46, National Archives and Records Administration, Washington, D.C.).

Finally, the headstone Bagley cites as evidence that Young excommunicated Gemmell "because of what he found out about Mountain Meadow Massacre" turns out not to have been installed until 1981. The headstone plaque refers readers to the Montana State Historical Society for details. But after the publication of Bagley's book, two of my research colleagues visited the historical society on separate occasions and found no evidence there to support the headstone's assertions beyond what has already been examined.

Post Hoc, Propter Hoc

Absent credible evidence that Pratt's death led directly to the massacre, why have people asserted such a connection? The answer is found in a common historical fallacy. After Pratt's death but before the massacre, a California newspaper predicted that the Mormons would wreak vengeance on travelers who passed through Utah.[48] When news of the massacre first reached California, journalists jumped on this explanation as the motive for the horrific killings.[49] The story was repeated so often thereafter that many writers took it for granted. After all, the sequence of events seemed compelling. Utah citizen Parley P. Pratt died at the hands of angry men in northwest Arkansas in May, and the members of a company from northwest Arkansas died at the hands of angry Utahns in September.

This conclusion is a fine example of the *post hoc, ergo propter* hoc fallacy, a logical error "that accepts as a cause something that

[48] An editorial in the *Daily Alta California* stated, "Whether the hot blood which must now be seething and boiling in the veins of Brigham Young and his satellites, at Salt Lake, is to be cooled by the murder of Gentiles who pass through their territory, whether the 'destroying angels' of Mormondom, are to be brought into requisition to make reprisals upon travelers, or whether, as has been done before, 'Saints' disguised as Indians are to constitute themselves the supposed ministers of God's vengeance in this case, we are not informed, but have no doubt that such thoughts, such intentions as these, are prevalent among those saintly villains, adulterers and seducers, of Salt Lake" ("The Killing of Pratt—Letter from Mr. McLean," *Alta California*, 9 July 1857). See also Bagley, *Blood of the Prophets*, 72.

[49] See "Horrible Massacre of Emigrants!"; "News from the South"; "Massacre on the Plains"; and "Massacre of Immigrants by the Indians."

merely occurred earlier in time."[50] In his book *Historians' Fallacies*, David Hackett Fischer wrote:

> The *fallacy of post hoc, propter hoc* is the mistaken idea that if event *B* happened after event *A*, it happened because of event *A*. An example is provided by a female passenger on board the Italian liner *Andrea Doria*. On the fatal night of *Doria*'s collision with the Swedish ship *Gripsholm*, off Nantucket in 1956, the lady retired to her cabin and flicked a light switch. Suddenly there was a great crash, and grinding metal, and passengers and crew ran screaming through the passageways. The lady burst from her cabin and explained to the first person in sight that she must have set the ship's emergency brake![51]

Over the past several years, my colleagues and I have scoured the country for information about the Mountain Meadows Massacre and its causes. We have studied the context in which the massacre occurred and found intertwining themes that contributed to the motives of the dozens of white men who participated in the killings. We have found sources in which massacre participants described their own motives or their compatriots' in the killings, sometimes in self-incriminating ways. The perpetrators said virtually nothing about Parley P. Pratt. Even Bagley, in noting vengeance as a causal factor, does not cite any sources from southern Utah claiming that Pratt's death motivated their actions.

Juanita Brooks, author of the 1950 landmark book *The Mountain Meadows Massacre*, acknowledged that Mormons living in southern Utah at the time of the massacre knew what happened to Pratt and that such knowledge could "have had . . . influence upon the feelings of the people." But she saw Pratt's murder as only one of many factors that precipitated the massacre. She wrote, "Exaggeration, misrepresentation, ungrounded fears, unreasoning hate, desire for revenge, yes, even the lust for the property of the emigrants, all combined to give justification which, once the crime was done, looked inadequate and flimsy indeed."[52]

---

[50] *Random House Webster's Unabridged Dictionary*, 2nd ed., 1511, s.v., "post hoc, ergo propter hoc."

[51] David Hackett Fischer, *Historians' Fallacies: Toward a Logic of Historical Thought* (New York: Harper & Row, 1970), 166.

[52] Juanita Brooks, *The Mountain Meadows Massacre*, 2nd ed. (1962; repr. Norman: University of Oklahoma Press, 1991), 57–59.

Careful research confirms Brooks's analysis. The factors contributing to the massacre were numerous and complex. But Pratt's death did not cause the massacre. It was simply one thread in a complex tapestry of events that formed the backdrop for the murders. Modern interpreters would do well to abandon the timeworn theory that the Mountain Meadows Massacre was simply an act of vengeance for the 1857 vigilante killing of a Latter-day Saint apostle in Arkansas.

CHAPTER 11

Finding Parley

A Family's Quest to Fulfill Parley P. Pratt's Dying Wish

Robert J. Grow

As he lay dying near Fine Springs, Arkansas, in 1857, Apostle Parley P. Pratt requested that his dying testimony be conveyed to the Church of Jesus Christ of Latter-day Saints (LDS Church) and that his body be taken to Utah where he could be buried near his family. In the succeeding 150 years, his descendants, who now number in the tens of thousands, have attempted to locate and remove his remains from the Wynn Family Cemetery in Fine Springs to the space reserved for him in the family plot in Salt Lake City. With encouragement from Latter-day Saint Church leaders, the Pratt family made major efforts to find Pratt's grave site from the 1890s through the 1950s. Logistical problems, the destruction of the cemetery during the Civil War, conflicting eyewitness accounts of the manner and place of his burial, and continued animosity against Mormonism resulting from the Mountain Meadows Massacre hindered these efforts. Nevertheless, the LDS Church and the family erected a monument in the Wynn Family Cemetery in the 1950s, approximately one hundred years after Pratt was killed. Between 2005 and 2008, his descendants (including myself) used all available historical records and recently developed technology, including ground-penetrating radar and electro-magnetic survey, to locate the probable location of his grave. In April 2008, an archaeological dig at the site of this probable grave provided further evidence that it was indeed Pratt's grave but yielded no identifiable human remains, suggesting that the acidic Arkansas clay had completely disintegrated his remains. The quest of his descendants to locate Pratt's grave over 150 years suggests the powerful meaning of his memory to his descendants and the broader Mormon community.

Death and Burial

The news of Pratt's death was a personal tragedy of monumental proportion to his family. On June 23, 1857, the day the news of Pratt's murder arrived in Salt Lake City, Apostle Wilford Woodruff recorded, "This was painful news to his Family." That day, Woodruff, along with Apostles Orson Hyde, George A. Smith, and Amasa Lyman, went to "visit the family & to comfort them on the Death of their Husband & Father. They were calm & composed."[1] Pratt's death left nine widows and twenty-three children without a father. Pratt had been preceded in death by his first wife, Thankful Halsey, and seven children.[2] At the time of his death, his oldest child, Parley, Jr., was twenty years old; his next oldest, Olivia, was fifteen; and his twenty-one other surviving children were ages twelve and under.[3]

The economic status of Pratt's family in 1857 was precarious at best, in large part because Pratt had devoted his life to Church service. His family, with few exceptions, remained poor for many years to come. When Eleanor McComb Pratt, Pratt's final wife, died in 1874, she was buried in the pauper's section of the Salt Lake City

[1] Scott G. Kenney, ed., *Wilford Woodruff's Journal, 1833–1898* (Midvale, Utah: Signature Books, 1983–1984), 5:62, entry for 23 June 1857.

[2] Pratt married a total of twelve wives during his life. Two wives—Mary Ann Frost and Martha Monks—had divorced or left him. See Steven Pratt's essay in this volume (chapter 2).

[3] Genealogical records kept by the Jared Pratt Family Association.

Cemetery; when Keziah Downes Pratt, another wife, died a few years after her, she was buried in what was likely a borrowed grave. Pratt's wives who did not remarry eventually purchased a family plot in the Salt Lake City Cemetery.[4] Even today, these wives have no individual headstones (only small footstones), suggesting the ongoing poverty of the family for decades after Pratt's death.[5] Notwithstanding the wives' poverty, they reserved a place in the family plot between them for Pratt to occupy when his dying wish was fulfilled.

In his final hour, Pratt's thoughts naturally turned to his family. Eyewitnesses to his statements before his death indicate that he made three requests: that his valuables be sent to his family in Salt Lake City; that his dying testimony be conveyed to his family and the Latter-day Saints; and that his body be taken to Utah. According to Eleanor McComb Pratt, who arrived on the scene of his murder within hours, Parley told the group of people who had gathered following Hector McLean's attack: "I have a family at Salt Lake City, Utah Territory and that is my home. My gold is in this pocket (pointing to his pants) and my gold watch is in this, and I want them with all my effects sent to my family in Salt Lake." His valuables, however, were not sent to his family but became the property of the state to pay the costs of the inquest after his death.[6] Eleanor feared that Parley's grave and body would be desecrated by local citizens, and soon after his death she wrote Apostle Erastus Snow, then the presiding authority of the Church in St. Louis, and asked that arrangements be made to remove Parley's body to the west. She inquired, "Can you send for the body of Brother Parley. What shall I do?"[7]

Eleanor's request indicates that her wish, and perhaps Parley's, was that his body be taken to Utah. A much more detailed account

---

[4] Cemetery records, Salt Lake City Cemetery.

[5] The Jared Pratt Family Association is currently planning to place new headstones on the graves of these women.

[6] Eleanor McComb Pratt, "Account of the Murder of Parley P. Pratt," ca. 1857–1860, 29–30, Church History Library, the Church of Jesus Christ of Latter-day Saints, Salt Lake City, Utah (hereafter LDS Church History Library).

[7] Eleanor McLean to Erastus Snow, 14 May 1857, Erastus Snow Papers, LDS Church History Library.

of Pratt's desire came from the recollection of John A. Peel, who had lived in western Arkansas and was among the large company that followed McLean and the other two primary assailants out of Van Buren, Arkansas, when it was learned that Pratt had been acquitted and released by Judge John B. Ogden. In 1896, Peel, then living in New Orleans, met a Mormon missionary, Elder Frank T. Pomeroy, who had arranged to rent a large conference hall from Peel. In the presence of "several gentlemen," Peel informed Pomeroy and his missionary companion "that he was present at the death of Parley P. Pratt and heard his dying statement." Peel then related, in substantial detail, the controversy between McLean and Pratt; although he clearly sympathized with McLean and told the account from his viewpoint, the relative accuracy of Peel's account suggests its credibility.[8]

Peel stated that after McLean had stabbed and shot Pratt, he and a group of other men arrived on the scene and "found Pratt sitting against a tree, he having crawled some distance from the road." Pratt told the men "he was going to die and desired us to communicate with the Mormon [wagon] train and have some of them return and take his body to Utah, and he desired us to send his dying statement to Brigham Young and the Church." Peel continued quoting Pratt: " 'I die,' said he, 'a firm believer in the Gospel of Jesus Christ as revealed through the Prophet Joseph Smith, and I wish you to carry this my dying testimony. I know that the Gospel is true and that Joseph Smith was a prophet of the Living God' and then added, 'I am dying a martyr to the faith.' His voice grew weaker and weaker and finally he breathed no more." Pomeroy transmitted Peel's account to Church authorities after the conclusion of his mission in 1898, which likely helped motivate efforts to recover Pratt's body in the early twentieth century.[9]

---

[8] Statement of Frank T. Pomeroy, 11 April 1898, "Journal History of the Church of Jesus Christ of Latter-day Saints," 11 April 1898, 4–6.

[9] Ibid. Although Peel included many accurate details, he erroneously believed that Pratt's final request had been fulfilled. He stated, "Mrs. McLean hired an ambulance and went out and brought his dead body into Van Buren. It was taken to the Mormon train and conveyed to Utah, Mrs. McLean and children accompanying it."

Historical records contain two starkly different accounts of Pratt's burial. According to Eleanor Pratt and reminiscences by local eyewitnesses, blacksmith Zealey Wynn witnessed the murder and gathered some neighbors. Though surprised to find Pratt alive, they cared for him in his final minutes. To this group, Pratt identified his assailant and made his final requests. According to Wynn's wife, Pratt had not "groaned or appeared to suffer much," but he "lay still and complained of nothing but thirst and his last breath was like a man going to sleep."[10] Eleanor and Elder George Higginson, a missionary who had been arrested along with Pratt, soon arrived; by this time, Pratt's body had been "cleanly washed and nicely shaved" and a "handsome shirt and material for a shroud" had been gathered. Assisted by the local marshal, Eleanor and Higginson prepared Pratt's body for burial in the manner of his faith. William Steward, a local resident who had known Pratt as a young man in New York, gave his own coffin for Pratt's burial. Because Eleanor depended on the marshal to escort her back to town, she left later that evening, before Pratt's burial, but "felt assured that all things would be as well done as the people could do it."[11] Accounts by local eyewitnesses indicate that Pratt was buried in the Wynn Family Cemetery after a short public service the day after his death.

George Higginson, Pratt's twenty-five-year-old missionary companion, gave a starkly different account of the burial many years later. Higginson had been chained to Pratt in Indian Territory (now Oklahoma) and forced to march to Van Buren even though he was accused of no crime. After Pratt was murdered, he accompanied Eleanor from Van Buren to the Wynn blacksmith shop where he helped prepare Pratt's body for burial. He wrote: "After his martyrdom I rode through the homes of the mobocrats and obtained possession of his corpse and buried it with a mob all around me at 10 o'clock of the night of the 14 of May, AD 1857, without the presence of a brother or sister. In this matter I presume I ran as much, if not more, risk than did B. H. Roberts [in] the

---

[10] Eleanor Pratt, "Account."

[11] Ibid.

matter of the Tennessee martyrs, but I never received a kind word or any recognition for my service in that direction and it has been remarked 'Died Parley as a fool dieth.'"[12]

The accounts suggest the possibility that both burials occurred: a public burial during the day and then a private reburial by Higginson to protect Pratt's remains (as the bodies of Joseph and Hyrum Smith had been secretly reburied after their murders in 1844). Higginson may have even intended to come back at some point and retrieve Pratt's body, as B. H. Roberts later did with the "Tennessee martyrs," when Roberts, an LDS Church leader, disguised himself to recover the bodies of two missionaries killed by a mob in Cane Creek, Tennessee, in 1884.

Despite the desires of Pratt, Eleanor, and Higginson, no attempt to remove Pratt's remains occurred. Transporting a body across the plains under any circumstances in the nineteenth century would have been a difficult undertaking. As such, Mormon pioneers invariably buried those who died while crossing the plains at the site of their death. In addition, the oncoming Utah War would have made any attempt to retrieve Pratt's remains from Arkansas impossible. The massacre of Arkansas emigrants in Utah in September 1857 at Mountain Meadows heightened the already substantial opposition to Mormonism in Arkansas for decades (and, to some extent, to the present). This opposition, combined with the poverty of the Pratt family and the geographical distance between Arkansas and Utah, impeded any desires of Pratt's wives and children to attempt to remove his body to Utah during the nineteenth century. The small Wynn Family Cemetery was used as a campground during the Civil War, causing substantial destruction and obscuring the location of Pratt's grave.

Early Attempts at Identifying Pratt's Grave

One Arkansas record published in 1928 does suggest some nineteenth-century searches for Pratt's grave: "For several years an

[12] George B. Higginson to Andrew Kimball, 1892, LDS Church History Library.

occasional Mormon evangelist would visit the grave of Pratt, but it was never marked by stone. Then came the Civil war and the frequent pilgrimages to the grave ceased. . . . As late as 1894," however, a "middle aged" Pratt descendant visited the local sheriff, Captain John Steward (the son of William Steward who as a sixteen-year-old boy had driven Parley's coffin to the cemetery) and offered $500 for the location of the grave. Steward, however, considered it an "impossible" task to locate precisely Pratt's grave and "he declined to consider the offer."[13]

A decade later, Pratt descendants made a more sustained effort to locate his grave when Samuel Russell, a grandson of Pratt, wrote to John Neal, ex-mayor of Van Buren, concerning the location of the grave. Russell gave Neal's response to his letter to the First Presidency of the LDS Church, who encouraged Russell in his efforts to locate Pratt's grave and move his body to Salt Lake City. The First Presidency, under the leadership of Church president Joseph F. Smith, suggested that Russell contact James G. Duffin, president of the Church's Southwestern States Mission, and ask him to "get one of the Elders laboring in the vicinity of Van Buren, Arkansas, to endeavor to find the grave of your grandfather, the later Elder Parley P. Pratt, with a view to bringing his remains to this city for interment. We commend your endeavors to accomplish this purpose and certainly hope they will meet with the success they merit."[14]

After he received Russell's request, President Duffin personally traveled to Van Buren in an attempt to locate Pratt's grave. While in Van Buren, Duffin spoke with three local residents who had relevant information. First, he met with James Orme, the local justice of the peace, who had conducted an inquest after Pratt's death and oversaw the preparations for his burial. Orme described Pratt's burial and confirmed the general location of his grave. Another resident, John Neal, who had firsthand knowledge of the events,

---

[13] Frank Anderson, "Memoirs of Meadow Massacre Recalled by Death of Berryville Woman," 1928.

[14] Joseph F. Smith and First Presidency to Elder Samuel Russell, 19 May 1902, LDS Church History Library.

concurred with Orme's account, though he added that the coroner's inquest under Orme's direction had also issued an indictment for murder against McLean. Finally, Duffin interviewed John Steward, still a resident of Van Buren and "very friendly disposed toward [the Saints]." Duffin asked all three about the "probability of locating the grave of Apostle Pratt." Orme "was very emphatic that it could not be definitely located," but both Neal and Steward (apparently giving a different response than he had earlier) told him otherwise: "There were two brothers by the name of Fine, living near the old grave yard who say that they can identify the grave, but I have not had time to visit them to find out definitely as to this," Duffin recounted.[15]

Samuel Russell apparently did not make any further attempts to locate Pratt's grave in 1902, though he renewed his quest a decade letter. In 1912, Russell again contacted Neal and asked for his assistance. He wrote, "Mr. Pratt was my grandfather and whatever the opinions of people may be concerning him, he was in many respects a great man and it is to be deplored that his last resting place has been so long unknown and neglected."[16] Russell subsequently traveled to Van Buren and interviewed several individuals who claimed to have knowledge of Pratt's death or burial. Two of the interviewees, Mary Frasier and John Steward, were teenagers when Pratt died and were participants in the events surrounding the burial. A number of other interviewees may or may not have had first-hand knowledge of the actual burial, but several had lived in the area of the graveyard (known alternately as Sherman's Graveyard, the Fine Springs Cemetery, or the Wynn Family Cemetery) for many decades. The graveyard itself had been sparsely used. These interviews and other historical accounts suggest that the cemetery contained only one other pre–Civil War grave besides Pratt's, and only a limited number of graves since that time.

---

[15] James Duffin to Anthon H. Lund, Church Historian, 16 December 1902, LDS Church History Library; and James G. Duffin, Journal, 3 September 1902, LDS Church History Library.

[16] Samuel Russell to John Neal, Van Buren, 7 July 1912, R. Steven Pratt Files, LDS Church History Library.

With respect to Pratt's burial, John Steward, then age seventy-two, recounted driving the "pine box" and "walnut coffin" (which was apparently placed within the pine box) his father had made for Pratt. He also provided several details about Pratt's grave site, stating that it was "across the field 100 yards northwest of the Baptist Church," a "little south of large red oak tree," "within 20 or 30 feet from thicket," about "40 or 50 yards west of Fayetteville road," and "in a grave by himself." This final detail suggested that Pratt's grave was somewhat removed from the other graves in the cemetery. (It is not surprising that Zealey Wynn, though he allowed Pratt to be buried in his family cemetery, would have wanted the controversial Mormon apostle buried at a distance from his family graves.) Mary Frasier, also then seventy-two, stated that she had gone "down to help cook as great crowds had assembled at Mr. Wynn's" following Pratt's death. According to her, he was buried in a public ceremony the "next evening about 3 o'clock." Her memory of the location of the grave also included several details, many that agreed with those provided by Steward, including that Pratt was "buried at the edge of a road 4 or 5 feet from road," "near a large red oak near foot of grave," and "in a place by himself, northeast from the thick part of the graveyard." Russell also interviewed John, Carol, and Hamilton Fine, who lived near the cemetery, though they apparently did not identify what they believed to be the exact site of the grave (as the 1902 Duffin account indicated they might).[17]

The next effort to locate Pratt's grave occurred a quarter century later in 1936–37 and involved Church members in the region, some local residents in the Van Buren/Fine Springs area, and the Pratt family. Several Church members in eastern Oklahoma—led by John W. Whipple, an attorney who had converted to the Church, served as branch president, and admired Pratt—traveled to Arkansas to locate Pratt's grave. Discovering anti-Mormon prejudice in the area, they disguised their identity as Church members. In this process, they met Hugh Park, the publisher of a local newspaper, the *Press Argus*, and his wife Ruie Ann. The Parks took the Church

[17] Statements concerning the burial place of Parley P. Pratt, 1912.

members to meet Carol Fine, then a very old and frail man who had lived in the area of Pratt's grave all his life. Although an infant at the time of Pratt's death, Fine claimed to know the exact location and stated that he had walked close enough to Pratt's grave each day while growing up to spit on it. Suspicious of the visitors, Fine initially refused to specify the location, though he finally identified what he believed to be the location of the grave as he and the others turned over stones in the undergrowth. Whipple wrote to Harold W. Pratt, a grandson of Pratt serving as LDS mission president in Mexico, that Pratt's body was "hidden in the secluded spot near Van Buren, Arkansas and in a locality where Mormon people," and Pratt "in particular," were "despised." Whipple added, "To make known to the public its location would mean that the grave would be destroyed."[18]

In 1937, Harold Pratt and his wife visited the grave site and took photographs to preserve the assumed location of Pratt's grave identified by Fine. Significantly, the location identified by Fine does not agree with the earlier details provided by John Steward, Mary Frasier, and others, and it lies more than one hundred feet northwest of the grave now believed to be Pratt's. No evidence indicates that those searching for Pratt's grave in 1936–37 were aware of the earlier interviews and investigations. According to Harold Pratt, the owner of the cemetery, Joseph Couch, who was a nephew of blacksmith Zealey Wynn, "manifested no ill feelings" toward his grandfather, "nor toward the Mormons." Couch had "only recently purchased the property" and told Harold "that he had desired to clean up and preserve the old cemetery, and would consider allowing the descendants of Parley P. Pratt to help him do this." Indeed, Couch was also willing to sell the cemetery to the Pratt family. Harold wrote two granddaughters of Parley Pratt who were quite active in the Pratt family organization, Una Viola Pratt Giles and Anna Amelia Pratt Romney, and suggested they lead an effort to raise funds to purchase the cemetery and "make

[18] John W. Whipple to Harold W. Pratt, 1 April 1937; Elias S. Woodruff to President Heber J. Grant and Counselors, 26 February 1937, LDS Church History Library; and Woodruff to Harold Pratt, 26 February 1937, LDS Church History Library.

Harold Pratt and his wife visit Parley P. Pratt's grave site in 1937. *Courtesy of the Church History Library, the Church of Jesus Christ of Latter-day Saints.*

some arrangements with Mr. Couch for its care," adding, "We will have it then, for the time when we feel it right to erect the monument." Harold thought that the alleged anti-Mormonism of the region had been overstated: "I believe from impressions gathered while in the vicinity that the Anti-mormon feeling is not as bitter as had been reported, and that it be overcome quite easily."[19] Notwithstanding Harold's recommendation, it appears the Pratt family took no immediate action to purchase the property.

In the late 1940s or early 1950s, Hugh and Ruie Ann Park attended a national newspaper convention in Salt Lake City. According to the Parks' daughter, at this convention Hugh suggested to some of the Mormon attendees that the "grave of Parley Parker Pratt should be marked. This stirred up considerable

[19] Harold W. Pratt to Una Pratt Giles and Anna Pratt Romney, 26 May 1937, R. Steven Pratt Files, LDS Church History Library.

Pratt monument as it appears today near the Rudy exit off I-540 in Arkansas. *Courtesy of Hyrum Bradshaw.*

interest and some of the officials of the Mormon Church contacted Mr. Park in regard to this. Ruie Ann Park located some elderly people in Crawford County who remembered where the grave was located."[20] These recollections, combined with the 1937 photographs, established the location then believed to be Pratt's grave. The Parks' interest thus helped motivate the Pratt family, with approval from the First Presidency, to move forward with

[20] Susan Stevenson Swinburn and Doris Stevenson West, compilers, *History in Headstones: A Complete Listing of all Marked Graves in Known Cemeteries of Crawford County, Arkansas* (Van Buren, Ark.: Press Argus, 1970).

identifying and preserving Pratt's grave site.[21] John Giles, the husband of Una Pratt Giles, had earlier assisted the LDS Church in locating and preserving other historic sites. On behalf of the family, he led this effort as well and hired the Putnam Funeral Home in Van Buren to oversee the onsite construction of a monument and the landscaping of the site. The monument was purchased by Giles and paid for by donations from the Pratt family and was subsequently donated to the LDS Church.[22]

The area originally purchased by Giles included only one actual headstone, which belonged to a Wynn family child. In addition, there may have been two other stones possibly identifying other graves located in the cemetery. In response, the area purchased by Giles was expanded to accommodate the location of those two possible graves so that they might be preserved as well. The family left a grassy area in front of the monument where they believed Pratt's grave was located. Although the family intended to dedicate the site (an LDS Church ritual intended to make sacred a place) when completed, Giles died and the dedication likely never occurred. From its construction in the 1950s until the present, the monument and surrounding area have been cared for by local LDS Church members in Arkansas. In 2003, LDS Church president Gordon B. Hinckley visited the site and directed the purchase of additional property to the south of the fenced monument area, including the area now believed to contain Pratt's grave.

Finding Pratt's Grave, 2005–2008

When I became president of the Jared Pratt Family Association in the 1980s, I was often accosted at reunions by very old members of the family asking, sometimes forcefully, if we should not fulfill Pratt's dying wish and move his remains to Salt Lake City.

[21] David O. McKay, Stephen Richards, and J. Reuben Clark to John Giles, 25 April 1951, R. Steven Pratt Files, LDS Church History Library.

[22] On the transfer of the property to the LDS Church, see Carl B. Pratt (acting as a lawyer for the Church) to Dorothy Giles Topham (a daughter of John and Una Giles), 25 April 1975, R. Steven Pratt Files, LDS Church History Library.

For years I resisted these efforts, telling them that I thought it was highly unlikely we could locate the exact grave or that we could find "enough of Parley to move." For nearly two decades I hoped that this issue would go away, to no avail, and I continued my resistance until late in 2005 when cousins Ernest Robison and Paul DeBry swept me up in their energetic effort to reevaluate the possibility.

In May 2005, DeBry, a great-great-grandson of Pratt, traveled to Pratt's grave site. His grandfather, Parker Pratt Robison, had been committed to Pratt's memory, republished some of his books, and told his grandchildren frequent stories about their ancestor. DeBry recounts that as he visited Pratt's grave site, he "relaxed and thought, 'at last, here I am. I think I will just sit back and enjoy the spirit of this sacred site.' To my amazement, I felt nothing! I knew that I felt nothing. I did not feel anything bad, I just did not feel anything. This concerned me greatly. All my life I had learned about and loved Parley. Now I was at one of the most sacred sites in his existence, his grave, and I felt nothing." When he returned home to Utah, Debry researched the history of Pratt's grave site and discovered that the site had likely never been dedicated. This prompted him to contact his first cousin Ernest Robison, who began to research all of the historical evidence regarding Pratt's grave. Robison quickly enlarged the scope of the project from the initial question of the dedication of the monument to the larger issue of accurately identifying Pratt's actual grave and possibly removing his remains to Utah. Robison located all of the historical evidence about Pratt's grave site, including the accounts produced by the earlier family efforts to locate it.[23]

Trained as a scientist, Robison sought to use scientific evidence to corroborate the historical accounts he had gathered about the location of Pratt's grave. Using all of the geographic clues in the historical evidences—including references to old roads and paths, distances from long-gone historical buildings, and allusions to other gravestones and large trees—Robison painstakingly

[23] Paul Debry, written account in my possession.

LDS Church president Gordon B. Hinckley at the Pratt monument near Rudy, Arkansas, March 2003. *Courtesy of Hyrum Bradshaw.*

correlated the historical data to suggest geographic parameters for the grave site. He then proposed using ground-penetrating radar and electromagnetic survey to find the actual grave within the parameters established by the historical evidence. Ground-penetrating radar can show soil disturbances in the shape of graves and is becoming a prominent tool in surveying old graveyards. Electromagnetic survey is a highly sophisticated form of metal detection. The correlation of these two methods would provide the best evidence possible of where graves were located.

The family association hired Hager Scientific, a leading Boston geosciences firm, to perform the ground-penetrating radar and electromagnetic survey. In the fall of 2006, Hager technicians, with the assistance of Robison, conducted both ground-penetrating radar and electromagnetic studies of the entire property owned by the Church as well as some adjacent properties. The two studies confirm the existence of three or four probable graves within the entire area and several other possible but unlikely graves. One grave, which is separated from the other graves by a considerable distance, is prominently located within the area identified by the historical records. The ground-penetrating radar and electromagnetic survey also suggested locations for former roads, paths, and large trees that are referred to in the historical accounts as landmarks. Based upon the historical records and the scientific studies, Hager, Robison, and others involved determined that this single grave is most likely Pratt's.[24]

Somewhat surprisingly, this grave is extremely shallow, only eighteen inches to two and a half feet deep, and does not lie in an east-west line typical in formal burial sites. In addition, the electromagnetic study shows that a circle of dirt about ten feet in diameter and six to twelve inches deep had at one time been completely disturbed around this grave, suggesting the scraping of dirt to cover it over. Relatively near this grave is another possible grave location identified by the electromagnetic technique; however, this location lacks the "classic ground-penetrating radar grave signature" that one would expect if it were an actual burial site with a body. The grave site believed to be Pratt's lay at the end of a path from this possible grave site. These findings provide some evidence that George Higginson may have reburied Parley Pratt following his public burial in order to protect his remains. The shallowness of Pratt's grave—and the scraping of dirt around it—additionally suggest such an action.

---

[24] Hager GeoScience, Inc., "Geophysical Investigation: Parley P. Pratt Grave Site, Alma, Arkansas," October 2006, report in my possession; and Ernest Parker Robison, "Ground Penetrating Radar and Electromagnetic Survey Report Concerning the Historic Wynn Graveyard and the Burial Site of Parley Parker Pratt," 10 March 2007, report of 111 pages in my possession.

Significantly, the grave believed to be Pratt's lay outside of the fenced area containing the monument to him and was only six inches from the southern boundary of the property line owned by the LDS Church after President Hinckley's directed purchase of additional land to the south in 2003. In April 2007, a historical conference was held in Fort Smith, Arkansas, which drew prominent scholars and several hundred attendees to discuss the life, times, and legacy of Parley P. Pratt. At that time, a group of family members and scholars visited what was believed to be Pratt's actual grave. It was apparent that light industrial development was likely proceeding on the adjoining property. The quiet countryside where Pratt was originally buried now lay a quarter-mile from a new freeway interchange where a large truck stop was under construction. Both family members and sympathetic scholars discussed the propriety of attempting to open Pratt's grave and move his remains to protect them from the encroaching industrialization and urbanization of the area.

In July 2007, the family organization held a major reunion of the Pratt family in Salt Lake City to commemorate the two hundredth anniversary of Pratt's birth and the 150th anniversary of his death. Besides the general family reunion, a special meeting for the descendants of Pratt was held to discuss and determine a course of action with respect to his grave. Approximately two hundred of Pratt's descendants from all over the western United States attended this meeting, including fourteen of his twenty-two or twenty-three surviving great-grandchildren. After fully considering the choices, attending family members voted unanimously to excavate the grave and attempt to move Pratt's remains to Salt Lake City. Arkansas law requires that a court order be obtained from an individual's next of kin in order to excavate and/or relocate a grave, if no death certificate was issued. Since Pratt died before the state of Arkansas issued death certificates, the family would need to obtain permission from an Arkansas court. Accordingly, the family organization began collecting affidavits that could be presented as representing the desires of Pratt's next of kin. Numerous family members volunteered contributions to cover the considerable costs associated with this effort.

As president of the family organization, I engaged the services of a highly respected law firm in Fort Smith, Arkansas to advise and represent the family. Because Pratt's probable grave is located on property owned by the LDS Church, I also contacted Elder Marlin K. Jensen, Church historian, and informed him of our plans. At his request, I provided copies of the scientific and historical studies for review within his department. In January 2008, I filed a legal motion in the Crawford County Court to allow the family to proceed, though the judge did not schedule the motion for hearing until early April. Because Mitt Romney, a descendant of Pratt, was then running for president, the family made no effort to expedite the hearing, reasoning that Romney's campaign (being waged, in part, against former Arkansas governor Mike Huckabee) and our own efforts might provoke unwanted media attention. Under Arkansas law, the next of kin, not the property owner, has the legal right to petition to excavate a grave. However, we knew that a judge would likely ask if the property owner had an objection to the excavation. As such, I asked the LDS Church to confirm that they had no objections to our proceeding, and they did so in late March.

On April 2, 2008, Judge Gary Cottrell heard the motion, which included over 130 signed affidavits of descendants, including seventeen of Pratt's surviving great-grandchildren, all that could be located. I asked Judge Cottrell to allow us to excavate Pratt's grave as a way of closing this chapter of our family's history. Although he expressed concern about disturbing any other graves, he ruled in favor of our motion. Cottrell acknowledged our "exemplary effort" in attempting to locate Pratt's grave and protect other possible grave sites from disturbance. He gave three reasons for his decision to allow us to excavate Pratt's grave: first, the grave was very shallow, had been "washed" by storms and surface water, and would likely be further destroyed over time; second, the proximity of the grave within a few inches of the property boundary further endangered the grave site; and third, the action represented the desire of the next of kin. After his ruling, the judge made an unusual personal statement. Although he had no involvement with the LDS Church, as a college student he had written a paper on what happened to Pratt in Van Buren. He stated that it had not been the region's "most heroic hour" and expressed his hope that maybe this would allow the local community to likewise close that chapter in their history.

Although we were relieved by the judge's decision, the nature of our effort changed dramatically at this hearing. Sitting as observers in the juror's box were reporters from the two local newspapers who had seen the notice of this hearing in the court's agenda. In addition, Elder Jensen and assistant church historian Richard Turley had been in Arkansas less than a week earlier to meet with descendants of the families involved in the Mountain Meadows Massacre and had informed reporters of our efforts to move Pratt's remains to Utah. The day before the hearing, I was contacted by a reporter for the largest Arkansas newspaper, the *Arkansas Democrat-Gazette*, who was also present at the hearing. I was very surprised at the extensive press coverage for the next three weeks. Our efforts quickly became front-page news in Arkansas (as well as lead stories on their TV news), and the coverage rippled back to Salt Lake City and was picked up by the Associated Press. Unlike the coverage 150 years ago, most of the press attention was supportive of the family's efforts.[25]

Beginning in the fall of 2007, a Utah-based volunteer team formed to conduct the excavation. The team was led by two archaeologists with doctoral degrees (one a Pratt descendant), a soil scientist, a surveyor, a videographer, experienced archaeological excavators, a site security expert, and support staff. Throughout the spring of

---

[25] Newspaper accounts include "Arkansas Judge Says Remains of Parley P. Pratt Can Be Moved to Utah," Associated Press, 3 April 2008; Kenneth Fry, "Body of Missionary to Be Exhumed," *Van Buren Press Argus-Courier*, 7 April 2008; Robert J. Smith, "Exhumation Begins for Parley Pratt," *Arkansas Democrat-Gazette*, published in *Deseret News*, 22 April 2008; Robert J. Smith, "Dig at Mormon Burial Unrewarded," *Arkansas Democrat Gazette*, 23 April 2008; and Rusty Garrett, "Exhumation Comes Up Empty," *Times Record* (Fort Smith, Arkansas), 23 April 2008.

The excavated grave is searched for evidence of human remains, April 2008. *Courtesy of Robert J. Grow.*

2008, the dig team formulated a complete archaeological plan for the excavation of Pratt's grave and was only awaiting the receipt of the court order. Just sixteen days following Cottrell's decision, the team arrived in Arkansas on Friday, April 18, and was joined by about fifteen descendants of Pratt. On Saturday, the site was resurveyed to correlate the dig site with the ground-penetrating radar and electromagnetic survey reports; the sod over the five-by-five-meter excavation site was also removed. Due to the risk of inclement weather, the entire excavation site was then covered by a large rented canopy. On Sunday, the entire group attended the Alma Ward of the LDS Church, where I thanked three generations of local Church members for caring for Pratt's grave site.

The excavation commenced in earnest on Monday morning and continued through Wednesday, April 23, when the grave was reclosed. The archaeological dig attracted a significant amount of media attention in Arkansas, with reporters and television crews visiting the site daily. In addition, a steady stream of local Mormons and other curious residents visited the dig site. These visitors included descendants of several individuals who had assisted Parley and Eleanor Pratt, including Judge John B. Ogden, William and John Steward, and Zealey Wynn. Digging in the hard, red Arkansas clay proved much more difficult than anticipated, particularly because the soil was heavily saturated with water from one of the wettest springs in recent history. The primary target area identified by the ground-penetrating radar as the likely grave was approximately six feet in length, oblong, and bowl shaped. While a larger area was excavated to six inches to create a formal dig site, this area was excavated to a depth of nearly three feet before we reached bedrock. It was readily apparent to the archaeologists, soil scientists, and diggers that the area identified by the ground-penetrating radar was filled with much softer, less compacted material, and much easier to dig than the surrounding clay, all indications that the area had been dug before. The material within this area also exhibited characteristics of being "mixed," an obvious sign to the scientists that it had been dug previously and was a grave. The careful excavation of the grave, including the meticulous sifting of soil from the likely grave site, yielded no discernable human remains. A local coroner and a representative of a local mortuary that had been involved in periodically moving historic graves confirmed that to their knowledge no grave older than ninety years had ever revealed identifiable human remains. Although we had hoped that the hard, red Arkansas clay would have protected Pratt's shallow grave, it was now clear that the acidic and water-saturated soil over the prior 150 years had completely disintegrated and absorbed Pratt's remains, a possibility we had recognized since the beginning of the process.

Understanding Pratt's Death

Thus, this most recent (and hopefully final) effort to identify Pratt's grave led to the very likely location of his grave but no discernable human remains. Perhaps more significantly, our quest led to an improved understanding of the circumstances of his relationship with Eleanor McComb and his death and burial in Arkansas. Misunderstandings of the circumstances of Pratt's death has sullied his reputation both inside and outside of the LDS Church community. Following his death, national newspapers celebrated what they viewed as the justified murder of a lustful polygamist. Latter-day Saints in general saw Pratt as a martyr. Nevertheless, within months of Pratt's death, Apostle George A. Smith stated that Pratt's disregard of his warnings had led to his unnecessary death, suggesting that Pratt had gone on what lawyers term a frolic, an unjustified diversion from his main mission.[26] In 1892, George Higginson stated, "It has been remarked 'Died Parley as a fool dieth.'"[27]

This suspicion about Pratt's action has remained to the present. My mother-in-law told me that Pratt had died because he was chasing another man's wife. More crassly, if in 2007 one performed a Google search on "Parley Pratt death," the second reference contained the following comment: "Anyone here know the REAL reason this son-of-a bitch was killed. . . . The assailant was none other than the HUSBAND of a woman that Parley Prick seduced into being his NINTH polygamous wife. IMO [in my opinion], Parley got what he deserved."[28] This comment was written in response to a "First Presidency" message entitled "A Testimony Vibrant and True" in the August 2005 *Ensign*, in which President Hinckley praised Pratt's missionary travels and his testimony of the Book of Mormon, and he referred to his death in Arkansas. A correct understanding of Pratt's actions and motivations indicate that Pratt viewed himself as acting honorably to defend a woman (to whom he was sealed) against the violent actions of her alcoholic former husband.

From another perspective, Pratt's descendants and other Mormons believed that the citizens of Arkansas had unanimously

[26] See Matthew J. Grow's essay in this volume (chapter 9).

[27] George B. Higginson to Andrew Kimball, 1892, LDS Church History Library.

[28] Comment by "Polygamy Porter," 16 July 2005, www.exmormons.org; and Gordon B. Hinckley, "A Testimony Vibrant and True," *Ensign* (August 2005).

cheered as McLean killed Pratt. My mother, who had long served as the genealogist of the Pratt Family Association, told me that Pratt was "disemboweled on the plains of Arkansas and left there to die." In reality, to my surprise, we discovered that several individuals in Arkansas exhibited significant personal courage in acting against the prevailing public sentiment and attempting to protect and assist Pratt, Eleanor, and George Higginson. They included the local judge, John B. Ogden, who considered his oath to uphold the law more important than the demands of an angry mob; Zealey Wynn, a blacksmith who cared for Pratt in his final moments after McLean attacked him on Wynn's property, opened his home for an inquest and preparation of the body for burial, and gave him a Christian burial in his own family plot; William and John Steward who provided William's personal coffin and helped ensure that Pratt received a proper burial; a hotel keeper, a Mr. Smith, who provided the linens Eleanor used to dress Pratt's body and who protected Eleanor against a threatened lynching; and other Arkansans who helped bury Pratt.

To comprehend Pratt's motivations, it is important to retrace briefly the story of his death with this improved understanding. In 1851, Eleanor McComb McLean and her husband Hector McLean, southerners who had migrated to San Francisco during the gold rush, attended a Mormon meeting in San Francisco. Eleanor soon converted to the Church while Hector remained steadfastly opposed to her conversion. According to Eleanor's testimony and other historical evidence, her husband was an abusive alcoholic. They had first separated in 1844, less than three years after their marriage, due to Hector's alcoholism. At that time, Eleanor and Hector exchanged letters in which she referred to the "vice to which you have become a prey" and he responded, "I have tried in vain, to live soberly and righteously before God and men, but cannot accomplish it." Once, upon discovering Eleanor singing a Mormon hymn, he beat her and threw her into the street, locking her out of her home.[29]

[29] Eleanor Pratt, "Account."

Eleanor nevertheless attended Church meetings and became an active part of the small group of Mormons in San Francisco. Another San Francisco Mormon, Caroline Barnes Crosby, recorded that Eleanor "attends our church and wishes to be baptised" but was "prevented by an unbelieving husband." In addition, Crosby noted that Eleanor and a few other "sisters" visited Crosby when she was sick.[30] Hector finally consented to Eleanor's baptism in 1854. After Eleanor's baptism, Parley arrived in San Francisco along with a plural wife, Elizabeth Brotherton, for a mission in 1854–1855; Parley attempted to mediate the marital disputes between Eleanor and Hector. In January 1855, Hector sent their three children to New Orleans, without Eleanor's knowledge, to live with her parents, ostensibly to protect them from Mormonism. Eleanor immediately sailed to New Orleans after her children; she considered Hector's acts as a final betrayal and viewed their marriage as over. Eleanor's parents also opposed her conversion to Mormonism and blocked her efforts to take her children to Utah.

As a woman and as a member of an unpopular religious minority, Eleanor had little chance of legally gaining custody of her own children from her parents or of obtaining a divorce from Hector. Before leaving New Orleans, Eleanor sought legal advice concerning whether she could regain custody of her children and was told that the likely outcome of a court proceeding was that her husband would have her committed to an insane asylum, as he and her brother had threatened to do several times before. Indeed, charges of religious excitement or frenzy were sometimes used to commit Mormons, Millerites, and other adherents of minority religious groups to asylums.[31]

After her unsuccessful attempt to regain custody of her children, Eleanor traveled to Utah in the summer of 1855, where

[30] Edward Leo Lyman, Susan Ward Payne, and S. George Ellsworth, *No Place to Call Home: The 1807–1857 Life Writings of Caroline Barnes Crosby, Chronicler of Outlying Mormon Communities* (Logan: Utah State University Press, 2005), 256, 264–65.

[31] Spencer Fluhman, *A Peculiar People: Anti-Mormonism and the Making of Religion in Nineteenth-Century America* (Chapel Hill: University of North Carolina Press, forthcoming), chapter 2.

she married Parley as a plural wife in a ceremony performed by Brigham Young. During the nineteenth century, the Latter-day Saints believed that the laws of God superseded the laws of men, and a divorce from Hector may have been viewed by Eleanor as an unnecessary formality (and impossible to gain). Prior to her arrival in Utah, Eleanor had not been romantically involved with Parley. Young also hired Eleanor as a schoolteacher to his own children.

In 1856, in the midst of the rising national clamor against the Mormons that preceded President James Buchanan's decision to send a federal army to Utah a year later, Brigham Young called Pratt on a mission to the eastern United States. Pratt's plural wife Ann Agatha Walker later recalled: "He came into my house one day about the middle of August, and said to me, 'Agatha, I have bad news for you.' . . . His words and manner sent a strange thrill through me. I said, 'What is it!' He replied, 'I am called to go on a mission.' I said, 'Why do you call it bad news? You have been on missions before.' He said, 'Because I feel as if I shall never come back.'"[32] While Pratt preached throughout the East during the fall of 1856 and the winter of 1856–57 (including stops in New York City, Cincinnati, and St. Louis), Eleanor traveled from Utah to New Orleans to recover her children. The children were not living with Hector; the oldest had been sent to boarding school in Ohio and the two younger children were in the care of Eleanor's parents. In today's legal setting, Hector would have been charged and prosecuted for kidnapping the children in San Francisco and holding them against their mother's will, and Eleanor's children would have been returned to her until a court decided the dispute between them. After retrieving her children by telling her parents she had renounced Mormonism, Eleanor headed toward Utah.

McLean blamed Pratt and Mormonism for the breakup of his family (though Eleanor repeatedly stated he had broken their marriage through his alcoholism, abuse, and religious intolerance). As such, McLean tracked Pratt during his eastern mission in order to exact revenge, almost catching up with him in St. Louis. Other

---

[32] Ann Agatha Walker Pratt, Reminiscences, LDS Church History Library.

Church leaders kept Brigham Young aware of Parley's efforts to assist Eleanor.[33] After Parley received word that Eleanor had started for Utah with her children, he met her in Oklahoma Indian Territory, where Hector obtained a warrant for their arrest by alleging they had stolen the clothes the children were wearing. On this flimsy charge, a U.S. marshal with a military escort arrested them, along with another missionary, George Higginson.

The trio was taken to Van Buren, Arkansas, for trial. Parley and Eleanor, through their conduct and declarations of innocence, impressed the local judge, John B. Ogden, who freed Eleanor and secretly acquitted Parley of the charges later that night. Early the next morning, on May 13, 1857, Judge Ogden released Parley and offered him a knife and pistol, knowing that Eleanor's former husband and others with him were waiting in Van Buren for an opportunity to kill him. Parley refused the weapons, saying, "Gentlemen, I do not rely on weapons of that kind. My trust is in my God!" Judge Ogden commented, "I never saw a man like him, so quiet, uncomplaining and free from every feeling of revenge."[34]

When McLean learned of Pratt's escape, he immediately followed with several associates. They caught up with Pratt twelve miles from Van Buren. McLean fired six shots. All missed, though some hit his coat and saddle. Pratt was then stabbed twice by McLean in the chest and left for dead. Ten minutes later, McLean returned and shot him at point-blank range in the neck. After Pratt's death, local residents—including the Wynns and Stewards—ensured that he received a proper burial and that Eleanor was protected.

Conclusion

If you were to ask me after all of this effort to locate and potentially move Pratt's grave, "Has it been worth it?" I would say, "Unequivocally, yes." We set out to fulfill a longstanding family obligation, a

[33] Erastus Snow to Brigham Young, 14 March 1857, Brigham Young Collection, LDS Church History Library.

[34] Eleanor Pratt, "Account."

A group of Pratt descendants stand behind the open excavation, April 2008. *Courtesy of Robert J. Grow.*

burden the family has felt for over 150 years. The family now knows it has done everything humanly possible and can lay down this burden. Perhaps more importantly, we went to remove our ancestor from a place that our family has always remembered and treated as hostile. Through our historical research, we discovered many "Arkansas heroes" who had assisted Parley and Eleanor. Likewise, during our excavation of Pratt's grave, we met literally hundreds of neighbors who came to observe and share stories as the excavation was occurring. Local newspapers and television stations in positive stories told of our efforts on Pratt's behalf. We went to Arkansas believing that Pratt was buried among his enemies but relearned of old friends who helped Parley and Eleanor in their darkest hour and made new friends for the family and the LDS Church.

After 150 years of inaccurate statements about Pratt's death, some of them openly slanderous, we have reconfirmed the truth that Pratt died as he had lived, keeping his promises to his family and to the cause he had long served. The effort to find Pratt's remains helped us rediscover a vast amount of new historical evidence about how Pratt lived as an apostle and died as a martyr to the gospel that he loved. Personally, I discovered that Pratt's dying statement had three components. First, he desired that his body be taken to Utah for burial. Second, he expressed concern for his family. Third, he bore a firm and final earthly witness that he was "dying a firm believer in the gospel of Jesus Christ as revealed through the Prophet Joseph Smith" and asked that this dying testimony be conveyed to the Church and Saints that he loved.[35] As a family, we believe that our efforts to clarify the historical record about his death permit Pratt's apostolic witness of the Restoration to continue to resonate down through time.

---

[35] Statement of Frank T. Pomeroy, 11 April 1898, "Journal History."

Contributors

GREGORY K. ARMSTRONG is a professor and chair of the Department of World Languages at the University of Arkansas–Fort Smith. He has published in *Foreign Language Annals*, *Modern Language Journal*, *Perspectives on Proficiency: Curriculum and Instruction*, *Hispania*, *Creative Approaches in Foreign Language Learning*, *Looking Back and Stepping Forward—75 Years of Service to the Profession*, and in the online library of the Association of Academic Programs in Latin America and the Caribbean. He also published an entry on the Church of Jesus Christ of Latter-day Saints in Arkansas in the *Arkansas Online Encyclopedia of History and Culture.* He earned his doctorate in Spanish language and literatures from Indiana University in 1981.

ALEXANDER L. BAUGH is a professor of Church history and doctrine, Brigham Young University. He received his bachelor's degree from Utah State University and his master's and doctorate degrees from Brigham Young University. He is a member of the Mormon History Association and the Mormon Historic Sites Foundation, and a member and past president of the John Whitmer Historical Association (2006–2007). He also serves as editor of *Mormon Historical Studies.*

MATTHEW J. GROW is director of publications for the Church History Department of the Church of Jesus Christ of Latter-day Saints. His forthcoming biography of Parley P. Pratt, written along with Terryl Givens, will be published by Oxford University Press in 2011. He is also the author of *"Liberty to the Downtrodden":*

Thomas L. Kane, Romantic Reformer (Yale University Press, 2009) and articles in various scholarly journals including *Journal of the Early Republic*, *Church History*, *American Nineteenth-Century History*, and *Journal of Mormon History*. He received his doctorate in American history from the University of Notre Dame in 2006.

Robert J. Grow holds degrees in engineering and law and has had a diverse career, including practicing law, being president of a large manufacturing company, and chairing a national trade association. He has been recognized as Utah's entrepreneur of the year. Grow is the founder of Envision Utah and during the last decade has been legal counsel for, or involved in the planning of, several of the largest potential real estate developments in the United States. He has been president of the Jared Pratt Family Association (a family organization for the descendants of Parley Pratt and his four brothers) since 1985 and presided, along with his wife Linda, over the Church of Jesus Christ of Latter-day Saints' California Sacramento Mission from 1999 to 2002.

David W. Grua is a doctoral student in American history at Texas Christian University. He received his master's degree in history from Brigham Young University. His publications have appeared in *BYU Studies*, *Mormon Historical Studies*, *Dialogue: A Journal of Mormon Thought*, *Nova Religio: The Journal of Alternative and Emergent Religions*, and *Federal History: A Journal of the History of the Federal Government.*

Patrick Q. Mason is an associate professor of North American religions and Howard W. Hunter Chair of Mormon Studies at Claremont Graduate University. He is the author of *The Mormon Menace: Violence and Anti-Mormonism in the Postbellum South* (Oxford University Press, 2011). He earned a doctorate in U.S. history from Notre Dame, and his interests include American religious history, African American history, and comparative religious violence and peacebuilding.

David Clark Knowlton is a professor of anthropology at Utah Valley University. He studies religion in Latin America and Mormonism in the United States.

R. Steven Pratt is a comptroller and resource manager for the U.S. Army and has had a thirty-six-year career with the U.S. government in Utah, Europe, and Texas. He is a graduate of Brigham Young University in U.S. history and holds a master's of business administration from Boston University and a graduate fellowship in government studies from Harvard University. He has written many articles on U.S./Mormon history and resource management. He is finishing up several books on Parley P. Pratt's papers for publication. Steve is a great-great-grandson of Parley P. Pratt and Belinda Marden Pratt.

Jan Shipps is a professor emerita of history and religious studies at Indiana University–Purdue University Indianapolis. She is the author of *Mormonism: The Story of a New Religious Tradition* (University of Illinois Press, 1987) and *Sojourner in the Promised Land: Forty Years Among the Mormons* (University of Illinois Press, 2000). Her new book project is titled "Being Mormon: The Latter-day Saints Since World War II."

Dennis J. Siler is associate professor of English at the University of Arkansas–Fort Smith, where he also serves as chair of the honors committee. He received his bachelor's in English from the University of Central Arkansas, his master's from Wake Forest University, and his doctorate from the University of Arkansas–Fayetteville. His publications include *The Influence of the Roman Poet Ovid on William Shakespeare's A Midsummer Night's Dream* (Edwin Mellen Press, 2010), as well as chapters on southern American dialects and numerous conference presentations on early modern literature and music.

Richard E. Turley Jr. is assistant Church historian and recorder for the Church of Jesus Christ of Latter-day Saints in Salt Lake City, Utah. His books include *Massacre at Mountain Meadows* (Oxford University Press, 2008) and *Mountain Meadows Massacre: The Andrew Jenson and David H. Morris Collections* (Brigham Young University Press and University of Utah Press, 2009).

Jordan Watkins is a doctoral student in American intellectual history at the University of Nevada–Las Vegas. He received his master's in history at Claremont Graduate University where he wrote his thesis—"American Wests: Three Nineteenth-Century Travel Writers and the Adaptation of a Region"—under the supervision of Richard L. Bushman. He is working on a dissertation topic in which he plans to outline the forms and trace the developments of historical consciousness in antebellum America.

David J. Whittaker is senior librarian and curator of nineteenth-century western and Mormon manuscripts, L. Tom Perry Special Collections, Harold B. Lee Library, and an associate professor of history, Brigham Young University. He served as president of the Mormon History Association from 1995 to 1996 and was a member of the board of directors, Society for the History of Authorship, Reading, and Publishing, 1999–2007. He has published a number of books and articles, including his work as editor and contributor in *Mormon Americana: A Guide to Sources and Collections in the United States* (Brigham Young University Studies Monographs, 1995), for which he received the Dwight L. Smith Award for the Best Bibliographical or Research Work in Western History, presented by the Western Historical Association, 1996.

Index